THE BONUS MARCH

Contributions in American History

Series Editor: Stanley I. Kutler

THE
BONUS MARCH

An Episode of
the Great Depression

Roger Daniels

Contributions in American History
Number 14

Greenwood Publishing Corporation
Westport, Connecticut

Library of Congress Catalog Card Number: 75-133497

SBN: 8371-5174-0

Greenwood Publishing Corporation
51 Riverside Avenue, Westport, Connecticut 06880

Printed in the United States of America

For Theodore Saloutos
Mentor and Friend

Contents

Illustrations

Acknowledgments

MODERN SCHOLARSHIP is a thoroughly collaborative process; even though only one name appears on the title page, any work of this nature is actually a product of many hands and minds. Most of my obligations I have acknowledged in the traditional way in the notes, but a number of my intellectual debts are so pressing that they command special mention here, although no mere catalog can possibly repay them.

Edwin Kaye of the UCLA Library staff first called my attention to the possibilities inherent in the Glassford Collections, and, over a period of years, helped me to acquire and borrow additional material. My student, Professor Leonard Leader of Immaculate Heart College, shared his observer's memory of the bonus march, ran to earth the Emanuel Levin Mss., and read, with his usual wit and intelligence, the entire manuscript. Two other students, David Disco and Mary Griset, explored specific topics in useful seminar papers.

Congressman Wright Patman not only took time to share his memories of the whole struggle for the bonus with me, but also allowed me full and unhampered access to his files.

He has not asked to see the work in advance; I hope it pleases him even though he cannot agree with all of it.

Since so much of this book is based on archival and manuscript materials, my debt to archivists and librarians across the country is obviously enormous. Sarah Jackson of the National Archives, Jack Haley of the University of Oklahoma, and Martin Schmidt of the University of Oregon were helpful far beyond even that high standard that generally prevails in such places. James E. O'Neill, Director of the Franklin D. Roosevelt Library at Hyde Park, was extremely cooperative in informing me of materials opened after my visit there and having them copied. Jerome Deyo and William Marshall at Hyde Park and Dwight W. Miller at The Herbert Hoover Presidential Library at West Branch also furnished particularly useful assistance. The Interlibrary Loan staff at UCLA, my home institution during most of the research, was diligent and persevering in tracking down odd items.

Many friends and colleagues were generous of their time and knowledge. Irving Bernstein, who first acquired and exploited the Glassford Collection, spoke to me at length about his meetings with the general. Morris Schonbach gave me wise counsel about extremist movements in the 1930s. John Shover read the whole manuscript critically and contributed significantly to its clarification. An early version was presented to a UCLA faculty seminar, and I profited from some of the comments. Phyllis Townsend, a University of Wyoming graduate student, ran down and selected most of the photographs with diligence and imagination. Frederick Hollander and Linda Nelson were energetic and committed research assistants, supported by UCLA and the University of Wyoming respectively. The research was supported by grants from the UCLA Faculty Senate Research Committee. Sally Peterson and Jane Delson typed the manuscript with intelligence.

At Greenwood Publishing Corporation, Beverly Miller was a most helpful editor and Herbert Cohen an understanding academic publisher.

In this, as in all my work, I have a very special collaborator, my wife Judith, who tears herself from Tudor-Stuart England to listen, read, probe, question, advise, and correct with patience and wisdom.

ROGER DANIELS
Laramie, Wyoming
March 1971

THE BONUS MARCH

1

Something
for the Boys

On July 28, 1932, one of the stranger events in American history occurred—the expulsion from the nation's capital of the self-styled Bonus Expeditionary Force of World War I veterans by infantry, cavalry, and tanks of the United States Army, under the direct supervision of Chief of Staff General Douglas MacArthur. This was the culmination of the bonus march—the veterans' two-month sit-in in the Washington area during the desolate summer of 1932. Perhaps no other incident better symbolizes the utter inability of Herbert Hoover's administration to understand and to cope with the unprecedented problems of the Great Depression.

Although the affair is mentioned in scores of histories and treated at some length in a few, it has never been subjected to a full-scale investigation. That, in the first instance, is the aim of this book. Although I am using this minor, if picturesque, incident as the point of primary focus, I hope in addition to illuminate several other topics of larger scope: the relationship of the veteran to society in general and the political process in particular; some similarities and differences between the old order and the New Deal; the ways in which authority dealt with mass social protest; the influence, real and imagined, of the American Communist party; and finally, the ways in which history becomes myth.

One must begin with the bonus marchers themselves. The veterans were trying to persuade Congress to accelerate payments due them in 1945 under the Adjusted Compensation Act of 1924; this act stemmed from the attempts of the Wilson administration to rationalize the treatment of the veteran and thus avoid what seemed to its leading figures the notorious excesses in pension legislation that followed the Civil War. To put all of this into some kind of meaningful frame of reference, it will be useful to examine briefly the history of veterans' legislation in America.

The general practice of pensioning or otherwise rewarding old soldiers goes back to antiquity. Grants of land, payments of money, preferment in public employment, or sometimes merely the right to beg in potentially lucrative sites are among the ways that governments rewarded the survivors of combat. More than mere gratitude was involved in such rewards, since disgruntled groups of veterans were always a potential danger to the state and often willing tools for demagogues anxious for political change. For governments dependent on suffrage, there is a further inducement to reward the former warrior: the existence of a bloc of veteran votes, real or imagined, actual or potential.

During our colonial period, Great Britain granted public lands to veterans for services performed, and, at the time of the French and Indian War, the authorities were using promises of land as a spur to enlistment. During the American Revolution, the Continental Congress continued this aspect of imperial military policy. The first congressional offer of land was not, as might be imagined, an effort to induce men to join the patriot cause, but rather was designed to seduce Hessians and others into deserting the British standard. Shortly

thereafter both Congress and certain of the better endowed
state governments offered bonuses in land to all who fought
the British.[1] Similar offers were made to those who served in
the War of 1812 and in the Mexican War. One authority
has calculated that under the six military bounty acts passed
between 1776 and 1855, nearly 75 million acres—an area larger
than all of New England plus New York State—were removed
from the public domain. A very small percentage of this land
was actually settled by the veteran grantees; in practice, most
turned their military warrants into ready cash by selling them
to land speculators, which was perhaps what Congress expected
them to do.[2] After all, the United States in those days had a
great deal of land, but very little hard cash.

In addition to the system of bonuses just sketched, there
was a parallel program of postwar compensation, the military
pension system. Before the Civil War, pensions were provided
for invalid veterans and the widows and orphans of veterans.
Most of the pension measures were adopted without much
controversy, but one of the earliest provoked an acrimonious
political struggle even though its advocates were led by that
august personage, General George Washington. What Washington originally proposed, early in the Revolution, was that
after the cessation of hostilities all officers should be placed
on half-pay for life, as was done in the mother country. The
storm that raged over this proposal was illustrative both of
the tensions that existed between the civilian and military
revolutionaries and the struggle between those with aristo-
cratic and those with more democratic predispositions. The
half-pay measure was rejected; in its place the Congress
adopted, after six years of controversy, the Commutation Act
of 1783, which provided five years of full pay for officers and
one year for enlisted men.

Forty-four years later, on the eve of the Age of Jackson, the
government was more democratically inclined. President John
Quincy Adams recommended that "justice" be done to the

survivors of the War for Independence, and, in May 1828, Congress indicated its agreement by voting full pay for life to all who fought in the Revolution, whether officer or enlisted.[3] Since there were then fewer than a thousand pensionable survivors, the economic impact of this was not very significant, but it did emphasize what became a distinct feature of future pension legislation: the tendency for Congress to become more and more generous as the war in question receded farther and farther into the past. Old soldiers faded away, but those who remained were more cherished. Even given this trend to be increasingly liberal with pensions, the total drain on the Treasury was still quite small: through 1860 the federal government had paid out less than $90 million in pensions.[4] Just before the Civil War broke out, the cost of veterans' pensions was a little over a million dollars annually, or less than 2 percent of federal expenditures. In view of its relative inconsequence, it is not surprising that the pension issue was of very little political significance in the years after 1783 and that the few organized veterans' groups played little part in national politics.

The Civil War, that great watershed in American history, changed every aspect of the pension situation and brought the veteran qua veteran into the center ring of American politics, where he has remained for more than a century.[5] The reasons for this change are both quantitative and qualitative. In the first place, that conflict directly involved a greater percentage of the population than any other American war, before or since, and inflicted a greater number of casualties. In the second place, it was politically advantageous for the minority Republican party to keep the partisan spirit alive as long as possible; in the decades immediately after the war, the GOP felt it could remain in power only if it continued to persuade significant numbers of non-Republican veterans that it was necessary to "vote as they shot." A third factor— perhaps the most important one in terms of explaining *why* the veteran issue persisted so long—was the rise of mass veterans' organizations whose survival was at least partially contingent on keeping the veteran issue before the public.

The first and most successful of these veterans' groups was the Grand Army of the Republic, the major organization of Union army veterans. Founded in Illinois by Radical Republican politicians in the winter of 1865–1866, it quickly spread throughout the old Northwest, absorbing other preexisting veterans' organizations in the process. By the time of the fall elections, a secret investigator sent out by President Andrew Johnson was worried about the possibility of a veterans' putsch in the Midwest and convinced himself that "Indiana needs reconstruction." [6] The radical victory in that election and in the presidential contest of 1868 was accompanied by a spectacular growth of the organization: by the year of Grant's first inauguration, the GAR had enrolled close to a quarter-of-a-million men. There ensued a slackening of interest and the organization suffered a steep ten-year decline, dropping to about 25,000 members in 1879. An even more spectacular growth came in the 1880s, and peak strength was reached in 1890 when more than 400,000 old soldiers belonged.[7] From that point, death and debility decreed a steady decline, but the organization continued to wield a significant influence into the twentieth century.

Veterans' organizations thrive for a number of reasons; politics, nostalgia, patriotism, and what a contemporary chronicler called "a craving for social intercourse" are contributing factors. These organizations also have distinct economic functions in addition to their social and political roles, and it is these functions that will be stressed here. At first, in the GAR, the economic emphasis was largely on benefits paid by the order itself—the Grand Army in many ways resembled and competed for members with the fraternal benefit societies that were proliferating at that time—but soon the major efforts were directed toward securing benefits from the federal gov-

ernment. As early as 1869, membership appeals emphasized
the role that the organization could play in obtaining economic benefits for disabled comrades and the dependents of
dead ones. There were also efforts made to provide for the
able-bodied. At its first national encampment, the GAR asked
for an equalization of bounties—essentially a bonus—which
would have paid the average veteran eight-and-a-third dollars
for each month of active service. Nine years of agitation on
this issue finally produced appropriate legislation from Congress in 1875, but Grant's veto killed that scheme.[8]

There were also attempts to follow earlier precedents and
secure special land grants for veterans, but the passage of the
Homestead Act in 1862 had made those precedents anachronistic. The numerous and influential supporters of the homestead principle, in Congress and out, were quick to point out
that another bounty act would result in land going to speculators rather than to settlers. A leading opponent of military
bounties, Radical Republican Congressman George W. Julian,
argued that it would be "a wanton conspiracy against . . . the
welfare of coming generations" to exhaust the public domain in
this way.[9] Continued pressure from the Grand Army did result
in an 1872 act that allowed homesteading veterans to count
their military service as if it had been spent in residence, but
the ex-soldiers' advocates were not satisfied. In the next year,
a bounty bill that would have put negotiable warrants for
160 acres into the hands of every Union veteran who served
more than ninety days passed the House but was defeated in
the Senate.[10] These largely unsuccessful efforts were, as it
turned out, essentially blind alleys. The main economic thrust
of the GAR was to be for successively larger and more comprehensive pensions.

The first postwar general pension act, however, was not
for the boys in blue but for the 17,000 survivors of the War
of 1812 who got pensions of $8 per month in 1872.[11] This
had little effect on the total cost of pensions and followed, in

its essentials and timing, the precedents of the War for Independence. But the so-called Arrears Act of 1879, the first great pension triumph of the GAR, broke many of these precedents and was the first of a series of measures passed between that date and 1917 that expanded the whole pension system and raised the nation's pension bill from about a tenth to almost half of all federal expenditures. What the Arrears Act did was to drop the long-standing rule that payments under any disability pension start from the date that the claim was established; instead, such pensions were now backdated to the time of discharge.[12] Further liberalizations took place in 1886 and 1888. In the former year, the general pension rate for widows and dependents was raised from $8 to $12 per month, and in the latter year many of the advantages of the Arrears Act were extended to widows. This resulted in some bizarre awards: in 1893, for example, a remarried widow of a Union captain who had died in 1871 without ever having applied for a pension was able to get, retroactively, nearly $4,000 for the period 1871–1887, the terminal date being that of her remarriage. Both this act and the Arrears Act greatly encouraged fraud, and the Commissioner of Pensions complained about the difficulties of its detection.[13]

In 1887 a general pension act was passed for survivors of the Mexican War along the lines of the 1812 pensions. This was only forty-one years after the war began. Actually, the bill would have passed sooner had not there been fear that many ex-Confederates would be the beneficiaries; it is significant that this act became law during a Democratic administration. Grover Cleveland signed the measure on January 29, 1887.[14] Thirteen days later, he vetoed a bill which would have given a $12 monthly stipend to Union army veterans "who are now disabled and dependent upon their own labor for support."[15] The veto, of course, infuriated many veterans' groups, and once again caused the glare of publicity to be focused briefly upon the Polish immigrant, George Brinski, who had been

Cleveland's substitute during the Civil War. These acts, along with the President's 227 separate painstaking vetoes of private pension bills and his executive order returning captured Confederate battle flags, helped to make pensions a partisan issue in national politics.[16]

The Republican platform of 1888 made this quite clear; it insisted that the nation's gratitude could not "be measured by laws" and that the pension system should be [17]

> so enlarged and extended as to provide against the possibility that any man who honorably wore the Federal uniform shall become the inmate of an almshouse, or dependent upon private charity. In the presence of an overflowing treasury it would be a public scandal to do less for those whose valorous service preserved the government. We denounce the hostile spirit shown by President Cleveland in his numerous vetoes of measures for pension relief, and the action of the Democratic House of Representatives in refusing even a consideration of general pension legislation.

In the same spirit, the national encampment of the GAR declared, just prior to the presidential elections, that "the time has come when the soldiers and sailors of the war for the preservation of the Union should receive . . . service pensions in accordance with established usage." [18] The resolution went on to specify a minimum pension of $8 monthly for all who served as little as sixty days, with a maximum—dependent on length of service—almost double the minimum.

After the election, the victorious Republicans did not go quite as far as the Grand Army had asked, but the famous billion-dollar Fifty-first Congress made good the pension promise of the Republican platform. The Pension Act of 1890, introduced into Congress by William McKinley, who seven years later would be the last Union veteran to enter the White House, was almost a pension for mere service. It provided that honorably discharged veterans with as little as ninety days of service "who are now or may hereafter be suffering from a mental or physical disability of a permanent character which incapacitates them from the performance of manual labor in such a degree as to render them unable to earn a support" should be eligible for pensions ranging from $6 to $12 monthly. Unremarried widows of veterans were entitled to $8 monthly, with an additional $2 per month for each child under sixteen years of age. No proof that the disability was connected with military service was required in the statute. In its administration, according to a leading authority, there was no inquiry into the capacity of the veteran to support himself. "The rich have been pensioned along with the poor. . . . Large numbers of persons, seemingly in normal health, have discovered in themselves ailments which would have passed unnoticed but for the pension laws." [19] The spirit in which the law was administered was more than generous. As ex-Corporal James Tanner, appointed Commissioner of Pensions by President Benjamin Harrison, understood his job, it was his "duty . . . to assist a worthy old claimant to prove his case rather than to hunt for technical reasons under the law to knock him out." [20]

The effects of the act of 1890 caused pension costs to sky-rocket: during the bleak and turbulent decade that followed, the relative cost of veterans' benefits was the highest in our history. In fiscal 1893, these payments accounted for 43 cents of every federal dollar spent.[21] It goes without saying that these monthly payments, however capriciously awarded, must have been a great help to hundreds of thousands of poor families during the depression of the 1890s.

In that decade, most of the nation probably approved this kind of expenditure (and would have been aghast at any suggestion of large-scale relief), but there were two significant and articulate groups who were opposed: the mugwumps and the Southern Democrats. Since the mugwump-type [22] has dominated our universities—and thus our written history—this high level of expenditure became and remains a national scandal. It is difficult to find a contemporary college text that does not agree substantially with Carl Schurz, who in 1894 denounced "the fraudulent practices of greedy speculators and pretenders" in striving for pensions.[23] That prince of mugwumps, Charles Francis Adams, went even further, insisting that "every dead-beat, and malingerer, every bummer, bounty-jumper, and suspected deserter . . . rush[ed] to the front as the greedy claimant of a public bounty." [24] The Southern resentment, which sometimes cloaked itself in mugwumpish protests against too much federal spending, really had its roots in sectional animosity. As one southerner put it to the 1908 Democratic National Convention, the postwar years "put Yankee Doodle on the pension list and Dixie on crutches." [25]

How did proponents of bigger and better pensions answer these and other critics? Largely by insisting, over and over again, that because the Union army, as one patriot later put it, "saved the nation, [its veterans had] a mortgage written in blood on every man, woman and child and on every acre of land in these United States." Most of the loudest pension supporters simply ignored the economy arguments of the mugwumps and other devotees of classical economics, but a few boldly counterattacked with arguments that viewed the disbursement of large sums of money to veterans as a positive good rather than as a necessary evil. In 1893, for example, GAR Commander in Chief Paul Van Der Voort claimed, in words that have a modern ring, that [26]

> the money disbursed to pensioners is an actual blessing to the country. It goes into the channels of trade. It makes money easy, and, in my judgement the amount scattered throughout the country by the action of the arrears of pensions bill was an actual benefit and prevented a financial crash.

For more than a decade after 1890, largely because of bad times, there was no further general pension legislation. Costs still continued to mount as the median age of Civil War veterans moved into the sixties. Then, starting in 1904, four consecutive presidential election years brought further liberalization of the rules. In 1904 Theodore Roosevelt's pension commissioner issued Order No. 78, which transformed, by administrative regulation, the Pension Act of 1890 into an outright service pension, something the Fifty-first Congress had been unwilling to do. It accomplished this simply by declaring that old age was, ipso facto, a disability. The commissioner determined that at 62 a man was 50 percent disabled, at 65, 75 percent disabled, and at 70, 100 percent disabled, and veterans on reaching these ages were entitled to $6, $8, and $12 per month respectively. A 1907 statute gave legislative recognition to this rule and upped the monthly ante to $12 at 62, $15 at 70, and $20 at 75. In 1908, widows' pensions were raised to $12 monthly and financial status was disregarded. In 1912 Congress again raised the payments, as the following table shows:

TABLE 1

Monthly Pensions Under Act of 1912

Age	90 Days	6 Months	1 Year	1.5 Years	2 Years	2.5 Years	3 Years
			Length of Service				
62	$13	$13.50	$14	$14.50	$15	$15.50	$16
66	15	15.50	16	16.50	17	18.00	19
70	18	19.00	20	21.50	23	24.00	25
75	21	22.50	24	27.00	30	30.00	30

In 1916 and 1917, Democratic Congresses raised the pensions of Civil War widows to $25 per month, regardless of age or financial status, as long as the marriage took place before June 27, 1905.[27] This last provision enabled some young women who were born in the 1890s to qualify for Civil War pensions. With this added generosity, pension expenditure continued to mount despite a steady decrease in the number of survivors; by fiscal 1917—before there were any World War I veterans—the nation's annual bill for veterans was nearly $170 million. Most of the proponents of these twentieth-century increases justified them on the grounds that the country could now afford the expense. As Senator Porter J. McCumber (R.-N.D.), chairman of the Senate Pension Committee, had put it in 1907: [28]

> The country . . . is wealthy. . . . Extravagances of every character are creeping into our legislation, extravagances which might well be abandoned until we have performed our entire duty toward the survivors of that war which made it possible that we have a country of this wealth and which could indulge in those extravagances.

The Congress, however, that put the capstone on federal largesse for the boys in blue and the girls they left behind them was also determined that history should not repeat itself. Imbued with that essentially progressive conviction that all fundamental problems could be solved by a statute, the Wilson administration devised a plan which it thought would take the veteran issue out of politics and, at the same time, provide a greater measure of economic justice during the present war, both for the fighting men and for their dependents. This hope, like so many hopes in that optimistic Indian summer of progressivism, was doomed to quick disappointment, but at least the legislation for the doughboys of 1917 did break with the traditions of the past and also provided basic principles of social justice on which a later generation could build.

The plan seems to have originated with Treasury Secretary William G. McAdoo,[29] who proposed to the President in June 1917 that the federal government insure the lives of soldiers and sailors and provide allotments for their dependents. His proposal arranged it so that the Treasury's Bureau of War Risk Insurance, set up in 1914 to insure ships and their cargoes, would become the insuring agency.[30] This unorthodox bypassing of the old Pension Bureau, a division of the Interior Department, was probably doubly motivated: in the first place, McAdoo naturally desired to enlarge his own department, and in the second place, as a southern Democrat, he had deep resentments about the whole Civil War pension system. In his memoirs, the efficiency-minded Secretary sneered that the existing pension system was "as scientific as the distribution of prizes from a Christmas tree." Under that system he felt "some men received too much, and others too little."[31] McAdoo planned to replace this with a dual system: the compulsory allotments plus voluntary insurance, both partially paid for by the man concerned and partially subsidized by the federal government. Typically, McAdoo called in the experts—specialists from the leading insurance companies, advisors from the Council of National Defense, including labor leader Samuel Gompers, progressive intellectuals like Julia Lathrop of the Children's Bureau, and a few college professors. The key draftsman was Julian W. Mack, a liberal upstate New York Democratic politician who, despite his seat on the federal circuit bench, served in several advisory capacities to the Wilson administration.

A different version of the origins of soldiers' insurance came from McAdoo's cabinet colleague, War Secretary Newton D. Baker. Almost two decades later he explained it, perhaps a little too patly, to Franklin D. Roosevelt as having been conceived as a means "to protect the country against a pension and a repetition of the difficulties and injustices of the Civil War pension episode." According to Baker:[32]

Mr. Samuel Gompers, as a member of the Advisory Committee of the Council of National Defense, had it practically worked out when Mr. McAdoo insisted upon the whole thing being brought into the Treasury Department and promoted as Treasury Depart-

ment legislation. When Mr. Gompers made his suggestion originally, it was for the express purpose of making World War pensions
forever impossible.

Regardless of where the measure originated—it might well
have had a dual origin—the resultant bill was a distinctly
"progressive" measure and one that has been ignored by students of progressivism.[33] It may not be too much to claim it
as one of the key statutes linking the New Freedom and the
New Deal. Perhaps more than any other act passed during the
presidency of Woodrow Wilson, it presaged the coming of
what is known as the welfare state. It was the first federal
statute to employ broadly the basic principles of social insurance and thus may be considered a direct ancestor of the
Social Security Act of 1935.

The very progressivism of the proposal drew some fire, particularly from insurance companies and their congressional
spokesmen. According to McAdoo's biographer, a committee
representing the insurance industry opposed the insurance
provisions entirely.[34] At the end of July, the Treasury Secretary wrote an open letter to Wilson which was in part an
answer to the industry and a good brief for the bill. Insisting
that the proposal was essentially a matter of justice, McAdoo
wrote:

> Its main purpose is to grant a reasonable Government indemnity
> against the losses and risks incurred in the discharge of a patriotic
> duty. . . . It provides not only for the man but for his family.
> . . . While in some respects the compensation system gives less
> than the present pension system, in other respects, especially in
> caring for the family after the man's death, it gives more.

The Secretary went on to point out that the insurance provision enabled every man to gain additional protection if he
wished. He argued that, since the government had abandoned

the volunteer system and instituted the draft, an even greater obligation rested on the government to take care of its soldiers and their dependents; he called upon Wilson to have the United States set an example in taking care of its men. Finally, McAdoo insisted, the whole program of compensation and insurance should be worked out before the troops went overseas so that every man might have "definite guarantees and assurances . . . not as charity; but as part of his deserved compensation for the extra-hazardous occupation into which his government has forced him." [35] The very precision and efficiency of McAdoo's language, the antithesis of the typical patriotic profusion, is an index both to his attempt to break with the traditions of the past and his devotion to efficiency, that tutelary deity of so much of the progressive movement.

Amidst an effective publicity campaign accompanied by visible support from the White House, a bill drafted by Judge Mack was introduced in the House, sent to the reliable Committee on Interstate and Foreign Commerce, given rather perfunctory hearings, reported, and debated in a little over sixty days. The administration's floor manager for the measure, Congressman Sam Rayburn of Texas (then in his third term), made it clear at the outset of debate that the government intended to "supersede the present pension laws." Somewhat uneasy at its compulsory features, Rayburn emphasized its voluntary aspects. He assured his colleagues that the government had no intention of going into the insurance business and admitted, in embarrassment, that "the enthusiasm of our socialistic friends . . . for this bill is because they believe it will be an entering wedge." Despite the blessings of Socialists like Congressman Meyer London of New York's Lower East Side, the umbrage taken by pension specialists who thought that the bill should have gone to the Committee on Pensions, the reluctance of some members of the old guard to change from a known to an unknown system, and the objections of a few ideological conservatives who deplored the compulsory aspects, the bill received overwhelming approval, both in the Congress and in the country at large. Even some diehard opponents of the administration, like ex-President Theodore Roosevelt, gave their support. Although there was quibbling over details and grumbling about procedures, the measure passed both houses of Congress without a dissenting vote.[36]

The new law provided that all enlisted men be included in a compulsory system of allotments and family allowances under which the government guaranteed $15 monthly to the wives of servicemen, $10 for the first child, $7.50 for the second, and $5 for each additional child up to a $50 overall maximum payment. There were similar allowances for other dependents. The enlisted man was forced to contribute half his pay (privates made $33 per month), with the government making up the difference, if any. A 1918 amendment liberalized the measure by limiting the compulsory deduction to a leveling $15 for all ranks. Although allotments seem commonplace today, this was a pioneering measure: in no previous war had governmental provision been made, during hostilities, for the dependents of fighting men.

There was also a schedule of payments to be made in case of the death or disablement in the line of duty of both officers and enlisted men. These schedules, based on those already worked out in existing workmen's compensation statutes, called for monthly compensation (not pension!) checks that ran from $25 for a childless widow to a maximum of $100 for certain disabled men.

The voluntary insurance aspects of the new law were supposed to equalize the difference between peacetime and wartime insurance rates. The soldier or sailor paid a premium of $8 per $1,000 annually up to a maximum of $10,000, approximately the rate a prime civilian risk would pay; when he could get it, a soldier had to pay about $58 per $1,000 for similar insurance from a commercial company. A maximum policy would yield a $25 monthly return to the beneficiary in case of death or total disability of the man insured. These payments would be over and above those due under the compulsory compensation program.

The allotments and family allowances officially ended in July 1921. The net cost to the government—not including administrative expenses—was $262 million; an even larger amount—$301 million—had been deducted from servicemen's pay. It is, of course, more difficult to draw up a balance sheet for the insurance aspects of the program, as some of the policies are still in force. Altogether some $40 billion worth of insurance was issued by the Bureau; by mid-1920, less than $4 billion remained in force, as most veterans, for one reason or another, failed to take advantage of the somewhat complex conversion procedures. Up to 1941, when another war complicated the accounting problems, insurance expenditures had exceeded premium receipts plus interest by some $1.7 billion. The net cost, then, of McAdoo's compensation-insurance plan was some $2 billion.[37]

A mere accounting cannot measure the value of any program of social insurance; it is obvious that the World War I programs afforded a greater measure of economic justice to the families of servicemen, although the rapid wartime inflation quickly reduced the allotments' purchasing power. The objectives of the framers were thus partially achieved, but, as tough-minded conservatives like Senator Reed Smoot of Utah had pointed out at the time, the naive hope that McAdoo's package was adequate insurance against future pension legislation was quickly blighted as the returning veterans began to clamor for more benefits and a new organization—the American Legion—proved to be a more insistent and anxious lobbyist than even the GAR had been.[38]

2

Adjusted Service Compensation

THE WILSON administration reopened the whole question of veterans' benefits. While the guns were still firing on the western front, several federal departments and agencies, clearly infused with what Richard Hofstadter has called the "myth of the yeoman," voiced interest in halting the steady drift of rural population to the cities. The problem of how to keep 'em down on the farm after they'd seen "Paree" concerned Pennsylvania Avenue even more than it did Tin Pan Alley.

Chief among the measures proposed in these Canute-like projects to keep America rural was the so-called Lane Plan of soldier resettlement, which combined patriotism, social nostalgia, reclamation of western deserts, and land speculation in approximately equal quantities. Its chief sponsor was Franklin K. Lane, the Democratic California Progressive who was Wilson's Interior Secretary until he resigned in 1920 to go to work for an oil company, while its chief legislative advocate was Frank Mondell, a conservative Wyoming Republican congressman. Lane insisted that his scheme, which was pushed by "service intellectuals" like Dr. Elwood K. Mead, was neither a "mere Utopian vision" nor a "bounty" for veterans, but rather a means for [1]

> the development of this country through the use of the returned soldier. . . . The United States lending its credit, may increase its resources and its population and the happiness of its people with a cost to itself of no more than the few hundred thousand dollars that it will take to study this problem.

Anachronistic as back-to-the-landism now seems, it was a quite understandable, if ineffective, response to industrialism, dating at least back to Feargus O'Connor and British Chartism in the early 1840s.[2] In this country such movements apparently date from the depression of the 1890s, which occurred as the closing of the frontier was being announced. Serious proposals for resettlement–conservation projects continued to be made throughout the 1920s, and, during the New Deal, some resettlement was actually effected. The Lane–Mondell plan afforded the first major legislative consideration of what was already a much discussed proposition. The Mondell bill had as its stated purpose the provision of "employment and rural homes" for veterans. It would have authorized the establishment of a $500 million National Soldier Settlement Fund administered by the Secretary of the Interior. The money was to be loaned to veteran applicants as forty-year mortgages drawing 4 percent interest for the purchase of "family-sized farms." The Secretary was also empowered to loan applicants up to 75 percent of the cost of certain improvements and equipment. This plan, first pushed by Lane in the spring of 1918, and endorsed by President Wilson in his message to Congress that December, was hailed by its proponents as both a method of relieving the unemployment that most felt was sure to follow the end of the war and a practical way to halt the depopulation of rural America. Yet, as its opponents were quick to point out, Lane's proposals would benefit only those

who had capital. Unlike the Homestead Act, to which its supporters compared it, the plan insisted that the settlers themselves eventually reimburse the government for all costs; in
addition, those who could not manage at least a $1,000 down
payment could not participate in the scheme. The Mondell
bill never came to a vote; recent scholarship attributes its
failure to the opposition of commercial farmers (and the
Department of Agriculture!) and to its clearly speculative
aspects. It also lacked, despite Lane's insistence to the contrary,
substantial support among the veterans themselves. They, like
most other Americans in the postwar era, were interested not
in seemingly idealistic schemes of agrarian reform, but in cash
payment for services rendered.[3]

The lame-duck Democratic Congress of 1918–1919 clearly
recognized that demand, and without administration sponsorship gave the boys a little mustering-out present. As Congressman George Huddleston (D-Ala.) later explained it, he was
shocked when the Senate put a rider on an appropriation bill
granting a month's pay to every veteran, because it gave so
much more to officers (up to $600 for a major general) than
to enlisted men ($30 for privates). It was his influence, he
claimed, that caused his colleague Claude Kitchin (D-N.C.)
to insist, in conference, that an egalitarian bill be passed. The
conferees agreed, and all veterans, officer and enlisted, were
awarded $60 as they were mustered out. That this was just a
stopgap measure, most of its proponents and opponents agreed.
By the late summer of 1919, three distinct positions had
evolved in regard to further veterans' benefits: there were those
who favored some kind of government-financed loan and those
who felt that the government had already done enough and
insisted that private capital could best handle the admittedly
difficult transition from war to peace if only the government
would leave it alone. The bonus advocates, most of whom
would also support loans, proposed stipends of varying
amounts, ranging from $25 for each month served to a fan-

tastic $5,000 per soldier. The most commonly discussed amount was $300. The advocates of low-interest government loans— 4 percent was the usual figure—proposed them not only for the purchase of farms, but also for purchase of homes and the establishment of businesses. The main theme, according to a congressional committee which surveyed the proposals, was "for the Nation to supply financial backing for every soldier who desires to engage in trade, industry or profession, of whatever nature." In addition, some states' righters instead proposed that the federal government appropriate a sum—Lane's $500 million was a popular figure—to be distributed among the states for them to use "in any way they consider best for the soldier's welfare." [4]

While the politicians were conducting fruitless discussions about how to provide for the returned soldier, the fledgling American Legion, destined to become the premier organization of World War I veterans, was beginning to shape its stand on the bonus. It is hard to overstate the Legion's legislative influence in the immediate postwar years, an influence based not only on its real power, but on its potential power as well. Today, when the Legion's flabby political muscle is, in essence, just that of another rightist pressure group, it is too easy to forget that many politicians expected that the Legion would assume the same kind of role in politics that the GAR had. It followed, then, that the White House would have a succession of ex-servicemen as tenants, and that the Legion would have a good deal to do with putting them there. This of course was not the case, and the "kingmakers" of the Legion establishment named only their own commanders. No member of the American Expeditionary Force reached the White House until 1945, and Harry Truman was hardly the kind of President the Legion wanted.

An incorrect reading of history can be just as influential as a correct one if men act on it, and many congressmen and would-be congressmen behaved for about two decades as if the American Legion were the political powerhouse they expected it to be. Congress chartered it and gave it special privileges; federal executive departments turned lists of government employees who were veterans over to Legion recruiters; the pompous pronouncements of its annual conventions were given much more attention than they deserved, and whoever happened to be the national commander became a one-year ex-officio expert on patriotism, morality, and textbooks.[5]

The Legion, despite continuous protestations to the contrary, was essentially a conservative, upper middle-class, white Protestant organization. It seems clear that most of its ex-officer leadership would have preferred to ignore the whole bonus question (or even oppose it), but on this issue the demands of the rank and file were too strong to resist. At its very first meeting in the United States, the so-called St. Louis caucus of May 1919, the leadership succeeded in tabling a bonus resolution, which asked for a $180 bonus for the average serviceman.[6] Six months later, however, just a year after the Armistice, the bonus question could no longer be shelved. The result was the adoption of a curiously worded resolution which insisted that "although the Legion was not founded for the purpose of promoting legislation in its selfish interest, yet it recognizes that our Government has an obligation to all service men and women to relieve the financial disadvantages incidental to their military service—an obligation second only to that of caring for the disabled and for the widows and orphans of those who sacrificed their lives and one already acknowledged by our allies—the American Legion feels that it cannot ask for legislation in its selfish interest, and leaves with confidence to the Congress the discharge of this obligation."[7]

The resolution also coined a new euphemism, "adjustment of compensation or extra pay," as a substitute for bonus; this soon evolved into "adjusted compensation" or "adjusted service compensation." The Legion never used the word bonus in its official propaganda, although the term was current among its membership, because it insisted that a bonus was a gratuity or a tip. All the "adjustment" was supposed to do was partially equalize the low pay received by soldiers as compared to the relatively higher pay received by workers in industry. In the hands of radicals, the bonus agitation could be yoked with an attack on war profiteers and big business, but in most Legion propaganda the invidious comparison was made with a steel worker or a coal miner, thus strengthening the prevailing antilabor bias in the predominantly small-town-oriented veterans' groups.

Whatever the less sophisticated Legionnaires may have made of the resolution, congressmen attuned to the Aesopian language of politics understood that the bonus was not yet a crucial issue and acted accordingly. No bonus bill was even voted on in 1919. But 1920 was an election year, and by May congressional Republicans had consolidated the Lane–Mondell plan and dozens of other proposals into one omnibus measure —the so-called Fordney Bill. It was managed by two midwestern reliables, Congressman Joseph W. Fordney of Michigan and Senator Porter J. McCumber of North Dakota, better known for their joint sponsorship of the protectionist tariff of 1921. The bill provided five separate options for the veteran: he could opt for

1. Immediate cash payment at a rate of $1 a day for domestic service and $1.25 for overseas service with maximums of $500 and $625.
2. Adjusted service certificates equal to adjusted service pay plus 40 percent, plus twenty years compound interest at 4½ percent payable twenty years after the passage of the act. This postponed payment would have totaled almost three-and-a-half times the adjusted service pay in option 1. There were also complex loan privileges and provisions

for immediate payment of total amount to the veteran's heirs in case of death, making this option a twenty-year endowment life insurance policy.

3. A kind of proto-G.I. Bill, by which the veteran could receive a $1.75 per diem during attendance in a course of approved vocational training, the total stipend not to exceed 140 percent of his adjusted service pay. [It should be noted that no provision was made for attending college. College men were officers, and vice versa.]

4. 140 percent of adjusted service pay to be applied to the purchase or improvement of a home or farm.

5. 140 percent of adjusted service pay to be used as an initial participation fee in a proposed "National Veterans' Resettlement Project," which was clearly an outgrowth of the Lane-Mondell proposals.

The Fordney Bill proposed to finance all this with a series of "victory taxes." These would consist of

1. Additional surtaxes on income over $5,000 for three years.
2. Additional taxes on the sale of stocks and bonds.
3. A tax on transactions at produce exchanges and boards of trade.
4. A tax on real estate transfers.
5. An additional tax on cigars, cigarettes and other manufactured tobacco products.
6. A special tax on stock dividends.

The "soak the rich" nature of the bill should be readily apparent. Its total cost was estimated at about $5 billion, but this was clearly a very rough estimate, being in part dependent upon how many veterans chose each option. No figure was named in the bill; instead the enabling clause authorized the appropriation of "such amount as may be necessary." The measure was opposed by the administration. Secretary of the

Treasury David F. Houston insisted that because of the strains of the war and reconversion on the economy, a bonus measure would be "highly unfortunate." Despite this negative administration reaction, Henry T. Rainey, ranking Democrat on the House Ways and Means Committee, himself author of a bill to pay the bonus by retroactive taxation of excess war profits at an 80 percent rate, called on his fellow Democrats to support the Republican bill as the measure most likely to pass. A majority of the Democrats followed him rather than the almost leaderless administration as the bill passed the House, 289 to 92, in late May. As most experienced observers expected, it died without even coming to a vote in the more conservative Senate.[8]

Despite strong advocacy by a number of individual delegates, neither party platform in 1920 came out for a soldier's bonus. Its most influential political proponent was William Jennings Bryan. The Great Commoner had come out for a bonus in April 1920, arguing that a war profits tax would be the best way to finance it. "Those who were made rich by the war," he insisted, "should furnish the money." [9] However, 1920 was not a Bryan year, and his fight for a bonus plank was thwarted by fiscal conservatives at the convention.[10] The Democratic platform did include support for a soldier settlement scheme; the GOP was satisfied merely to remind veterans that "Republicans are not ungrateful." [11]

The convention of the American Legion, however, meeting in late September, took its first entirely unambiguous stand on the bonus by giving "unqualified approval" to the measure passed by the House.[12] Perhaps in response to this pressure, the pliant Republican candidate seemed to endorse the bonus late in the campaign. Speaking in Cincinnati, Warren G. Harding pointed out that a Republican House had passed the bonus bill—something Republican orators had been telling veteran voters throughout the summer—and went on to say that he thought it "ought to pass," although, he claimed, "the patriotic men of the American Legion wouldn't have cared to have us pass a bonus bill last summer when our war bonds were 15 to 20 below par." [13] But with the Democratic party in the hands of fiscal conservatives like James M. Cox and Carter Glass, the bonus could not become a real campaign issue.[14] Probably more Republicans than Democrats favored the cash bonus, if only because many southern Democrats, haunted as always by the race issue, were afraid of too much easy money spoiling their Negroes. Small as the cash bonus was, it was considerably larger than the annual cash income of most southern Negroes.

When the heavily Republican Sixty-seventh Congress met in special session just after Harding's inauguration, a new Fordney-McCumber bonus bill was high on the list of legislation expected to pass. The only significant difference between this bill and the one that had passed the House in 1920 was that the new bill had no tax provisions. It was planned to leave to later legislation, or perhaps even later Congresses, to decide how to raise the $5 billion that might eventually be required.[15] The first clear indication that there would be administration opposition came in early July when Secretary of the Treasury Andrew W. Mellon declared that, in view of the financial difficulties accompanying the return of "normalcy," "the best interests of the country demand that action be deferred upon the soldiers' bonus." The bonus, according to Mellon, would probably cause "renewed inflation, increased commodity prices and unsettled business conditions." In addition, the Pittsburgh banker insisted that service "performed as the highest duty of citizenship . . . can never be measured in terms of money." [16] Mellon's warnings had little impact; the bill still seemed headed for Senate passage. Ten days after Mellon's letter, the President himself intervened. Today, when all his vices have been long exposed and his few virtues forgotten, Waren G. Harding seems merely a pitiful, contemptible figure. But in July 1921, he was fresh from an electoral triumph of landslide proportions. For all his obvious weaknesses and pliability, Harding did on occasion exhibit strength. The bonus fight shows him at his most influential. To stop the bill he did what no President before or since has even attempted; he appeared in person before the upper chamber and asked its members to recommit a bill that had already been reported out of committee and was nearing a vote that was all but certain to be favorable.

In his appeal to his former colleagues, Harding performed variations on the same economy theme his Secretary of the Treasury had introduced, and it cannot be doubted that the basic idea was Mellon's. "The enactment of the compensation bill," he insisted, "would greatly emperil the financial stability of our country." Like Mellon, he did not rule out a bonus in happier financial times, but insisted that with the government paying 5¾ percent interest on short-term bills, no new major financial commitments should be undertaken. "Generous treatment" to able-bodied veterans, he argued, "would be a mark of the nation's gratitude," not "the payment of a debt." [17]

Although the Senate had previously voted, 46 to 4, to take up the bonus bill, the President's wishes were promptly obeyed, despite claims by Georgia's irascible Tom Watson that Harding's unprecedented visit was "unconstitutional." On July 15, by a vote of 47 to 29, the bill was sent back to the Finance Committee, where it stayed bottled up for the rest of the session. The administration was deserted by a number of Republican Senators, mostly midwesterners; without the support of eleven conservative Democrats, mostly southerners, the motion would have failed.

This vote, and other votes on similar measures, suggests that the anti-general-welfare coalition between fiscal conservatives of both parties is a product of the early 1920s, not the late 1930s. Probonus Republicans felt that as soon as the nation's finances were restructured, the administration would support a bonus. There were several efforts to salvage some kind of bonus in that session, including a bill by Congressman Hamilton Fish (R.-N.Y.), a founder of the American Legion, that would have put all interest collected on the war debts and owed the United States by its allies into a special fund for the payment of adjusted compensation.[18]

The American Legion, meeting in October, officially "deplored" the action of the President and Congress in sidetracking the bonus. Although there were many, if not a majority, among the delegates who wanted a stronger statement, the Legion merely went on record as reaffirming its support for the adjusted compensation bill with its several options.[19]

When the Congress met in December 1921, in its regular session, the passage of some kind of bonus bill seemed almost a foregone conclusion. The Republican steering committee, meeting on January 25, 1922, named the bonus as one of the ten most pressing legislative topics, and the House Ways and Means Committee set to work to produce a bill. The 1922 measure, also managed by Fordney and McCumber, again narrowed somewhat the scope of the original 1920 measure. First, the cash option was eliminated, except for those entitled to only $50 or less. Veterans who were in need could borrow up to 50 percent of the loan basis of their certificates from any bank, at a rate of interest not to exceed the current Federal Reserve rediscount rate plus 2 percent. The loan value of a certificate was to be figured on an actuarial basis; a man with the maximum amount of service, who would have been entitled to $625 adjusted service pay, would get instead a certificate with a face (that is, maturity) value of $1,884.15, that sum being collectible twenty years later. But its initial loan value was only $312.50, and that not until two years after the issuance date of the certificate. The home loan, resettlement, and vocational training options remained essentially as before. Like its immediate predecessor, the 1922 bill contained no revenue features. Its proponents assumed an eventual $4 billion cost—about a billion less than the previous bill; but—and this seemed its greatest virtue to many—there would be very little immediate expense, e.g., an estimated $125 million for the first year of operation.[20]

This modified bonus bill seemed at first to have smooth sailing, despite the fact that President Harding had, in mid-February, suggested a general sales tax, and warned that, if the Congress was not willing to vote such a tax, "it would be wise to let the legislation go over until there is a situation which will justify the large outlay." [21] In March, however, Speaker Nicholas Longworth assured the House that, on the basis of several conversations with the President, he would be "greatly surprised" if the pending bonus measure failed to win the Chief Executive's approval.[22] There was a great deal of pressure for the bill; a conservative Oregon Republican claimed that various members were saying privately:[23]

> The bill is an insult to every World War veteran, a shameful disgrace to Congress and the Nation, but I will vote for it.
>
> I do not believe that the measure is a good one, but the soldier boys at home want it, and let them have it.
>
> I know that it is a bad measure, but I have made a pledge to support it, and I shall have to keep the pledge.
>
> Any man who votes against the bill will be defeated. I shall vote for it.
>
> It may be statesmanship to oppose this bill, but there is such a thing as a statesman without a job.
>
> The bill is damned bunk, but the Legion demands it.

The tactics adopted by the Republican House leadership suggest the steamroller: it was introduced under a special "gag" rule—no amendments were allowed and only four hours of debate were permitted. As Democrat James Byrnes

(S.C.), who voted for the bill, later complained, his party was "confronted with the proposition . . . of either voting for their bill or voting against it, which if defeated means no [bonus] legislation whatsoever." The bill passed overwhelmingly, 333 to 70, getting the assent of a majority of both parties.[24]

It then went to the Senate, where, according to Senator Pat Harrison (D.-Miss.), it was kept sleeping in the Senate Finance Committee. In mid-April, a conference of Senate Republicans resolved to "pass a soldiers' compensation bill" during the 1922 session.[25] In June, the President made it known that "under no circumstances" should the bonus question be brought before the Senate until the tariff issue had been settled. Senator McCumber, who was the sponsor of both measures, wanted it taken up immediately and insisted that the "honor of the Republican party" was at stake.[26] Honor or no honor, the bonus bill was kept in committee until mid-August. There, although the bill was opposed by some fiscal conservatives, the majority clearly seemed to agree with Senator Arthur Capper (R.-Kan.), who insisted that the bonus was "nothing more than a square deal for the men who did the fighting." On the last day of August the bill, slightly amended, passed the Senate, 47 to 22.

In the discussion of the conference report necessary to reconcile differences between the House and Senate versions, the possibility of a presidential veto was raised. Senator McCumber, pointing to the more than two-thirds majority in each house, calmly assured his colleagues and the nation that there were "enough votes in the two Houses to make this bill a law" whatever Warren Harding might do. The Congress gave final approval on September 15.[27] Five days later the President sent back a veto message which was a calm and reasoned exposition of the conservative fiscal objections to the bill and almost certainly had been drafted in the Treasury Department.[28]

Harding reiterated the national gratitude to the veteran, but insisted that fiscal responsibility came first. According to the President, the bill said in substance that "we do not have the cash; we do not believe in a tax levy to meet the situation, but here is our note; you may have our credit for half its worth." Nowhere in the message, of course, did he suggest any of the soak-the-rich taxes that had been so popular during the war or connect the administration's tax reduction program with its inability to pay. Not realizing the scandals which would soon engulf the Veterans' Bureau, he also pointed with pride to what the government had done for the disabled veteran. Harding closed his veto message with a peroration that could serve as an epitaph to the whole short-sighted fiscal policy of the 1920s: expressing his regret in disappointing many ex-servicemen and his embarrassment at being "out of accord with the majority of Congress," he insisted that he was merely doing his duty.

> The simple truth is that this bill proposes a Government obligation of more than four billions without a provision of funds for the extraordinary expenditure, which the executive branch of the Government must finance in the face of difficult financial problems, and the complete defeat of our commitment to effect economies. I would rather appeal, therefore, to the candid reflections of Congress and the country, and to the ex-service men in particular, as to the course better suited to further the welfare of our country. These ex-soldiers who served so gallantly in the war, and who are to be so conspicuous in the progress of the Republic in the half century before us, must know that nations can only survive where taxation is restrained from the limits of oppression, where the Public Treasury is locked against class legislation, but ever open to public necessity and prepared to meet all essential obligations. Such a policy makes a better country for which to fight or to have fought, and affords a surer abiding place in which to live and attain.

The House quickly overrode the veto, 258 to 54, as some Democrats who had opposed the bill did not want to support a Republican president in difficulty with his own party. The more obedient Senate, however, preferred to switch rather than fight, and sustained the veto by 44 to 28, a margin of four votes.[29]

The Legion and other probonus forces intensified their efforts after this somewhat unexpected setback. The Legion convention reaffirmed its stand in favor of the bonus, but was constrained by its leadership from an outright attack on either the President or his party. Although during the 1922 campaign some Democrats used the failure of the GOP to fulfill its bonus promises as a talking point, and Legion publicists insisted that the defeat of certain congressmen and senators was due to their failure to take the "right" position on the bonus, it is really impossible to evaluate the effect of an isolated issue in a tangled off-year election which had normal results—that is the party in power lost seats, in this case 76 in the House and 8 in the Senate.[30] By the time the new Congress met, in December 1923, the bonus had become one of the two or three truly major issues; the fact that 1924 was a presidential year served to heighten the political tension. In the months preceding the opening of Congress, the public debate on the bonus reached a new peak, and this is perhaps the most logical place to summarize the pro and con arguments and indicate alignment of the major forces and individuals.

The greatest single voice for the bonus, of course, remained the American Legion, whose stand became less ambiguous with every convention. It prepared a comprehensive brief which argued that the majority of the population wanted the bonus, that the claim was a just and honorable one, that the principle of adjusted compensation had been long established in this country and had been voted by most of our allies. In addition, the Legion pointed out that the federal government had adjusted the compensation of railroads (which had been seized and operated by the government) and war contractors by about $750 million each. The Legion, of course, continued to ring all the changes on the "we owe our boys a debt that can never be paid" theme, and insisted, with some reason, that with the postwar slump over and a boom well under way, the country could easily afford the bonus; in addition, its argument ran, the expenditure of this money by the veterans would stimulate the building trades and industry, increase employment, benefit merchants and serve as a "general stimulus to the tide of prosperity."

The bonus opposition was led, as we have seen, by economic conservatives, particularly big businessmen and the very rich. Their chief voice was, of course, the Pittsburgh millionaire Andrew W. Mellon who, as Secretary of the Treasury, represented his constituency even more faithfully than the Legion represented its own. An admiring family memoir assures us that Mellon was "horrified" by the bonus campaign and that the grounds of his opposition were not just the economics of the matter. He feared that if the bonus were paid to millions of young Americans their "careers might be blighted for years by such ill-advised, reckless, and needless spending." In statement after statement, Mellon attacked the bonus, insisting that the nation could have either more tax reduction or the bonus, but not both. Mellon's 1923–1924 tax reduction program called for the elimination of a number of minor excise taxes and a substantial reduction in the income tax rates, a reduction intended to benefit primarily those in the higher brackets.

Conservatives also organized the Ex-Servicemen's Anti-Bonus League, a largely letterhead organization, which characterized the Legion's campaign as "a disgraceful display of inordinate greed" and insisted that able-bodied veterans still "in the years of their strong young manhood" had no claim whatsoever on the government.[31] The economy-oriented National Industrial Conference Board concluded that the bonus could not [32]

> be justified on grounds of economic equity and fairness to the veterans or to the general population, while it would lay upon the country a financial burden which would adversely affect the interests of the nation as well as of the veterans and might tend to hamper the nation's efforts in behalf of the incapacitated veterans at present and of the needy or aged veterans in the future. Sentimental considerations, therefore, can afford the only grounds on which the adoption of the Soldiers' Bonus must rest.

Individual businessmen also joined the verbal battle. Camera magnate George Eastman opposed the bonus because it would make "mercenaries out of our patriotic boys," while Pierre S. DuPont, whose chemical company was a major beneficiary of wartime prosperity, argued that able-bodied veterans were "the most favored class in the United States, having health, youth and opportunity" and therefore did not need the bonus.[33] With business and its organizations lined up almost solidly against the bonus, it should come as no surprise to learn that most of the nation's press also opposed it.[34] The major exception to this generalization were the newspapers owned by William Randolph Hearst, which insisted that both national honor and the people's will called for the payment of the bonus. Most of the leading progressives, Democratic and Republican, agreed. Amos Pinchot claimed that since we treated returning soldiers like "tramps" when they came home, they were due "a bonus and an apology combined." [35] But it was the cowboy-humorist Will Rogers who best caught the country's mood. He supported the bonus because he thought the boys deserved it, and he brushed aside one prop of the conservative argument effectively in pointing out: [36] "That old alibi about the country not being able to pay is all applesauce. . . . This country is not broke, automobile manufacturers are three months behind in their orders, and whisky was never as high in its life."

The opening gun of the last battle for the passage of a bonus bill was fired by the new President, Calvin Coolidge. In his very first message to Congress he stated with typical Yankee bluntness: "I do not favor the granting of a bonus." [37] Later he argued that although the veterans were "entitled to the highest honor . . . the service they rendered was of such a nature that it cannot be recompensed to them by the payment of money. America was not waging war for the purpose of securing personal gain." [38] Despite the opposition of the accidental President, who would soon get the nomination and the presidency in his own right, a majority of his party seemed to favor the passage of a bonus bill before the November elections. As the most powerful midwestern voice of the GOP put it, the bonus would pass the Congress, even over a veto if necessary, because "it offers far too popular an issue for a Democratic candidate for the Republican party to take an opposite stand." [39] One such candidate was William G. McAdoo. As wartime Secretary of the Treasury, he had wanted to keep the veteran question out of postwar politics, but as the leading Democratic hopeful he favored "paying the bonus in cash and getting it behind us." He proposed funding that payment with an issue of fifty-year bonds.[40]

In Congress charges flew back and forth. Senator James Reed (D.-Mo.) asked the Senate to investigate "whether there is an organized effort being made to control opinion and the action of Congress . . . and whether the profiteers of the war are now contributing to defeat the soldiers' adjusted compensation bill." [41] In the lower chamber, freshman Congressman William Connery (D.-Mass.) went even further, charging that "a well-organized, concerted conspiracy, concocted by the big moneyed interests" was trying to defeat the bonus.[42] A midwestern Democrat saw the conspiracy a bit differently. Congressman Edgar Howard of Nebraska, who neither understood nor trusted the complex funding side of the bonus measure, insisted that the technical aspects of the bill made it a "legislative bastard, conceived in the fertile brain of a professional profiteering patriot, and accouched on a damask divan in the gold room of the House of Morgan & Co., attended by a galaxy of accouchers appointed by Treasury Secretary Mellon and approved by the President of the United States." [43]

Fiscal conservatives, of course, saw it another way. Senator Furnifold M. Simmons (D.-N.C.) complained about "bushels of . . . telegrams" from the American Legion,[44] while the *Wall Street Journal* saw the bonus advocates making "a last desperate attack from their Hindenburg line" and argued that the veterans were "panhandlers" seeking an "unearned and undefensible dole." [45]

At the more rational level, the performance of the nation's economy made it much harder for Mellon's arguments to have their previous effect, and bonus supporters were quick to point out how faulty the Secretary's figures had been in the past. Harding had used Mellon's estimate of a $650 million deficit for fiscal 1923 as a major buttress of his bonus veto, but there had in fact been a surplus of $310 million. This "billion dollar error," as it was called, did much to dim the luster of "the greatest Secretary of the Treasury since Alexander Hamilton," as the publicists of the Republican National Committee liked to call him.[46] In addition there were appeals to precedent. Senator Royal S. Copeland (D.-N.Y.) remarked that Lee, Grant, and Lincoln had all received some kind of bonus, while Arkansas' junior Senator Thaddeus Caraway played on a then popular prejudice by pointing out that "men like Jack Dempsey, who went into the shipyards instead of the trenches . . . got a bonus [of] about $14 a day for staying in a place of safety." [47]

Despite all the wind on Capitol Hill, the bonus ship sailed its prescribed course. The House Ways and Means Committee made the 1924 bill even more palatable by stripping from it the vocational-, farm-, home-aid options. What remained was simply the insurance provisions of the 1923 measure, with similar borrowing privileges, death benefit and deferred twenty-year lump-sum payment. The cash-option plan was brought up again, and this reopened question became perhaps the sorest point of the 1924 debate. Some bonus proponents saw the reintroduction of the cash option as further proof of a conspiracy against the bonus. Professional lobbyist Aaron Sapiro, chairman of the Legion's National Legislative Committee, was afraid that the "cash-option clause [would] defeat any real chance for securing adjusted compensation." [48]

The stripped-down measure passed the House 355 to 54 in mid-March; a month later the Senate, after a brisk fight on the Democratic-sponsored cash-option plan, rejected it and passed the House measure by a lopsided 67 to 17 vote.[49] By early May, minor differences between the two houses had been ironed out and the measure went to the White House. After almost two weeks of suspense—the close-mouthed Coolidge had kept even leaders of his own party guessing [50]—the President returned the bill with a stinging veto message. According to Silent Cal, the bonus bill offended not only the principles of good government and economy, but of morality, patriotism, and Americanism.

"Patriotism," said Coolidge, who had remained a civilian during two wars fought while he was of military age, "which is bought and paid for is not patriotism. . . . This bill would condemn those who are weak to turn over a part of their earnings to those who are strong. Our country can not afford it. The veterans as a whole do not want it. All our American principles are opposed to it. There is no moral justification for it." [51]

The congressional reaction was sharp; many congressmen seemed surprised at the tone of the message, if not its substance. New York's insurgent Republican Fiorello La Guardia,

for example, declared himself "hurt . . . offended . . . sad-
dened" because the veto message "placed a question mark on
the honorable discharge granted to 4,000,000 gallant American
soldiers." [52] The House, to no one's surprise, overwhelmingly
voted to override, 313 to 78.[53] The Senate, however, remained
a question mark, and some bonus proponents, disappointed
so many times previously, were anxious up to the last minute.
Administration pressures, however, could change only five
votes as the Senate overrode by a three-vote margin, 59 to 26.[54]
The bonus fight was over, or so it seemed.

What exactly had been won? Much of the original rationale for the bonus had been lost. It was supposed, in the first
instance, to help the returning doughboy readjust to civilian
life; yet the bonus, as finally passed almost six years after the
armistice, would not pay off for most veterans until 1945,
by which time, of course, an entirely new crop of veterans
would be attempting the difficult postwar reconversion. The
loan privileges, rather severe by present standards (until the
interest rate was lowered in the early years of the Depression,
the prevailing rate was around 7 percent), did not even begin
until 1927. The assumptions behind the 1924 bill, like most
American assumptions in the 1920s, were fallacious; its
sponsors assumed that prosperity would continue and that
the money would be most useful to the ageing veteran in
1945. As it happened, the possession of what was essentially
a postdated check was to prove a severe irritant when the
economic disasters that followed the Great Crash caused
veterans, along with other Americans, to question many of
the assumptions of the prosperity decade. But all this was
in the future. To the Legion leadership, and probably to
most veterans, it seemed a famous victory; probably no one
in America had the slightest inkling of the amount of bitter-
ness that this victory would unleash.

3

Wright Patman
and the Fight
for the Bonus

FOR THE NEXT six years the bonus issue was almost dormant, with Congress passing a few minor statutory liberalizations, such as follow almost every major legislative breakthrough. Outside of Congress there was no noticeable demand for further action. Only with the impact of the first shock waves of the Great Depression did veterans, and those who claimed to speak for them, reactivate the bonus issue; they soon came to want immediate cash payment which would enable the veteran to cash in his certificate at once for the same sum which the law promised him in 1945. As the pinch of the Depression grew tighter, more and more veterans grew conscious of the postdated check they were carrying around, and many of them wanted to change the rules. This was, of course, abhorrent to the administration, fiscal conservatives of both parties, and, interestingly enough, many, if not most, of the progressives in and out of Congress. All vigorously opposed what they characterized as "class legislation," and "a raid on the treasury" cries echoed repeatedly by most of the nation's press.

Even before the crash came, there were scattered and desultory efforts to get immediate cash payment. The first bill calling for this was introduced in May 1929 by Senator Smith W. Brookhart (R.-Iowa), one of the midwestern insurgents who so troubled the calm of the Senate. The same bill was introduced into the House a few days later by a freshman representative, Wright Patman (D.-Tex.), who would later become the acknowledged leader in the fight for the bonus. None of the three bills offered in the special session called by President Hoover in early 1929 even got out of committee; the same was true for the nine bills offered in the post-crash session which adjourned in July 1930 for the summer recess.[1]

In October, the American Legion convention in Boston took time out from horseplay, patriotism, and nativism to debate the newly revived bonus question. A number of resolutions calling for immediate cash payment were bottled up by the Committee on National Legislation, which was obedient to the conservative Legion leadership. Two resolutions of the bonus were raised from the floor: one calling for payment of 80 percent of face value in 1931 was voted down decisively, 967 to 244, while another calling for abolition of interest in loans made on the certificates was amended to call for a reduction to 4 percent with no compounding and then passed without a recorded vote.[2]

The congressional elections of 1930 came as a shock to the orthodox; the Democrats picked up 53 seats and control of the House for the first time since 1916, and their gain of eight in the upper chamber left the GOP only an uncertain one-vote advantage. When the lame-duck session of the old Congress met in December, no fewer than twenty-one bonus bills were introduced, including measures sponsored by such Republican stalwarts as Senator Arthur H. Vandenberg of Michigan and Congressman B. Carroll Reece of Tennessee, who had just suffered what would be his only defeat in a congressional career that ran from 1921 to 1947.[3] Pressure from the floor, from dissident Legion posts, from the Hearst newspapers, and from the country at large made it difficult for the Republican leadership to continue to do nothing. It was also clear that if the Republicans wanted to make any political capital out of the bonus issue they would have to act before the Democrats took over the House.

Meanwhile, the hierarchy of the American Legion was also beginning to feel the pressure. Mail, petitions, mass meetings, and Washington-bound delegations of veterans made it clear to those whose political ears were close to the ground that something had to be done. On January 21, 1931, in the largest demonstration yet, a group of a thousand veterans marched through Washington and delivered a petition calling for immediate and cash payment into the willing hands of Congressman Patman.[4] Four days later, the Legion's national executive committee met at its Indianapolis headquarters in a stormy all-day session and passed two unanimous resolutions constructed to conceal serious differences. In the first, the group affirmed its authority to "interpret" the seemingly unambiguous action of the Boston convention, which just four months previously had tabled all discussion of significant bonus modification. Then, subscribing to the "stimulation" theory that the bonus would "materially assist in the relief of present distressful economic conditions and put new life into American business," they endorsed "immediate cash retirement," a phrase hitherto unknown. It seemed to mean immediate payment of the accrued value of the certificates, or about 25 percent of face value, and thus corresponded to some of the more conservative bills already introduced into Congress. This would have cost about $900 million.[5]

In the closing days of January and early February, the House Ways and Means Committee held hearings on the whole subject of adjusted compensation. Most of the testimony was predictable; the Legion spokesmen, "without choosing as between any of the specific bills now pending," made it clear that the veterans of the nation wanted more, while administration spokesmen insisted that nothing at all should be done.

The only new idea, and one that quickly bore fruit, sprang from that source of so much of welfare capitalism during the new era, Owen D. Young of General Electric, a veteran of various public and quasi-public commissions since the Wilson administration. Young, an expert at fiscal hocus-pocus, as his plan on the war debts indicated, proposed that the loan basis be arbitrarily upped to 50 percent which would give the average veteran about $500 ($280 if he had already borrowed the maximum allowable). This would have the advantage of giving the veterans a little cake—the amount of their loan—but would also allow them to keep the insurance provisions of their certificates in force, as a retirement would not. The sanction of a great captain of industry gave this scheme irresistible political appeal to the hard-pressed legislators, and almost as soon as it was proposed, it began to draw support from individual congressmen and the veterans' lobby.[6]

The leadership of the executive branch, however, saw the matter in a different light and continued to oppose any significant modification. "It is neither sound nor equitable," Andrew Mellon, ignoring Young's alternative, wrote to Oregon Republican Willis C. Hawley, Chairman of the House Ways and Means Committee, "for the Government to invite the veterans to cash in their endowment insurance policies and so to forego the benefits of future protection." The Secretary of the Treasury continually argued that the 1924 legislation had settled the issue forever, and delighted in pointing out that a sum paid out in 1930 or 1931 was really a great deal more than that same sum paid out in 1945. Even more irritating was his bland refusal even to discuss the rapid deterioration of economic conditions which threw the assumptions of 1924 in an entirely different light. As Congressman Hamilton Fish (R.-N.Y.) put it, Mellon avoided "any discussion of the urgent needs of the veterans who are un-employed," and whether or not the accelerated payments might stimulate business.[7]

In mid-February the House leadership was ready to move; Hawley himself introduced a bill that increased the loan basis of the certificates to 50 percent of face value (the maximum loan was then 22½ percent) and lowered the interest rate on such loans from 6 percent to 4½ percent. If all eligible holders borrowed the maximum amount, this could cost $1.6 billion. Just four days after it had been introduced, Hawley's measure was reported favorably out of committee under the familiar "gag" rule—forty minutes of debate and no amendments. The bill was passed overwhelmingly, 363 to 39, with 24 not voting. The Senate was almost as swift, passing the bill three days later, 72 to 12, with 12 not voting. Only 15 of the Senate's 56 Republicans either voted or were paired against the bill, while one Democrat, William King of Utah, was negatively registered.[8]

What the *New York Times* called "The Inevitable Veto" followed a week later.[9] President Hoover in his message echoed many of the views voiced by his Treasury Secretary, but un-like Mellon he did take notice of the arguments made for the bill.[10] He dismissed the claim that veterans were in need, asserting that unemployed veterans were "being provided the basic necessities of life by the devoted communities in those parts of the country affected by the depression or drought." The stimulation argument he rejected with logic curious even for him. If the veterans spent their bonus money on the necessities of life, "there would be no stimulation of business. The theory of stimulation is based upon the anticipation of wasteful expenditure. It can be of no assistance in the return of real prosperity." But in the final analysis, Hoover's veto really rested on moral rather than economic arguments. Even more important than the issue itself, the President felt, was the dangerous precedent it would create by opening the Federal Treasury to a thousand purposes, many admirable in their intentions but in which the proponents fail or do not care to see that with such beginnings many of them consume more and more of the savings and the labor of our people. In aggregate they threaten burdens beyond the ability of our country normally to bear; and, of far higher importance, each of them breaks the barriers of self-reliance and self-support in our people.

Neither the economics nor the morality moved many Congressmen; although a few Republicans faithfully switched their votes, a majority of the President's party in each house voted to override, and the liberalized loan provisions became law on February 27, 1931.[11] That same day Hawley announced that the first loan on the new basis had already been approved by the Veterans Administration, whose agile Director, Brigadier General Frank T. Hines, demonstrated a capacity for bureaucratic survival surpassed only by J. Edgar Hoover.[12]

Five days later the Seventy-first Congress passed out of existence, and the administration had what it obviously regarded as a nine-month respite from congressional interference. This period, from March to December 1931, is a crucial period in the Great Depression and thus in American history. It was during 1931 that significant numbers of influential Americans became thoroughly convinced that the economic crisis was not just another depression; it was during 1931 that significant numbers of people began to blame the nation's ills on Herbert Hoover; and finally, it was in that same period, especially during the nine-month congressional recess, that the bonus issue was again made a major national concern.

It became one, in the final analysis, because a few influential and energetic Congressmen made the cause of the bonus their own. Two well-established Democratic Congressmen, William P. Connery of Massachusetts and John E. Rankin of Mississippi, were quite important, but by December 1931, Wright Patman, with only one term of Congress behind him, had become the acknowledged leader of the bonus forces.

The almost unprecedented preeminence gained by Patman, a very junior member in a body that prized seniority, can be explained only by observing that Patman very quickly made the issue uniquely his own. He was born in rural northeast Texas in 1893, received a law degree, worked in the county attorney's office, served in the army during the war, and in the Texas legislature afterwards. Before being elected to Congress, he had been district attorney for five years. He was a Baptist, a 32d degree Mason, a prohibitionist, and a former post commander of the American Legion.

Patman's socioeconomic views can best be described as neo-populist. He was first elected on a platform that called for farm relief of a substantial nature, states' rights, world peace by taking the profit out of war and drafting capital as well as labor, a square deal to all ex-servicemen, economical administration of government, strict and rigid immigration laws, prohibition, and increased personal exemptions in income tax. The platform declared the candidate hostile to monopolies, trusts, branch banking, centralization, gambling in products of the soil, and excessive and discriminatory freight rates.[13] If one keeps in mind that the original populist movement was concerned essentially with land, money, and transportation, Patman's intellectual debt to populism is unmistakable. There has been a great deal written during the last decade about the nativistic aspects of populism, and essentially ahistoric arguments have been adduced to fabricate a link between the agrarian reform movements of the late 1890s, and fascist, anti-Semitic, anti-intellectual movements of the 1930s, 1940s and 1950s.[14] A close examination of Patman's writings, speeches, and papers discloses absolutely nothing of an antidemocratic nature, save for the inevitable touch of negrophobia. There is a strain of economic nationalism, but if one were to write off as antidemocratic and anti-intellectual everyone who exhibited that tendency, there would be precious little left in either the democratic or intellectual traditions.

Since Patman finally evolved a position which yoked the

demand for immediate cash payment of the bonus with a plan
to expand the currency, those few historians who have written
about him seem to assume that his agitation for the bonus
was essentially a means to further his inflationist ends.[15] The
record shows otherwise; his first bill, introduced in May 1929,
called for financing the bonus by an issue of fifteen-year bonds,
a thoroughly orthodox means of payment. His first argument
in favor of cash payment stressed justice and propounded no
economic panacea, although it did show an enthusiasm for
soaking the rich. Patman insisted, quite plausibly, that the
adjustment should have been figured from January 1, 1918
(a later calculation convinced him that June 5, 1918, the
median point of service, was a better date), and that the veterans were entitled to 6 percent rather than 4 percent interest
on the money they failed to get. If these changes were made
retroactively to right the wrong that had been done the veteran
in 1924, the face value of the bonus would be due in 1929,
according to the Texan's figuring. He delighted in pointing
out that the railroads and war contractors had had their compensation adjusted retroactively. The country could easily
afford it, his 1929 argument continued. The war had cost
$36 billion, and he estimated that half of it had gone to make
millionaires.[16]

Patman helped to create organizations to work for the bonus
both inside and outside of Congress. In March 1930, he took
the first steps to organize a steering committee of congressmen
to guide bonus legislation; by the next year about thirty
representatives and senators were meeting regularly to plan
strategy and tactics.[17] He also made wide use of the mails and
his congressional privileges; about 50,000 copies of a bonus
speech he made in the House were mailed under frank to
"every part of the US." [18] By this time, of course, the depression had made an impact on his thinking, and he was beginning to argue that the bonus payment would stimulate the
whole sagging economy. Although quite unhappy that the 1930
Legion convention, which he attended, had failed to endorse

cash payment, he tried to make what capital he could of its one positive bonus action.

In mid-October, Patman sent a letter to all Democratic congressional nominees telling them how to use the bonus issue in the final weeks of the campaign. He pointed out that, despite the national convention's failure to act, state Legion groups in New York, Massachusetts, and Texas had all voted for immediate cash payment. The Boston convention's proposal to lower the interest rate (Patman put it "in order that the veterans may borrow their own money at 4 percent simple interest") would, he argued, "open up for consideration the whole adjusted compensation law and give us an opportunity to convince Congress that the certificates should be paid off instead. . . ." Patman volunteered to act as a clearing house for probonus activities and invited anyone to write him for either information or support.[19]

Early in the lame-duck session of 1930–1931, Patman reiterated his bonus demand. Immediate payment, he insisted, would relieve unemployment and distress and restore prosperity without additional taxation. Either short-term certificates (presumably to circulate) or long-term bonds would be acceptable to him as a source of financing. The country's two basic problems, as he saw them, were "underconsumption" and the fact that the "per capita circulation of money was too low." As the year closed, the Texan began to zero in on the man who soon became his favorite devil, Andrew W. Mellon. While his remarks about the Secretary of the Treasury never had the biting vindictiveness that his comrade-in-arms John Rankin delighted in ("If I had my way we would put a wound stripe on his purse big enough to be seen from Pittsburgh to Philadelphia."), it is clear that Mellon became for him the personification of eastern bankerdom. The whole nation, he felt, was

suffering from an overdose of Mellonism. Predatory wealth will remain in control of our Government as long as Andrew W. Mellon is Secretary of the Treasury. He is the worst enemy of the wage earners, farmers, and veterans. . . . He always places property rights above human rights.[20]

In February 1931, when it was clear that his bill would again fail to get out of committee—he had filed a discharge petition but couldn't get a majority of the House to sign it—Patman joined with Rankin and Connery to denounce as an enemy of the veteran the Legion's legislative representative, John Thomas Taylor, who had been working for Owen Young's loan proposal and against immediate payment. The "rank and file" of the Legion, the congressmen claimed, wanted payment now. Patman had earlier made it quite clear that he would be satisfied with nothing less than full payment, although he was pleased that the loan basis was increased.[21]

Patman worked all during the long 1931 recess writing letters, making speeches, and organizing probonus groups. In mid-June he was a featured speaker during a Chicago conference which created a Veterans Prosperity Committee, a pressure group devoted to organizing probonus sentiment, circulating petitions, and acting as a pressure group inside the American Legion. The committee's literature announced that the Texan intended to address as many meetings as possible on this subject and invited speaking invitations for him.[22] By the time the Legion met in September, Patman was in touch with and had helped to organize similar groups all over the country.[23]

The Legion's convention was held in Detroit that year, and in his welcoming address, Mayor Frank Murphy, the future New Deal Attorney General and Supreme Court Justice, appended to the usual platitudes of the occasion an exhortation for social justice and an indirect plea for the bonus, as he told his comrades that it was "their plain duty to come out on the firing line in the interest of the jobless veteran and brother, denied the right to work because of social and economic conditions . . . for which he is in no wise to blame."

The mayor made it clear that he felt that much of the blame should fall on what he described as "a government unconcerned." [24]

Later the same day the head of that government came to Detroit to make a different kind of exhortation. Hoover had come for one thing: to ask the Legion not to press the immediate payment issue. The Chief Executive arrived without ceremony and received a cool, thirty-second ovation. Lauding the past patriotism of the Legionnaires, he talked to them of the "even greater service" they could now perform.

That is disinterested opposition by you to additional demands upon the Nation until we have won this war against world depression. I am not speaking alone of veterans' legislation which has been urged for action at the convention, but I am speaking equally of demands for every other project proposed in the country which would require increased Federal expenditure.

As he concluded, a leather-lunged Legionnaire bellowed: "We want a beer!" setting off a "wet" demonstration that masked the President's departure.[25] Despite the obvious lack of enthusiasm for the President's counsel, the Legion leadership loyally brought in a resolution tailored to Herbert Hoover's conservative specifications. It called upon

the able-bodied men of America, rich and poor, veteran, civilian and state[s]men, to refrain from placing unnecessary financial burdens upon National, State, or municipal governments and to unite their efforts as they all did in 1917 to the end that the war against depression be victoriously concluded, prosperity and happiness restored.

A minority resolution, which Wright Patman helped draft, called for immediate cash payment. Patman himself, a delegate from Texas, in the longest single speech in favor of it argued mainly on the grounds that it was a debt owed to the veterans, that the country could afford it, and that circulation of the $2 billion that it would cost would be a blessing for the economy. As was almost always the case in Legion conventions, the view of the leadership prevailed, but the vote—902 to 507—demonstrated that more than a third of the delegates were tired of restraint. It is safe to assume that the same was true for an even larger segment of the rank and file.[26]

Although unsuccessful with the major veterans' organizations, the bonus propagandists had earlier scored a significant success with the second ranking veterans group, the Veterans of Foreign Wars, which then had fewer than 200,000 members as opposed to the Legion's million. Although they had taken a full cash payment stand as early as 1930, it was only at the VFW 1931 convention in Kansas City (a county judge named Harry S Truman was chairman of the local arrangements committee) that a militant probonus group of officers was elected. Under the leadership of their new commander in chief, Darold D. De Coe, and a rising young politician, James E. Van Zandt, who would be elected as a Republican congressman from Pennsylvania in 1938, the VFW became one of the chief lobbying groups for the bonus. Their Washington office became the headquarters of the probonus groups, and special funds were raised to support a nationwide petition campaign and other publicity devices. The VFW makes a curious ideological contrast to the better established Legion. Its leaders tended to be younger, its economic demands were more radical, and it was much more likely to be critical of the status quo; yet, like the Legion, it was hypernationalistic, superpatriotic, and utterly contemptuous of the more libertarian portions of the American Constitution. (In 1933, for example, its convention resolved without a dissenting voice that no member of the American Civil Liberties Union should be employed as a teacher.) Even with such a "respectable" and active ally, however, Patman clearly faced an uphill fight.[27]

The Texan, of course, was not discouraged. He spent the rest of the fall lining up support for the bill he intended to introduce. In late October he wrote to William Randolph Hearst asking the publisher for support. "Your newspapers accomplished more for [the veterans'] cause," the Congressman told the lord of San Simeon, "than all the other newspapers in the United States combined." Speaking of his plans for the immediate future, he assured Hearst that "the greatest campaign for the passage of legislation in the history of our country will commence during the next thirty or forty-five days. Organizations are being perfected all over the nation." He wanted the publisher to amend his pet scheme—a $5 billion bond issue for public works—so that $2 billion of it would be earmarked for the payment of adjusted service compensation; in return, Patman suggested, it would be easy to swing veteran support behind the package. Nothing came of this proposal, but it is important, I think, to show how relatively orthodox Patman's fiscal views then were; at a later date a bond issue would be anathema to him.[28]

Herbert Hoover—the first Republican since Taft to face a Congress his party did not control—met the bonus issue head-on in his State of the Union message. Acknowledging that "there will be demands for further veterans' legislation," he pointed out that the nation's annual expenditure on veterans was more than a billion dollars, and he reiterated his opposition "to any extension of these expenditures until the country has recovered from the present situation."[29] The President was quite right about the demand for veterans' legislation; no fewer than 34 separate bills affecting adjusted service compensation were introduced in the first session of the Seventy-second Congress, but the one upon which most of the attention was focused was the so-called Patman bill, which he managed to get numbered H.R. 1. This was the first of several bills that the Texan introduced during the 1931–1932 session; all called for immediate cash payment, but there is a distinct progression in the sections of the bills providing for the method of payment. H.R. 1 called for the issuance of Treasury notes in denominations of $1, $2, $5, $10, $20, $25, $50, $100, $500, and $1,000; these notes would be full legal tender, non-interest-bearing, and exempt from all taxes. This part of his proposal was later modified in H.R. 7726; in its final form this bill would pay the bonus with Treasury notes almost indistinguishable from other currency. At the same time it called for the issuance of 3½ percent United States bonds in like amount, to be sold only if the purchasing power of the dollar should fall as much as 2 percent below its value in 1926.[30]

The difference in sophistication between these two provisions should be apparent even to the reader wholly innocent of monetary views. The first was rather crude Coxeyish inflation, with the creation of a deliberately conspicuous new breed of currency. The second created the same amount of "fiat" money, but with as little fuss as possible, and appended to it, as a sort of pedigree of orthodoxy, a rather complicated proposition looking hopefully toward a steep rise in commodity prices. (In 1926 farm prices had been at 145 percent of parity, that is, the average price received during 1910–1914; in 1931, the figure was depressed to 87 percent, and, as it turned out, the 1926 figure would not again be passed until the war year of 1942.)

Still a third Patman-authored measure, introduced in July 1932, at the very end of the session, shows in its title the expansion of the congressman's thinking. All his earlier measures had been titled simply "To provide for the immediate payment to veterans of the face value of their adjusted-service certificates"; this last bill was "To provide for controlled expansion of the currency, increase in commodity prices, relief of unemployment, and the immediate payment. . . ." Sometime during 1931–1932, Patman's crusade changed its direction. The original limited, if costly, objective had been justice for the ex-serviceman; the new goal involved a change in the nation's monetary system. The pragmatic warrior for the veteran had become a true believer battling to change the orientation of the entire country. The concern here will be exclusively with the bonus fight, but this larger struggle, which still goes on, must at least be noted in passing.[31]

Patman's original bill stayed bottled up in the House Ways and Means Committee almost five months; this did not stop it from becoming a national issue. Patman himself was a whole host; in addition to speeches, interjections, and interpellations on the floor of the House, he continued his extensive speaking engagements. In December 1932 and January 1933, he and Van Zandt of the VFW addressed veterans' rallies in Providence, Columbus, Chicago, Milwaukee, St. Paul, Minneapolis, Des Moines, St. Joseph, Kansas City, St. Louis, and Indianapolis, and he and other bonus advocates also spoke several times on nationwide radio hookups. The VFW was circulating thousands of petitions calling for immediate payment. Patman also tried, without success, to get Governor Franklin D. Roosevelt of New York to support the bonus campaign.[32]

In addition to his bonus activities, Patman also launched a full-scale impeachment process against Andrew Mellon for violation of an ancient conflict of interest statute forbidding the Secretary of the Treasury from participation in any business, which was ended only by the Secretary's resignation to become Ambassador to Great Britain. Patman also joined in the long-standing struggle for federal insurance of bank deposits, attempted to inhibit the sale of worthless securities, and proposed a far-reaching investigation into "monetary, banking, currency and financial systems." [33]

The arguments for the bonus were essentially the same, but the steadily deteriorating economic conditions made them stand out in even bolder relief. In addition, 1932 was an election year, and one in which the Democrats had high hopes of regaining the White House. Yet, despite these favorable factors, political pundits predicted that the bonus measure would not even pass the House; should it do so, Senate passage was viewed as well-nigh impossible, and, in any event, an almost certain veto awaited it at the White House.

The passage of the 50 percent loan bill the previous session gave Patman one additional talking point. For the veteran who borrowed the maximum, he pointed out, compound interest on his loan would eventually eat up the other 50 percent. In one radio speech he denied that the veterans were either "treasury raiders" or "bonus racketeers"; in another, he argued that the nation needed more money in circulation (the bonus, he claimed, would add about $18 per capita), and, if his Treasury note plan were used, the veterans could be paid off painlessly, "without a bond issue, without additional taxes, and without paying interest." The $2.2 billion note issue, he admitted, would cause "a moderate inflation" but would "in no way endanger the gold standard." In a later broadcast, he returned to this theme; the United States, he insisted, was on a "double gold standard"; by this he meant that the federal gold reserve of $4 billion was sufficient to support a circulation of $10 billion in currency, yet only $5.5 billion was in circulation. Therefore, he argued, his proposal to issue a mere $2.2 billion in new currency was not in any way a fiat money proposal.

Insistent on his own remedies, Patman was scornful of others. When the administration sponsored a measure to set up a Reconstruction Finance Corporation to lend money to banks, corporations, and governmental bodies, Patman protested against its theory, as he puts it, that money "should percolate on down to the people." He wanted the money to go directly to them without the intervention of banks, insurance companies, or even the state and city governments. He took up pages of the *Congressional Record* with a table compiled by the Veterans Administration showing just how much would go to each county in the United States if the bonus were paid in full (Cook County, Illinois, would have gotten $82 million; Storey County, Nevada, $14,567.28). In addition, he insisted, much of the RFC money would go "to pay dividends on watered stocks and bonds" and wind up in the hands of "the house of Morgan, the Mellons, Kuhn, Loeb & Co., and other international bankers." He found it particularly galling that this bill (which had a $2 billion price tag, almost identical with his bonus measure) could pass with very little said about "the budget not being balanced." The $2 billion for the RFC, he complained, was not intended to pay a debt; since the bonus was a debt, it should have been paid first. Later he made similar complaints about the bill creating a $1 billion Federal Home Loan bank.[34]

If Patman's arguments stressed the plausibility and justice of his measure, certain of his allies emphasized the unprecedented nature of the emergency. Some, like John Rankin, used what William Leuchtenberg has called the analogue of war:

> Let no man deceive himself. This country is at war! We are at war with depression, we are at war with poverty, we are at war with hunger, we are at war with privation, with human misery and with all the kindred evils that this unprecedented panic has produced.

Congressman Fred M. Vinson (D.-Ken.) answered critics of the measure, who prophesied that, if passed, it would bring near chaos, by asserting simply that "we have already arrived at the brink of ruin." And in perhaps the most emotional appeal, inflationist Senator Elmer Thomas (D.-Okla.) implied that if Congress did not give the veterans the bonus they might foment revolution. "In the jungles where the bananas and coconuts are plentiful do the monkeys starve?" he asked his colleagues. "Are not the citizens of America as intelligent as the monkeys of Africa? . . . These men will not starve." [35]

To all of these arguments, of course, the guardians of the

status quo had answers. Ogden Mills, who took over at the Treasury after Mellon's resignation, was willing to admit that economic distress existed. Just before Christmas he told the New York Economic Club:

> It is true that a distressingly large minority of the wage earners of the country are now out of work. But we must not forget that a majority still have enough work to make a living. We have lost much; but we have infinitely more to lose.

Another New Yorker, Congressman Hamilton Fish, long-time friend of the veteran, whose positive contribution to the bonus controversy was a repeated insistence that the Allied War Debts, that chimera of the 1920s, be used to pay off the bonus, also came down for fiscal orthodoxy.

> In the last analysis, [the struggle against the Patman bill was] the same old fight of soft money against sound money. We are already in the midst of a severe panic, but if the proposed financial heresy of printing two more billions of paper money is carried out it will mean the collapse of the dollar and American credit that will make the present panic look like a new-born babe.

It was not just the orthodox and the conservative who opposed the bonus; to the progressive, to the mugwump, to many a liberal northern Democrat like Franklin D. Roosevelt, the bonus bill seemed to be just another piece of special-interest legislation. As Senator George W. Norris (R.-Neb.) put it, after pointing out that veterans constituted perhaps one-third of the unemployed:

> If there were no unemployment outside of the ranks of the veterans of the World War, I would not hesitate to vote for this bill . . . [but] if we pass this bill it will be an impossibility to pass an unemployment bill at this session. . . .

His fellow progressive, Congressman Fiorello La Guardia (R.-N.Y.) was much blunter; the fiery little ex-major snarled that Patman's bill would

> pay over $2,400,000,000 to less than 4 per cent of the population. . . . [It] will not solve a single problem with which Congress and the country are confronted. With 8,000,000 unemployed men and women in the country, I for one refuse to sacrifice them for any such sordid, selfish purpose.

A third facet of progressive opposition was displayed by Senator Robert M. La Follette, Jr. (R.-Wis.). In a speech that demonstrated his vaunted independence, he insisted that he was not "frightened by the cry of inflation raised against this bill. It is the type of inflation provided that I am not ready to accept." According to his view, the Depression was going to get worse for at least two more years, and the government ought to husband its resources for the emergencies to come. Although he opposed the Patman view, he had nothing substantial to offer to replace it. He was sure that "in a long period of depression there is an amount of credit which the Government can obtain [but] I do not know how much that amount is, and neither does any other living man in or out of this chamber." [36]

Some northern Democrats, in an obvious vote-catching device, declared themselves ready to support payment of "immediate surrender value," but since any veteran could borrow about twice the surrender value, this was an empty gesture. No one ever anticipated that the veterans pay the loans back, and the reports of the Veterans Administration fail to indicate that any did.[37]

Press opinion was almost universally hostile to the probonus forces, with the notable exception of the Hearst chain, then still a power in Democratic politics. Arthur Brisbane's comment that the administration's policy was "Billions for high finance, but not a dollar for soldiers" was a typical Hearstian comment.[38]

Before passing to an account of the legislative progress of Patman's doomed measure and the sequence of events which the struggle for it set in motion, it might be well to examine the whole inflationist controversy with the hindsight of three-and-a-half decades. Most historians have been less than kind to Patman and the other inflationists; writing either from the standpoint of FDR and seeing the inflationists as part of the politics of upheaval threatening to overthrow the President, or as opponents of most of the New Deal changes, none have tried to see the period from this particular point of view. When not ignored, as is usual, Patman is written off as a "professional veteran." [39] Yet today, when the acceleration of payments to veterans has become a standard method of stimulating the economy, it is not as clear as it once seemed to be that the Patman proposals had no value. In fact, one of the most recent and most sophisticated analysts of the American economy, Professor Douglas North, has argued just the opposite. Suggesting that conservative fiscal policy may have prevented the New Deal from becoming a true social revolution, he points out that in only two years of the 1930s—1931 and 1936—was federal fiscal policy significantly more expansive than in 1929 and that in both cases the expansion was caused in large part by veterans' bonus payments passed over presidential vetoes.[40]

Patman and his fellow inflationists, who were in a long American tradition of monetary radicalism, in some respects anticipated the Keynesian revolution in economic thought, which, despite many comments to the contrary, never succeeded in becoming the economic philosophy of the New Deal. If Patman and his fellows were correct, or partially correct, in their diagnosis and prescription, it must be pointed out that they claimed rejuvenating powers for their economic tonic that it just did not have. Injecting $2.2 billion into the economy in the spring of 1932 would certainly have had a stimulating effect, but it is reasonably clear that the economy needed a good deal more than a mild tonic. Since, as John Kenneth Galbraith has put it, the economy was fundamentally unsound, corrective surgery rather than a stimulant was required.

Although many of the bills had been introduced the first day of the session, it was only in April 1932 that the House Committee on Ways and Means held hearings on a number of pay-the-bonus-now proposals. A few days previously the White House, in a highly unusual step, released a presidential statement reaffirming Hoover's opposition to the bonus.[41]

> Informal polls of the House of Representatives have created apprehension in the country that a further bonus bill of $2,000,000,000 or thereabouts for World War Veterans will be passed.
>
> I wish to state again that I am absolutely opposed to any such legislation. . . . I do not believe that any such legislation can become law.
>
> Such action would undo every effort that is being made to reduce Government expenditures and balance the budget. The first duty of every citizen of the United States is to build up and sustain the credit of the United States Government. Such an action would irretrievably undermine it.

The following week the White House was able to announce that National Commander Harry L. Stevens had informed the President that the American Legion stood "solidly behind him" in opposition to any further bonus legislation. This was perhaps arranged to counteract the effect of the VFW petition drive, which was climaxed by a thousand veterans marching to the Capitol to present petitions for cash payment supposedly signed by two-and-a-half million ex-servicemen.[42]

When the hearings finally took place, there were few surprises. Congressman Patman made a long preliminary statement. As far as the press was concerned, the most interesting witness was Father Charles E. Coughlin of Royal Oak, Michigan. The radio priest, not yet notorious, had already built up a mass following—he claimed a clearly absurd figure of 60 million listeners—who enjoyed his denunciations of "world bankers" and his obviously sincere regard for the poor. Coughlin, an avowed inflationist with a strong silver bias, testified for the bonus, as did George LeBlanc and Robert Harriss, two renegade minor members of the New York financial community who were the radio priest's chief monetary advisors; John A. Simpson of the Farmers' Union, a heterodox farm group; General Jacob Coxey, of Coxey's Army fame (1894), who had just taken over as mayor of Massillon, Ohio; and former Senator Robert L. Owen of Oklahoma, a leading proponent of an expansive monetary policy, whose reputation as a coauthor of the Federal Reserve Act gave him much prestige.

As opposed to these mavericks, the committee heard the several voices of the academy and high finance. Although some of the more orthodox experts favored inflation—or to use the then popular term "reflation," meaning a controlled inflation—none thought that the Patman bill was a particularly good way of achieving it. Williford I. King of New York University, who insisted that nothing was "more important at the present time" than "a reasonable expansion of the currency," nevertheless thought the Patman bill "would probably do great harm to the American people." Irving Fisher of Yale, the most noted of the academic inflationists, expressed fear that the psychological effect of paying the bonus—"giving away when we ought to be economizing"—might in the long run prove "deflationary in its net effect." If the "radicals" among the economists tended to view the bill with alarm, the more orthodox held up their hands in utter horror. Edwin W. Kemmerer of Princeton feared that even the "anticipated passage" of a bonus bill would destroy "the little financial confidence that is left," while E. A. Goldenweiser of the Federal Reserve Board felt it "would prolong the depression." One of his chiefs, Eugene Meyer, a governor of the Federal Reserve Board, invoked Gresham's Law (bad money drives out good) and implied that a massive outflow of gold would ensue if the Patman bill became law.[43]

Despite the overwhelming negative weight of academic opinion, ten of the fifteen Democrats on the Ways and Means Committee voted to support the bill; their five fiscally conservative colleagues, however, joined the ten members of the Republican minority to bring in an adverse report. The majority argued that American soldiers had been taken care of with "great liberality"; nevertheless, "if the financial condition of the country would permit it," they would report the bill favorably. They were convinced that "fiat money" ought not to be issued "in this, the greatest and richest country in the world." Despite the claims of the inflationists, the majority insisted that there was no shortage of currency, and concluded with the familiar platitude that what was really needed was "a restoration of confidence in order to get back to normal."

The minority report agreed that a restoration of confidence was necessary, but insisted that it could come about only when "commodity values are restored through an expansion of the circulating medium." The Treasury notes called for in the bill, it insisted, would be "sound money." It concluded with an argument that the proposed legislation would afford relief "not alone to the veterans . . . but to the entire Nation." [44]

The committee brought in its adverse report on May 7; in order to bring it before the House, it was necessary for Patman to file a discharge petition. Under the rules that the House had adopted for the first time in that session, only 145 signatures were necessary to bring a measure before the Congress; this was a temporary liberalization of the rules. In previous sessions the signatures of a majority of congressmen had been required, that is, 218 signatures; during the New Deal, the more restrictive rule was restored as a method of dealing with the often restive agrarian–inflationist bloc in the lower house.[45] Patman's petition was placed in the well of the House on May 10; when Congress took its short Memorial Day recess, fewer than a hundred had signed, and many doubted whether the requisite number would ever be obtained.

However, at the end of May, the whole balance of the bonus question was upset by an extraparliamentary event—the arrival of the major contingent of what Pelham Glassford named the Bonus Expeditionary Force.

4

On to Washington

THE STANDARD accounts of the origin of the bonus march run
something like this: In the spring of 1932, a group of unemployed veterans in far-off Portland, Oregon, somehow conceived the idea of a march on Washington, D.C. About 300
set out in box cars for the nation's capital. When uncoopera-
tive railroad officials attempted to halt their journey, they
seized the trains and bluffed their way through. Arriving in
Washington with their dynamic leader, Walter W. Waters, a
former cannery superintendent, their example inspired thousands of other veterans, and soon about 20,000 bonus seekers
were encamped in and around Washington. The major source
for this has been the ghost-written memoir of Waters himself. Although in its general outline it conforms to reality,
there are significant differences between the story Waters and
his professional collaborator produced and what really happened.

It would be convenient to be able to demonstrate that the
bonus march was planned and arranged in advance, but this
seems not to be the case. Neither, however, did the march just
happen. Like most events, it was deeply rooted in the past and

triggered by current events. The most important causative factor of the march was, of course, the Depression itself. Added to this was the intense feeling of injustice that the whole bungled bonus controversy produced in unemployed veterans, the long tradition of dramatic protest that was so much a part of both American and far western history, the essentially optimistic nature of the average American—an optimism that would impel him upon what was clearly a pointless pilgrimage—and a sort of mindless activism that insisted that it was better to do something, even if it turned out to be wrong. Added to all the above was an immense amount of probonus propaganda in print, and, perhaps even more important, over the airwaves. Unemployed men and their families spent a good deal of time listening to the radio during the Great Depression, and what they heard tended to have a much higher radical content than what they read. Not only did the major radio networks give both sides of the bonus question a thorough airing, but they also provided national forums for radio rabble-rousers. Some, like Father Charles Coughlin and Senator Huey Long, spoke over coast-to-coast hookups; others, like the Kansas Goat-gland quack John R. Brinkley and the fundamentalist preacher Bob Schuler (Savonarola in Los Angeles one critic called him), performed on the state and regional level. All, however, found willing ears. Their varied messages had one common theme: contempt for conventional politics and a call, implicit or explicit, for direct action.[1]

The years of the Depression produced a great deal of direct action, as had the decade before it. The years of prosperity saw prohibition-spawned gangster violence in the cities, and Ku Klux Klan violence in the small towns and countryside. The Klan was deemed respectable enough to stage a parade 25,000 strong in full regalia up Pennsylvania Avenue in the summer of 1925, the first such demonstration since 1913, when suffragettes had similarly paraded. (It is instructive to note that while no one bothered the Klan, the women were spat upon, slapped, reviled, and pelted with lighted cigar butts by the capital's outraged masculinity.) The first socially significant violence of the Depression centered around Communist- and Socialist-led unemployed demonstrations on March 6, 1930; throughout that spring and summer, sporadic urban violence continued, and during the winter it got worse. According to Louis Adamic, an astute labor journalist who studied the papers of New York, Chicago, Detroit, Cleveland, and Philadelphia, significant press coverage of unemployment bore a direct relationship to the incidence of mass demonstrations and other unrest: [2]

> Millions of jobless and work-eager people were not newsworthy in the eyes of the press in any big way, or at least the press did not become acutely cognizant of their existence and their plight until the situation was dramatized or intensified with violence and bloodshed. Quietly suffering millions are not news; they are not dramatic enough. When one of them commits suicide in some alley, he gets possibly three lines on page ten. But when a mob raids a food store, or a few of them get their heads banged up, that is front-page news; that is dramatic.

By Adamic's reckoning, unemployment was "front-page stuff" about two days a week throughout the winter of 1930–1931.

The next winter, the third of the Depression, was even worse. The first notable demonstration was a "National Hunger March" on Washington on December 7, 1931. Ostensibly led by Herbert Benjamin of the Unemployed Councils, it was in fact a Communist-sponsored demonstration; most of its participants from all over the country were party members, and perhaps a majority were party functionaries. The modus operandi for this and other Communist marches—nobody really marched, but instead hired trucks and buses—was a quick descent upon Washington, the garnering of national publicity, and then a return home to the mundane task of preparing for the revolution in less spectacular ways. The 1931 Hunger March was a flop, with only 1,600 participants and no spectacular incidents. It was quickly followed in January 1932 by a self-styled "patriotic" demonstration of the unemployed led by a demagogic Pittsburgh priest, James R. Cox; 15,000 of his followers made a three-day pilgrimage by truck to Washington. The cleric was photographed with Pennsylvania politicians and had an audience with the President. (A few days after his return to Pittsburgh, the self-styled "Shepherd of the Unemployed" told a rally of 55,000 that he would form a jobless party and run for President. He did organize a group called the Blue Shirts and started a presidential campaign. His campaign collapsed in September in Tucumcari, New Mexico, due to lack of funds, and Cox eventually endorsed Franklin Roosevelt.)

The Washington demonstrations were all peaceful, but in much of the rest of the nation there was sporadic violence. At the beginning of March, to cite one instance, the Dearborn, Michigan, police fired on a demonstration of the unemployed outside the Ford Motor Company plant: four unemployed workers were killed and some fifty injured. In Frankfort, Kentucky, Jackson, Mississippi, and Philadelphia, angry taxpayers marched on the seats of government—the Kentuckians were so aroused that they "demolished" the governor's mansion. At least one liberal commentator called for more demonstrations. It seemed to Heywood Broun that "the only mistake starving unemployed of this country have made is that they did not march on Washington and under the windows of Mr. Hoover in the White House display banners reading 'We are Belgians.' " [3]

It is against this background of social upheaval that the bonus-seeking activities of the veterans' groups can be understood. The Communist party, correctly sensing the discontent among former soldiers, tried without much success to enlist veterans in a party-dominated front organization—the Workers' Ex-Servicemen's League (WESL or "Weasels" for short). Originally formed in 1930 as a defense group (perhaps the party eventually wanted to emulate the paramilitary formations of central Europe), after uniformed veterans (mostly Legionnaires) had repeatedly attacked meetings, the WESL achieved a short-lived prominence in 1931–1935, and then faded out of sight. It originally was interested solely in party matters like antiwar demonstrations, Negro–white solidarity, and the defense of the Chinese Soviets. In early 1931, however, it began to talk about payment of the bonus, while continuing to advocate the rest of the party line. Its leading spokesman was Emanuel Levin, a party functionary whose peacetime hitch in the Marine Corps had been shortened by a purchased discharge. In the spring of 1932 there were WESL bonus demonstrations in New York, Chicago, Cleveland, and Toledo. (Even these were politicized; New York marchers carried signs insisting "We fought the last war for the capitalists; the next war for the working class.") Despite its small membership (less than 1,000 nationwide), the WESL decided to sponsor a bonus march on Washington on June 8; it was clearly planned as a summer replacement for the December "Hunger March" and in all probability would have been the same kind of futile demonstration.

By that time the so-called Bonus Expeditionary Force had already arrived in strength. The Communists would later claim that the whole affair was done on their initiative; the Hoover administration agreed—the bonus march was, it felt, essentially a Communist conspiracy. In the 1940s and 1950s the same charges were made by Communist renegades in confessions and before congressional committees, and today this belief is held as an article of faith by the extreme right. Arthur Schlesinger, Jr., on the other hand, has written that: [4]

it may be said definitely that (a) the [bonus march] originated spontaneously and the Communists were latecomers in their effort to exploit it, (b) the B.E.F. leaders were openly and militantly anti-Communist, (c) the Communists represented at no time more than a miniscule and beleaguered minority, and (d) there would have been a Bonus March if there had been no Communist party in existence.

A detailed examination of the *Daily Worker* and other Communist publications shows that part of Professor Schlesinger's conclusion is untenable, although his major point is well taken. Mention of a possible bonus march on May 10 and a full-fledged call for nationwide participation on May 17 are conclusive evidence that the WESL Bonus March was independent of the "original" contingent which started from Portland, Oregon, without fanfare on May 11 or 12 and got no eastern publicity until May 19. If the Communists were not the latecomers in the bonus parade that Professor Schlesinger makes them, it does not follow that the Communist party must be given "credit" for everyone who marched. The several bonus marches were, like the American economy, unplanned and uncoordinated. As will be shown, the Communist influence among the veterans of the bonus march was almost as small as it was in the nation at large (in November the party's presidential ticket, William Z. Foster and James Ford, would get about one-quarter of one percent of the popular vote). They were largely without imagination, and most of their propaganda was couched in a jargon unintelligible and abhorrent to the average veteran. Their bonus march would have been a tiny, bureaucratic demonstration manned largely by party functionaries and their friends. When instead, through no effort of theirs, the bonus movement became one of the genuine mass movements about which Marxist theoreticians love to pontificate, the party was neither willing nor able to adapt its creaky apparatus to the unforeseen situation. Unable to shape events, it was equally incapable of capitalizing upon them. The American Communist party is usually denounced as conspiratorial, ruthless, and slavish; not often enough is it pointed out that even at the moment of the greatest crisis of American capitalism its most salient characteristic was impotence.[5]

The Communists, however, were not the pioneers of the veteran protest march. Groups of veterans had been making pilgrimages and descents on Washington since early in the Depression. Some of these incidents, like the VFW petition presentation on January 21, 1931, mentioned earlier, were well organized and received considerable publicity; others were barely noticed outside of the localities from which they came. In the same month, for example, about three hundred Philadelphia war veterans set out from Independence Hall to hike to Washington. The vast majority of the self-styled "bonus brigade" dropped out on the very first day, and even the twenty-six who actually got to Washington four days later did some riding en route. Their leader, John Alferi, a painter who hadn't had a job in six months, told reporters that they wished "simply to make a gesture." He reported being treated with "kindness and courtesy" everywhere. In Washington the Philadelphians were housed in the Salvation Army shelter and then went to Capitol Hill to call on Wright Patman. "By coincidence," according to one account, "General" Jacob Coxey was in the Congressman's office at the time. Train rides home were arranged for the marchers; their leader flew back, thanks to a publicity-seeking air service.[6] But even more important as a precedent for the spectacular 1932 demonstration was a round trip from Portland, Oregon, to Washington the next winter.

Its leader, Eldon J. Munce, was fond of describing it later as the "first bonus march." Munce led a little group of about forty veterans out of Portland in late November, 1931. Riding in boxcars and on the rods, they arrived in Washington just after Congress convened, called on friendly members of the Oregon delegation, talked up the bonus, laid a wreath on the

Tomb of the Unknown Soldier, and after a couple of weeks, returned by coach thanks to financial support raised by Senator Frederick Steiwer, an Oregon Republican who was up for reelection that year. As the chief of the *Portland Oregonian's* Washington bureau later remembered them, they were a "forlorn . . . little band . . . discouraged and homesick." On leaving Washington early in January, they had high praise for Steiwer, who gave them a letter testifying that they had "conducted themselves most worthily" in Washington, and promised the Senator that they would never do it again. When the Oregon delegation of the BEF arrived in Washington five months later, an even dozen of its members were veterans of this earlier, seemingly insignificant march.[7] Their stories about the good treatment they had received cannot have been a deterrent to the second group of Portland pilgrims. But before turning to that more significant journey, it will be useful to try to determine why Portland, of all the cities in the country, should supply the initial impetus for what became a nationwide movement.

Oregon had a rather prosaic and unsensational political past. Although it had been one of the seedbeds of the progressive movement—William U'Ren, the father of the recall, referendum, and initiative, had been its leader—the state had quickly settled down into a mildly progressive Republican mold: Charles McNary, cosponsor of the most significant farm relief proposal of the 1920s and Wendell Wilkie's running mate in 1940, was its outstanding political figure during the interwar years. Much of the Pacific Northwest's radicalism had come from neighboring Washington, a stronghold of the IWW, locale of the 1919 Seattle general strike, and, in 1932, undergoing a political revolution in which Seattle's organized unemployed and other radical groups captured and revitalized the state's Democratic party. (James A. Farley, FDR's conservative Postmaster General, would later sneer about the "Soviet of Washington.") Yet the bonus march came out of conservative Oregon rather than radical Washington. Why? Clearly the movement could have started anywhere, and to a degree, at least, its origin was somewhat fortuitous. But the point of origin would have had some of the characteristics of Portland.[8]

In the first place, there was geography. A bonus march from Philadelphia, New York, or even Chicago would not have stirred the imagination (or the feet) of the nation in the way that a transcontinental trek did. In a railroad age, with inadequate highways, the Pacific slope seemed much more separated from the east coast than it does today. The very fact that Oregon and Portland had no dynamic radical movement with a local focus was another contributing factor. Energies that might have been used in more constructive ways were channelled instead into the bonus crusade. In addition, the political climate in Portland was open and friendly to the veteran. In mid-February, for example, when a local veterans' organization marched on the city council asking it to endorse a demand for immediate cash payment, the Council agreed to petition Congress to do just that, and the mayor then led the several hundred assembled veterans in singing "America." Local newspapers and radio were willing to give publicity to an offbeat veterans' movement, partly because both the city and state American Legion were on record in favor of immediate cash payment in opposition to the national position.[9]

Added to all this was the fact that Oregon's veterans were among the most fortunate in the country, as far as state benefits were concerned. A postwar referendum had approved a state bonus of $15 for every month's service after the first sixty days, veterans could borrow up to $3,000 on real property at low long-term rates (i.e., 28 years at 4 percent), and there was even a rudimentary "G.I. Bill" which allowed veterans going to an approved school or college to draw up to $25 per month for subsistence. These benefits probably not only tended to make Oregon veterans more aware of possible benefits than those from some less generous state—78 percent of Oregon veterans had borrowed to the legal limit on their bonus certificates, as against a national average of less than 70 percent—but probably conditioned them to expect a little more.[10]

In Portland, where almost a third of Oregon's 950,000 residents lived, the unemployed—estimated at about 30,000 that spring—were aided by a relief program far more extensive than most, although it admittedly was palpably inadequate to meet the demands placed upon it. Work and home relief were supported solely by local funds, public and private, and these just could not carry the burden properly. Portland voters had approved a million dollar relief bond issue in early 1931, but the funds lasted less than a year. The relief rolls continued to rise—March 1932 saw twice as many applicants as a year earlier—while real estate taxes, the chief source of governmental funds, became harder to collect—the statewide delinquency rate doubled in the same period, from 15 percent to 30 percent. Caught in this two-way squeeze, the local Civic Emergency Committee was forced to limit severely the amount of relief and set up strict eligibility rules. Applicants for work relief must have been residents of the county for at least six months, be married men with families or single men with dependents, unemployed, and in need. As little as $20 monthly income from any source cancelled eligibility. Although 15,000 heads of families were registered for work, by April only 1,100 could be employed. These fortunates could earn $24 every six or seven weeks. Mayor George L. Baker, calling the need "desperate," admitted the inadequacy of the local program and called for federal assistance. In addition, the Bureau of Public Welfare gave food orders to the destitute. A man with a wife, two children, and a dependent mother-in-law was given a $4 weekly food order. Local relief workers knew it wasn't enough, but, as one put it, "the money has to stretch." In addition to residents, Portland, like most other western cities, had a large transient population which it tried to care for; in the year ending in June 1932, various institutions in Portland supplied over 600,000 free meals and 200,000 free beds.[11]

Is it any wonder then, that unemployed, useless feeling men in the prime of life should be restless as the third winter of the Depression turned into spring? Most of the men eventually attracted to the bonus march were not from the very bottom layers of society; although few were college educated, even fewer were illiterate. Most seem to have worked at relatively decent jobs until the Depression and seemed to maintain essentially lower middle-class attitudes towards themselves, society, and the future. If they only had their bonus, they mused as they lounged listlessly in the early sunlight in the downtown "Plaza blocks" which came to be the open air forum of Portland's veteran unemployed. What could a veteran with dependents do with the few hundred dollars immediate cash payment would give him? Well, for just $470 he could buy a brand new Chevrolet pickup truck, and with a new truck a man could do a little hauling, a little contracting, and have reliable transportation besides. What if he had a family? Could he leave them? Could they be any worse off? Work relief was almost impossible to get (few if any of those who left Portland seem to have been getting it) and the Home relief would continue. Some of the BEFers justified their desertion by reasoning that their families would be taken care of by the local authorities and they could "live on the country" until their bonus was paid.[12] A Washington journalist who covered the BEF called them "the army of bewilderment." [13] Thomas R. Henry of the *Washington Star* wrote:

> Nearly all have one thing in common—a curious melancholy, a sense of the futility of the individual struggle, a consciousness of being in the grip of cruel, incomprehensible forces. Their presence here is a supreme escape gesture. . . . They are fixing on a symbol—the symbol of the security and plenty of happier days. This symbol happens to be Uncle Sam and the war period with its

military relief from responsibility. . . . This bonus march might well be described as a flight from reality—a flight from hunger, from the cries of starving children, the humiliation of accepting money from worn, querulous women, from the harsh rebuffs of prospective employers.

But perhaps the feelings of the men were summed up best in a simple sign one BEFer hung outside his Anacostia shack: [14] "War is hell, but loafing is worse."

If loafing was worse than hell, a cross-country boxcar adventure might be better than either. The first public statement of a plan to march on Washington from Portland in the spring of 1932 that I have been able to discover appeared in the *Portland Oregonian* of April 29, in a little item on page 17 of a twenty-page paper. It announced a meeting to plan a march on Washington early in May and expressed hope that a larger contingent than the one which had left in November could be mustered. A later and more detailed story talked about a march by four or five thousand. One Edgar (Edward) W. White, public relations manager, talked to the press. Other leaders bore more martial titles: Chester (Charles) A. Hazen was commander in chief (he made at least one radio appeal for volunteers on Portland station KWFF) and H. B. Dewitz, field marshal. The curious thing about the leaders just named is that none of them got anywhere near Washington. They seem to have been promoters willing to make a dollar out of the misery of others; they collected money and food and held benefits, allegedly all for the marchers. Hazen was later charged with larceny. The captains and lieutenants—there were twenty of them and I suspect they were those who signed up first—included many who later became leaders en route and in Washington. W. W. Waters was the third listed captain (in his book he said he was "assistant field marshal"). After several delays the march departed, less than 300 strong, on May 11 or 12 (the Portland papers are exasperatingly silent or vague on this and many other early details) via boxcars. Hazen and presumably some of his henchmen went on by car. In Pocatello, Idaho, Hazen either resigned or was deposed, and Walter W. Waters became the new chief.[15]

Waters is still a shadowy figure. Thanks to Army Intelligence, which eventually checked on all the bonus march leaders, we know that he had no obvious subversive links or criminal record. Born in 1898, he entered the Idaho National Guard in 1916, was federalized with it during the trouble with Mexico (he did not serve on the border), was mustered out of federal service in January 1917, and back in again at the end of March. He served in the Medical Detachment of the 146th Field Artillery, spent almost eighteen months overseas where he was promoted to sergeant, and was discharged in mid-1919. His character was recorded as "excellent" and there is no mention of any combat service, although Waters, who never mentioned that his service was as a medic, liked to give the impression that he had been a fighting man. By his own account he drifted from job to job ("My inability to take root in fertile soil may have been due to the unsettling effects of the War on me."), broke with his family, and lived and was married under an assumed name. He said he went to work at a cannery near Portland at some unspecified date in the 1920s and worked his way up to assistant cannery superintendent until he lost that job in December 1930, due to the depression. He wrote later that he and his wife had gone through a thousand dollars of savings and were "penniless" by March 1932. A fellow marcher later remembered Waters' telling how he and his wife had to make a Christmas dinner out of fried potatoes.[16]

After he had become nationally prominent, a Portland newspaperman interviewed some of his local friends and acquaintances, and, although the reporter wrote an uncritical puff, some of its details just do not check out with Waters' memoir. While Waters wrote that he had been assistant superintendent in a cannery "near Portland," his Portland contacts had been told that he was a "cannery superintendent" in Wenatchee, Washington, almost 200 miles away. Even more important than this discrepancy, which after all was based on hearsay, is evidence that he did work in a cannery while in Portland during the fall of 1931, but as an ordinary employee, not as a superintendent. Waters seems also to have been a sometime car salesman and would-be entrepreneur; his wife worked as a store-window demonstrator.[17] While the actual differences may seem minor, they all point to an entirely different type than Waters has usually been pictured. Instead of the classic middle-class symbol of the depression—successful young executive out of work through no fault of his own—we see instead a glib talker, a reasonable man with a good front, for whom nothing had clicked in a dozen years of prosperity and depression. Yet despite his consistent lack of success, Waters retained enough confidence, gall, and charisma to take over a small group of disorganized men and make them the focus of a national movement.

Some of Waters' adjustment problems may well have been psychological; he writes guardedly about an unspecified illness—"my health failed"—just after his army discharge. At various times during his months of fame, there are hints of ill-health, nerves, and chronic instability. His portrait, with deep, brooding eyes, suggests both brilliance and instability.

A physically attractive six-footer, Waters habitually wore boots, riding breeches, white shirt with a bow tie, a jacket, and no hat. He seems a familiar type—the handsome, articulate, mercurial chap for whom everything should go right, but somehow doesn't. He was the image both of the petit-bourgeois respectability tinged with glamour that the BEFers hoped to regain and of the youth that was already past them. This, plus a good, loud speaking voice, a knack for the right phrase, and a nature just authoritarian enough to provide the illusion of security that so many of the marchers sought, made misfit Waters, for a few short weeks at least, Commander Waters, leader of men.

After the reorganization at Pocatello, the march proceeded at a good clip. Western railroads and railroaders were used to providing free rides and the group's advance man, former locomotive engineer, A. F. Taylor, proved adept at organizing support from Legion posts, civic groups, and even police forces along the line of march. At Cheyenne, Wyoming, for example, local organizations provided so much food that one marcher remembered it as a banquet. A week after their departure from Portland, the marchers reached the east bank of the Missouri, at Council Bluffs, Iowa. There they met their first roadblock and received, for the first time, nationwide press coverage. The first week of the journey, which covered about 2,000 miles, had been peaceful and thus was not news by the standards of the American press.

At Council Bluffs, on May 19, and in St. Louis and East St. Louis a few days later, railroad executives and local law enforcement officials made half-hearted efforts to stop the progress of the Oregon bonus march. When these efforts failed, it was as if a green light had been flashed on all across the nation. For the rest of the spring and early summer, neither local officials nor the railroads themselves placed any substantial barriers between groups of veterans and the nation's capital. In fact, in more cases than not, their clearly illegal passage was aided and abetted by the authorities along the way. It was much simpler to pass the problem on to Washington than to attempt to deal with it locally.

At Council Bluffs, officials of the Wabash Railroad at first refused to allow empty boxcars to be placed on the train going to St. Louis. According to Waters, neither the sheriff nor the police would assist the railroad in halting the march. The Oregonians' "Transportation Committee," composed in part of ex-railroad men, uncoupled cars, and disconnected air brakes (not without assistance from the train crews, one suspects), until the Wabash officials gave in and allowed the men to board empties which were attached to a St. Louis-bound train.

In St. Louis the freight train with its extralegal passengers
was met by local police; although Waters remembered that
"the entire police force of St. Louis" was there, the papers
talked about thirty policemen. In the St. Louis yards, where
the bonus army rested for a day, Waters met the press for the
first time and got his name mentioned by the wire services. In
that freight yard press conference on May 20, Waters was
quoted as saying: "I don't know when we'll get to Washington
but we're going to stay there until the bonus bill is passed if
it takes until 1945." This is the first public intimation that
the bonus march from Oregon was not to be just another
quick descent on Washington. It is impossible to say whether
this had been agreed on in advance or whether Waters just
blurted it out on the spur of the moment. It is perhaps more
than coincidental that the morning papers of the previous day
had carried a small Associated Press story about the arrival
in Washington on May 18 of a group of twenty-five Tennessee
veterans who parked their truck with a "We want our bonus"
sign on it near the White House. They told reporters that
they were from Post 1289 of the Veterans of Foreign Wars
and that they wouldn't go back to Chattanooga until "we get
our bonus." Waters, much more an imitator than an innovator,
may well have seen this story and seized upon it. Certainly the
Communists did. In the *Daily Worker* of May 20, a representative of the WESL sent greetings to the VFW men in the
capital and stated:

> When they say they are going to stay until they get the money,
> they have the right line. That's what we all intend to do. Tell
> the veterans to get behind the march to Washington. All the
> veterans who are unattached should start for Washington now.
> We will all be in Washington June 8. We will get our back pay
> when we get there this time, for we are going prepared to stay
> until we get it.

Whoever originated it (and the idea may have had several independent origins), the idea of staying in Washington proved highly popular and caught the imagination of veterans all over the country. It was spread largely by the national news media, who from late May on made the bonus march one of the five big continuing domestic stories of 1932, along with the Depression, the election, the Lindbergh kidnapping, and the Culbertson-Lens-Jacoby marathon bridge match.

In the full glare of publicity the Oregonians walked across one of the Mississippi River bridges to get to the East St. Louis, Illinois, freight yards of the Baltimore and Ohio railroad on May 21. The B&O was determined that the men should not ride its trains and sent its chief of detectives to make sure that the road's policy was carried out. An appeal was also made to the governor of Illinois, Louis L. Emmerson, to help railroad police hold the line. But 1932 was a gubernatorial election year in Illinois, and the governor was loath to take any aggressive action against the veterans (he lost the election anyway). He did call out the National Guard, but it was on a stand-by basis, and he made no attempt to evict the bonus marchers from the railroad's property. The chief of the state police also refused to act. The veterans had been orderly, he told reporters, and besides, he insisted, his jurisdiction was limited to the state's highways. An impasse ensued, with Waters' transportation committee inhibiting the departure of all B&O freights for the east, but unable themselves to move. After two days, the Oregonians managed to seize a freight train, but that got them only as far as Caseyville, some seven miles out of town. Threatened with arrest, Waters resigned as commander in chief and went ahead by bus. Finally, on May 24, the Illinois governor broke the impasse by using the National Guard, not to evict the veteran trespassers, but to truck them to the Indiana state line. The governors of Indiana, Ohio, Pennsylvania, and Maryland, none of whom wanted to have three hundred organized out-of-state veterans on his hands, quickly followed suit, and on May 29, 1932, eighteen trucks of the Maryland National Guard delivered the Oregon contingent—somewhat augmented along the way but minus its leader Waters—to the boundary line of the District of Columbia. They had traversed the country in twenty days and become, in sense, celebrities.[18]

By the time of the Oregonians' arrival, many groups were already marching, and, as we have seen, some had already arrived. The trickle was soon to become a flood; "Stay til we get our bonus" and "Stay til 1945" became popular slogans and the bonus movement became a real mass movement. It is impossible here to chronicle all the varied columns, contingents, groups, and individuals who began to head toward Washington in ever-increasing numbers.

How many came? No precise answer can be given to that question. The range of estimates runs from a palpably inadequate 5,000 or 6,000 by some right-wing critics to a superabundant 80,000 ventured by a professional historian. Waters later claimed to have a list of 28,540 names, addresses, and service numbers, which, he thought, comprised a roster of "perhaps half of the total." More reasonable is the estimate made by General Pelham D. Glassford, the capital's police chief, whose educated guess was that there were, at the height of the movement in mid-July, "more than 20,000 veterans" in Washington. Since some men were coming and going all the time, this almost surely means that more than 25,000 individuals were in the nation's capital at one time or another during June and July 1932 and that another 10,000 to 15,000 probably started out and never arrived at their goal. If these assumptions are accurate, there were then a total of 40,000 bonus marchers, 25,000 of whom made it all the way to Washington; the peak BEF population of 21,000 or 22,000 was reached about the time Congress adjourned on July 17. (There had been an earlier peak of about 20,000 in late June.) [19]

Apart from Waters' list, which he broke down by states,

and the daily estimates made by Glassford's police, there is one other piece of statistical evidence available, but it must be used with great caution. Congress, as we shall see, eventually passed a bill which allowed BEFers to borrow against their adjusted compensation certificates to finance a railroad ticket out of Washington. It is important to realize that they were given travel orders and not cash. A total of 5,109 veterans took advantage of this offer and thus had their names, service numbers, and destinations recorded by the Veterans Administration. This is the only list the federal government ever had and it did some strange and wonderful things with it. It should be noted, first of all, that this represents between 20 percent and 25 percent of the whole BEF, but it is not necessarily a representative sample. It is probably biased in favor of those less deeply committed to the bonus struggle, toward those who were a long way from home, and toward those who were somewhat deficient in what the President liked to call "rugged individualism." (I am assuming, not unreasonably I think, that the "rugged individualist" so dear to Hoover would have ridden the rods or hitchhiked in preference to taking what seemed like a government handout. Those who took the travel orders were actually borrowing their own money and had every reason to believe that they would pay interest on their loans. The President, as we shall see in Chapter 8, made different character assumptions about those who did and did not choose to ride home on credit.) [20]

The relatively small numbers from adjacent states (Pennsylvania accounted for only 5 percent of the VA's travelers, but 16½ percent of Waters' list), and the relatively high numbers from far away places (California was the destination of 17 percent of those who got travel orders, but was the point of origin of only 5 percent of Waters' list) set forth the geographical bias clearly. Both lists show that New England was underrepresented (only 100 on the VA list and 625 on Waters' list, a little over 2 percent in each instance, although the region had more than 6 percent of the nation's population). Apart from that, most bonus marchers hailed from the industrial states and can be presumed to be essentially urban.

The VA list, in addition, tells us some other things about the men. Thirty-six had been commissioned officers (1 major, 4 captains and thirty-one lieutenants), 878 had been sergeants and corporals, and an overwhelming 4,192 had been private soldiers. Almost 90 percent had served in the army, and more than 65 percent of the total had gone overseas, a greater percentage than prevailed in the armed forces as a whole. One other generalization can be made about the composition of the bonus army: in a strictly segregated era, the several hundred Negroes in the bonus army were surprisingly well integrated. Roy Wilkins, sent down to look things over for the NAACP, reported on this unexpected situation. Jim Crow was "absent with leave" in most of the camps of the bonus army, although segregation was present in some of the southern delegations and there were some self-segregated Negro groups. Wilkins failed to note that there were no Negroes in positions of leadership, except among the Communist group.[21]

Although most of those who came to Washington after the first groups were relatively unheralded, a few groups did attract unusual attention. There was, for instance, a Texas contingent, headed by a woman—"a Joan of Arc in overalls" the press called her, and with picturesque livestock—a burro named Patman and a goat named Hoover. There were Communist contingents from Detroit, Cleveland, Chicago, and New York, each spoiling for trouble. And finally, although they arrived quite late, there was the largest group of all— more than a thousand Southern Californians under the leadership of Royal W. Robertson.

Robertson, who had to wear a large neck brace, made a pathetic figure and most assumed that he had been a casualty; actually he had served in the navy and never gone to sea. His compensable injury—he drew a pension and had a number of private pension bills to increase it unsucccessfully introduced in his behalf—resulted from falling out of a hammock while in training. A small-time local politician, active in veterans' affairs, Robertson took charge of a group of thirteen veterans who camped in a vacant lot in downtown Los Angeles, and announced that they were prepared to "march on Washington" and join the BEF. By the middle of June, 2,500 had "registered and pledged to travel." Since even in 1932 Los Angeles was a city on wheels, this column of bonus marchers was motorized. After fending off, somehow, a flank attack of "75 representatives of automobile finance companies," the Southern California contingent set off for San Bernardino in 350 cars and trucks of varying reliability, after a parade through the downtown section and a send-off by the mayor, who implored them to do nothing that "would disgrace the name of Los Angeles," whatever that might be. Although reports of number vary, apparently about 2,000 men left California for Phoenix, Arizona, where the governor had promised them the use of the fairgrounds. Like the other units marching on the capital, Robertson's group tried, with some success, to live off the land. Veterans' and civic groups along the way furnished a little food and some gasoline and sometimes even gave cash. By the time they reached El Paso, many of the vehicles had broken down and freight trains became the major means of transportation. Despite being split by the usual dissension and accusations—over authority and the use of whatever money was collected (Robertson was widely reported to have a treasury of some $2,500)—Robertson led the vanguard of perhaps 1,500 men across the District line on July 9, some six weeks after their departure from the West Coast.

In these and other less spectacular ways, bonus marchers came, singly and in groups, from all parts of the country. Many probably believed that the leaders of the march really had a plan. Robertson, himself a major leader, apparently

believed when he started that the BEF was a real organization.[22]

> We naturally believed that [Waters and the others] had some
> business ability and a definite legislative program [and that] we
> might strengthen the organization and force Congress to pass the
> bonus bill at once. . . .

Robertson and others were misled by the glib phrases of
the press and the ersatz titles that Waters and the others
appropriated. "Bonus Expeditionary Force," "Commander in
Chief," "Regimental Commander," and similar terms with
which the stories about the veterans were studded, gave the
whole affair an illusion of solidity and stability that must
have seemed attractive to unemployed veterans looking
desperately for something meaningful and useful to do with
their lives. For many veterans, the bonus march seemed an
opportunity and a haven; but for the authorities in Washington, it was a frightening and dangerous spectacle.

5

Pelham Glassford
and the BEF

OFFICIAL Washington became aware of the bonus marchers while they were still en route.[1] The knowledge came, not from any official source, but from a story in the Washington Sunday *Star* of May 22, which featured a delegation of Philadelphians and only mentioned the Oregonians under Waters in passing.[2] Two days later, when it became apparent from other press reports that thousands of veterans might eventually converge on the capital, the first tentative plans were made for their reception and accommodation. Inconceivable as it may seem today, the only public official in all of Washington who had the wit to initiate any action was the relatively new chief of the District of Columbia police force, Brigadier General Pelham D. Glassford. No one else was willing to take any responsibility; no one else seemed to understand, during that whole demoralizing summer, that exceptional times called for exceptional measures.

Part of the problem was institutional. The city of Washington was and remains today a power vacuum. Governed by Congress instead of by its citizens, who gave up all semblance

87

of home rule in 1871 rather than risk the Negro officials that newly enfranchised freedmen surely would have eventually elected, the city was administered by a three-man commission. These men were direct appointees of the President. In 1932 all three were appointees of Herbert Hoover and conservative representatives of the old order. Significantly, none was a politician with the politician's art of compromise; instead, each was a technician and embodied in one way or another the progressive ideal of efficiency. The president of the Board of Commissioners was Dr. Luther H. Reichelderfer, a retired physician, a past president of the District's medical society, and a reserve officer who had served as a lieutenant colonel in France. The second commissioner, in charge of police and fire matters, was a retired army officer, Major General Herbert B. Crosby. The third commissioner, traditionally a Corps of Engineers officer on active duty, was Major John C. Gotwals, in charge of sanitation and public works. He seems to have taken no active part in the decisions relating to the bonus marchers. When, late in 1931, it was necessary to appoint a new chief of police (the precise title in Washington was Major and Superintendent of Police, but to avoid confusion, normal American usage—that is, to call the uniformed head of the force "chief"—will be followed), the inefficiency and corruption of the Washington force dictated a noncareer candidate. It is not surprising that such a group selected an army officer rather than one trained in law enforcement. Major General Crosby, probably to his lasting regret, talked an old army acquaintance, Pelham D. Glassford, into taking the job late in 1931.

Glassford's appointment was originally viewed with some skepticism in most quarters in Washington. Senior police officials, of course, deeply resented him; liberals and those conservatives who had an abiding mistrust of the military expressed fear that the new chief would be an autocrat; and many practical persons wondered just what qualifications a sol-

dier had for the job, doubts that were not eased when the newly
appointed chief told inquiring reporters that having gotten a
speeding ticket or two represented the sum total of his police
experience and thus constituted his "qualifications" for the
job. However bad the appointment might look on paper, it
turned out to be a very good one. The former soldier soon
won an exceptional degree of acceptance in almost all of
Washington's mutually exclusive circles. This acceptance and
the success that it symbolized stemmed largely from the fact
that, despite an orthodox and brilliant military career, Glassford was a far from ordinary soldier.

The scion of a military family—his father had fought
Geronimo and served as chief signal officer of volunteers during the Spanish-American War, while his brother William
attended Annapolis and became an admiral during World
War II—Pelham Glassford was born in 1883, and raised
largely in the free and easy society of Denver, Colorado. He
was graduated eighteenth in a class of 124 at West Point in
1904, leading the corps in Spanish and drawing. (His most
distinguished classmate was "Vinegar Joe" Stilwell, who
ranked thirty-second.) His early tours of duty included service
in Hawaii, the Philippines, and on the Mexican border, as
well as a stint on the faculty at West Point. During World
War I he commanded the 103rd Field Artillery in France, and
in October 1918, became the youngest brigadier general of
the American Expeditionary Force. Service in the peacetime
army apparently was dull for Glassford, despite such choice
assignments as the Army War College and the Chief of Staff's
office, which gave him a familiarity with Washington social
life. His professional career boring, his personal life disintegrating (his wife and mother of his three children would be
granted a divorce in August 1932), Glassford voluntarily
retired in 1931 after twenty-seven years of active duty, on an
annual pension of $3,920.[3]

It is not clear what he intended to do or even if he had

precise plans, but his later statements that he meant to retire to the family ranch in Arizona for the rest of his life cannot be taken seriously. Underneath his austere exterior—in his late forties Glassford was still slim and carried his six-foot-three frame straight as a ramrod—there was a disinctly flamboyant, bohemian streak, as well as a deep-seated humanitarian impulse. In addition, he possessed a constantly inquiring mind which even three decades of military service could not stifle. While he was on the faculty at West Point, he conducted, on his own, pioneering experiments in sending wireless messages from a moving automobile. In his report he commented astutely on the possible military uses of both the motor vehicle and radio. ("I have had to terminate the experiments," he informed the Adjutant General, "because I sold my car.") [4] The general was a persistent amateur painter who eventually had his work exhibited. He devoted some of his leaves to slaking his thirst for new experiences: one was spent as a reporter for Hearst's *San Francisco Examiner,* another working for a circus. The flamboyant side of the new police chief was quickly remarked in the capital: he took to riding around on a big, blue motorcycle that soon became his trademark. His social life also attracted some attention: one Washington gossip dubbed him the "debutante's delight" and remarked on seeing his roadster—like the motorcycle, quite distinctive—parked in front of various ladies' doors in the wee hours of the morning (on the eve of the New Deal, Washington still had many of the hallmarks of a small town).[5] If Glassford's unorthodoxies drew disapproval from some quarters, his engaging personality soon won him a host of friends and admirers. He was a genuinely popular man who deserved his army nickname of "Happy." His somewhat frivolous side was quickly noticed in the capital—it was almost impossible not to notice it—but his real abilities were just as quickly tested and proven.

Before Glassford had been chief a month, the first severe

test occurred—the Communist-inspired Hunger March which greeted the opening of Congress in December 1931. Although similar demonstrations in other cities were terrorized and brutalized by the police (which served the Communist cause well), Glassford, somehow, understood what most Americans in authority could not get through their heads, that this kind of repression was not only pointless but actually self-defeating. Under his personal direction—astride the ever-present blue motorcycle—a distinctly reluctant District police force treated the marching reds with relatively scrupulous correctness: they were watched closely but not molested. Glassford insisted publicly that, since the Communist party was legal and on the ballot like other parties, the police should do nothing to inhibit a Communist-led parade as long as it was orderly. The lack of violence in Washington as compared with other cities drew much favorable notice.[6] This solid performance in the one serious early test of his ability, plus his flair for publicity in an era lacking in colorful personalities, delighted the local newspapermen, who firmly established him as a dynamic and colorful personality. By May, even though he had been on the job only six months, Glassford already seemed to be a Washington fixture.

On May 24, two days after he read about the bonus marchers in the paper, Glassford began to act. On his own initiative he issued a statement to the press that no food was available. At the same time, he began to make plans to feed and shelter the men who, he was convinced, would come and had to be taken care of. He called on Secretary of War Patrick J. Hurley and tried to obtain from him the use of tents, cots, bedsacks, rolling kitchens, and other equipment from the plentiful stocks on hand at the various military encampments around the capital. Hurley flatly refused, saying, as Glassford remembered it, that "the Federal Government could not recognize the invasion." Glassford also called on Daniel Willard, president of the Baltimore and Ohio Railroad, who agreed to continue to do everything possible to keep the marching veterans off the nation's railroads.[7]

The next day Glassford went up to Capitol Hill to talk to leading legislators. He tried, without success, to convince Senator James Watson, a senior Republican, and Congressman Henry T. Rainey, Democratic majority leader, that it would be good tactics to unbottle the Patman bill from the Ways and Means Committee and have it put to the vote. (Presumably it would be voted down.) This, Glassford argued, would put a damper on the invasion. From his knowledge of the psychology of the average veteran, he felt that the bonus bill would serve as a magnet for footloose veterans as long as it remained unfinished business. Having failed to get results with one branch of the government, Glassford tried the other, and presented the same arguments to Walter Newton, the President's secretary, with the same negative results. The administration insisted that it could do nothing. Actually, the administration was secretly taking what it felt to be protective measures, but the preventive ones were ignored. It seems clear that if the nation's leaders had taken Pelham Glassford's advice in the closing days of May, the bonus invasion might well have been kept on a very small scale, and one of the uglier incidents of our history might have been avoided. In this, as in almost every other crisis in human affairs, there were some who saw clearly an alternative more felicitous than that chosen. But Glassford's words fell upon deaf ears.

Later that afternoon the police chief met with a more sympathetic group, representatives of the capital's welfare agencies and veterans' organizations. The group, seemingly with the tacit approval of Commissioner Crosby who also attended, decided on a two-fold course of action. They would all vigorously augment Glassford's propaganda campaign aimed at discouraging veterans from coming; at the same time, however, they agreed to try to house and feed those who actually did come. The capital's social workers, public and private, knew full well that the responsibility was theirs and that it could not be gainsaid with rhetoric about "non-recognition." [8]

Official Washington, unfortunately, was not yet aware that the old order had passed. After the social workers left, the two retired generals had a heated argument. As Glassford later reconstructed their dialogue, Commissioner Crosby wanted him to treat the bonus marchers just like any other "floaters."

"If you feed and house them," he argued, "others will come by the thousands."

"It would be far better," Glassford replied, "to have 10,000 orderly veterans under control than 5,000 hungry, desperate men breaking into stores and committing other depredations."

"What is the police force for?" sneered the Commissioner.

"Are you making a suggestion or issuing an order?"

"In the Army, it has been my experience that a suggestion is obeyed just the same as an order."

"We're not in the Army now," snapped Glassford, just like an ordinary G.I. and admittedly hot under the collar. "I cannot follow suggestions. If you desire to take the responsibility yourself for such a policy all you have to do is to issue written orders and they will be carried out. In the absence of such orders I shall take what I consider the correct course." [9]

For almost two months, with few formal directives forthcoming, the police chief was allowed to set public policy for the nation's capital, although it was soon clear to all close observers that he had incurred the wrath of his superiors, both those in the Old District Building and the one in the White House. Senator Watson, an administration spokesman, warned him privately that "the President has taken a great dislike to you." After one of his fruitless attempts to get the President to talk to a BEF delegation (Glassford himself never got past presidential secretary Walter Newton), the chief was told that the President would fire him if he didn't change his essentially friendly attitude toward the BEFers.[10]

These administration attitudes were certainly not representative of national feeling, nor even of conservative Republican feeling. More typical of the latter was an editorial in the *Washington Star*, which, after denouncing the whole idea of marching on Washington as irresponsible and a "lark," soberly observed: [11]

Because of this irresponsible spirit and because the word "veteran" seems to confer upon the marchers a certain immunity from interference, the police department is making extraordinary arrangements to see that the demonstration is kept within bounds.

The practical problem for which no solution has yet been advanced, is how to feed these men—for they must be fed. Washington's charitable and welfare organizations are hard pressed to make both ends meet in caring for the deserving cases that properly rest as a responsibility upon the community. . . . Two of the states through which the marchers have passed on their slow trek eastward—Illinois and Indiana—have provided the men with transportation and food and passed them over to the next state. There will be no passing them along when they get to Washington. And as the exclusive government of the District, including the appropriation of its money, rests with Congress, that body should pause long enough to take cognizance of the situation in advance and determine what is to be done. It should not take many minutes to authorize the War Department, for instance, to set up kitchens and furnish the men with food, allow them a reasonable length of time to stage their demonstration and to get out of town. No such authorization may be necessary, but there should be as carefully laid plans for seeing that the men are adequately fed and housed as for seeing that they follow prescribed routes should they have a parade. And all the responsibility should not be placed on the local community.

Conservative and Republican though it was, the power structure of the city of Washington was quick to look for federal aid. This was neither unreasonable nor exceptional. Since, in America, relief has traditionally been a local affair, it was the cities which first felt the main thrust of the Depression. The urban reaction was, throughout the nation, an appeal for increased relief spending, from city, from state, and, eventually, from the federal government. The rural reaction, on the other hand, was, in part at least, an appeal for a cessation of certain governmental actions, for mortgage and tax moratoriums, the withholding of produce from the market and other actions typical of distressed propertyholders and businessmen. The bonus marchers were almost exclusively urban and small town in origin—what farmer could take time off in late spring?—and their reaction, although extreme, was fully consistent with the urban pattern.

While Washingtonians, like most Americans, were largely sympathetic toward the marchers, they felt that it was unfair that a burden national in character should be thrust upon their locality. Even without the bonus marchers, Washington had troubles of its own, like any other large city in the country. (Not quite like any other city, however, since Washington's major industry, the federal government, was not depressed. In 1932 there were 73,000 federal employees in the District, nearly 8,000 more than in the last year of the Coolidge administration.) Despite this expansion, and the large-scale public building program in the Federal Triangle which employed perhaps 10,000 men, "relief rolls lengthened while want and nameless fears turned tempers edgy." That many property owners were in bad straits is demonstrated by the utility companies' growing delinquent lists: 14 percent of the city's water bills were more than a month overdue. On Anacostia Flats, soon to become the major BEF encampment, subsistence gardens were set up on federal land for the unemployed with the Department of Agriculture furnishing seeds and expert advice. Washington's inadequate relief system was severely taxed before the influx of thousands of veterans.

Nationally, the picture was worse. By mid-spring, *Business Week* accurately observed that both private agencies and local governments had nearly exhausted their resources and warned of an impending "complete breakdown." Against this nation-wide distress, it was unrealistic of the Washingtonians to expect hard-pressed officials elsewhere to do much to stem the tide of bonus marchers. While a few railroads—like the B&O —refused to let groups of veterans ride, others did little or nothing to stop them. On June 3, for example, fifty-five veterans arrived from Ohio in an empty Pennsylvania Rail-road boxcar; a friendly trainman had even supplied them with a waybill marked "livestock—55 veterans." The bonus march, once it began to get nationwide publicity, rapidly snow-balled into a quasi-spontaneous mass movement involving thousands, most of whom came to Washington in relatively autonomous small groups.[12] But once they got to Washington, they became an army.

This army was first organized on Thursday, May 26, when more than 500 veterans met outdoors at Judiciary Square in downtown Washington. (The Oregonians, at this time, were still in Indiana.) It is not known who called this meeting, but before it was over Pelham Glassford clearly emerged as the man in charge. Arriving out of uniform—"nattily clad in grey" according to the *Star*—to "keep an eye" on the veterans, he wound up making two speeches and so impressed the men that they elected him secretary-treasurer of the organization he urged them to form—the Bonus Expeditionary Force. The men pledged to cooperate with the police and to respect the law and reaffirmed what Glassford called their "Americanism." Glassford was friendly, if firm, and frankly admitted a possible conflict of interest:

Fellow veterans and comrades, . . . I shall be very glad to do everything I can for you. I can't tell you how much in sympathy

I am with you and all others who are unemployed. I shall be very glad to accept this responsibility, but hope that you will appoint two or three of your own men to assist me.

General Glassford also made it clear that none of the District's scanty relief funds could be used, but did promise to help them tap private money and spoke of organizing benefits. His forthright approach immediately gained him a secure place in the affections of the men: some were soon even talking about Glassford for President. The fact that he was General Glassford rather than Chief Glassford and that he was himself an overseas veteran surely contributed to what would be called his favorable image today. A cynic might argue that Glassford helped the veterans only to manipulate them, but a sounder appraisal would note the consistent ambivalence of Glassford's role ("Waters and I were friendly enemies"). He wanted to help them *and* manipulate them. He wished they would go away but would help them as long as they stayed, and thus perhaps lengthened that stay. Although he was a soldier and something of a disciplinarian, he was willing to tolerate a certain amount of disorder. In the final analysis he was also a policeman: as he readily admitted, he was always prepared to use force if necessary. His seemingly incongruous role as secretary-treasurer of the BEF actually reinforced both sets of values. By organizing the marchers into a cohesive group amenable to discipline and by raising money and supplies for them, he was not only ministering to their needs but also making trouble much less likely. This pragmatism—the cynic would say opportunism—was a hallmark of Glassford's behavior all summer. For a time it met with great success. This success was due not only to the essential good sense of the policy, but also to the fact that Glassford worked very hard at it.[13]

By May 28 he was talking publicly about a "campaign of discouragement" and had already planned to try to accommodate the veterans in a number of vacant and abandoned buildings around the city, and, if these sites proved inadequate, to settle the overflow on federal land on the Anacostia Flats, happily separated from downtown Washington by Anacostia Creek and a drawbridge which could be raised if necessary. By noon of the next day, he could report to the press that a central commissary had been established and a fund-raising campaign had begun. Food procurement was put under the charge of a local food broker named De Ford, who had run a similar operation during the visit of Father Cox's "Jobless Army." Glassford, unable to get equipment from the War Department directly, was successful in obtaining two rolling kitchens from the Washington National Guard, whose commander, Major General Anton Stephan, was a personal friend. Glassford advanced $120 out of his own pocket to purchase food from the army commissary at Ft. Myer. He also managed to get food wholesalers to contribute 200 pounds of beef and 100 pounds of coffee and got the promise of day-old bread donations from eleven bakeries. To avoid overtaxing local hospitals, an arrangement was made whereby the local Marine Corps Reserve unit set up a dispensary staffed by volunteer doctors and three enlisted men called to active duty for the purpose. Sick calls were held twice daily as long as the BEF was in town; the absence of any large-scale illness during the summer is probably due in large part to this early preventive measure. After a typical day the dispensary reported "42 men at sick call last night, five teeth extracted and two minor operations performed."

While making these arrangements for the veterans, Glassford tried to reassure Washingtonians about the pending invasion. He pointed out that "the men have a right to be here" and called on local citizens to contribute to their support, but at the same time insisted that there would come a point "beyond which the residents should not be asked to contribute." From that undefined point on, Glassford felt, the responsibility shifted to the federal government.[14]

All of the preparations described above had begun before

the Oregonians arrived. When they arrived on May 29 in trucks belonging to the Maryland National Guard, there were still fewer than a thousand veterans in the capital. The Volunteers of America fed the Westerners a meal (about whose quality they complained bitterly) of vegetable soup, bread, and milk; then they got an orientation from one of Glassford's men, Patrolman J. E. Bennett.

"You're welcome here," the policeman began, "but the minute you start mixing with Reds and Socialists, out you go. If you get mixed up with that gang, you're through here. The Marine barracks are across the street, the Navy yard is a couple of blocks away, and there's lots of Army posts around. We don't want to call them, and we won't call them as long as you fellows act like gentlemen."

Rather than being resented, these admonitions were cheered by the BEFers, who quickly assured Bennett of their patriotism. "If we find any Red agitators," one of them vowed, "we'll take care of them ourselves. . . . We came here under the same flag for which we fought."

The next day, Bennett, normally a member of the traffic division and a veteran like all other police selected by Glassford to work with the BEF, reported to his chief that "a full military setup" had been established. Each of the several buildings where men were quartered would have to turn in a daily morning report which would keep the police informed about the number of veterans in the city. Bennett also explained the culinary details—two meals a day at an estimated cost of 32 cents a man (the current army ration cost 38 cents a man)—and explained how veterans were being put to work at various housekeeping and sanitary chores under the supervision of the police.[15] Although the food expenditure seems pitifully small, it was probably adequate. Cheap Washington restaurants were then offering a meal of half a fried chicken, bread, butter, and coffee for twenty cents.[16]

The same day—Memorial Day—Glassford won his first of

many skirmishes with federal authority. As we have seen, Secretary of War Hurley, acting for the administration, had refused absolutely to assist in caring for the veterans. After the Oregonians had spent one night sleeping on the floor, Glassford wired Hurley (and released the wire to the press in time for the afternoon papers):

> FAILURE OF THE WAR DEPARTMENT TO FURNISH ONE THOUSAND BED SACKS AS PER MY WRITTEN REQUEST OF MAY TWENTY EIGHTH RESULTED IN APPROXIMATELY FOUR HUNDRED VETERANS BEING REQUIRED TO SLEEP ON HARD FLOORS LAST NIGHT. REQUEST ISSUE OF BED SACKS TO POLICE DEPARTMENT IN THIS EMERGENCY BE EXPEDITED.

Just after the afternoon papers hit the streets, the Secretary of the General Staff himself telephoned police headquarters to say that two thousand bed sacks could be picked up immediately at Ft. Myer.[17]

On the last day of the month Glassford was able to announce his most important single stroke in his campaign to control the BEF. In an "Information Notice" for the press, written out in his own hand, the chief declared:[18]

4:15 P.M.

> W. W. Waters accepted appointment as Comdr. in Chief Veterans Bonus Expeditionary Force to organize all units arriving same as Oregon group—This accepted upon a strict diciplinary [sic] agreement—including the elimination of radicals.

This was an important victory for Glassford, because Waters was an instrument ideally suited to his needs. Dynamic and militant enough to appeal to the rank and file, he was at the same time plastic enough to be used by Glassford. Waters' middle-class values and his staunch anticommunism made him, in most instances, submissive to higher authority. For

Glassford, having most of the day-to-day orders come from Waters and agents appointed by him was obviously much more satisfactory than trying to run the whole show from police headquarters. For Waters, the support of Pelham Glassford meant that, without any further effort or campaign on his part, he had become the head of a growing movement. The situation was obviously quite satisfactory to each and neither ever seriously complained about the arrangement.

Having taken care of food and leadership, Glassford also provided places for the veterans to stay. At the start of the second week of the BEF occupation, the number of bonus marchers in Washington had grown to 3,000 and—as every paper now reported—thousands more were on the way. During the first week, most of the marchers had been billeted in empty and partially demolished buildings around the city; from then on, the majority were to be concentrated on the vacant Anacostia Flats outside the city, where they erected a motley community known as Camp Marks, named for Police Captain S. J. Marks, the friendly commander of the neighboring 11th precinct. There some mess and toilet facilities were being constructed with lumber and labor that was partly donated and partly paid for out of District funds. Glassford originally intended to have lumber and tar paper shelters erected to house the marchers, and he personally drew up plans, but the commissioners vetoed that project. The men on the flats had to do it themselves out of whatever materials they could scrounge. Just when Glassford began to think about Anacostia is not clear, but one early leader of the BEF remembered that the chief had taken him and other leaders to inspect the site on May 27. Although Anacostia was federal property, Glassford found another army friend in a key position, and somehow persuaded Major General U. S. Grant III, who was Director of Public Buildings and Public Parks of the National Capital, to agree informally to make "no objection . . . to the use of certain public parks . . . for the temporary encampment" of the BEF, even though such use was against the wishes of the administration and in direct violation of federal law.[19]

But at the same time he was doing all of this, Glassford was preparing for the worst. On June 3—just eight days after his first meeting with the veterans in Judiciary Square—he wrote a report which, alone of his papers for this period, he labeled "SECRET." In it, he described his welfare activities and gave vent to his apprehensions. In an uncharacteristically gloomy mood that Friday, he described his policy of segregating the "bonafide veterans" of the BEF from the Communist group, and then admitted that he thought trouble was just around the corner.[20]

Although no disorders have occurred, the plan of the Police Department is to assemble all disaffected groups at Anacostia Park and should emergency arise to hold the Eleventh Street Bridge against a riotous invasion across the Anacostia River. Plans and preparations are being made to this end, including plans for the use of tear gas: at the same time a force of police will be held in readiness on the east side of Anacostia River [e.g., on the Flats] in order to localize any riot that may occur, to prevent access to the bridges further north. . . .

As soon as funds available have been exhausted and no more food can be furnished by this department we believe that an emergency situation will exist. Such a situation may develop as early as noon tomorrow.

Recommendation: That preparations be made by the Commissioners to declare an emergency, and to provide for the use of the National Guard, or to place in effect "The White Plan". [The "White Plan" was the official designation by the War Department for the plan to be followed by the regular army in quelling domestic insurrection.]

The early June crisis that Glassford feared never materialized, but the whole month saw a steady rise in the strength
of the BEF. The Board of Commissioners, although they dis-
approved of their subordinate's policies, did little to inhibit
the steady increment of the bonus army. Their major actions,
if they can be called that, were to continue to urge the
railroads to deny passage to groups of marchers and to send
telegrams to all state governors on June 10 asking the state
executives "not to facilitate or encourage" any more veterans
coming to Washington and to use their "facilities to return
them to their homes." While a number of the governors
promised to stop helping veterans to cross their states, only
New York's Franklin Delano Roosevelt took any positive action. He wired that he was sending an official of his Temporary Emergency Relief Administration to the capital to bring
back any New Yorkers who wanted transportation home. Few,
if any, accepted the offer. More typical, if somewhat franker
than most, was the response of Governor William G. Conley
of West Virginia, who explained his refusal to cooperate
actively by arguing that "if we furnish free transportation to
one class of citizens, why should we not offer it to all other
classes of citizens who may want a free trip?" The Commissioners also enlisted the help of the American Railroad Association, which asked its member roads to cooperate with the
government. After this early June "flurry" of executive action,
the Commissioners did nothing for more than a month, although they continued to leak their dissatisfaction with Glassford to the press.[21]

Given, in effect, a free hand, the chief continued to impro-
vise, although the bonus army, as it grew, underwent a distinct
mutation. With growing numbers, perhaps twenty thousand
by mid-June, came an increasingly efficient internal organization and a seeming semipermanency which frightened some
District officials and residents. Others, however, were sympathetic, and still others amused: strange as it may seem, the

bonus army, no longer regarded as "visitors," had become an army of occupation, and a trip out to Anacostia had become a prime tourist attraction. There, despite all the grimness, a distinct carnival atmosphere prevailed. There was a large wooden speaker's platform constantly in use (somehow it reminded reporter John Dos Passos of an old-fashioned gallows). One veteran arranged an elaborate "cemetery" with prominent graves marked "Hoover" and "Mellon." Another marcher had himself "buried alive" daily: he could be seen through a wooden tube for a "donation"; while a third, combining necessity with a macabre sense of humor, made his home in a coffin he had picked up somewhere. A number made money by "panhandling"; others sold a newspaper that the veterans put out. The vast majority, however, were wholly dependent upon donated cash, food, and services. Although the financial and supply crises continued, there was always enough for one more meal.

By June 20, when he made the fullest accounting of which there is a record, Glassford had received $12,895.56 in contributions, $5,000 of it in one check from the radio priest Father Charles E. Coughlin, who wired "absolute instructions that they who benefit by this donation keep clear of all communistic leaders and all communistic suggestions." Other funds came from more secular sources and with no strings at all: three Washington benefits—an "uncensored" burlesque show at the Gayety Theater, a boxing card staged at the Washington Senators ballpark, and a wrestling exhibition featuring Jim Londos—netted some $1,500 while another $500 was raised by the District post of the VFW. The rest came in small amounts, the overwhelming amount of it from residents of the capital. While there is no record of funds handled after June 20, by which time Glassford had turned over his fiduciary functions to Waters and his staff, it is clear that the total cost of maintaining the BEF must have been well over $100,000.

Glassford's accounting—which showed about $5,500 still in the kitty—listed food as the biggest item of expense, comprising about 75 percent of expenditures, although it must be remembered that much food was donated and that many contributions of food and money did not go through police hands. (Evalyn Walsh McLean turned up late one night with a thousand sandwiches.) Other major expenses included lumber, tents, medical supplies, and transportation costs. The dilapidated vehicles used by the veterans consumed 140 gallons of gas and 21 quarts of oil daily. Not all of the money was used for necessities; a bill in Glassford's papers records the purchase of two bats and two balls for $3.20; more urgent, perhaps, was $7.50 for five gallons of "kil-bug." Expense money was also granted to groups if they would go home: the precise amounts were apparently subject to negotiation. One man was given $23 to go back to New Orleans, while six others driving to Columbus, Georgia, got only a total of $5.00 for gas and oil.[22]

The BEF, with the aid of Glassford and his helpful patrolmen, soon got a functioning organization going. What Waters liked to call his GHQ (general headquarters) was located in the downtown Washington home of Don Zelaya, son of a Central American politician, a concert pianist, and, more important, a West Point classmate and old friend of Pelham Glassford. Waters and the upper echelons of his staff clearly lived better than the average marcher. Besides sleeping indoors in a real bed, the commander in chief made a number of foraging, recruiting, and publicity trips to New York, Philadelphia, and other eastern cities, and always had enough money to use commercial transportation and to stay in decent hotels. Unlike most of the marchers, whose clothes grew progressively more shabby, Waters was always neat, pressed, and usually wore a clean white shirt. The conclusion is inescapable that all of his expenses were financed by contributions and that his style of life was substantially improved.

The BEF commander was subject to a good deal of criticism

from within his army, not only from the Communists, who quickly and characteristically styled him a "fascist," but also from some of the more militant marchers who simply resented his dictatorial style (he was often compared to Mussolini), his hobnobbing with Glassford and other "enemies," and his essentially passive policy. These criticisms would cause Waters to resign twice, but in each instance he was able quickly to reestablish his authority, largely because he was the only marcher with a broad following, the only marcher whose name was generally known, both inside the BEF and to the public.[23]

After the first few chaotic days, the incoming veterans were handled with efficiency and dispatch. If they arrived by truck, District police, alerted by Maryland or Virginia officials, would meet them at the District line and escort them to Anacostia. If they came by boxcar, railroad officials would similarly notify the police. Once at Anacostia, each veteran had to prove to the BEF officials that he had a right to be there: discharges and bonus certificates were carefully examined, for no nonveterans were wanted. The police department furnished typewriters, stationery, and other office supplies. If a man arrived without proper papers, he was sent to the Veterans Administration, which went out of its way to provide identification. Once he had passed scrutiny, he was sworn into the BEF and issued a membership card, which he had to show at every meal. The oath bound him to support the Constitution and the flag and to oppose those who were against the bonus. To enforce its regulations, Glassford allowed the BEF to appoint "Military Police," who were loosely supervised by the patrolman whom Glassford assigned to regular duty at each encampment. Visitors to the army continually commented on the orderliness of the assemblage. As one minor federal official remarked: [24]

> Upon approaching the camp, we found all entrances were guarded by M.P.'s who directed everyone to the main entrance. These guards were a polite lot, more polite, I should say, than many . . . traffic officers.

However polite they may have been to respectable visitors, the MPs were not at all gentle to those they regarded as "reds." According to a letter in the Communist daily: [25]

When we get in here, the stool pigeons point us out to the M.P.'s and they took us to the commander of the camp. He says, "You're a damn red. All right, men, give him the works." The strong arm squad take you in a car and beat you before turning you loose. . . . A preacher came down and told us that we must take our bibles and pray. A veteran was put out of the camp for telling him to go to hell.

On several occasions Glassford had to interfere with the vigilante-like treatment that Waters and his MP's meted out to "reds," real and imagined. Glassford's own views on the Communists, although much more tolerant than those of most American police officials, were not as unambiguously civil libertarian as they have been painted.[26] He wrote in the fall of 1932:

From the point of view of the police, the Communists presented a specific problem. The Communist party is not outlawed. It is running candidates for President and Vice President and for other offices. It appears in the ballots under the emblem of the Arm and Sickle. It has constitutional rights that must be protected until those rights are withdrawn by due process of law. It is a curious thing that while the avowed purpose of the Communist party is the overthrow of our present social structure, the law confers upon it the protection of the Constitution it seeks to destroy and guarantees it the fundamental rights of free speech, free press and free assembly.

The Communists sought to carry their propaganda into the camps of the regular B.E.F. The police discouraged this as much as possible. There the Metropolitan Police under my command had to stop, as a matter of law, the B.E.F. military police carried on.

The B.E.F. military police was created by the veterans to maintain law and order in the camps and billets; it assisted in directing traffic and maintained an embargo against the introduction into the camps of liquor and firearms. One of its chief activities was preventing the spread of Communist and radical propaganda.

Of necessity, the Metropolitan Police adopted the inflexible policy of treating all veterans alike, irrespective of race, religious or political affiliation. One of the first difficulties arose when Waters refused to give rations to the Communist group among the veterans. Since the feeding of the men had fallen on my shoulders, I insisted that the Communists be fed as were the other veterans. Waters reluctantly yielded in this. . . .

[Communist leaders often protested] against the tactics of the B.E.F. military police in preventing distribution of [their] party's literature in the camps. Frequently, when [their] agents invaded the camps, they were seized by the military police and beaten up. . . .

They were granted permits for meetings any time they applied for them. Words never yet broke bones and speech is a safety valve. My subordinates did not agree and it was often difficult to see that this policy prevailed. As it was, the meetings were never molested by the police; they were attended by not more than 50 bona fide veterans and a maximum of 200 curious onlookers. . . .

Every effort of the Communists to infect the veterans with their ideas failed. Their plans, never of a menacing nature, were known beforehand and frustrated by the regular police, aided constantly by the B.E.F. military police.

Glassford's estimate of the Communist strength was essentially correct, although he may have understated slightly their number when he claimed that only about 45 "actual communists" and 150 of "their unintelligent followers" were in the BEF. But the importance of the Communists in the BEF cannot be gauged by numbers alone: they were important because they were feared and because these fears were acted upon and used as a pretext for action. As early as May 28, under the leadership of the peacetime marine, Emanuel Levin, the WESL was quickly transformed into a Provisional Bonus March Committee which the *Daily Worker* absurdly claimed was "leading" the march. Actually the Communist committee was largely a "paper" organization which used the same Washington address as a number of other front groups. By early June, however, tough Communist contingents from Detroit, Chicago, and Cleveland arrived, and John Pace, a hitherto obscure Detroit party member with a real war record, became the public leader of the Communist forces in Washington. During the whole summer the party press shamelessly magnified their influence a hundredfold. General Secretary of the party Earl Browder, with the facile opportunism that has characterized his whole career, claimed that the WESL had initiated the entire bonus movement, and, using a very cloudy crystal ball, saw the BEF as the harbinger of the "greater Workers' Expeditionary Force which will march along the road to the revolutionary solution of the crisis." [27]

These exaggerated claims of the early 1930s have found curious echoes. Some conservatives and rightists, then and now, and with a variety of motives ranging from pure funk to calculated exaggeration, have accepted and even further blown up the party's self-magnification. No one can doubt that the hard-core party cadres devoutly wished that a truly revolutionary situation would develop and that many of them daydreamed about becoming the American Lenin or Trotsky and turning the BEF into a soviet of workers and farmers. To mistake these Mitty-like fantasies for historical reality is ludicrous; that many on the right in this country continue to do just that is a rather telling comment on the tenacity of their grasp on reality.[28]

Yet, having said all this, the Communist presence was important; it sharply delimited the alternatives available to those in charge and enabled them better to indulge in socially dangerous delusions. Glassford was deluged with advice on the subject. A member of the Michigan State Police wrote to let him know "confidentially" how things were handled in Michigan. "We had a little trouble here in Lansing wich [sic] the reds but on the second visit a few of the boys took the leader for a short ride, they have not returned."

Similar views existed within the Washington force, and, if the police there were somewhat inhibited by Glassford's relatively libertarian views, they persistently went beyond the bounds of law in harassing red agitators, real and imagined. Here, to cite one instance, is a detective's report to Glassford: [29]

1. Marion Watkins, colored, 28 years, of 905 I Street, N.W. arrested June 21st 1932 selling pamphlets—'Veterans Close Ranks' issued by Workers Ex-Servicemen's League, #1 Union Square, New York City, Room 715—on 9th Street, N.W. between E and F Streets which were suggestively Communistic, revolutionary in aim and undermining to the principles of the United States Government.

2. He was detained at #1 Precinct and two copies of pamphlet given to Assistant District Attorney Schwartz for review and recommendation.

3. June 23rd 1932, Mr. Schwartz stated that the substance of the pamphlet contained no violation of the law and did not justify preosecution. [sic]

4. In the meantime Precinct Detective Wanamaker, #1 Precinct, desired that Watkins be held for him for questioning. Watkins was turned over to Wanamaker on June 23rd 1932 and released by him at 9:30 A.M., June 25th, 1932.

Thus Watkins spent four days and nights in jail for absolutely nothing and no formal charges were ever placed against him. If he did not condone this kind of harassment, Glassford

did little to check it. In addition, he was determined to iso-
late the Communists from the other marchers and to minimize
their influence as much as possible. At a very early date he
decided to billet all identifiable Communist groups—that is,
those publicly adhering to the WESL or the Provisional Bonus
March Committee—in a separate area in downtown Washington. The inspiration for this may well have come from the
Communists themselves. The first WESL Washington leaflet—
dated May 28 but apparently written a few days later—was
headed "Do NOT Let the Bonus Enemies Divide Us." It demanded housing "in a central location group together closely
[sic]" and, further indicative of the limited original aims of the
Communist party, called for all veterans to stay until June 8,
the date originally set for their one-day demonstration. While
Waters and others developed slogans calling for the marchers
to "Stay til we get our bonus" or "Stay til 1945," the WESL
group was saying "One monster demonstration is what we
want." As late as June 3, the *Daily Worker* was promulgating
essentially the same line. It instructed prospective marchers
as follows: [30]

1. Contact the Provisional Bonus March Committee upon arrival
   in the capital.

2. Beware of police attempts to inhibit communication.

3. Demand a central location in downtown Washington.

4. Be sure to get a Provisional Bonus March Committee identification card.

5. Ignore rumors . . . make no statements to the press.

6. Demand quarters unsegregated either by race or political
   affiliation.

The publicity which the Communists gave to their plans

and public announcements of tactics made it easy for Glass-ford to thwart them. Since the Communist-led delegations were obedient to their orders and demanded, upon arrival, to be put in touch with their local people, it was simple for the police to quarter them in a separate and relatively isolated billet. Although they had at first insisted on being quartered in downtown Washington and protested against the proposed camp at Anacostia, after it became clear that Camp Marks would be the most heavily populated of the encampments they vainly protested their exclusion.

Having isolated them by fiat, Glassford preempted their "monster" demonstration scheduled for June 8. He encouraged Waters to have the BEF parade on June 7. Perhaps 5,000 of Waters' men turned out to march down Pennsylvania Avenue on the eve of the scheduled Communist party demonstration. Floyd Gibbons, writing for the friendly Hearst papers, called it a "ghost parade," while Thomas Henry in the *Star* felt that it was "the saddest parade Washington ever has known." Most of the hundred thousand spectators seemed to sympathize with the gaunt, ragged veterans, many of whom could no longer move at the military pace. Pathetic or not, the parade clearly turned out many, many more veterans than the Com-munists could hope to muster; the June 8 demonstration, until then the major goal of the party's outmaneuvered tac-ticians, was quietly abandoned.[31]

Public sympathy for the bonus marchers was not confined to Washington; by early June, it seems clear, the BEF had cap-tured the emotions of most of the country. Though Congress-man Hamilton Fish (R.-N.Y.), the premier red-hunter of his day, could insist that most of the marchers had been "duped by Communist agitators," even he readily admitted that "prob-ably 95 percent" of the veterans were loyal Americans. Fish never went out to Anacostia to see for himself, but a steady stream of celebrities did go to see and be seen. The Pittsburgh rabble-rouser, Father Cox, himself a virulent anti-Communist,

scoffed at the red influence charge and urged the men to stick
it out in an appearance that was a thinly disguised boost for
his own ridiculous presidential candidacy. Unlike Coughlin,
he had no largesse to distribute, but he lent the men moral
support while pronouncing the two major parties "doomed,"
denouncing the "present dictatorship of this country by Wall
Street," and predicting that "if the bonus marchers stood firm,"
half a million or so veterans would join them.

Although the bonus march was largely an urban manifes-
tation, it drew much of its political support from rural
America. John A. Simpson, president of the National Farmers' Union, Jeff Davis, self-styled king of the hoboes, and
"General" Jacob S. Coxey, who must have seen fascinating
parallels between the BEF and his own "army" of 1894, came
out to look around and were apparently sympathetic, but did
not talk for publication. Oklahoma's Governor William H.
"Alfalfa Bill" Murray, an avowed candidate for the Democratic presidential nomination, not only voiced approval for
the march, but suggested that other "hungry folks" might soon
augment the veterans, while in Iowa, Milo Reno's Farmers'
Holiday Association telegraphed best wishes and offered to
supply plenty of food, if only the railroads would ship it east
free of charge. And, most impressive of all, volunteers and
donations from all over the country continued to stream
toward Washington. This broad national support is not reflected in the editorial columns of the nation's press: most
newspapers, always excepting the powerful Hearst chain, continued to oppose the bonus. Their news columns, on the other
hand, reflected the deep-felt sympathy of the Washington press
corps. Had there been a national referendum on paying the
bonus that spring, it would have passed easily. But the bonus
marchers had not come to Washington to win a popularity
contest or to influence public opinion. They had come to get
Congress to pay the bonus.[32]

The congressional temper by mid-1932 was somewhat short;

it had been a long and frustrating session, and most members were impatient to get on with the political campaign. The earliest congressional reactions, not surprisingly, were those of annoyance and embarrassment. House majority leader Henry T. Rainey (D.-Ill.) labeled the whole march "futile" and declared that "never since the children marched to the holy land has there been a march so foolish." Other Congressmen, like Hamilton Fish and Thomas L. Blanton (D.-Tex.), saw the march as a sinister "show of force" and an attempt "to browbeat Congress." Even long-standing friends of the bonus were non-plussed. John E. Rankin (D.-Miss.), chairman of the House Veterans Committee, asked publicly that no more marchers come and pleaded with those already in Washington to return home.[33] Wright Patman, although surprised at the event, defended the bonus marchers.

"I had no part in the coming of the bonus army," the Texan observed with legalistic accuracy, although it could be argued that his long struggle for the bonus and his ceaseless agitation of what was, for the time being at least, a lost cause, made him an accessory before the fact. "I will not give any encouragement to any others joining this force," he continued. But he would not ask the men to go home or ask others not to come. He insisted that the veterans had a perfect right to petition their government in person, and, in an analogy that had been used in the 1890s to justify Coxey's Army, and was to be reiterated constantly during the debates to come, he claimed that they had as much right as any other lobbyists to come to Washington. He also insisted that the BEF "must not be allowed to starve on the Capitol steps." [34]

The first legislative attempt to do something about the march came in the Senate on Memorial Day, when Edward P. Costigan (D.-Colo.), acting on Glassford's advice, introduced a bill providing for emergency relief in the District and making a special appropriation of "$75,000 for nonresident, homeless transients moving to, within and through" the national capital. Opposed by the Senate leadership, this bill never even came to a vote.[35] In the House, Patman's discharge petition, which had lain largely unnoticed in the well of the House for three weeks and which most observers thought would never get the requisite 145 signatures, suddenly became quite popular. Three legislative days after the BEF had arrived, the petition had been completed. It took a bipartisan effort: 34 of the 145 signatures were those of Republicans. The petition drew heavily on southern support, with considerable strength shown in the Midwest and on the Pacific Coast. Representatives from the Northeast were least willing to sign.[36]

Once discharge had occurred, and the House was committed to a record vote on paying the bonus, it quickly became apparent to insiders that the bonus was again a live issue. Insiders expected that it would be impossible for the majority of the House to vote against the veterans, even though it was clear that the majority would have preferred not to vote at all. It was also clear that the bill would fail in the Senate, if it ever came to a vote there. And should a miracle occur in the upper house, a most unlikely place for divine intervention, a presidential veto had been promised and no conceivable set of circumstances could deprive President Hoover of the support of thirty-three senators, the number necessary to sustain a veto. The legislative maneuverings over the bonus were thus a charade whose predetermined denouement was known to most of the actors. The spectators, however, particularly the veteran spectators, were naive men of faith, and the charade seemed high drama to them as they listened to agitators, encouraged each other, and made the daily pilgrimage up Capitol Hill to parade, buttonhole Congressmen, and jam the congressional galleries.

They heard what sounded like a full-scale debate, despite the seeming certainty of the outcome. Patman's petition, filed on June 4, came up for debate on June 13, when a motion to discharge the bonus bill from the Rules Committee was automatically in order. In his summation Patman promised that his bill would be more palatable to the fiscally orthodox and claimed that in fighting for the bill he was seeking not only justice for the veteran but also "a fair price for corn, cotton, wheat, hogs, cattle, land, agricultural products, and for fair wages for labor in our great factories. This bill will accomplish that result. If it passes, this panic will disappear and prosperity will return." The House, as expected, voted for discharge and then resolved to take up the bonus bill itself the next day under a "gag" rule allowing a total of four hours of debate.[37]

On June 14 the debate commenced, before packed and somewhat noisy galleries which drew repeated admonitions from the Speaker. As promised, the bill was amended to make it conform more closely to the fiscal superstitions of the time. The bill, it will be remembered, had called simply for the Treasury to print a new kind of money, Treasury notes, in sufficient quantity to pay the bonus. There were no provisions in the bill for taking the notes out of circulation; it was an inflationist measure, pure and simple. The substitute provision, which had been agreed to in advance by Patman and the other managers of the measure, was modeled after the Owen plan. The same amount of notes was to be issued by the Treasury, but they were to be "printed in the same size, of the same denominations, and of the same form as Treasury notes, omitting the reference to any Federal Reserve bank." To seem to back this money, the bill directed the Treasury to issue an equal amount of $3\frac{1}{2}$ percent 20-year bonds, the proceeds from which would be used to retire the notes issued to pay the bonus. Although many fiscal conservatives professed not to see any difference between the two versions, it apparently enabled many Congressmen, perhaps a crucial number, to vote for the bonus without damaging their allegedly tender fiscal consciences.[38]

The debate was strictly ersatz drama, as most speakers trotted out the same set speeches they had been using for several congresses. Toward midafternoon the drama became real, when Edward E. Eslick, an obscure Tennessee Democrat in his fourth term and sixtieth year, collapsed on the floor of the House in the midst of a hackneyed argument in favor of the bonus. He died a few moments later. The House quickly adjourned for the day, but resumed debate on June 15. The vote was as expected, 211 to 176, or, if one counts pairs, 232 to 197. Again, a heavily Democratic but still bipartisan group prevailed. Of 219 Democrats recorded, 168 voted or were paired in favor, and 50 were opposed. Of the 210 Republicans, 63 favored while 147 opposed. While most of the House opposition can be labeled "conservative" or "orthodox," some progressives, like Fiorello La Guardia, voted "no." The New Yorker explained his vote by arguing that the bonus "would not solve a single problem with which Congress and the country are confronted." [39]

As the bill went to the Senate, excitement among the BEF rose to its highest pitch, as more and more veterans continued to stream into Washington and few left. The day the Senate got the bill, at least 15,000 veterans were milling around downtown Washington and their slightly ominous presence caused the Senate, for once, to move with haste. Reed Smoot of Utah promised that his Finance Committee would report on the bill within a day or two. What he wanted, he explained, was a quick vote, and he suggested that "every Senator" desired the same thing. The assumption was, of course, that once the bonus had been disposed of, the BEF would go home. [40]

Waters, who understood the political realities better than most of his rank and file, tried to counter the feared reaction before it set in. On the morning of June 15, the day the House would pass the bill and send it to the Senate, Waters issued an order to be read in all billets. [41]

To All Commanders and Group Leaders:

There is going to be a determined effort on the part of the bonus enemies to bring about the evacuation of Washington by the BEF.

They are particularly hoping to start this disbanding of the veterans immediately after adjournment of the House and Senate. National General Headquarters will be in accord with the evacuation provided the bonus bill is passed. However, if the bill is pigeonholed or if for any reason it fails to pass National General Headquarters will not officially countenance the return home of the groups at present in Washington, D.C. General Headquarters BEF has from the beginning emphatically stated that if necessary we will stay on the job until 1945. That attitude is unchanged. No matter what the fate of the bonus bill at the present session of Congress, it is the positive intention of National General Headquarters BEF to use every inducement in its power to prevail upon the rank and file of the veterans throughout the U.S. to come to Washington, D.C., and stay in Washington, D.C., until this fight is won.

W. W. Waters
National Commander, BEF

On June 16 Senator Smoot was as good as his word, and the bill was brought to the floor with an adverse report from the Senate Finance Committee. At the request of its proponents, debate was postponed to the next day. Friday, June 17, saw the legislative farce concluded while some 8,000 BEFers gathered on and around the Capitol steps. There were a few set speeches, and some of the liberal-progressive members explained their votes at length. Four Democratic senators, Wagner and Copeland of New York and Walsh and Coolidge of Massachusetts, issued a joint statement declaring that next winter, when a presumably Democratic administration would become the "last hope of a distressed people," the country would need an "unimpaired treasury." They therefore, "against all the dictates of . . . personal desire" could not support paying the bonus in full.[42]

A number of Senate progressives, including Norris and La Follette, attempted to make it clear that the votes they were going to cast against the bonus were motivated by the belief that payment of the bonus would prevent any significant relief measure from passing Congress. Norris said that he would vote for the bonus only as a "last resort," which he thought had not yet arrived. La Follette, who paid tribute to the BEF as a "cross section of the backbone" of the nation, felt "infinite regret" that his commitment to federal unemployment relief legislation and a large public works program did not allow him to vote for the bonus.

Burton K. Wheeler (D.-Mont.) tried to answer his progressive brethren. The Montanan said that he agreed with those who said [43]

> that we ought to provide work rather than give money to these ex-soldiers. If I could see a ray of hope in this Congress that some means would be found to put more money into circulation other than by the method here proposed, I would not vote for the pending bill. If some proposal should be offered by those who have spoken, and I felt sure that we could pass such legislation and give employment to the men on the streets tonight, and to the veterans, I would not vote for this legislation. But nothing has been offered, and every program that has been suggested for the purpose of putting men to work, public construction, bond issues for that purpose, has been denounced. . . .
>
> I have sat here waiting month after month and week after week and day after day in vain for the great engineer at the other end of Pennsylvania Avenue to come forward with some proposal for taking care not only of these ex-soldiers, not only of these veterans, but of the other thousands and millions of men and women of this country who are anxious and willing to work, but nothing has been done and nothing will be done.

After a few hours of voluntarily curtailed debate—at times the noise of the milling veterans outside drifted into the Senate chamber—the vote came in the evening of June 17.

Yet despite its predetermined outcome, there was a great deal of tension inside the chamber as well as out. As Senator Hiram Johnson (R.-Cal.) described it in a letter to his son: [44]

> We had yesterday and last night a scene here at the Capitol that probably has never been witnessed before in this city, and which to an imaginative old fellow like myself was intensely interesting. You have read, of course, of the war veterans who have marched into Washington, demanding their bonus payment. Yesterday, the matter came before the senate, and they during the day, marched to the Capitol steps. After exhausting all the space casual visitors are permitted to occupy in the gallery of the senate, the vast crowd remained until after nine o'clock last night immediately in front of the Capitol awaiting final action by the Senate. With my peculiar sensibilities you realize I was torn with conflicting emotions. Those men ought not to have come here in the first instance, they should have not swarmed down upon the Capitol, and no legislator should respond to their mere numbers or their veiled threats. They constitute but a small part of the unemployed of the Nation, and but a small part of those whose distress is appealing. Nevertheless, they present a picture of human misery, and if I could have seen any way in which they could have been afforded relief without jeopardizing the whole financial fabric of the Nation I would have voted with them. Their presence, although, in my opinion it threatens no particular ill, is ominous. If the farmers of this Nation who are suffering united, as these men have united, and with the same abandon, started a march upon the Capitol, and joined ranks with those of the city whose souls have been seared with misery during the past few years, it would not be difficult for a real revolution to start in this country. . . . Thoughtful men in the congress, and we have been so extremely engaged that few have had time to think at all, view the presence of these veterans in such numbers, and their insistence upon a demand, which, in justice to the Nation, could not be accorded them, as evidence of the economic disease from which the Nation is suffering.

Only 28 of the 96 senators were in favor of the bill—18 Democrats, 9 Republicans, and Hendrik Shipstead of Minnesota, the lone Farmer-Labor senator. The neopopulist geographical pattern of southern and western support for the bonus was even more pronounced in the Senate. North of the Mason-Dixon line, no senator east of Indiana voted for the bonus. Eight of the 9 Republicans were midwesterners, while 11 of the 18 Democrats were southerners.[45]

Outside the Capitol the news of the vote came, somehow, as a shock to the gathered veterans. Their commander, Waters, made the announcement: [46]

> Prepare yourselves for a disappointment, men. . . . The Bonus has been defeated. . . . This is only a temporary setback. We are going to get more and more men and we are going to stay here until we change the minds of these guys. You're ten times better Americans than the Senators that voted against the bill.

His announcement was followed by a tense silence. No one seemed to know what to do. One journalist was reminded of "the mobs of the French Revolution; the crash of the Kerensky Government in Russia; the Spanish uprising." He was convinced that the assembled veterans could have, "had they wished, by sheer force of numbers swept away every obstruction." According to Waters, the spell was broken when he took the advice of Elsie Robinson, a saccharine Hearst columnist, who whispered the suggestion that he have the men sing "America." This struck just the right note and after the rendition the men quickly broke up and headed toward their billets. No single incident more clearly indicates the nonrevolutionary character of the BEF. Bewildered rather than angry, none of them—not even the Communists—seems to have thought of storming the Capitol. Most of the revolutionary ideas were in the minds of the defenders of the old order, including many of Glassford's subordinates.[47]

Particularly nervous was Inspector L. I. H. Edwards, one of the officers who had been passed over when Glassford was made chief. To frustrate Waters' directive that all bonus marchers assemble before the Capitol to hear the final vote, Edwards had the drawbridge between Anacostia and the city raised, stranding about half the BEF in Camp Marks and playing havoc with homeward-bound traffic. To quell the resulting mutterings about a "double cross" which threatened future cooperation between the BEF and the police, Glassford wrote a formal apology and had it published. In it he disavowed personal responsibility for the incident and admitted to Waters that "it was a mistake to have done so and the entire Police Department realizes it as such." [48]

Believing that the worst was over, much of Washington breathed a sigh of relief. Praising the soldierly way in which the men took their bad news, the *Star* editorialized: "If they go now every hand will be turned to help them. Their return will be likened to the return of an army from battle, where honor has been won."

Even some congressional friends of the BEF expected them to disperse after the vote. Senator Elmer Thomas (D.-Okla.), the staunchest bonus advocate in the upper chamber, had assured his colleagues that as soon as Congress gave them "an answer . . . they would commence immediately to make their plans for evacuation of this so-called camp." [49]

The expectation of quick departure was, of course, a vain hope. As a visiting sociologist had pointed out a few days earlier, the departure of what he styled an "army of occupation" might create even more serious problems than its advent.[50] The professor was right. The petition became a siege. Congressional rejection of the bonus settled nothing: it merely put the ball back in Glassford's court.

6

The Siege
of Washington

PELHAM GLASSFORD was surprised neither by the vote nor by the fact that many veterans stayed on in Washington (in fact, the bonus army continued to grow after the Senate rejected Patman's bill), for he had assumed for some time that this would be the case. Speaking at Anacostia, as he often did, the day before the Senate voted, he assured the BEF:

> You men have as much right to be here as anyone else. I'll admit I've been trying to get some of you to go home to make room for others who are coming in. At 11 o'clock every morning we have trucks available with sufficient rations for those who want to go. But I want to tell you boys who want to stay here we'll keep on feeding you as long as a cent remains, and we'll do the best we can for you. Commander Waters and myself . . . are still playing our little chess game.

Glassford coupled this nonhostile posture with a continuing campaign of discouragement, including a venture in psychological warfare. He had military bands serenade Camp Marks

regularly and made sure that their repertoire featured sentimental selections like "Keep the Home Fires Burning" and
"There's a Long, Long Trail A-Winding." When Waters and
other leaders of the BEF refused to distribute his mimeographed appeal for the bonus army to return "to the States
from which they came," Glassford had 3,000 copies dropped
on the Anacostia encampment from an airplane.

Behind the scenes, he and Waters had apparently agreed that
it would be best if the bulk of the BEF disbanded fairly soon.
Despite the bravado about "Stay til 1945," which Waters and
others continued to spout, it is clear that the outdoor encampment could not have lasted through the winter. Both of the
"friendly enemies" understood this and seem to have envisaged
a semipermanent BEF of perhaps a thousand or so staying in
the capital, with the majority of the army disbanding by
gradual attrition rather than by evacuation. The police chief
wanted all of the bonus marchers on the other side of the
Anacostia River, where "they would be isolated from the heart
of the city, from the constant mass of curious and sympathetic
visitors, and from all the glamour that intrigued their fancy." [1]
To this end Glassford was instrumental in securing for the
BEF the use of a thirty-acre plot of private property toward
the outskirts of Washington, which was named Camp Bartlett
after its donor, John Henry Bartlett, a most unlikely "angel"
for a protest group. A former Republican governor of New
Hampshire, Bartlett had enjoyed high-level executive appointments under all three Republican presidents of the 1920s. As
he explained his actions later, in a book severely critical of the
administration: [2]

For nearly eight weeks I had personally visited the larger camps
and conversed at more or less length with a great many of the
veterans, not only with their leaders but with their privates, and
with the women and children. I became acquainted with them,
so that whenever I went many of them recognized me by name. In

fact, I was more or less in the habit of carrying things to them. They RESPONDED TO KINDNESS as gratefully as any people I ever knew.

They were persons who needed kindness. They were not ignorant. There were COLLEGE GRADUATES among them. There were men who had been FOREMEN IN SHOPS AND MINES, who had owned FARMS, and, in fact, they represented in education, industry, ideals, and all, about the same qualities that we would find among people generally. But they looked pale, ragged, gaunt, and dejected.

Another possible semipermanent campsite had been acquired when General Stephan, Glassford's friend who commanded the District's National Guard, agreed to allow the BEFers to use Camp Simms, a guard installation in the vicinity of Anacostia.

Glassford's hopes that the bonus army could be dispersed relatively quickly, first to the new suburban camps and then to their homes, were short-lived. As soon as the bonus bill was voted down, the chief arranged with the Pennsylvania and B&O railroads to give a special cent-a-mile rate for home-ward bound marchers, about one-third of the normal fare. Glassford, of course, was willing to use BEF relief funds for this purpose, but not even the lure of a ride home "on the cushions" tempted many marchers; some of the few who went seem to have done so to be able to recruit others. In any event, the army continued to grow. By June 25, Glassford seemed convinced that many thousands would just stay, despite the continuing efforts to get them to leave.[3]

"It is a fact," he reported to the Commissioners, "that these efforts will bring scant results and we will have on our hands for many weeks, if not months, several thousands of veterans." He also assumed that thousands of nonveteran unemployed would come to Washington for the opening of the lame-duck session of Congress in December. He proposed, therefore, that the District Commissioners try to get the federal demolition program delayed so that marchers quartered in partially demolished buildings could remain there and that they finance the building of "barracks at some location such as Camp Bartlett."

This the Commissioners refused to do. They did not want to make any provision for a semipermanent army of occupation. Glassford personally argued his case before them in a stormy session on June 27. At that time he estimated that a hard core of five or six thousand BEFers would remain for "many weeks or months." The Commissioners, and particularly General Crosby, not only rejected the police chief's proposals, but they once again made it clear that they blamed the continued presence of the veterans on him and his too lenient policies. As Glassford recorded the meeting in a document he labeled "Memorandum for Record": [4]

> Commissioner Crosby stated that police ordinances were being waived or suspended in permitting the veterans to occupy camps for more than 24 hours where these camps are not provided with sewerage; that buildings were being occupied by the veterans without proper authority and that they were not entitled to any assistance from the District Government or in providing more permanent shelter.
>
> Commissioner Crosby's attitude was critical of the Police Department in that force had not been used to prevent the veterans from occupying buildings which had not been designated for their occupancy. He stated that the general sense of the Bonus Expeditionary Force was that they had the "Police Chief's goat," and that they would no doubt do as they pleased until police authority was exerted to prevent them. He said they would have to be ejected from certain of the buildings. I told him that this would require turning out the National Guard or federal troops to quell certain riots that might ensue. His reply was that "we have a police force." It was perfectly apparent that General Crosby was not in sympathy with the policy that has been pursued by the

Major and Superintendent of Police in the handling of the Veteran Situation. It was further apparent that he advocated, without assuming any responsibility therefor, the use of force.

It was not just General Crosby who anticipated the use of force: talk about eventual violence was everywhere—in the newspapers, in the halls of Congress, and in the squalid camps of the bonus army itself. Despite this verbal restiveness, the BEF continued to squat passively in the Anacostia mud. When Glassford made one of his periodic announcements about dwindling contributions and food supplies and concluded, as he usually did, that the veterans ought to go home, one marcher responded that "there's a lot of warehouses and stores in this town that are stuffed full of food and we're not going to starve."

Waters, who tried to stem the tide of restlessness by ordering regular close-order drill, seemed to be going along with Glassford's gradual dispersal policy. This and other grievances brought about an ouster move in late June. Among the leaders who spoke against him was Joe Angelo, of Camden, New Jersey, a holder of the Distinguished Service Cross and the most decorated man in the BEF. (Several accounts talk about Congressional Medal of Honor winners, but none were present.) Angelo argued:

> Waters swore to us when we made him boss that we would all stay here until 1945, if we did not get our bonus. Is he trying to sell out to the cops? Well, he won't get away with it.

Other criticisms came from the Communists, who continued to brand him "fascist," and from some of the more militant marchers who resented his dictatorial style, his hobnobbing with Glassford and other "enemies," and, perhaps most of all, his essentially passive policy. Sensing the deterioration of his position, Waters suddenly resigned on June 26 before the movement to depose him had gotten up a full head of steam and before the various dissident groups had been able to agree on a mutually acceptable replacement. In his "farewell" address, the BEF commander insisted:

> I did not . . . seek . . . this position. Nor did I accept it with any thought of personal gain or aggrandizement. . . . I accepted the position of national commander of the B.E.F., tendered some weeks ago. . . I have made many mistakes but I hardly believe my sincerity is open to question.

Waters proposed that the "rank and file . . . now in Washington should be permitted" to elect a national commander. Waters made it clear that he was a candidate, and, not surprisingly, he was elected overwhelmingly. Actually, while there were some individuals who had a following among this or that group, Waters was the only marcher whose name was generally known, both inside the scattered BEF and to the public. His leadership confirmed by the ballot, Waters proceeded to banish some of the dissident leaders and to entrench himself and his supporters more firmly in control of all but the Communist elements of the bonus army.[5]

As the congressional session ground on to adjournment—with the presidential campaign already in progress there was much restiveness among the legislators—Glassford lobbied hard to get some legislation passed for the relief of the BEF. His pet scheme, which he quickly dropped, was a "back to the land" proposition which would have dispersed the veterans to their respective states and there settled them on government-owned subsistence plots of three to ten acres in size.[6] He could also make practical proposals: largely as the result of Glassford's urging, Congress did pass, by joint resolution, a measure which provided railroad fare (or an equivalent sum for gas and oil) and a seventy-five-cent-per-day subsistence allowance for any honorably discharged wartime veteran who wanted to go home. The resolution established a cut-off date of July 25, nine days after Congress adjourned. Eventually some 5,000 bonus marchers received such transportation from the Veterans Administration, at a cost of about $70,000. Since the congressional action failed to make any provision for women and children, the American Red Cross, which had refused to do anything for the bonus army while it was in Washington, financed the journey home of nearly 500 wives and children of returning veterans.[7] In addition, Congress liberalized the terms under which a veteran could borrow on his adjusted service certificate, the most significant change being a lowering of the interest rate from 4½ to 3½ percent.[8]

While the lawmakers were throwing their departing sops to the bonus army, the veterans, or some of them, were abandoning their passive policy and pursuing a course of limited activism. This new activism was certainly stimulated if not sparked by the arrival on July 9 of the Los Angeles contingent headed by Royal Robertson, the ex-sailor with the neck brace. He and his men refused to conform to the patterns that Glassford and Waters had so carefully established. Instead of allowing themselves to be shunted into one of the established camps and being swallowed up in the mass of other men, Robertson and his several hundred followers insisted on a separate billet in downtown Washington. As the Californian put it: [9]

My men will refuse to follow Waters as long as he continues with a stew-and-beans mooching policy. The public is supporting these men here and my men feel they should try to do something constructive instead of sitting in a puddle and whittling a stick until 1945.

Robertson's idea of something constructive turned out to be picketing the Capitol and sleeping on the Capitol grounds. This threw the authorities there into anxious confusion. By a legal anomaly, the Capitol and its grounds were not under the jurisdiction of Glassford's metropolitan police but were supposed to be policed by the separate Capitol police force under the direction of the Capitol Police Board, a body consisting of the sergeants-at-arms of the two houses and the Capitol architect. All were patronage appointments; the board took its orders from the Speaker of the House and the Vice President, who were, in 1932, of different political parties. To add a further note of confusion, Glassford and the uniformed head of the Capitol force, Captain S. J. Gnash, did not get along and seem not even to have been on speaking terms.

On July 12, Robertson received permission from Vice President Charles Curtis to parade to the Capitol and there present a petition. Glassford discovered that the Californians planned to take their bed rolls with them and stage what we would now call a "sleep-in" on the Capitol grounds. After a quick conference with Curtis, Glassford and twenty of his policemen, whom he ordered to disarm, halted Robertson's 400-man parade at the edge of the Capitol grounds. After a parley they agreed to have their bedding sent back on a police truck and proceeded to present their petition. After presenting it, Robertson's men remained all night on the Capitol grounds, sleeping on the sidewalks and lawns without molestation.

The next day, with Robertson's men still picketing, Curtis and House Speaker John Nance Garner personally instructed Glassford that they expected him to enforce the regulations— that is, not let the veterans sleep on the grass—but admonished him to prevent violence. When apprised of this by Glassford, the Californian asked if there were any regulation against walking through the grounds. When Glassford said that there was not, Robertson decided to start what the press quickly dubbed the "Death March." About 360 veterans walked all night on the sidewalks that interlace the Capitol grounds. To make sure that the grass remained unslept upon, the sprinkler system was turned on and left on all night. It was a pitiful spectacle. Thomas Henry of the *Star* thought it was a "supreme dramatic gesture" and described the "men in bare feet, in stocking feet, with toes sticking through their shoes . . . most with faces fixed on the ground."

The death marchers were orderly; in fact, Glassford had more trouble with the several thousand curious spectators than with the veterans. The chief admitted that although most of the men actually marched in single file and thus probably constituted an illegal procession, he felt that the latitude Speaker Garner had given him justified his stretching of the regulations. Besides, he noted, they were easier to control that way. Easy to control or not, Glassford didn't get to bed until 5:00 A.M., and was up again three hours later.

When he got to police headquarters he found that the liberties he had taken with regulations had not been appreciated everywhere. At a Capitol Police Board meeting that afternoon (July 14), he found that its members, particularly Senate Sergeant-at-Arms David S. Barry, were deeply fearful that Congress would not be able to adjourn without serious disorder and wanted federal troops called out to protect the legislators. They were not only disturbed by the continued presence of Robertson's men, but by a Communist handbill which called an illegal meeting on the Capitol grounds for the following morning. The handbill, couched in the imperative throughout, in typical pseudobolshevik style, insisted repeatedly that "Congress must not adjourn until the bonus is granted in full to every veteran." Glassford tried to allay the fears of the seventy-three-year-old Barry and his cohorts by pointing out the relative insignificance of the Communist forces and apparently thought he had sufficiently calmed them.

Later that afternoon Commissioner Crosby summoned Glassford to a meeting in Chief of Staff Douglas MacArthur's office in the old War, Navy, State Building behind the White House. Those in attendance included Deputy Chief of Staff George Van Horn Moseley and General Perry L. Miles, the ranking area troop commander. While MacArthur was outlining the procedures necessary for calling out federal troops and how he would use them, Admiral Henry V. Butler arrived with the startling news that the marines had been called out and that sixty of them were on the way to the Capitol to clear its grounds. No one in the room seemed to know who was responsible, but the admiral agreed to recall the men.

A hurried trip to the Capitol revealed that the culprit was Charles Curtis, perhaps the least accomplished Vice President of this century. (As the leading authority on Curtis has written, "Curtis took virtually no part in the Hoover administration. His advice was seldom sought and had it been sought he would have had little to contribute.") Curtis insisted to Glassford that the police chief was, in effect, under his orders, and he ordered him to rid the Capitol grounds of all veterans. Unable to reason with the irascible seventy-two-year-old Kansan, Glassford went over his head; using Senator Hiram Bingham as an intermediary, he eventually received compromise instructions from the White House, which merely called for the clearing of the plaza in front of the Capitol. This Glassford's men accomplished without difficulty. Robertson's men continued to march around the remainder of the grounds for the second night, but were not allowed to sleep on the grass. The next day, as Glassford had predicted, the WESL-run demonstration fizzled. About 165 men gathered and tried to march onto the Capitol grounds. The police shunted them to the steps of the Library of Congress across the street, where they were allowed to make speeches. A delegation of 36, allegedly representing 36 states, attempted to march on the Capitol to present its petition. The police allowed five to proceed. The red threat, for that day at least, was over. While all this was going on, Robertson demonstrated his anticommunism by withdrawing his men from that part of the Capitol grounds which adjoined the WESL demonstration.[10]

Glassford's handling of the situation at the Capitol, successful as it seems in retrospect, drew the fire of the Capitol Police Board, which issued a statement to the press insisting that the laws were being flouted and that the usurping police chief had "wholly without authority suspended the law." Glassford replied in kind, pointing out that the officials at the Capitol had asked for police protection. Since this placed the responsibility for law and order on his shoulders, Glassford insisted that his judgment must prevail and that his aim was to enforce only "such regulations . . . as would be possible without inviting violence." The aged triumvirate of the police board had the letter of the law on their side; the chief had common sense on his.[11]

The dramatic action of Robertson and his "death marchers" created problems for Waters as well as for the authorities. The new activism threw into sharp relief the passive policy of Waters and the bulk of the BEF. Understanding this and sensing a feeling within the bonus army that something ought to be done, Waters temporarily abandoned his policy of co-operation on July 16, the day that Congress was slated to adjourn. Early that morning a large contingent of BEFers (Waters later claimed 17,000 although the *Star*'s estimate of 3,000 is about right) assembled in front of the Capitol. A police line had been established, keeping the demonstrators some distance from the building, but the men wanted to demonstrate on the Capitol steps, as they had been allowed to do in June when the Senate voted down the bonus. This Glassford would not permit; there was apparently some fear that there would be an attempt to break into the legislative chambers. When Waters arrived at about 10 A.M., he found his men restive but restrained. He then made his one rebellious gesture of the summer: with four followers, he deliberately broke through police lines and dashed for the Capitol steps, with the rest of the men beginning to follow. The police quickly caught and arrested the five-man spearhead; the rest of the 3,000 simply sat down and yelled, "We want Waters!" over and over again. Although Glassford believed at the time that a riot had been "narrowly averted," he later realized that it was not really a serious matter:

> The only thing left to do was to keep the demonstrators under good natured control until they wore themselves out. . . . I knew it merely to be a dramatic effort on the part of Waters to restore the prestige and notoriety that had been shorn from him by the more energetic Robertson.

Glassford's account is probably a little wiser after the fact than he was at the time. The good-natured control included a number of concessions. Waters was taken out of sight, but after a quick session of what the press called a "Kangaroo Court," presided over by Glassford, the quintet was released with only an admonition. The bonus marchers were then allowed to occupy most of the Capitol steps as long as aisles were left on either side. All of this came to pass without any violence whatsoever, vindicating Glassford's fabian policy of selective law enforcement.

Part of his success must have been due to the fact that most of the real militants, including all of the WESL people, had decided to protest at the other end of Pennsylvania Avenue. Although today picketing the White House is an almost constant phenomenon, in the days of Herbert Hoover this simple act of protest was not permitted. At noon a placid delegation of Waters' men had tried to present a petition at the White House, but the President would not even allow it to be received by his staff. The BEFers left quickly without creating any disturbance. Several hours later, Glassford, still in charge at the Capitol, which seemed to be the focal point of unrest, received word from both Commissioner Crosby and a Captain Carroll of the Park Police (another separate Washington police force) that President Hoover would not permit parading or picketing in front of the White House. Richard Jervis, of the White House Secret Service detail, told one of Glassford's subordinates that one of the President's secretaries, Lawrence Richey, had informed him that picketing or parading was not to be permitted for several square blocks around the presidential residence. What was feared, apparently, was that the President might be interfered with on his annual ceremonial trip to the Capitol at adjournment. Commissioner Crosby telephoned Glassford that although violence was not desired, it should be used if necessary.

Learning a lesson from his brush with the Capitol Police Board, Glassford insisted on getting his orders in writing. In a formal memorandum to the District Commissioners he asked that in view of the dual legal responsibility—the Park Police were responsible for the White House grounds and the Metropolitan Police for the surrounding area—one force or the other be given sole jurisdiction. He also asked "that these orders contain specific instructions as to the extent to which violence may be used." In addition to sending this to the Commissioners at about 6 P.M., he also telephoned Senator Bingham and let him know what was going on. Probably as a result of his call to Bingham, Senator George H. Moses (R.-N.H.) telephoned Glassford to say that "the President of the United States does not desire violence." (This kind of Byzantine indirectness was typical of the Hoover years.)

Understandably dissatisfied with these contradictory verbal instructions, Glassford went to Crosby's home at about 9 P.M. that evening. The Commissioner wrote out, on the back of an envelope, detailed instructions making the Metropolitan Police responsible for the front and the two sides of the White House and leaving the rear and interior grounds to the Park Police. That serious trouble was envisaged can be seen from the rest of the instructions:

In event of a call for Federal troops responsibility shall pass to the Commander thereof.

Under no circumstances is congregation or parading to be permitted inside of the lines established by the various police contingents. While all unnecessary use of force will be avoided force will if necessary be used to prevent the congregation of unauthorized groups.

After all these elaborate preparations, the events of the evening of July 16 were distinctly anticlimactic. A little after 10 P.M. there was a small commotion outside the White House, as a probonus demonstration was attempted. Three men— none of whom seems to have had Communist connections— were arrested. A little later John Pace of the WESL tried to get a demonstration started at 15th and H, more than a block away, but as soon as some thirty radicals had gathered, Glassford's police broke it up without arresting anyone. According to the police chief, there were many more curious spectators than demonstrators dispersed that evening. Congress adjourned in relative quiet at 11:30 P.M.; it did so without President Hoover's customary presence. At the last minute, and probably to the great relief of the Secret Service, the President chose not to make the short ride, although a police motorcycle escort had been held in readiness at the White House most of the evening.[12]

The adjournment of Congress was, in effect, the public burial of the bonus for 1932, and for many members of the BEF it was a signal to lift the siege. On Monday morning, July 18, more than a thousand veterans lined up at the Veterans Administration to get their tickets home. Commenting on this, Glassford told the press, with an optimism he did not believe, that the exodus was very significant and probably denoted the "beginning of the end." Actually the end of the congressional session served as a green light for the administration to begin strong pressure to get the bonus army out of Washington. Some constitutional scruple about " the right of the people peacefully to assemble, and to petition the government for a redress of their grievances," as the First Amendment puts it, apparently served to inhibit any positive presidential dispersal action as long as Congress was in session. The President also evidently decided to respect the July 25 deadline laid down by the congressional joint resolution authorizing the payment of railroad fares. After that date, however, the veterans were to be moved out of town as soon as possible. In the closing days of the session many congressmen came to realize this. Wright Patman merely said publicly what others whispered privately: "I understand it is rumored that the President, as soon as the Congress adjourns, is going to order these veterans . . . out of the city. I hope that rumor is not true." Reiterating his desire that the bonus army disband, the Texan realized that many would stay. "There are men here," he pointed out, "who do not have a home." There was no reason, he felt, forcibly to evict them, and he hoped that "extreme means" would not be used to do so.

There were many men in the bonus army who were not going to go home willingly. One of them wrote to the *Star:*

Why should we go home? In Detroit, where I come from, the Fisher Lodge has closed, the thousands of men who were cared for there have been turned out to shift for themselves as best they can. The city of Detroit has no funds to care for the unemployed. . . . Since the Spring of 1930 I have been unable to secure a position of any kind. I am married and have two children. My savings were exhausted in the Summer of 1931; since that time I don't know how I and my family have lived—I should not say lived, that's not the word—existed.

As a construction superintendent or foreman worth $350 per month in 1930 it seems to me by all fair rules of the game I should be worth at least something at present, if nothing more than to keep body and soul together. . . . No job—no home—no money —I might as well be here, and here I shall stay even if in jail.

Men like that were not likely to be sent home by a proclamation; and it was men like that who formed the hard core of the BEF. It was knowledge of their presence that led Glassford to write that "tragedy hovered over Washington from the moment Congress adjourned." [13]

There was tragicomedy as well. Waters, despite his mock heroics before the Capitol, continued to face serious dissension from within the ranks of his shrinking army, dissension not only over tactics, but over money. In late June a group of former newspapermen, some of whom had grandiose political ambitions, put out a small tabloid which they called the *BEF News*. Peddled on the streets at five and ten cents by the veterans themselves, who sometimes would enter stores and offices in groups and refuse to leave until a certain number of copies had been purchased, the project scored a modest financial success, although the claim of its editor, Joseph Heffernan, former mayor of Youngstown, Ohio, that the press run was 50,000, seems highly improbable. The Ohioan hoped that the BEF would be the catalyst for a "national movement," something like the unemployed leagues which had sprung up in Seattle. The sweet smell of success caused a rift among the editorial board, and soon ugly charges about embezzlement ($1,200 was the figure mentioned) were bandied back and forth. In July a rival sheet, also named the *BEF News,* appeared; while the original continued to be "official" and supported Waters, the second attacked him ("Demand Waters Resign—Cowardice Exposed" was a typical headline) and, for a while, seemed to be boosting Royal W. Robertson. The Californian, however, left for California on July 23, leaving the anti-Waters group again without a well-known name.[14]

Throughout the week following the adjournment of Congress the attrition of the bonus army continued; probably about a thousand men a day were leaving Washington. According to Waters the strength of the BEF dropped as follows:

July 16   22,374

July 18	20,593
July 20	18,508
July 24	14,403
July 26	14,925

These figures are certainly too high, particularly the latter ones, but they do reflect the scale of the shrinkage. By the end of the encampment there were certainly fewer than 10,000 marchers still present.[15]

Among those who talked to the veterans that last week, none was more flamboyant than Smedly D. Butler, the very antithesis of a Marine Corps Major General, although that is exactly what he was. A veteran of many campaigns of pacification in the banana republics and the Caribbean, his testimony in the later 1930s describing the corps as a servant of finance capital made him the favorite military figure of the isolationist left. His remarks to the BEF were equally unorthodox. He spent the night of July 19 bivouacked with the army at Camp Marks, after having told them that, like "every man who ever wore the uniform," they were different from other men. The general, who appeared under BEF auspices, put forth the new Waters line: [16]

Most of you ought to go home, but you ought to leave some of you here in the front line trenches. . . . George Washington's army went home in the fall of the winter of Valley Forge, but by God they came back in the spring and chewed up the enemy. You are in a beautiful position. Just hang on to it.

Whether the Glassford-Waters policy would have eventually prevailed will never be known. Although it seemed to be working well enough—the BEF was dispersing and by July 28 it would be at a little more than one-third of its peak strength—the President of the United States wanted faster action.

Shortly after Congress adjourned, the administration put into operation a concerted plan for the eviction and dispersal of the bonus army. Perhaps thinking that legal threats would spur acceptance of free transportation home, the early moves were publicized. The first step that can be documented consisted of three letters written on July 20 by Assistant Secretary of the Treasury Ferry K. Heath. Addressed to Glassford, the District Commissioners, and a firm of building contractors, they revoked permission, which the Treasury had granted in early June, for bonus marchers to occupy a group of partially demolished buildings on lower Pennsylvania Avenue near the Capitol. Walt Whitman had lived in one of these buildings for a time during the Civil War, and earlier another had been a gambling establishment named "The Palace of Fortune." The bonus marchers had named the area Camp Glassford. By late June some 1,100 men were billeted there. The Treasury letters set no deadline for evacuation, and the explicit rationale for the request was "to proceed immediately with the completion" of the demolition, so that actual construction could begin.

Glassford, who had no inkling that the letter from Heath was the start of a campaign, reacted routinely. He passed the order from the Treasury, which he received on the morning of July 21, on to Waters and supplied what he thought were reasonable deadlines: the evacuation of the downtown block was to begin by noon the following day, and be completed by midnight of July 24. The final paragraph of Glassford's order to the BEF shows that he regarded it as a routine matter:

It is recommended that the veterans quartered in this area be urged to take advantage of the transportation home available until midnight, July 25th, 1932. It will be necessary for those who do not take advantage of this transportation to find accommodations elsewhere. In this connection you are advised that no public buildings or public space will be occupied by veterans unless authority is granted by Police Headquarters, and no private buildings or grounds will be occupied without written authority from the owners thereof.

That same afternoon, July 21, Glassford was summoned to the Commissioner's office. They had received additional letters: another one from the Treasury reiterating the request of the previous day; one from A. J. Brylawski of Warner Brothers Theaters asking for evacuation of his company's property adjoining the government-owned site on Pennsylvania Avenue; and, most significantly, a letter from Ulysses S. Grant III, Director of Public Buildings and Public Parks of the National Capital, asking for evacuation of the major encampment at Anacostia and all other property under his jurisdiction. None of the letters set deadlines, but the Commissioners had supplied their own. Glassford was handed a typewritten order by General Crosby. It fixed the deadline for evacuation of the Pennsylvania Avenue buildings at midnight July 22—less than thirty-six hours away—and ordered the return of all National Guard equipment by noon, August 1, and the evacuation of all park areas, including Anacostia, by noon, August 4. Glassford was instructed to make "no exceptions" in the enforcement of the evacuation. Whatever chances had existed for a gradual and peaceful evacuation—which was in fact proceeding—would be destroyed by the Commissioners' order. It issued an ultimatum, drew a line, and set the stage for a confrontation. Glassford tried to convince the Commissioners of "the great danger inherent" in this new departure, but without success. Their minds were made up, or had been made up for them.[17]

The Commissioners' order seemed to strip Glassford of all

discretion, since it was framed as a set of instructions to him and specifically forbade him from making any exceptions whatsoever. The police chief, however, had doubts about the legality of the instructions, doubts that revolved around the Commissioners' authority over federal property. He went from the Commissioners' office to the office of the District's Corporation Counsel—who apparently had not been consulted—to question the legality of his instructions. The next morning Glassford, the legal staff of the Commissioners, representatives of the federal District Attorney's office, and a lawyer from the Treasury, all agreed that the order was illegal. Glassford so informed his superiors. In his letter he warned Crosby and the others that [18]

> From police investigation the bonus marchers are known to be preparing for passive resistance against forcible ejection . . . and are believed to be preparing to bring reinforcements from other camps and billets to oppose ejection by force if necessary.
>
> The situation is fraught with potentialities of riot and bloodshed should any attempt be made in an illegal manner to evacuate the buildings in question by midnight this date.
>
> RECOMMENDATION:
>
> That the evacuation of the buildings and grounds under the jurisdiction of the Treasury Department be postponed pending legal action initiated by that department. . . .

Overruled by their own lawyers, the Commissioners formally withdrew the offending order, but reiterated the demand that National Guard equipment be returned by August 1. Now that the issue had been joined, the focus of the ejection attempt narrowed to Camp Glassford, the group of buildings on lower Pennsylvania Avenue. Like a chess game in which all the pieces are concentrated to control a key square, the area in question quickly assumed a symbolic significance entirely disproportionate to its real importance. The buildings were occupied by the Sixth Regiment, BEF, a unit largely southern, the nucleus having been a group of unemployed Texas oil field workers. Man for man, they were probably as combative as any element in the bonus army.

The next day, a Saturday, the Treasury, apparently not fully synchronized with the Commissioners, served written notice on Waters to evacuate all land and premises under Treasury jurisdiction by midnight the following Monday, July 25. That morning, Waters, accompanied by an attorney, Herbert S. Ward, received a twenty-four-hour stay from the Treasury. On July 26, the Treasury again postponed the showdown by formally requesting police protection from the Commissioners "to prevent any interference with the contractor and his workmen" in carrying out the demolition work. On July 27, however, the contractors refused to proceed, because, they said, their insurance carrier threatened to cancel their insurance if they did.[19]

By this time the eviction procedure seemed almost farcical, and the bonus marchers cannot be blamed if they concluded that the government was not really serious about getting them out of Washington. After all, their entire two-month stay had been punctuated with deadlines and ultimatums changed in their favor. The federal authorities, however, were determined to have a showdown.

On July 27 the frustrated administration forces regrouped. The planning, which had previously been left to the Treasury, was now taken over by the Justice and War departments. Assistant Attorney General Nugent Dodds informed his chief that "apparently there is no statute in the District of Columbia concerning resistance to arrest unless the resistance proceeds to the point of using personal violence upon the officer attempting to make the arrest." The Justice Department at least contemplated making mass arrests, for Dodds gave Attorney General William D. Mitchell the capacity of the work house (about one hundred vacancies) and pointed out that "there is nothing at all to prevent setting up tents for taking care of almost any reasonable number. . . . Occoquan [work house] could handle [a large number of prisoners] at least during the summer and fall months, when heated quarters are unnecessary." Working in conjunction with the Attorney General, Acting Director of Public Parks E. N. Chisolm requested the United States Marshal "to cause the [bonus marchers] to be ejected and removed" from Anacostia and other public parks, and the Treasury Department furnished the Attorney General with an annotated map indicating the order in which the areas were to be evacuated. The Treasury similarly determined priorities for the evacuation of the various building sites which it owned. The Judge Advocate General of the Army prepared elaborate memoranda outlining legal procedures to be taken should the troops be called out and also prepared a draft of a presidential proclamation doing so.[20]

As it turned out, the administration was overtaken by events—events which it had precipitated—and the evacuation of the bonus marchers was more hurried and haphazard than originally anticipated. While all these plans were being made secretly in various federal offices, Pelham Glassford and other district officials were involved in a busy round of consultation and preparation. July 27 was spent in conferences. Glassford and his personal attorney, James Easby-Smith, had succeeded in persuading the federal lawyers that repossession should be confined initially to a small part of the Pennsylvania Avenue site and then gradually extended to the entire Camp Glassford area. The police chief seems not to have been aware of the federal plans for total evacuation. The Commissioners issued a written order instructing Glassford "to render all protection necessary to the Treasury . . . making arrests for violations of the law committed in the presence of police officers, and protecting such property as may be repossessed against unlawful reoccupancy." For some reason, which the available documents do not illuminate, the federal officials did not take the normal step of getting a court order. Perhaps they feared the law's delay.

Faced with what he feared would be a showdown, Glassford brought Waters to District headquarters for a late afternoon conference with the Commissioners. The Commissioners refused even to be in the same room with the BEF commander, but did agree to have the police chief relay messages between them. As Waters later described the nonmeeting: [21]

> The General [Glassford] would go into the Commissioners' office, get their statement, return to me, then take back my comments to the gentlemen in the next room. It isn't every ex-sergeant that can have an ex-General for a messenger boy.

According to both Waters and Glassford, Waters expressed willingness to cooperate in evacuating the area, although the Commissioners did not allow the police chief to inform Waters of the already-agreed-upon operations scheduled for the next day. Despite Waters' expressed willingness to begin evacuation, the Commissioners refused to deviate from their timetable. Had it been dictated by higher authority? There is no direct evidence of this, but it is interesting to note that the draft presidential proclamation which Secretary of War Hurley sent over to the White House left the day blank but wrote in the month "July."

Ignorant of their plans, Waters agreed to move 200 men from the Pennsylvania Avenue area the next day, but could not be persuaded to agree to General Crosby's relayed deadline of 4:00 P.M. Friday, July 29, for complete evacuation of the area. Waters gave as his reason that he intended to move all the men from there to Camp Bartlett and that there were not yet enough facilities at the outlying billet. Finally Waters promised to try to have all the men gone from Camp Glassford by 7:30 A.M. the following Monday, August 1. The BEF commander had every reason to believe when he left the District Building in the late afternoon of July 27 that he had reached an agreement with the District Commissioners. The Commissioners continued to perfect their plan for partial eviction at ten o'clock the following morning. Crosby and Reichelderfer evidently regarded the plan as a military operation and felt that their deliberate duplicity was fully justified. Glassford was a part of this duplicity—however reluctantly— a fact he never made clear in his published accounts.

Glassford went to great pains to assure himself of the legality of the proposed action. After the government lawyers had worked it all out, he called District Attorney Leo Rover for a final check. Rover assured him that the proposed action was quite legal, and that anyone refusing to be evicted, or who assisted in any resistance to the eviction, was subject to arrest under the District code. Finally satisfied of the legality of the proposed action, the police chief made every effort to make it a bloodless one. As much as he disagreed with the plan of attack, there is no evidence that he ever thought seriously of resigning in protest. Perhaps he reasoned that if the execution were in his hands, the chances of bloodshed and riot were much less than if the operation were conducted by his subordinates, many of whom were spoiling for a fight.

Early the next morning, still ignorant of the Commissioners' true intentions, Waters appeared at Camp Glassford to try to produce the partial evacuation he had promised. In his memoir he states flatly that despite some heckling when he proposed that 200 men make a token evacuation, "I was going to get the 200 without difficulty." A contemporary police report gives a different and probably more accurate account. According to Private J. O. Patton, the officer regularly assigned to Camp Glassford, Waters arrived at about 8:15 A.M. and sought out the camp commander, a bonus marcher named J. W. Wilford. To get privacy, Waters and Wilford, accompanied by the policeman, retired to a car parked in front of a neighboring undertaking parlor.

Waters told Wilford that he had made arrangements for the immediate removal of 200 men to Camp Bartlett and that transportation was available. Wilford told Waters that the men wouldn't go, because Bartlett was out of the city. Officer Patton chimed in that it was within the city limits. Wilford rejoined that in any event it was too far from everything, which was one of its virtues in Glassford's eyes. Finally Wilford passed the word to his men about Waters' agreement; it was greeted with much disapproval. At about this point the facile Waters, not wanting to jeopardize his standing with the men, abandoned the effort and made a militant speech, which Patton reported as follows:

> Men, I have not changed my mind about moving. We do not intend to move until they provide us with proper shelter and food, and we can remain here and be "locked up", then they will have to provide for us. However if the Army comes they will move us and you can depend on that.

Perhaps a thousand men were present for the speech and, still according to Patton, voted by acclamation to remain in Camp Glassford.

At this point, about 9:55 A.M., in accordance with the Commissioner's instructions, a volunteer civilian aide to Glassford, Aldace Walker, arrived, accompanied by a lawyer. He told Patton that he had to talk to Waters privately, and the policeman interrupted Waters' speech and brought him to the chief's messenger. Walker then told the BEF commander what was to ensue. Waters returned to the rostrum and told the assembled bonus marchers what was about to happen and counseled passive resistance. According to a prearranged plan, some seventy men took up positions in the building to be cleared and waited for the arrival of the police.[22]

Glassford had made careful, if somewhat overly secretive, preparations for the piecemeal eviction. Inspector Edwards, who was to supervise the actual proceedings, didn't get any of the details until the morning of July 28. At 9:30 A.M. Glassford instructed him and the hundred-man detail under his command with a military-style blackboard briefing. Glassford himself, never one to give either the dirty work or the limelight to a subordinate, was to direct a twelve-man squad in the actual evicting; the rest, under Edwards, were to rope off the area and keep other bonus marchers and the curious out. The operation was initially directed at a partially demolished National Guard Armory occupying half of the block; it was planned to use the same procedure later in clearing several small commercial structures that comprised the other half. Glassford made no provision for raising the drawbridge separating the Anacostia camps from the city proper. Whether it was oversight or policy cannot now be determined, but it was a costly error.

The clearing of the old armory went pretty much according to plan. As the BEF area commander later wrote:

> On the morning of the 28th, there was no unusual excitement and no thought of resistance among our men. They felt that last minute negotiations would secure a delay. . . . They had been instructed that, if these failed and the Treasury Department agents came, they were to leave the building peaceably with these agents. This is exactly what happened. . . .

One man, a Negro and obviously not a member of the all-white southern unit, went limp and had to be carried out; the BEF later claimed that he was a "plant" from the Department of Justice, whose agents were also alleged to have started the trouble. There is no evidence to support this plot theory. Waters, who had spoken earlier in the day about being the first to be arrested, left for Camp Marks about the time the police arrived. Once across the river, he made a number of speeches suggesting that the men go downtown where the action was. Waters returned to the downtown area until the shooting started, and then seems to have gone into hiding. In any event, he exercised no leadership during any of the crucial incidents from noon on. It was probably this critical failure of leadership that Glassford had in mind when he commented: "When I needed his cooperation most, Waters failed me." [23]

The first phase of the police operation was completed before noon: the old armory and a space around it had been completely cleared of veteran squatters. Glassford planned to apply the same techniques to the rest of the block after lunch. Toward noon, however, BEFers from Anacostia and the other outlying camps began arriving by the hundreds. Private Patton, who had been assigned to the BEF all summer and knew the men well, gave the best first-hand account of what happened in a report that Glassford removed from the files and never fully utilized.[42]

At about 12.00 Noon, a group of men, about 35 in number, came across the park area bounded by 3rd and 4½ Streets, Maine and Missouri Avenues, N.W. I recognized this group as followers of Pace and Levine [Levin], namely the Workers Ex-servicemen's League—a Rank and File organization known to be Communists. . . . Shortly thereafter several truck loads of veterans from Camp Marks disembarked on 3rd Street, N.W. between Pennsylvania and Missouri Avenues and were clamorously greeted by the bonus marchers of Camp Glassford. A group of 25 bonus marchers led by a white man carrying a flag began forging their way through a crowd of bonus marchers assembled around the building and were met at the police line by Major and Superintendent Glassford who told them that they could not proceed further. One of the men of this group, a white man named McCoy—known as a Communist, tore the Major's police badge from his shirt and struck him. The individual carrying the American flag immediately attacked an officer and bricks and stones began to fly from all directions. This melee last[ed] for approximately five minutes during which time three or four men were arrested, the majority of the assailants made their escape into the crowd. From my observation I would say that these individuals who threw the bricks and stones were ones who had come to Camp Glassford for that express purpose.

Glassford himself brought the fracas to an abrupt end by physically separating some of the combatants. "This game is getting dangerous," he shouted, "and it's getting time for lunch." Glassford's coolness prevented what could have been a serious disorder. There were several thousand BEFers in the immediate area, although the chief estimated, somewhat conservatively, that "not more than fifty" actually participated in the flurry of brick throwing and fighting. Glassford himself showed extreme grace under pressure (although one doubts newsman Paul Anderson's widely quoted description of the chief who "smiled when a brickbat hit him in the chest"), and the restraint of his hundred-odd men was even more remarkable. Not only were no shots fired, but apparently no one so much as unholstered a pistol, even though many of them were struck with bricks and other missiles that were naturally abundant on the rubble-strewn block. The aggressive actions of the Communists were typical of their tactics in such situations; there was nothing wrong with heaving a brick at the class enemy. Glassford's suppression of the report best documenting their agency in starting some of the trouble can probably be explained by the later actions of the administration in trying to "pin" all of the trouble on the reds. Glassford, trying to refute the administration's irresponsible charges, did not want to reveal anything that would give them the slightest credence.

After the commotion died down, the police and Treasury officials got lunch in relays. Glassford reported in person to the Commissioners at District headquarters. Exactly what happened there is in dispute. Commissioners Reichelderfer and Crosby and Crosby's aide, Police Lieutenant Ira Keck, all later bore witness that Glassford had asked for federal troops. Glassford and his volunteer aide, Aldace Walker, testified to the contrary. Everyone in authority, the two Commissioners, five of Glassford's ranking subordinates, and even Glassford's aide, Walker, thought that troops should be called out.

Glassford insisted that he told the commissioners that the police would be able to hold the area that they had repossessed, "but that if any further repossession was insisted on the Federal forces should be called." He believed that, being badly outnumbered at the site of the trouble, riot and bloodshed would result if further repossession were attempted. Glassford left the office without any decision having been made. A few minutes later, Commissioners Reichelderfer and Crosby traveled the few blocks from their office to the trouble site to see for themselves. They left, according to Glassford, without telling him what they intended to do. As soon as they returned to their office, they called for federal troops.

It is impossible to settle definitively the question of whether Glassford asked that troops be requested, but the logic of the situation supports his version. It is difficult to see why, if Glassford had, as they later insisted, asked for troops, Reichelderfer and Crosby found it necessary to make a personal reconnaissance. Their original letter to the President, it should be noted, carefully did not say that Glassford had actually asked for troops. The Commissioners wrote (in the follow-up formal letter which was written after a telephonic request had been acted upon) that a "serious riot" had occurred, that the police were outnumbered and that

> it is the opinion of the Major and Superintendent of Police, in which the Commissioners concur, that it will be impossible for the Police Department to maintain law and order except by the free use of firearms which will make the situation a dangerous one; it

is believed however, that the presence of Federal troops in some number will obviate the seriousness of the situation and result in far less violence and bloodshed.

To Crosby and Reichelderfer, the maintenance of law and order was synonymous with continuing the eviction process immediately. Since Glassford admitted that this could not be done peacefully, law and order had broken down, even though an uneasy truce continued at Camp Glassford. This author suspects that when the battle was over and the President and his advisors discovered that the Commissioners had somewhat misled them about Glassford's views, or, conversely, when the Commissioners discovered or were told that they had placed the President of the United States in an ambiguous position, they stretched the truth somewhat, and got Keck, who as a career man deeply resented Glassford, to back up their story. It is possible, of course, that there was a communication breakdown and that the whole dispute was based on a misunderstanding or even that Glassford and Walker were lying, but the evidence suggests otherwise. In addition, although Glassford was, as this author has shown, capable of stretching the truth and concealing inconvenient facts, this author can find no instance of his having told a direct lie. The administration forces, on the other hand, soon became engaged in a long campaign to falsify the historical record.[25]

Apart from the question of whether Glassford agreed, how justified was the decision to call out troops? The situation in downtown Washington was certainly serious. Several thousand adult males assembled belligerently in the heart of a great city is always fraught with the danger of violence, whether the people in question are veterans, strikers, the poor, or college students. However, in view of the level of physical violence which American cities found tolerable during the Depression, the situation in Washington does not seem to have warranted the amount of force used.

Could Glassford have handled things better? Perhaps. Certainly his preparations on July 28 can be faulted. Had he successfully isolated the Camp Glassford area and kept the rest of the bonus army away, the operation might have been a success. Wilford, the area commander, made this argument, pointing out that the trouble had been caused not by the men who were being evicted, but by their allies from other camps. Yet it is difficult to be very censorious of Glassford, and impossible to imagine that anyone else in authority could have done as much to keep the peace. What is to be wondered at is that he kept it so long.

Unbeknown to him, the troops had been requested before 1:45 P.M. A few minutes later, fatal violence erupted for the only time—violence whose timing provided two convenient corpses for those who sought to justify the administration's action. Between 1:45 and 2:00 P.M. (Patton says 2:15, but this is clearly too late), a quarrel somehow erupted—Glassford called it a "spontaneous brawl."

Glassford later testified: [26]

While waiting around for the veterans to disperse shortly after [the] visit of the Commissioners . . . suddenly I saw a commotion over in the direction of the Ford [garage]. . . . There was some kind of a scramble between two veterans on the sidewalk and some police officers were taking a hand. Suddenly . . . I heard a shot [and] saw Officer Shina[u]lt being attacked by a number of civilians. . . . One man had a club and was beating him. Another was choking him. About this time a garbage pail dropped down from above, adding to the confusion, and a few bricks. . . . Shinault, who is rather a powerful man, shook himself free and drew a revolver. As he did so I saw a veteran start toward him, and Shinault fired. I saw the veteran collapse. I heard another shot. I yelled to Shinault, "Put up that gun; stop that shooting." Shinault looked up at me in a very wildeyed manner and pointed his gun in my direction. I dodged behind [a] pillar momentarily and heard another shot or two, jumped back . . . and again yelled, "Stop that shooting. You men get back where you belong" (because other men, policemen, were crowding into the scene of this shooting). This ended the shooting. . . . [ellipsis in original] I saw a man in civilian clothes with a gun in his hand. I yelled to him to put that gun back in his pocket. He did so.

The best corroborating eyewitness account was volunteered to Glassford three days after the event by an apparently disinterested citizen. Bruce E. Clark, an engineer-builder according to his letterhead, wrote: [27]

At about 1:45 P.M. on Thursday afternoon, I arrived in my car at the intersection of 4th. Street and Pennsylvania Avenue Northwest. I was directed by a Traffic Policeman stationed on that corner to proceed down 4th. Street, which I did. Upon arriving at the first Temporary Government Building down 4th Street I parked my car and proceeded on foot to Missouri Avenue between 3rd. and 4th. Streets N.W. I saw a great commotion in the middle of this block and then went to the Alley near the rear of 332 Pennsylvania Ave. N.W. Almost coincident with my arrival there, I saw a number of Policemen coming from the direction of the Northeast portion of the above mentioned block and form themselves in a double line in the Alley adjacent to premises 332 Pennsylvania Ave. In a few minutes they marched off accompanied by several men in civilian clothes and accompanied also by you, to the rear of 346 Pennsylvania Ave. I noticed that there was a rope stretched from, I should judge 3rd. Street, along the Alley to 4th. Street. Behind this rope was congregated a crowd of men, I would say about a thousand or more. They were jeering, shaking their fists and many of them cursing the Policemen. Many of them had bricks in their hands. The police in the meantime had arrived at the rear of premises 346. They were then aligned, by what I judged to be a Sergeant of Police, on the Alley side of the rope above mentioned and about three feet apart facing the crowd. All at once there arose a yell and I saw a mass of men running down the Alley from 3rd Street toward 346. I noticed that they appeared to be in a very angry mood. In rushing through the Alley they brushed the police aside and kept going to the side steps of 346. I should have said that before this took place I had seen you and several policemen and the men in Civilian clothes enter 346, go to the top story and then I noticed, what I judged to be so called Bonus men, begin to leave the building in great numbers. In the meantime, however, this rushing mob had arrived and I saw Police station themselves on the stairs near the bottom and I could plainly hear those officers say "You cannot come in here." I heard yelling replies such as "The Hell we can't." I saw then what appeared to be a great huddle at the foot of those stairs as if there were a fight going on and all the time officers on the stairs were trying to prevent the mob from rushing them. All at once I saw an officer on the stairs, about eight feet from the bottom, draw his pistol, take aim and fire toward the foot of the above mentioned stairs. The crowd of jeering, fighting men—immediately after this shot was fired—scattered out and soon disappeared into the crowd. Not all of them however. Soon after this shot was fired I heard two or three more in quick succession. By this time the building 346 seemed to be cleared. I then saw you accompanied by several officers and several men who I judged to be the Bonus men come from the building. I heard you say to one of them who seemed to be hard of hearing, "Come to my office this evening." I then left for my home.

In this short melee, one veteran, William Huska, was dead; another, Eric Carlson, was wounded, fatally as it turned out; and three policemen were injured badly enough to be sent to the hospital. Huska and Carlson, both overseas veterans and neither a Communist, were the only two bonus marchers whose bonus was collected that summer. Almost as soon as Glassford had quieted things down—he later testified that he was contemplating a tear gas attack in order to clear the disputed block completely—he learned, first from a newspaper-man and then from Assistant Attorney General Nugent Dodds, that the troops had been called out. Glassford headed up Pennsylvania Avenue to meet Chief of Staff Douglas Mac-Arthur. The ball was out of Glassford's court and in the army's.

7

The Battle of Washington

THE ARMY HAD been prepared for trouble with the bonus marchers almost from the beginning. The War Department, publicly and repeatedly, refused to give any aid or comfort to the men who had helped make the world safe for democracy only fourteen years before. In two instances, however, the army did lend a helping hand, if a reluctant one. Glassford, as we have seen, practically had to blackmail Secretary Hurley into releasing the bed sacks. Less publicly, the army yielded in mid-June to a Glassford-inspired request from Brigadier General Frank Hines, and allowed the Veterans' Administrator to set up a hospital-dispensary for bonus marchers at Fort Hunt, Virginia. Apart from these two actions, the army maintained its unfriendly public posture—the top brass of the army, that is. Enlisted men and junior officers tended to be friendly, so friendly that in the early days of the occupation of Washington the authorities found it necessary to bar bonus marchers from military installations, because so many of them were being illegally fed at mess halls.[1]

By early June the War Department was concerned enough to order an armored car and a truck-mounted 75-millimeter artillery piece with a hundred rounds of shrapnel ammunition brought secretly from the Aberdeen (Md.) Proving Grounds. ("If questioned," the movement order specified, "the personnel in charge will state that the armored car T-4 is en route to Fort Knox and the Truck Mount T-6 is en route to Fort Bragg.") Since the armored car was kept right behind the White House, this crude attempt at news management failed, and pictures of the vehicle and accurate speculation as to its purpose soon appeared in the press.[2]

The movement of vehicles was one part of a revision of the secret "White Plan" for the nation's capital, a revision whose major assumptions are worth quoting:

a. The greater part of the bonus marchers thus far have resisted all attempts of the Communists to gain control of them but there are a number of well known Communist leaders here and they are claiming credit for the instigation of the march.

b. Any demonstration therefore will almost certainly contain ex-soldiers without a desire for Communist affiliations and Communists themselves who will try by overt acts, possibly of violence, to commit the veterans.

c. Our operations, therefore, should contemplate giving an opportunity to the non-Communistic veterans to disperse, but of course the tactics employed must depend on the commander on the spot and the character of the emergency.

d. For this reason, tear gas grenades are provided which would be used in sufficient numbers to be effective if the character of the disorder did not require more drastic action at once.

e. The White House, Treasury Buildings, Bureau of Engraving and Printing and the Capitol are critical points and their protection primarily must be foreseen.

The rest of the plan set up emergency command posts and message centers, ordered the issuance of ammunition and supplies, named assembly points, and decreed the maintenance of a constant state of readiness. (Apparently the troops who marched in the Flag Day parade that June carried live ammunition!) Yet, like most other military plans, these proper and somewhat restrained precautions were virtually ignored when trouble came. MacArthur, as we shall see, made no serious effort either to separate non-Communist veterans or to get them to disperse. Why he failed to do so is difficult if not impossible to determine definitively, but certainly a procession of lurid and provocative reports from Army Intelligence streaming across his desk had something to do with the official change of attitude.[3]

Army Intelligence began to take an active interest in the bonus marchers on June 10. If the other staff sections planned reasonably, G-2 often operated in a cloud-cuckooland uniquely its own. Its files on the bonus march are still sealed from the impious or perhaps subversive eyes of the historical researcher, but happily there are declassified carbon copies of many of its reports in other files. On June 10, the same day that the Commissioners were using Western Union to ask the state governors to hold back the marching veterans, the Chief of Army Intelligence radioed, in secret code, a request to all Corps Area commanders:

> With reference to any movement of veteran bonus marchers to Washington originating or passing through your corps area, it is desired that a brief radio report in secret code be made to War Department indicating presence, if any, of communistic elements and names of leaders of known communistic leanings. Your detailed report will follow by air mail.

Most of the replies to this were reasonably sane, if not too astute. Ninth Corps Area for example, could not discover when the Oregon contingent left Portland, a fact that was reported in the local newspapers. It did correctly evaluate the political complexion of Royal W. Robertson's Californians, pointing out not only the absence of Communist activity, but also that its leader was "firm in stand that [Communists] will not be tolerated." In neighboring Eighth Corps, however, an almost undiluted paranoia prevailed. The intelligence reports emanating from Fort Sam Houston, Texas, are simply incredible, and lend verisimilitude to at least the last proviso of the army legend that the brainy go to the engineers, the brave to the infantry, the deaf to the artillery, and the stupid to intelligence. In any event, the Texas-based intelligence experts convinced themselves that the Californians were dangerous Communists (with a leader named Royal P. Robinson) and that Metro-Goldwyn-Mayer was financing the whole movement. In case Washington didn't know what it was, Colonel James Totten told them:

> Metro-Goldwyn-Mayer Picture Corporation is known to be 100 per cent Jewish as to controlling personnel, and that high officers of this company are in politics. An unconfirmed rumor circulated many months ago, stated that agents of U.S.S.R. had contacted motion picture companies in California, and contributed to some of them with a view to inserting propaganda and support of U.S.S.R. policies.

Other reports spoke of machine guns in the hands of bonus marchers, forged discharges available for fifty cents from "any pawn broker in Chicago" (this from an officer in Philadelphia), while another report, early in July, claimed that Waters had the "assistance of gunmen from New York and Washington . . . [and] that the first blood shed by the Bonus Army in Washington is to be the signal for a communist uprising in all large cities."

The sources for these reports were varied: in some cases from "trusted agents mingling with the marchers," in others from reserve officers, American Legion officials, and from professional antiradical groups like Harry A. Jung's American

Vigilant Intelligence Federation. It is impossible to say how much weight MacArthur and Hurley gave to the more lurid aspects of these reports, but the assumption that they gave them some credence, and that this credence percolated through the whole administration, does much to explain official behavior on July 28 and after.[4]

By late July the army had been in a state of readiness for almost two months. Chief of Staff Douglas MacArthur, not standing on ceremony, had conferred with Waters twice during that time, including a disputed meeting on July 26. Waters remembered that the general had promised that in case the troops were called, the BEF would be allowed to make an orderly retreat, while in his memoirs the general recalled that Waters promised to withdraw his men without violence once the troops were called out. Waters implies bad faith on MacArthur's part, but, by his own admission, he was in hiding by the time the troops arrived, and there was no one either to parley with the general or to lead a retreat. Glassford, too, had conferences with the chief of staff, and found him sympathetic, particularly when contrasted with the outright hostility of Secretary of War Patrick J. Hurley.[5]

The hostile Secretary was certainly one of the major influences on the President's decision, although Washington gossip also gave a leading role to Secretary of the Treasury Ogden Mills, probably, after the President, the most powerful man in the government. In calling out the armed forces, the administration neglected certain legal details. The procedure for the use of troops in civilian affairs is a complicated one, and technically, at least, the President violated the law which prescribes that a proclamation be issued announcing the advent of federal forces. Such a proclamation was actually drafted (in the War Department rather than in the Department of State) but Hoover, somehow, never used it. It called upon "all persons now in the District of Columbia [to desist from] unlawful obstructions, combinations and assemblages

. . . and [to] retire peacefully to their respective abodes, in whatever state or territory situated." [6]

Besides drafting this proclamation, the army's top lawyer, Major General Blanton Winship, the Judge Advocate General, sent MacArthur at least three long memoranda carefully outlining the legal situation and suggesting proper procedures. These memos, fully consistent with the revised "White Plan" for the capital, assumed that any military operation would proceed along the following lines: [7]

a. Mobilization within the District of Columbia of a military force sufficient in number and equipment to enforce such orders as the President may issue;

b. Issuance to the Chief of the Metropolitan Police Force of the District of Columbia of appropriate directions with reference to dealing with the so-called Bonus Expeditionary Force;

c. An address by the Chief of Staff to the known leaders of the Bonus Expeditionary Force substantially as outlined in my previous memorandum, offering the members of the Bonus Expeditionary Force an opportunity to be transported to, or in the direction of, their respective homes;

d. Conveyance of all members of the Bonus Expeditionary Force accepting such offer to their respective home states in trucks operated and escorted by Regular Army personnel;

e. Should any substantial number of the Bonus Expeditionary Force refuse to leave the District of Columbia, issuance by the President of a proclamation in form substantially as heretofore recommended by me; and

f. Arrest and compulsory conveyance under guard of all persons associated with the Bonus Expeditionary Force refusing to leave the District of Columbia to their respective home states in trucks operated and guarded by Regular Army personnel.

Thus, the general staff envisaged a cautious but firm employment of troops, with alternatives being offered to the bonus marchers even after the military put in an appearance. When the army did move, however, it was guided not by conservative staff officers, but by Chief of Staff Douglas MacArthur himself, even then an exponent of total victory rather than negotiated settlements. It is, of course, impossible to say why MacArthur deviated from the general staff plan, but something of his mood can be gathered from his official report to Secretary of War Hurley (which was removed from the National Archives). "For many weeks," the chief of staff wrote, "members of the Bonus Army had seen all their wishes and desires . . . acceded to by civil officials." This being the case, MacArthur apparently felt that the time for talk had passed, and once the troops were summoned he followed only his own counsel.[8]

Much of the actual summoning process was by means of that bane of the historian, the telephone. We can, however, construct a rather precise timetable because a warrant officer in the army message center in the Munitions Building kept a log of all calls that went through there. The Commissioners must have made their telephonic request for troops from the War Department at about 1:30 P.M., because at 1:35 P.M. Mac-Arthur called to order the troops in the area placed on alert. Five minutes later, before the fatal shooting incident occurred, MacArthur called again to order the troops to move into the city. What must have happened is that the Commissioners called the War Department and the War Department called the President. Hoover gave verbal approval, but asked for a letter which the Commissioners provided.

The President:

The Commissioners of the District of Columbia regret to inform you that during the past few hours circumstances of a serious character have arisen in the District of Columbia which have been the cause of unlawful acts of large numbers of so-called "bonus marchers," who have been in Washington for some time past.

This morning, officials of the Treasury Department, seeking to clear certain areas within the Government Triangle in which there were numbers of these bonus marchers, met with resistance. They called upon the Metropolitan Police Force for assistance and a serious riot occurred. Several members of the Metropolitan Police were injured, one reported seriously. The total number of bonus marchers greatly outnumbered the police; the situation is made more difficult by the fact that this area contains thousands of brickbats and these were used by the rioters in their attack upon the police.

In view of the above, it is the opinion of the Major and Superintendent of Police, in which the Commissioners concur, that it will be impossible for the Police Department to maintain law and order except by the free use of firearms which will make the situation a dangerous one; it is believed however, that the presence of Federal troops in some number will obviate the seriousness of the situation and result in far less violence and bloodshed.

The Commissioners of the District of Columbia, therefore, request that they be given the assistance of Federal troops in maintaining law and order in the District of Columbia.

Very sincerely yours,

L. H. Reichelderfer, President
Board of Commissioners of the
District of Columbia

Hurley later issued the following typewritten order:

Washington, D.C.
July 28, 1932

TO: General Douglas MacArthur, Chief of Staff, U.S. Army

The President has just informed me that the civil government of the District of Columbia has reported to him that it is unable to maintain law and order in the District.

You will have United States troops proceed immediately to the scene of disorder. Cooperate fully with the District of Columbia police force which is now in charge. Surround the affected area and clear it without delay.

Turn over all prisoners to the civil authorities.

In your orders insist that any women and children who may be in the affected area be accorded every consideration and kindness. Use all humanity consistent with the due execution of this order.

On the original order, now in the files of the War Department in the National Archives, there is, just below the date, inked in an unidentifiable hand, "2:55 P.M." All hitherto published descriptions of this document have treated this addition as if it were an integral part of the original order. Most accounts of the disorders assume or state that the decision to call out troops was made after the killings, a chronology the 2:55 P.M. time line supports. But the message center records, plus the various reports of unit commanders, all prove that the troops were set in motion before 2:00 P.M. In addition, the fact that the Commissioner's letter to Hoover, whenever it was written, contained no reference to the shooting incident, is further indication that it was the morning brick-throwing episode, and not the afternoon shooting, that triggered the request for troops. And finally, the official White House statement, made according to the *Star* at 4:22 P.M., just eight minutes before the troops moved down Pennsylvania Avenue, discussed only the morning incident, and spoke of injuries not to marchers but to the policemen, one of whom was supposedly near death.

For some days, police authorities and Treasury officials have been endeavoring to persuade the so-called bonus marchers to evacuate

certain buildings which they were occupying without permission.
. . . This morning the occupants of these buildings were notified
to evacuate and at the request of the police did evacuate the
buildings concerned. Thereafter, however, several thousand men
from different camps marched in and attacked the police with
brickbats and otherwise injuring several policemen, one probably
fatally.

Yet every defense of the administration and all but one of the
historical accounts have assumed or stated that it was the
shooting that drove President Hoover to the extreme step.[9]

Once he had taken it, the army of course had no choice.
MacArthur, never one to hide his light under a bushel, personally accompanied the troops, although actual operational
command was exercised by Brigadier General Perry L. Miles.[10]
A number of myths have sprung up about MacArthur's
participation, some of them invented and spread by journalists, others by historians. It is often asserted that the whole
operation was held up while someone went over to Fort Myer
to get MacArthur's fanciest uniform; Pulitzer Prize winner
Thomas L. Stokes wrote of "his chest glistening with medals,"
while Professor Arthur M. Schlesinger, Jr., has described how
MacArthur "seized his riding crop, mounted his horse, and
took personal command." [11] The general almost certainly
changed clothes that day, simply because the Quaker President had a standing rule that general staff officers wear civilian
clothes in the capital, and it would have been inappropriate
to wear civvies while accompanying troops. Rather than
medals, he wore the five rows of ribbons to which he was
entitled. MacArthur traveled in a staff car; in fact, the former
engineer officer almost never rode a horse, apparently because
he didn't like them. I mention this not just to shame previous
slovenly practice, but because in concentrating on irrelevant
details most historians have missed the significant fact: the
operation as conducted bore little resemblance to that envis-

aged by Hurley's order (apparently dictated by Hoover himself).

The order called for cooperation with the police; MacArthur superseded their functions and gave them a subsidiary role. The order called for the affected area to be surrounded; the troops instead cleared it. The order envisaged the taking of prisoners; none were taken. The order referred only to the affected area; MacArthur cleared the entire District. As we will see, Hoover, after the fact, ratified the actions of his insubordinate subordinates, and the complaints about the disobedience in his memoirs have been all but ignored. It is clear that the President had a distinctly more limited kind of operation in mind. However, once the word had been passed, the military took the bit in its teeth, and, as later Presidents discovered, it was not easy to hold a checkrein on Douglas MacArthur.

Glassford found MacArthur between two o'clock and three o'clock that afternoon, at the ellipse behind the White House which was the staging area for the troops. The chief of staff told him: [12]

> We are going to break the back of the B.E.F. Within a short time we will move down Pennsylvania Avenue, sweep through the billets there, and then clean out the other camps. The operation will be continuous. It will all be done tonight.

The troops began arriving before four o'clock; by four-thirty they were ready to move up the avenue usually devoted to ceremonial marches. The cavalry, 200 strong, led off, with five tanks, followed by some 300 infantry; altogether some 600 troops were actively employed, although they had additional logistical support, and several times that number were either in reserve or en route to the capital from neighboring Maryland and Virginia installations.

The "Battle of Washington," as it has been called, was not

really much of a battle. No one was killed and not a shot was fired. Saber, bayonet, and, above all, tear gas were liberally employed by the army. The bonus marchers, who offered no organized resistance, hurled bricks and imprecations at the troops, with slight effect. Although the operational commander, General Miles, asserts in his official report that the bonus marchers at Camp Glassford "were called upon to evacuate, which they refused to do," the reports made to him by his subordinate commanders do not bear this out. The troops seem to have gone into action almost immediately. The cavalry commander wrote that at about five o'clock, only a few minutes after the troops arrived, "the mob became increasingly hostile and it was apparent the unless it was dispersed it would charge the troops." The cavalry then went to work. With drawn sabers, and frequent exercise of both the flat and the point, they forced most of the marchers away from the Camp Glassford area. The cavalrymen quickly destroyed whatever active spirit of resistance existed. According to the squadron's commander, "The continued cry was 'to get down off your horse and fight fair.' "

Naturally the cavalry didn't try to evict the men from the buildings themselves. The infantry did that, largely with tear gas, which was used somewhat indiscriminately throughout the encounter. Some fifteen hundred grenades, bombs and candles were expended in the few hours of the operation.

The downtown area was cleared in a little over an hour. The troops faced not only the missiles and insults of the BEFers, but also unfriendly natives. Occurring as it did at the height of evening rush hour, there were crowds of bystanders, largely government employees. These civilians were said to have "decidedly hostile" attitudes towards the army, and one commander even reported that they "joined the Bonus Marchers in insulting language toward the troops." But neither sticks nor stones, nor names, can slow the advance of well-disciplined troops. By about seven o'clock most of the billets in Washington proper had been cleared and many destroyed. Troops had seized the bridge to Anacostia at the onset of the operation, and toward evening three tanks were placed upon it.

The soldiers took a supper break and, after giving the people at Camp Marks an extra hour to evacuate, began clearing the Anacostia Flats camp at 11:15 P.M. Boos, curses, and one shower of rocks were the only resistance encountered, although there continued to be unfounded rumors about guns in the hands of bonus marchers. At some time during the day, to cite only one instance, Colonel Alfred T. Smith, who headed the army's G-2 section, had passed the word to MacArthur that he had heard (source unstated) that Atwell, the Camp Marks commander, had told all men having firearms to use them against the first troops to cross the Anacostia River bridge. The operations across the river went even more smoothly than the evictions in town. By a little after midnight the camp was completely cleared, and most of the refugees from it had trudged up badly named Good Hope Hill and over the District line into Maryland and safety. By 2:00 A.M. all troops not on guard duty were bedded down for the night.

If, from a military point of view, the "battle" went well and was rather efficiently conducted, it nevertheless went against all American traditions. The disorder in downtown Washington, provoked by federal authority, the burning of shacks, the occasional manhandling of civilian spectators and even reporters, and, perhaps above all, the obvious disparity between the amount of force apparently necessary and the amount of force used, left a very bad taste in the public mouth, a bad taste that the anti-Hoover forces were quick to intensify in an election year. Had the troops merely restored "law and order" by completing the eviction at Camp Glassford, a different reaction would probably have ensued.[13]

It is clear that MacArthur had planned, from the beginning,

to force the evacuation of the Anacostia Camp. What has not been made clear by previous historians is that the President of the United States had not wanted it that way. In his *Memoirs,* Hoover wrote, somewhat guardedly: [14]

> Certain of my directions to the Secretary of War, however, were not carried out. Those directions limited action to seeing to it that the disturbing factions returned to their camps outside the business district. I did not wish them driven from their camps, as I proposed that the next day we would surround the camps and determine more accurately the number of Communists and ex-convicts among the marchers. Our military officers, however, having them on the move, pushed them outside the District of Columbia.

Theodore G. Joslin, one of Hoover's secretaries, reported later that the President acted reluctantly and that he had heard his chief "ask Secretary Hurley that the troops should be moved into the trouble area without firearms," and later in his narrative implies that Hoover wanted the soldiers to use sticks.[15]

A more shocking revelation, however, was made by Major General George Van Horn Moseley in his papers, now in the Library of Congress. Moseley, a skilled officer, was Deputy Chief of Staff during the bonus march. Long known within the army as an anti-Semite, he later became a leading American Fascist. According to his statements, he had consistently urged a more active policy upon his immediate chief and the President, but his advice had been just as consistently rejected. The crucial part of his testimony concerns the evening of July 28, and deserves to be quoted in full: [16]

> Sometime after the troops had completed their mission on Pennsylvania Avenue and before they had crossed the Anacostia Bridge with the view of cleaning out the camp on the other side, Mr. Hurley, the Secretary of War, directed me to inform General

MacArthur that the President did not wish the troops to cross the bridge that night to force the evacuation of the Anacostia Camp. I left my office, contacted General MacArthur, and as we walked away, alone, from the others, I delivered that message to him and discussed it with him. He was very much annoyed in having his plans interfered with in any way until they were executed completely. As I told him, I was only instructed to deliver the message to him, and having done that, I returned to my office. Later, I was asked from the White House if I had delivered the message, and I stated that I had. Still later, I was instructed to repeat the message and to assure myself that General MacArthur received it before he crossed the Anacostia Bridge. I sent Colonel Clement H. Wright, then Secretary of the General Staff, to repeat the message to MacArthur and explain the situation as I had it from the White House. Colonel Wright contacted General Mac-Arthur immediately and explained the situation to him fully. As I now recall, Colonel Wright reported to me that the troops then had not crossed the Anacostia Bridge, but were advancing on the bridge. In any event, General MacArthur went on with his plan, carrying it through and compelling the complete evacuation of the large Anacostia Camp, which held most of the veterans. A mission of this kind was a very disagreeable one for the Army, but it was executed with precision and efficiency and entirely without blood-shed.

If this memorandum is accurate, and there is every reason to believe that it is, although there is no directly corroborating evidence, it illustrates nicely Douglas MacArthur's ideas about the relationship between the Commander in Chief and the Commander of the Army. MacArthur, it seems, was willing to accept a properly subordinate role until a military opera-tion was actually begun: then he would brook no interference. It is fascinating to speculate about this brush between the President and the general and to wonder to what degree the successful defiance of presidential instructions about crossing one river influenced the attempt, almost twenty years later, to force a later President to allow him—or at least his airplanes —to cross another. Equally fascinating is the question of why Hoover allowed MacArthur to be insubordinate with impunity. It is not hard to come up with a plausible answer to the latter question, although it is, in large part, guesswork.

Hoover regarded his whole presidency as an ordeal, as something to be endured stoically, as his particular cross to bear. A student of history, he had an almost uncanny knack of reading history wrong. It seems clear from his various statements that he regarded the BEF—which he never visited nor allowed to visit him—as a dangerous threat, not to him, but to the nation. He felt, I think, that the situation in Washington in 1932 was somewhat analogous to that in Petrograd in 1917, and he did not want to be the Kerensky of the American revolution, which he regarded as a distinct possibility. His use of troops at the slightest pretext came neither from cruelty nor callousness—the Quaker President was a sincere humanitarian—but from a fundamental misunderstanding of the nature of American society, a misunderstanding which shouts from almost every page of his *Memoirs*. Those who wrote, then and later, that the expulsion of the bonus army was an appeal for political popularity, the opening gun of Hoover's presidential campaign, have done Hoover a grievous injustice.[17] Whatever sins Herbert Clark Hoover may have committed, being a politician was not one of them. A politician might have thrown the insubordinate MacArthur to the wolves, but Hoover, who demanded and got an amazing degree of loyalty from most of his subordinates, reciprocated that loyalty. A Christian with perhaps more than a touch of masochism, he did nothing to transfer the onus of the midnight rout from Anacostia onto the splendid scapegoat that his chief of staff could have provided.

It was, above all, that midnight operation at Anacostia, an operation that sent men, women, and children staggering across country in the middle of the night, which filled much of the nation with horror, and, in some cases, real loathing. After Anacostia, Herbert Hoover became the most hated President in office since Andrew Johnson.

The army was, at first, quite proud of what it had done, and in the days immediately following, the brass hats wrote a number of letters congratulating one another on how splendid it all had been.

General MacArthur felt that the whole operation was well done. In his official report, submitted two weeks after the event, he stated that the troops performed their allotted tasks

rapidly and efficiently, but with maximum consideration for the members of the riotous groups consistent with their compulsory eviction. The results speak for themselves. Within a few hours a riot rapidly assuming alarming proportions was completely quelled, and from the moment troops arrived at the scene of the disorder no soldier or civilian received a permanent or dangerous injury. Thus a most disagreeable task was performed in such a way as to leave behind it a minimum of unpleasant aftermath and legitimate resentment.

One troop commander suggested that the operation be given wide publicity to convince the general public that the regular army would "act relentlessly" in any future disorder. The Third Cavalry, a regiment with a proud history of real combat, even issued a general order "to commemorate" what it felt was a "highly meritorious achievement," little realizing that the sordid "battle" of Washington would be the last mounted engagement the United States Cavalry would ever have.[18]

While the army was mopping up at Anacostia, MacArthur and Hurley held a joint press conference back in town. MacArthur's florid performance clearly prefigured the well-known communiques which poured out of his various headquarters after Pearl Harbor.

"That mob down there was a bad looking mob," MacArthur

told the reporters, most of whom knew a good deal more about the bonus marchers than he did. "It was animated by the essence of revolution." Claiming that the veterans had mistaken the "gentleness" with which they had been treated for "weakness," the chief of staff gave his opinion that "had the President not acted today, had he permitted this thing to go on for 24 hours more, he would have been faced with a grave situation which would have caused a real battle." The general claimed that "beyond the shadow of a doubt" the BEF thought they were about to take over the government, directly or indirectly. MacArthur styled the marchers "insurrectionists" and assured the press that there were "few veteran soldiers in the group we cleared out today . . . if there was one man in ten in that group today who is a veteran it would surprise me." Then came an all-too-typical piece of MacArthur baroque: [19]

> I have never seen greater relief on the part of the distressed populace than I saw today. I have released in my day more than one community which had been held in the grip of a foreign enemy. I have gone into villages that for three and one half years had been under the domination of the soldiers of a foreign nation. I know what gratitude means along that line. I have never seen, even in those days, such expressions of gratitude as I heard from the crowds today.

In the face of such bald misstatements, there is little the historian can say. Perhaps one word from the comment in the *Baltimore Sun*—"Horsefeathers"—is most appropriate.[20] One cannot but wonder, however, what would have happened if MacArthur's florid and persuasive rhetorical talents had been employed at Camp Glassford to urge the men to leave peaceably. As we have seen, the chief of staff rejected that alternative. After all, one does not make patriotic appeals to insurrectionists.

In the days immediately following the expulsion—in fact even before it really began—the administration, at every level, excoriated the BEF and tried, with conspicuous lack of success, to convince the American public that what had happened in Washington was necessary. The President himself led the way. Although Hoover called for an official investigation into the whole affair by the Attorney General, the President had already propounded what was to become the official line. In the White House statement of the afternoon of July 28, the President said that "a considerable part of those [BEFers] remaining are not veterans; many are Communists and persons with criminal records." [21] The next day, in a stern public letter to the Commissioners, Hoover reiterated this theory. He also made it clear that he felt that the Commissioners and Glassford had been too lenient. The veterans, the President wrote, "were undoubtedly led to believe that the civil authorities could be intimidated with impunity because of attempts to conciliate by lax enforcement of city ordinances and laws in many directions." Then, perhaps trying to strike a note which would get the same happy public response that had greeted Calvin Coolidge's immortal bromide about the Boston police strike, Hoover closed with the pronouncement that "there is no group, no matter what its origin, that can be allowed to violate the laws of this city or to intimidate the government." [22]

It was only on August 3, however, that what became the official "line" on calling out the troops was formally developed by the administration. On that day Secretary of War Hurley released a long statement which, for the first time in an official document, related in causal sequence the calling out of troops to the fatal 2:00 P.M. fracas and put forth the false 2:55 P.M. dateline in the troop order. This belated manipulation of the facts was prefaced by the bald assertion that its issuance was "owing to the apparently deliberate propaganda and misrepresentations that are being circulated." The crucial paragraphs of Hurley's statement are those which relate the calling out of the troops to the afternoon events.[23]

During the morning of the 28th of July, the police again appeared and asked the marchers to vacate the premises where the new buildings were to be erected. The marchers refused to vacate. The police attempted to oust them. The marchers then attacked the police. Thousands of veterans and agitators who were encamped south of the Anacostia River marched into Washington and joined in the attack on the police.

A definite organized attack of several thousand men was then made upon the police. The leaders of the veterans protested to their followers and to the public that this attack was led by radicals and that the veterans participating in the attack were not under the control of their veteran leaders but were entirely controlled by Red agitators whose sole purpose was to bring about disorder, riots, bloodshed and death.

During the riot of the morning of the 28th of July, no lives were lost, though several policemen were seriously injured. Later in the day a second riot occurred. Thereupon the Commissioners of the District of Columbia advised the President (in writing) that a riot was in progress, blood had been shed, a number of police and rioters had been injured, and one person had been killed. (Another who was wounded at that time has since died.) The Commissioners of the District of Columbia advised the President that the civil government was unable to restore law and order. The Commissioners of the District of Columbia then requested the President to bring to the scene of disorder United States troops for the purpose of stopping the riot and protecting the lives of the people. Thereupon, with the riot still in progress, at 2:55 P.M. on the 28th of July, as Secretary of War, I issued the following order: [Hurley then quoted the whole order].

After the arrival of the United States troops, a force of about six hundred men, not one shot was fired and no person was seriously injured. Law and order was promptly restored.

On July 29, the day after the riot, law and order had been quite lawless. In the morning the troops completed desultory mopping-up operations and returned to their barracks by mid-afternoon. Martial law had never been declared, although some civilian activities were interfered with. While the army was completing its task, District and federal law enforcement officers disregarded almost completely even the notion of due process of law. The Washington police reverted to pre-Glassfordian tactics; the police chief was nowhere to be seen that day. His force, without his approval or knowledge, arrested and jailed twenty-six Communist leaders, including James W. Ford, the party's vice presidential candidate. All eventually had to be released, as there was no law violation with which they could successfully be charged.

Less fortunate were some two hundred presumed radicals and veterans whom the police rounded up, marched through the streets, and summarily expelled from the District. Maryland didn't want them either, so many were packed into trucks and hauled away, like so much garbage. Naturally, there is no precise record of the results of such an operation; many of the deportees were undoubtedly "on the bum" and used to such treatment. An Associated Press dispatch of four days later from Indianapolis, Indiana, gives an inkling of what happened. According to the story, some of those arrested had no connection with either radicalism or the BEF. It dwelt in particular on the plight of a bearded gentleman who said he was H. H. Moore, a book salesman from Augusta, Georgia, and who had a suitcase full of advertising literature to prove it. According to Moore, the police dragnet swept up "everyone without a Prince Albert coat or the credentials of a Senator. . . . I want to go back, but they keep shoving me in trucks." Another man, who said he was working for a wallpaper company, claimed he was picked up by police while coming home from a dance, while still a third said he was a member of the District National Guard.

Glassford, furious at the roundup he had not authorized, publicily reprimanded the inspector in charge, but softened his criticism when he learned that the raid had been instigated by federal officials in charge of immigration and intelligence and that there was an old standing departmental order for the police to cooperate with all requests from federal law enforcement officials, without questioning their legality. It is instructive to note that the press and public were so inured to illegal police procedure that these scandalous deportations caused practically no excitement.[24]

Two controversies arising out of the use of troops did spring up immediately, and these attracted a great deal of attention: one concerned the allegedly indiscriminate use of gas, the other the mass burning of the shacks the bonus marchers called home. The tear gas controversy arose from the close proximity of civilians to much of the action and the fact that there were several hundred women and children with the bonus army. Undoubtedly both inaccuracy and wind drift caused much of the irritant to be "wasted" on spectators. One story claimed that Senator Hiram Bingham was one of those affected. The public reaction to the use of gas can be understood only if one realizes the horror with which gas was held after World War I, in which it was perhaps the most awful weapon. In addition, it was quickly alleged and widely believed that the army—and by extension Herbert Hoover— gassed babies. First spread by the Hearst-owned *Washington Times,* the false atrocity story was given its widest currency by Pulitzer Prize winner Paul Y. Anderson in *The Nation.* In a story titled "Tear-Gas, Bayonets and Votes: The President Opens His Reelection Campaign," the newsman, himself an eyewitness, wrote of an "eleven-weeks-old baby in a grave condition from gas, shock and exposure; one eight-year-old boy partly blinded by gas; . . . one bystander shot through the shoulder, one veteran's ear severed with a cavalry saber." [25]

These atrocities, particularly the baby and the earless veteran, have become stock figures in most accounts of the BEF. The veteran, along with the eight-year-old boy and the obviously fictitious bystander (the army fired no shots), is strangely nameless. One would think that if he had existed, he would have come forth, like the immortal Jenkins, and claimed the fame that was his due. Part of the story may have come from the boasting of the then Major George S. Patton, the swashbuckling armored commander of World War II, who rode with the cavalry that day and told many yarns about his heroics. One of his comrades in arms, who also became a general, later wrote that [26]

> Major Patton's exploits of the afternoon are already too surrounded by the legends that he always created to make possible a guaranteed factual account. . . . The stories of his snipping off ears without touching any other part of a man's body can be disbelieved.

However shadowy the other victims, the gassed baby is all too real. On August 9, Bernard Myers, aged twelve weeks, the son of a bonus marcher from Reading, Pennsylvania, died in Washington's Gallinger Hospital. There is no evidence, other than journalistic assertions, that his death was in any way connected with tear gas. The *Star* reported he died of a "stomach ailment," and an army investigation, a week before he died, reported a hospital diagnosis of enteritis, an intestinal disorder. The army doctor who investigated agreed and reported further: [27]

> One thing certain—the child does not appear to present any symptoms of injury from Chloracetophenone [tear gas]. . . . There were no symptoms present of inflammatory reaction around the eyelids, or any evidence of conjunctival congestion, and a

complete absence of dermatitis, a condition that certainly would have been present if a child of this age had been exposed to a toxic concentration of chloracetophenone.

The question of the shack burning was more complicated. Several of the unit commanders' reports, written a day or so after the battle, quite casually mention "destroying" the camps of the bonus marchers. Even before the eviction was complete, however, MacArthur, in that unfortunate midnight press conference, had denied army responsibility for any destruction. In answer to the question, "Who fired the camp?" the general replied simply, "They must have fired it themselves." Five days later, Secretary Hurley was even more certain. "The statements made to the effect that the billets of the marchers were fired by the troops is a falsehood," Hurley insisted. The Oklahoman even knew the politics of the arsonists: "The billets were fired by retreating radicals." [28]

Unfortunately for the credibility of the administration, there existed both still and motion picture evidence to the contrary, and some of this evidence was soon released. As Howard Brubaker later remarked in the *New Yorker,* continued denials of army responsibility made it clear that Hoover's cabinet didn't waste time "looking at newsreels." When the irrefutable evidence began to pop up—and to be published—the army did a little investigating and quickly discovered that the men at the top had been talking through their hats. In the first place, it developed that some of the shacks had been deliberately set ablaze by soldiers in response to orders from their officers, who, seeing some billets burning, assumed that there were orders to burn them all and acted accordingly. In the second place, on-the-spot observations and later experiments demonstrated that much of the army's chemical warfare equipment was both defective and incendiary. Most of the army's casualties came from gas grenades and candles that did more damage to their wielders than to those they were used against; in addition, certain types of candles and grenades set the shacks and other rubble afire. In a memorandum written in late September, General Miles, the operational commander, assumed "full responsibility" for the burning, which he thought was caused in the first instance by the gas candles and grenades, and then spread by soldiers erroneously assuming that in so doing they were following orders. Hurley, however, never released this report. Despite the fact that the Washington press identified one of the soldiers who was photographed putting a torch to a shack, and finally got the War Department to admit that some of the shacks had been deliberately set afire by troops, the Secretary of War continued publicly to back up the off-the-cuff comments of the chief of staff. Six months later Hurley could still write: [29]

> On an abundance of evidence that I believe is true, I am convinced that the general burning of the shacks at the camps was not initiated by the military.

These minor controversies over military details soon paled into insignificance. For a short while after the battle of Washington, national attention focused on what was left of the rapidly disintegrating bonus army. Then the war of words began in earnest as the BEF and all it represented became an issue in the presidential campaign of 1932.

8

The Aftermath
of Battle

MANY OF THE refugees from Washington headed for Johnstown, Pennsylvania, nearly two hundred miles away, where
a futile, week-long attempt was made to pull the disintegrating
BEF back together. They had been invited there a few days
previously, in what must have been a mere rhetorical gesture,
by the town's flamboyant mayor, an ex-prize fighter named
Eddie McCloskey. McCloskey, a penny ante demagogue, had
been elected mayor in 1931 on a far-fetched program that
called for ending unemployment by building sidewalks from
Maine to California, abolishing chambers of commerce because they frightened business, killing prohibition by having
it strictly enforced by the United States Army, and organizing
great caravans of the unemployed to march on Washington.
Finding McCloskey a kindred spirit—the mayor had visited
Anacostia in mid-July—Waters passed the word that Johnstown was the place to go, although he never went there
himself.

While many of the bonus marchers just "melted away," the
majority of those left seem to have headed for Johnstown.
Some went in their own cars and trucks, others hitchhiked or

182

rode freights, and still others seem to have been transported on Maryland National Guard trucks, as Governor Albert Ritchie was determined not to have any large BEF encampment in the "Free State." Some bona fide Maryland residents claimed to have been transported out of their home state against their wishes. In any event, when 5,000 or 6,000 destitute and bedraggled bonus marchers began to trickle into the small city (population 67,000), its residents naturally felt that a second Johnstown flood was occurring. The mayor had made speeches and issued press releases, but had made no real arrangements to accommodate the influx. A camp of sorts was set up at the Ideal Amusement Park, five miles outside of town.

Conditions at the pleasure park were far from ideal. Even the mayor quickly soured on his invited guests ("God sent you to Johnstown. Now I'm going to send you home."), while the local newspaper excoriated them as "thieves, plug-uglies, [and] degenerates," from whom the community must be protected. [1] Pennsylvania's Governor Gifford Pinchot, an old-line Bull Moose Progressive who had retained his aggressive idealism, sent state troopers to maintain order, but issued no threats and took no steps toward eviction. He also sent sympathetic investigators from the State Welfare Commission, and from the report of one of them, who visited the camp on August 3, we get the best picture of conditions there.

Water and toilet facilities were severely limited, food supplies were skimpy, and the housing conditions deplorable; yet, and this is a damning comment on conditions in the United States in the summer of 1932, there was "a definite reluctance to leave," a distinct feeling that however bad it was, there were at least some comforts at Johnstown. The social worker found that most of those at Johnstown were from formerly respectable lower-middle-class families, and that the weeks at Anacostia had constituted, for many, a distinct bettering of their standard of living—the health of many of the children had actually improved there.

"From different people," Welfare Commission member J. Prentice Murphy reported, "one got stories which indicated long unemployment, from one to two years." The families he talked to seemed to be "people who had had their homes, been independent at one time, and who had lost their savings. They gave evidence of having enjoyed and treasured family life. . . . They spoke with restraint, some certainly were folks who read and liked books." Then, in true social worker fashion, he gave a series of capsule case histories:

> Man, wife, seven children from Pennsylvania; baby quite ill in Washington; long period of unemployment; has received poor relief; no one to go back to in home town; relatives all poor; this family is going to wander.

> Father, mother, five children; mother pregnant, the youngest child, a girl, had convulsions the night before; man a baker; lost his house in New York State; was evicted; he is going to wife's relatives in Virginia.

> Man, wife, four children; carpenter from Camden, N.J.; they have lovely children; parents are neat, intelligent people; children have been in better health since they went to Washington; often went without meals before going there; was in service 16 months; has some hope of a job; in the meantime may go to a camp of the B.E.F. in New Jersey.

> Man, wife, five children; long unemployment, desperately poor; man greatly discouraged; the little four-year-old daughter said she loved to have her mother read from a book about Jesus and the Lord. This family came from Baltimore; put on trucks at Washington; was not permitted to get off at a point near Baltimore; their baby has been sick in the Memorial Hospital, Johnstown.

Murphy estimated that 2,500 to 3,000 persons were still at Ideal Park by the time he arrived and that perhaps 1,500 to 2,000 had already left. He was impressed that there were "no obviously immoral women" and "apparently no illicit sex." Every one of about 75 men whom he questioned was able to produce a discharge certificate. He was also particularly struck by the difficulty that most of the people had in comprehending that when the government talked about insurrectionists and dangerous reds, it was talking about them. This they found incomprehensible, and understandably so. Largely "100 percent Americans," who despised any hint of foreign ideology and who never once made an appeal to organized labor or any radical group, the BEFers just could not understand how anyone could doubt their loyalty. Back in their home towns, most of them were likely candidates for any civic-vigilante action, like running a union organizer out of town or breaking up a Socialist meeting. Like Dreyfus, who allegedly would not have been a Dreyfusard had he not been Dreyfus, most of them had never participated in anything faintly resembling a protest movement before, and would not do so again.[2]

In Waters' absence, his chief of staff, Doak Carter, a Kentuckian who had seen only twenty-one days of federal service in 1916 before getting a medical discharge, tried to assume leadership. It seemed important to a number of people, including Carter, that the BEF remain in being. Waters was trying to make arrangements for a "permanent" camp at Catonsville, Maryland, arrangements which Governor Ritchie successfully frustrated. Waters had also flirted with a "shirt" organization à la Mussolini, the Khaki Shirts. Another shirted leader, Father Cox of Pittsburgh, whose Blue Shirts would soon nominate him for the presidency, made a 3:00 A.M. visit to Johnstown to attempt to get the bonus marchers to join forces with his unemployed. If they would do so, the political priest offered to give the vice presidential slot on his Jobless party ticket to a bonus marcher. He was quickly shouted down, probably as much for his collar as for his politics.

Carter dreamed up a scheme with a Los Angeles promoter to settle the BEF in Mexico as part of a "back-to-the-farm" movement south of the border. The scheme was discussed enough to draw a formal veto from Mexican President Ortiz Rubio; Carter later planned a more modest transfer from Johnstown to West Virginia, but this too never came about. By August 3, Waters, realizing the utter futility of trying to keep the remnants of his army together, gave, from his Washington headquarters, the order to disband, arguing that the most effective move would be for everyone to return home and start little BEF camps; he went on a lecture tour. Carter, who was allegedly living in the best hotel in Johnstown, "rebelled" against Waters' order and tried to keep the group together. It was no use. Deprived of effective leadership, official sanction, logistical support and, above all, the sense of purpose and glamour that the occupation of the national capital had provided, the soldiers of the bonus army just faded away, aided, in the end, by special B&O and Pennsylvania railroad trains partially paid for by local businessmen. The Ideal Amusement Park was evacuated by August 6.[3]

Four days later, forty-three members of the Portland contingent arrived home, attracting a little more attention than when they had left, three months before. A Portland reporter described them as "dusty, tired, looking somewhat the worse for wear." Yet, enough pride and discipline remained for them to form a column of twos and march, after a fashion, out of the depot. Their leader, Arthur Wilson, insisted that the BEF would live on,[4] and told the press:

> We are going to form Bonus Army camps in every city in the United States and some in Mexico. We are going to have state departments and a national department. We are going to keep this movement going until we get what we think is due us.

The urge to make something permanent out of the wreckage of the BEF, to set up a national veterans' organization that would rival the American Legion, was probably chimerical at best. From its very inception the Legion had received impressive fiscal and political support from nationally important individuals and groups, while the BEF had to depend on charity. Some slight chance of success for a permanent BEF might have existed had the Legion remained adamant in its antibonus stand, but when the Legion at its 1932 convention —held ironically in Portland, Oregon—got on the bonus bandwagon, whatever chances there had been for a new organization were blighted. Yet fragmented bits of the BEF did survive. The files of Congressman Wright Patman, who remained the major congressional bonus advocate, contain dozens of letterheads showing that at least token BEF encampments were scattered over the country as late as 1934, and a few BEFers joined Milo Reno's Farmer Holiday Movement. As a real force, the BEF received its death blow from MacArthur at Anacostia, and died, nine days later, in the squalor of the Ideal Amusement Park. The BEF itself was dead, but what was done to it was still a live issue.[5]

That the bonus march controversy was kept alive until after the November presidential elections was due in no small part to the inept maneuverings of the Hoover administration, which consistently mismanaged its public relations. First, the matter was turned over to the Washington, D.C., grand jury, even though all of the "suspects" had been systematically dispersed by MacArthur's troops. The hearing, which opened on July 29, continued intermittently until August 15. It opened with an optimistic and highly improper charge by Justice Luhring of the District Supreme Court, who began by calling the attention of the already empaneled grand jurors to the stories in the press and concluded by letting them know what his wishes were in the matter:

It is reported that the mob guilty of violence included few exservicemen, and was made up mainly of communists and other disorderly elements. I hope you will find that this is so and that few men who have worn the nation's uniform engaged in this violent attack upon law and order. In the confusion not many arrests have been made, and it is said that many of the most violent disturbers and criminal elements in the unlawful gathering have already scattered and escaped from the city, but it may be possible yet to identify and apprehend them and bring them to justice.

The grand jury investigation was thought important enough to rate the personal attention of Nugent Dodds, an Assistant Attorney General of the United States, as well as Leo Rover, the local Federal Attorney. They carefully made sure that the grand jurors heard little testimony favorable to the bonus marchers. Pelham Glassford was called, but not any of his "crime prevention detail," that is, those men who were assigned to the camps and knew the BEF best; nor did any member of the BEF testify. Instead, there was paraded before the grand jury a succession of "friendly" witnesses: two District Commissioners, several high-ranking police officials, all of them anti-Glassford, two army officers, and a sprinkling of shopkeepers and filling station attendants from the downtown riot area. The questioning was not designed to elicit all the information, but to support the administration's contention that the calling of troops was necessary to suppress a riot of Communists, criminals, and riffraff. Dr. Reichelderfer went to great lengths—at least to the brink of perjury—to make it appear that the call for troops followed rather than preceded the fatal incident. General Crosby, who was more circumspect, managed not to disturb that impression. Both Dodds and Rover were careful not to ask the army officers who testified just when they left Ft. Myer; their failure to mention this routine chronological detail, a detail that appears in the reports the same officers turned in to the chief of staff, strongly suggests that they had been briefed on what to say and what not to say. All of this, of course, was meant to maintain the illusion that the troops did not move until after 2:55 P.M., when Hurley's order was supposed to have been issued. Contrary to Justice Luhring's hopes, the grand jury was not able to make any positive findings. It did not even consider the shootings per se, as a coroner's jury had already found that Patrolman George Shinault had committed justifiable homicide in the line of duty when he shot bonus marchers William Huska and Eric Carlson. The administration wanted to focus no light on these unfortunate bonus marchers, because they were a distinct embarrassment to the theory propounded by the President. Both were veterans of overseas combat and neither had either a criminal record or verifiable Communist connections. Both were eventually buried in Arlington Cemetary with the full military honors that their service merited.[6]

Also inconvenient for the official theory of radical non-veterans as troublemakers was the fact that all five men who were arrested during the early morning rioting, two for refusing to evacuate and three for disorderly conduct in the first brick-throwing melee, were bona fide veterans with no known radical connections. That two of the five were Negro probably says more about the prejudices of Washington police than it does about Negro militance. The first two were quickly sentenced to six months in jail, but released in less than a month. The other three were indicted, but apparently never came to trial. Glassford himself eventually recommended that their cases be nol-prossed on the following grounds: [7]

1. They were only three of many.
2. All three were overseas veterans, one holding the Distinguished Service Cross.
3. Although the rioting was allegedly started by Communists, none of the three had Communist or WESL connections; in addition, he noted, all arrested Communists had been released.
4. The prosecution of these three men would make them martyrs.

As we have seen, the President himself had laid down the official administration line about the bonus march even while the eviction was proceeding. In retrospect, it is clear that the administration would have been much better off if it had left the matter alone, but Hoover and his associates had an abundance of self-righteousness and a compulsive desire for public vindication. Besides, the whole BEF fiasco was most inconvenient to the theories that the soothsayers of the Republican party were propounding about the administration and its function. Just two weeks before the Battle of Washington, for example, Secretary Hurley had assured the Ohio State convention of the GOP that the Hoover administration was a success because the President's policies had been vindicated. Proof of this, according to the Secretary of War, was self-evident:

> We have prevented disorders, riots, and social upheavals. We have cared for the needy. We are in a depression, but we have averted panic and catastrophe. . . . While twenty revolutions have shaken the foundations of other nations . . . the United States, under the administration of Herbert Hoover, is tranquil, solvent, and confident.

In a similar vein, Andrew Mellon, now Ambassador to Great Britain, had assured the annual Lord Mayor's luncheon that "deflation in America is proceeding calmly and in an orderly manner, without strikes or riots or any of the violence that in times past have accompanied such drastic readjustments in the Nation's economic life." [8]

Since the use of federal troops in the national capital called even these negative virtues into question, it is easy to understand why the administration felt desperately that it had to discredit the BEF as the criminal, Communist conspiracy which many of them sincerely believed it was. The President, himself, made this clear the day after the eviction, when, in the same release which announced that an investigation was already in progress, the President said that "it is my sincere hope that those agitators who inspired yesterday's attack" would quickly be identified and brought to justice. He particularly deplored the disorders because he regarded "order and civic tranquility" as the "first requisites" of what he always styled "economic reconstruction." When coupled with his earlier statement that "a considerable part [of the bonus army] are not veterans; many are communists and persons with criminal records," it is apparent that Hoover had already made up his mind.[9]

When, then, he ordered his Attorney General, William De Witt Mitchell, a Minnesota lawyer-politician, to conduct an investigation, he left his subordinate few real choices. He could either concoct a report that would conform with Hoover's preconceptions, or he could refute the head of his party in the midst of a presidential campaign. Given the American political system which makes the head of the Department of Justice a partisan politico, it should be obvious that the result of any such investigation would more likely be a lawyer's brief than an impartial inquest. In addition, many subordinate figures in the government knew exactly what kind of testimony was desired and, steeped in the techniques of bureaucratic survival, gave that testimony. A good example is the Health Officer of the District, Dr. Fowler. On July 4, he summarized the reports made by his inspectors regarding the six major camps of the bonus marchers for Commissioner Reichelderfer. He gave them a surprisingly clean bill of health reporting that the inspection showed "all of them to be kept in a good sanitary condition considering the facilities available, with the exception of a vacant building. . . . This vacant building is open to the public and is being used for toilet purposes by the Bonus Marchers." The building was quickly cleaned up. Two months later, however, Health Officer Fowler told a different story in a letter to the Attorney General.[10]

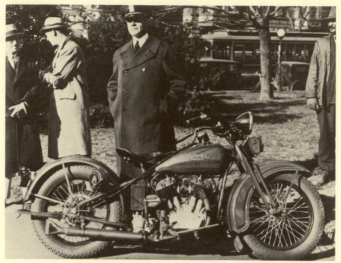

General Pelham D. Glassford.

*Secretary of War
Patrick J. Hurley.*

*President Herbert Hoover, in an
uncharacteristic pose.*

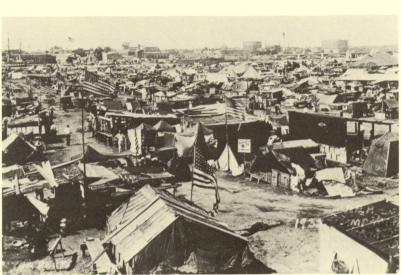

Camp Marks, Anacostia Flats, shortly before July 28, 1932.

Doctor Luther H. Reichelderfer.   *Major General Herbert C. Crosby.*

Glassford's Unfriendly Enemies: District Commissioners Reichelderfer and Crosby.

W. W. Waters.

General Glassford tours Anacostia Flats.

BEF Commander W. W. Waters (third from left) and staff talk with a newly arrived bonus marcher.

194

Bonus marchers pose by the partially demolished building that became the focal point of the eviction of the BEF. Huska and Carlson were killed at the foot of the staircase in the left background.

The first and nonfatal clash between bonus marchers and police July 28, 1932.

*An immaculate
General Douglas MacArthur
takes a coffee break near the bridge
to Anacostia, July 28, 1932. The
unidentified civilian, probably a
reporter, seems to have something
stronger than coffee.*

United States Army troops routing out gassed bonus marchers, July 28, 1932.

196

Shacks burning at Anacostia Flats, July 28, 1932.

Camp Marks, Anacostia Flats, shortly after July 28, 1932.

The sanitary conditions were necessarily very bad. Open latrines were freely used, and of course, flies and vermin infested the camps. The fact that it was warm weather increased the dangers incident to such practices, as well, causing in many instances foul oders [sic]. . . .

There was no time during the weeks that the Bonus Army was here when its presence, under the conditions that existed, was not an extreme menace to the public health.

After some forty days, and just on the eve of the 1932 American Legion convention (about which more later), the Attorney General produced his report. Both from internal evidence and from those working papers which survive and are open to scholars, it is apparent not only that it is the partisan brief that one would expect in the circumstances, but also that it is a deliberately mendacious document, containing untruths, half-truths, and significant omissions. The report, which ran only to seven-and-a-half legal-size pages, was released by the White House on September 12. The crux of it was that "a very much larger proportion of the Bonus Army than was realized at the time consisted of ex-convicts, persons with criminal records, radicals, and non-service men." To support this charge there was presented a statistical table which showed that of 4,723 identifiable members of the BEF, some 829, or 17.4 percent, were convicted criminals. The report stated that these men had been identified by fingerprints, but the archival materials demonstrate that, in at least some instances, mere telegraphic communication to hometown law enforcement officials was used to gather data. Since the veterans had been identified only by name (in some cases local officials wired back about several criminals with identical or similar names), identification was far from precise. Military as well as civilian "crimes" were tabulated, so that any doughboy who had been court-martialed for anything—insubordination, drunkenness, AWOL—was solemnly listed as having a "criminal record," although this is not apparent from the report itself. Many civilian peccadilloes were similarly listed as "crimes": the unemployed veteran who was unable to meet child support payments in violation of a court order was recorded as having committed an "offense against the family and children," and according to the chief law officer of the United States, fourteen veterans had been found guilty of "suspicion and investigation," presumably in some of the more benighted jurisdictions. When obvious military offenses (some are dumped into civilian categories), misdemeanors, prohibition violations (mere possession of beer, wine, or liquor was a crime from 1919 to 1933), and the crime of being poor and homeless are deducted from the total, nearly half of the alleged criminality of the BEF disappears.

Even if Mitchell's figures were accurate, they demonstrated nothing about the men who bore the brunt of the Battle of Washington, because the "sample" of 4,723 that the Department of Justice analysed was the list of men who had received money from the Veterans Administration to get home, and were presumably no longer in the capital when the trouble started. Mitchell tried to get around this difficulty with a single sentence which tortured both logic and syntax:

> When it is realized that the men who applied for loans to go home after Congress adjourned were the most sensible and the least disorderly, that many with criminal records no doubt refrained from disclosing their identity for any purpose, and a considerable portion of the Bonus Army were not ex-service men and included radicals, and disorderly elements which always congregate under such conditions, it is probable that the Bonus Army brought into Washington the largest aggregation of criminals that had ever been assembled in the city at any one time.

The question of nonveterans was a sticky one for the Attorney General; his method—use of a VA list—meant that his main sample was 100 percent veteran. Yet his chief had insisted that "a considerable part" were nonveterans, something of which there was no real record. Here he had to resort to a different sample: the early muster rosters of the BEF itself, which had been compiled by Glassford's police up to June 12. Of the 3,656 names on the list, some 877, a little less than one-fourth (Mitchell's report, deficient even in arithmetic, says a little "more"), could not positively be identified as veterans. Actually, as Mitchell knew, these figures are not as significant as they seem. As VA Chief General Frank T. Hines had explained to Hoover at the time, the records of both the VA and the War Department were not organized in a way to make a name search meaningful, and some names that were not found in one place were found in another. Of the 877 unidentified names, Hines quite specifically wrote: "I question whether this figure may properly be used to indicate the number of non-veterans in this group in the light of inadequate identifying data in a number of these cases." Mitchell had Hines' letter before him when he put his report together. Mitchell wrote: "It is possible that some of the 877 were ex-service men and could not be identified because of meagre information, but the bulk of them were evidently imposters."

The rest of the report stressed Communist influence—"a very large body of Communists and radicals"—the long-suffering patience of Washington officialdom, ignored Glassford's public denial that he had asked for troops, and criticized the police force's handling of the riot. In his conclusion, the Attorney General argued that Hoover's action in calling out the army had prevented a "calamity" and insisted that future mass gatherings in the national capital should be prohibited.[11]

The report brought forth a storm of protest, and from a public relations point of view was a disaster. As that old cynic H. L. Mencken pointed out, the press, with few exceptions, had given "hearty cheers" when Hoover sent in the troops. He continued, with his usual hyperbole: [12]

Hoover had to defame the poor idiots he had gassed, and presently there was a sharp reaction. . . . [T]he calm and implacable statesman, bent only upon preserving public order, revealed himself overnight as a peevish and unfair partisan, fevered by transparently discreditable fears.

What impelled the President to release the report and thus rekindle the fires of controversy? Certainly the desire for self-justification was a factor; still another was the wish to influence the American Legion convention, which was expected to endorse immediate payment of the bonus and perhaps to criticize the administration's handling of the eviction. Still a third, as Hoover himself put it, was "to correct the many misstatements of fact as to this incident with which the country has been flooded," while a fourth motive certainly involved the presidential election. Early in August, Henry J. Allen, former governor of Kansas and then serving as director of publicity for the Republican National Committee, had expressed concern over the public relations aspects of the bonus affair.[13] The general insensitivity of the White House retinue, an insensitivity which, coupled with the President's personal misconceptions about the nature of American society, often led the administration to put its worst foot forward, can be indicated by the way it reacted to liberal protests over the eviction of the bonus army. Two examples will have to suffice.

In mid-August, with a great deal of preliminary publicity, Sherwood Anderson led a delegation of well-known writers with liberal or radical inclinations to the White House to protest the evictions. Predictably, the weary titan in the White House was "too busy" to see them. Hoover, as Arthur M. Schlesinger, Jr., has pointed out, had time for wrestling champions, sorority girls, teen-aged contest winners, and the like, but never found time for the BEF. To add insult to injury in this instance, one of his secretaries, Theodore Joslin, read the angry authors a little homily on their "duty" that would have been cheered at most Kiwanis Clubs, but was almost sure to antagonize further the already hostile writers.[14]

> I would like to talk to you as an individual rather than in an official capacity. I want to give you my personal view as a fellow craftsman. It is your duty to spread the truth. If you do so you will relate that from 3,000 to 4,000 men, turning from their own leaders to the leadership of radicals and Communists, made an organized attack on the police of the District of Columbia. In this attack they injured a score of policemen. They overwhelmed the police and two rioters were killed. The officials of the District of Columbia demanded in writing to the President that being unable to preserve order in the Capital of the Nation troops should be sent to prevent further disorder and loss of life. The first duty of the President of the United States is to maintain order. He acted unhesitatingly. From the moment the troops entered the city not a shot was fired, not a man injured. Law and order were promptly restored. The great bulk of demonstrators, instead of being evacuated, fled the city. The[y] knew the consequences of their rioting. They were afraid to be brought before the proper tribunals. They beat it. There were thousands of good and innocent men among them. But this republic is founded on order and not upon mob attack on the police. If you do your duty you will tell these indisputable facts to the American people.

Similarly, when the American Civil Liberties Union filed a formal protest, another presidential secretary, Lawrence Richey, sent it to the chief of staff for comment.[15] Douglas MacArthur wrote:

> My own recommendation would be to ignore it. The signers thereto are all well-known, and some of them notorious exponents of various types of radicalism. It is useless to argue with them and anything that is said would be misconstrued, warped, and serve as an instrumentality in opposition to the present administration.

. . . The Civil Liberties Union have [sic] made frequent attacks upon the Army in every possible way. Their basic purpose, of course, is the destruction of all constituted authority. The War Department has long since made it a policy not to acknowledge any of the communications it receives from such a source.

Richey and the President followed MacArthur's advice. With advisors who thought that sophisticated New York writers could be swayed by Rotary rhetoric and that the ACLU was a bunch of anarchists, is it any wonder that the administration's public relations went awry?

Mimeographed copies of Attorney General Mitchell's report were given to the press on September 10, but the release date was the following Monday, which, not at all coincidently, was the opening day of the American Legion convention. The press, duller and more formally ethical then than now, respected the release date, although a friendly reporter tipped Pelham Glassford off to what was coming. A brief presidential statement accompanied the report, highlighting what Hoover called "the extraordinary proportion of criminal, communist and non-veteran elements amongst the marchers." It made the front pages all over the country—1069 WITH POLICE RECORDS, MANY REDS IN BONUS ARMY, MITCHELL REPORT ASSERTS was the *New York Times* headline—and reactivated the whole bonus controversy.[16] Of course, the Legionnaires would have stirred it up anyway, and perhaps the administration felt it should fire the first shot in the renewed propaganda war that was sure to come. The shot backfired: not only did it fail to inhibit the Legion's action and fail to narrow the growing credibility gap the administration was experiencing, but it also brought Pelham Glassford into the lists.

The police chief, except for a few guarded comments to reporters on the day of battle, had maintained a careful silence; as he wrote the friendly editor of a Washington scandal sheet in late August, "I am very hesitant to make any statements at this time, and have been very careful not to express any opinions." [17] At about the same time he turned down an invitation to address the National Convention of the American Legion. Externally at least, Glassford was being a good soldier. Behind the scenes, however, he was marshalling evidence for a sustained defense of his own position and an attack on the Commissioners and the administration. What he would have done had the administration kept its peace is, of course, pure conjecture, but I imagine he would have said little or nothing. The direct and implied criticism of him by the Attorney General, added to the resentment that he must have felt when the federal government took more testimony from his subordinates than from him, stung him to an immediate riposte.

Glassford's statement, which was also page one news, concentrated on two aspects of Mitchell's report: the statement that he had asked for troops, which the chief continued to deny, and the Attorney General's statistics alleging a high degree of criminality in the BEF, which Glassford countered by showing what offenses they had actually committed in the nation's capital. These statistics had been furnished to the Justice Department before the report was issued, but since they did not support the official thesis, Mitchell only alluded to them. The police data showed 341 arrests of "visiting veterans" prior to the day of the riots—that is, from the end of May to the end of July. All but a dozen of these were for minor offenses or no offense at all: 203 involved liquor, 101 investigation only (remember Marion Watkins), 12 for vagrancy and panhandling, 11 for parading, speaking, and passing out leaflets without a permit, 1 for not having a Washington, D.C., driver's license, and 1 hapless vet who was arrested on the awesome charge of "destroying government trees." The twelve truly criminal charges mostly involved physical violence against other veterans: there was one murder, seven men were arrested for assault, two for destroying private property, one for "permitting obscene and indecent acts," and one on a bad check charge. The *New York Times* caught the gist of his argument well with its headline—ACTUAL CRIMINALS IN BONUS ARMY 12 GLASSFORD ASSERTS. The police chief traded public recriminations with the District Commissioners and the Justice Department for a couple of days and then went back to running the police force.[18] But, he suspected correctly, his days in that job were numbered. His papers show an overwhelming amount of public approval, some of it from antiadministration Republicans. Since the chief was one of the authentic heroes of the Depression, his word in a hero-worshipping nation carried a good deal of weight. *Editor & Publisher,* not exactly a radical organ, spoke for much of the nation when it editorialized: "No one knows the BEF story as well as Gen. Glassford. His word is final." [19]

Meanwhile, the American Legion convention got underway at Portland, Oregon; many of the delegates slept on the 20,000 cots and sets of bedding provided at no cost by the army with congressional sanction. The more militant VFW convention, meeting earlier in the month in Sacramento, California, had reaffirmed its probonus stand, and censured the administration for "the unhumanitarian and un-American manner" in which the BEF was evacuated. The administration feared, and with good reason, that the much larger and more influential Legion might follow suit. The passage of a probonus resolution was a near certainty; at least thirty-five state Legion organizations had already gone on record favoring immediate payment. Forces led by Congressman Wright Patman, who had spoken to the VFW, were also pressing for a censure resolution at Portland. In addition, Patman was leading a campaign to break the power of the Legion oligarchy by electing an Oklahoma publisher, Raymond Fields, as national commander. "Among the higher-ups in the Legion," Patman had written before he left for the West Coast, "I will be just as welcome as a skunk." He felt that it was distinctly possible to "kick the old gang over" and "elect a former private national commander." As he explained it to a receptive Portland newspaperman, he and Fields had been fighting for the bonus and more democratic control of the Legion for some time. "[In 1930] they gagged us at Boston and wouldn't let us get on the floor. [In 1931] we thought we had it won at Detroit until President Hoover came there and some of the delegations disregarded their instructions. This time we believe we are going to win." [20]

The administration antibonus forces at the convention were led by Pat Hurley himself, with an assist from former national commander Hanford MacNider, who resigned as ambassador to Canada to participate in the 1932 campaign. It was clear from the beginning however that it was to be not only a bonus year, but a Democratic one as well in the normally Republican Legion. Josephus Daniels, Wilson's Secretary of the Navy, and soon to be FDR's ambassador to Mexico, took some thinly veiled slaps at the administration by attacking those who denounced veterans as "unpatriotic lobbyists," "raiders of the Treasury," or "Communists." Another Democratic stalwart, Boston's James Michael Curley, never one for subtlety, bluntly spoke of "victims . . . shot down like dogs in the Capital of the Nation." It was Floyd Gibbons, the flamboyant one-eyed Hearst war correspondent, who became the real spokesman for the antiadministration forces. At the National Commander's dinner, the war correspondent and the Secretary of War engaged in an acrimonious debate on a coast-to-coast hookup; Gibbons later presented his side in an address to the convention, a tearjerker which spoke of "five or seven thousand hungry ghosts of the glorious old American Expeditionary Force," while Hurley had to be satisfied with sending a mimeographed statement to each convention delegate, which "in the interest of truth and accuracy" recapitulated the administration line. Gibbons definitely had the better of the exchange: as Will Rogers noted, "Pat got away with his life but no votes." A censure resolution was forestalled, however, and was kept from the floor, much to the chagrin of Wright Patman. The Legion did come out for immediate cash payment by an overwhelming 1,167 to 109 roll call vote.[21]

The bonus itself was not an effective issue in the presidential campaign that year, for the simple reason that Franklin Roosevelt and Herbert Hoover each opposed paying it, and neither party platform had even mentioned it. Roosevelt, after being criticized by Republican orators for not making a public statement on the bonus during the campaign, came out against payment "until the government has a surplus," a position he would maintain after the election. On the bonus itself then, there was little to choose between the candidates. Hoover, however, had made himself the enemy of most American veterans by ordering the expulsion of the BEF and then, as Mencken put it, defaming them afterwards. In his *Memoirs,* the bitter ex-President wrote:

> The misrepresentation of the bonus incident for political purposes surpassed any similar action in American history. Not only did Roosevelt use the incident in the 1932 campaign, but Democratic orators continued to use it for twenty years after. . . . I was portrayed as a murderer and an enemy of the veterans. A large part of the veterans believe to this day that men who served their country in war were shot down in the streets of Washington by the Regular Army at my orders.

The historian must question Hoover's hyperbole. Many things have been more misrepresented during political campaigns, including Al Smith's subservience to the Pope. Besides, FDR himself never once mentioned the BEF during the campaign. Yet, Hoover's observation has a good deal of truth in it. The whole bonus march left a bad taste in the nation's mouth and certainly cost Hoover a great many votes. He would have been defeated if not a single veteran had come to Washington;

the bonus march just contributed an indeterminable minor fraction of the seven-million-vote victory margin that the Democratic candidate ran up that November.[22] Democratic partisans used the incident again and again; but the most damaging blows were struck by Pelham Glassford.

As we have seen, Glassford tried to go back to being a good police chief and, after his initial ripostes at the Mitchell report, kept his peace. To many in the administration, however, his very presence in Washington was an affront. On October 20, without any warning, the District Commissioners asked for, received, and accepted Glassford's resignation. What impelled the firing at that particular time—almost three months after the riot, more than a month after the controversy over the Mitchell report, and less than three weeks before the presidential election—remains obscure. There is, in the files of the District Commissioners, a letter from presidential secretary Walter Newton, dated October 13, forwarding a particularly intemperate complaint about Glassford from Congressman John G. Shafer (R.-Wis.) ending with the recommendation that "he should be kicked out of office and let him continue his cooperation with the bonus organization and the Democratic party." However logical the firing may have been—Glassford had felt that his days were numbered even before the riot—it was politically stupid. In the first place it seemed to most of those who were not Hoover partisans as a petty act against a man who had done an outstanding job. In the second place, it gave Glassford the freedom to attack the administration to his heart's content. And attack he did.[23]

His major salvo was a series of eight articles that were nationally syndicated by the Hearst newspapers and given front page play throughout the country, the last one appearing two days before the election. The articles were commissioned by William Randolph Hearst himself, acting through his Washington publisher, Eleanor "Cissy" Patterson. If the purpose and timing of the articles were not patent, Glassford spelled it out in a letter to Hearst later. (Hearst, somewhat typically, had not paid Glassford all the general thought he had coming.) "Election was fast approaching," Glassford reminded the publisher, "and there was very little time to delay if the articles were to have the intended political effect." Glassford received some professional help from the Hearst staff, but the bulk of the articles was his own work. They form a reasonably reliable narrative account of the whole bonus incident, but are definitely slanted to throw Herbert Hoover and all his political minions in the worst possible light. As an old soldier, Glassford could not bring himself to say much in criticism of the army. The headlines that accompanied "General Glassford's Story," as it was called, are perhaps the best summary: [24]

HOOVER'S REGIME SET BONUS ARMY RIOTING, SAYS GEN. GLASSFORD

SUPERIORS DENIED HIM SUPPORT IN B.E.F. CRISIS, SAYS GLASSFORD

GLASSFORD, HANDLING 2 ARMIES, HAMPERED BY OFFICIAL "SNIPING"

PRESIDENT AIDED REDS BY ATTACK ON B.E.F., GLASSFORD DECLARES

B.E.F.'S "DEATH MARCH" BEFORE THE CAPITOL PUT POLICE BOARD IN PANIC

COMMISSIONERS' MINDS "MADE UP" FOR THEM ON B.E.F., SAYS GLASSFORD

B.E.F. DEATHS BORN OF FEAR AND POLITICS

GEN. GLASSFORD UPSETS HOOVER ALIBIS ON RIOTS

The general also made some political appearances, most notably at a preelection mass meeting in Philadelphia. Although affecting a nonpartisan stance ("I am not in politics. I am neither a democrat, a republican, a socialist, nor a communist."), Glassford was in fact making an effective and somewhat demagogic attack on Herbert Hoover.[25]

I have been criticized in administration circles for too much lenience, too much hospitality, too much kindness towards these men, but in this policy I had taken a leaf from the book of Mr. Herbert Hoover in the humanitarian relief work he accomplished in Belgium and Russia. The outstanding difference in this case is that the relief was not for foreigners but for American citizens who had served their country in the greatest war in history, many of them decorated for valor.

. . . It was not my problem to solve the economic situation which brought these veterans to Washington: I was astonished that the Administration which has the problem of solving a serious nationwide economic problem applicable to 120 million people, should acknowledge its inability to solve this relatively insignificant one of less than 8,000 destitute veterans, by running them out of the District of Columbia at the point of the bayonet.

The President of the United States is traditionally and in fact the Commander-in-Chief of the Army and Navy. You Veterans who have borne arms in the defense of the country must still revere him as your supreme commander. He must stand in your minds for the high ideals of freedom and patriotism upon which this great nation was conceived by our forefathers. Armed with the most modern implements of warfare, the peacetime army of our present Commander-in-Chief, Herbert Hoover, on July 28th last, drove from the National Capital at the point of the bayonet the disarmed, disavowed and destitute army of Woodrow Wilson.

9

Franklin Roosevelt
and the Bonus

Since Congress had not been in session when the remnants
of the BEF had been expelled, there had been no coalescence
of congressional sentiment at the time. A few congressmen
made indignant statements to the press. Fiorello La Guardia
sent off a tempestuous telegram to Hoover insisting that "Soup
is cheaper than tear bombs and bread better than bullets in
maintaining law and order in these times of depression, unemployment and hunger" but most congressmen were more concerned with the impending election than with the battle of
Washington.[1] In early December, when the lame-duck Congress assembled during the uneasy and ill-tempered interregnum between the old order and the New Deal, few wanted
to rake up old bitternesses by asking embarrassing questions
about the battle of Washington. An exception to the rule was
crusty Senator Kenneth McKellar (D.-Tenn.), who introduced
a resolution calling for a committee of five senators to investigate the acts of the District Commissioners, Glassford, Hurley,
MacArthur, and all other officials, federal or district, involved
in "causing or planning or inciting or directing the attack on

211

the ex-service men and women and children . . . on July 28, 1932, and having been commonly called a riot." The Senator proposed that all committee sessions be public and included a set of twenty-two well-framed interrogatories about the causes, chronology, and constitutionality of the eviction. This was obviously not a matter the rest of the Senate wished to pursue, and McKellar's proposal was quickly shunted to the tame Military Affairs Committee, where it died quietly.[2]

The story was much the same in the lower house. Congressman Loring M. Black (D.-N.Y.) made a short speech in late December characterizing the expulsion of the BEF as the "greatest crime in history," and was particularly exercised that the administration had waited until the Congress had adjourned before moving. "Nobody in executive authority dared . . . to harass these men while Congress was in session." Black felt that the House should "ventilate" the whole affair, but neither he nor any other representative made any formal proposal.[3] Most of the bonus advocates seemed to feel that it was not good strategy to couple the continuing campaign for immediate cash payment with an investigation of the events of the past summer, which would probably alienate some of the Republican senators and representatives whose votes would be needed. Wright Patman, still the chief congressional voice of the average veteran, made this quite clear in a mid-December speech on a nationwide radio hookup. The Texan's arguments were much the same, but he not only chose not to mention the expulsion of the previous summer, but explicitly opposed any repetition of a bonus march, insisting that "a march on Washington by destitute veterans will be injurious to the cause of all veterans." [4] No veterans came that winter, although a group of Communist hunger marchers did put on a one-day demonstration in early December.[5]

By the time the new administration came into power, of course, the entire American economy seemed to be grinding to a halt. Full or partial payment of the bonus certainly would have been one way to inject a vast amount of purchasing power directly into the veins of the economy and one that would have involved an absolutely minimal administrative overhead. But it was a method never seriously considered by FDR or any of the leading New Dealers. To the President and his advisers, still embracing much of the conventional wisdom of the old order, the demands of the veterans for further benefits seemed like an unprincipled raid on the Treasury. Even those like Rex Tugwell and, later, Harry Hopkins, who were most committed to what we would call the welfare state, were less than sympathetic to special benefits for able-bodied veterans. Rather than prepay the bonus, the New Dealers instead proposed to cut severely existing benefits. During the campaign, and particularly in the Pittsburgh speech in which he reiterated his opposition to the bonus, Franklin Roosevelt had criticized the spendthrift Hoover administration and promised economy in government and a balanced budget.[6] The New Dealers, of course, outspent Hoover, and probably should have spent more than they did, but simultaneously with new spending programs the President proposed certain economies, economies that were directed at veterans' benefits and the salaries of government employees. In his very first use of the radio after the inaugural, FDR, appearing jointly with Louis Johnson, American Legion Commander, asked for support from American Legionnaires who knew "the meaning of sacrifice and who in every emergency have given splendid and generous service." [7] On March 10 he sent a message to Congress insisting on "drastic economies in government." Arguing, in words most reassuring to fiscal conservatives, that "too often in recent history liberal governments have been wrecked on rocks of loose fiscal policy," he called for "new legislation calling for broad principles for the granting of pensions and other veterans benefits . . . [and] relating to the salary of civil and military employees of the government . . . giving to the Executive the authority to prescribe the administrative details." [8]

Just what was encompassed by the casual phrase "administrative details" had been explained the previous evening at a White House conference for selected congressional leaders, presided over by the President and Lewis Douglas, his economy-minded budget director. Under the proposed legislation, most of the statutes concerning Spanish-American and World War pensions were simply repealed. Authority to decide just what classes of veterans should continue to receive pensions and how much each should draw was transferred from the Congress to the President, who was to be inhibited only by a very broad fiscal range—$6 and $275 a month were stipulated as minimum and maximum amounts. Douglas and General Hines, who continued as Veterans Administrator, estimated that they could save some $400 million to $460 million out of the nearly $900 million annual bill for veterans' benefits and indicated, roughly, where and how the cuts would come.[9] FDR was thus asking not only that the economy axe be liberally applied, but also that his authority be distinctly enlarged.

Debate commenced on both sides of the Capitol on March 11. In the House, the bill was reported out under a two-hour "gag" rule. Before the miniature debate began, the Democrats, who outnumbered the Republicans 310 to 117, met in caucus to discuss the measure. A motion to adopt the so-called Browning amendment, which would have limited cuts of existing pensions to 25 percent, passed, 174 to 112, but since it did not secure the two-thirds necessary to bind the Democrats, it insured that most Democrats would follow Roosevelt's lead, however reluctantly. The White House bill was introduced as "A Bill to Maintain the Credit of the United States Government," and drew its vocal support from two types of representative: those who wanted to stand by the President—("In Roosevelt I trust"—Congressman Edward A. Kenny [D.-N.J.])—and those who were for economy at all costs. These groups comprised a majority of each party as the measure passed, the very day it was introduced, 266 to 139. Of those opposed, almost two-thirds were Democrats, and most of the opposition from both sides of the aisle came from the hard-core veteran bloc, including a number of neopopulists and currency expanders, like Wright Patman and William Lemke (R.-N.D.). Joining them in opposition were some conservatives who felt concerned about the unprecedented peacetime delegation of power to the President.[10]

The more leisurely Senate took four days to dispose of the Economy Act and even found time for a brief public hearing on the morning of March 11. The Legion's chief lobbyist made a plea for "human lives and human happiness," warned against giving too much power to the President and above all asked for delay. In addition, the Legion got in touch with every post in the country and called for an "immediate barrage" of telegrams and other forms of pressure to blunt the economy offensive against established pensions. The pressure was not without effect. Senator Harry Ashurst (D.-Ariz.), for example, said he was being "swamped" with wires, but in reply noted that "a crisis of tremendous proportions" called for "sacrifices" from "all citizens," and asked his correspondents to have faith in FDR.[11]

> President Roosevelt is probably the best friend of the ex-service men ever in the White House. He has suffered and knows how to sympathize with suffering. Please assure veterans and all others to trust him.

When the talking stopped, the Senate overwhelmingly passed the Economy Act on March 15 by a vote of 62 to 13; it received the approval of a majority of both parties. The key vote, however, was on the so-called Connolly Amendment, which would have limited the cut to 25 percent for pensions involving service-connected disabilities. The Legion, by this time, was willing to accept a 25 percent cut across the board, and supported the amendment. It lost, but the vote, 28 to 45, is the

best indicator of proveteran sentiment in the Senate.¹² The
Legion Commander, Louis A. Johnson, later to be an ineffective Assistant Secretary of War and a befuddled Secretary of
Defense, used all his political skills effectively to make much
of the pension cut illusory. The very day the bill passed the
Senate, Johnson, who had not publicly participated in the
hopeless fight against the bill, pledged the support of the
Legion to the Commander in Chief, declared that it had "every
faith in the discretion, fairness and the justice with which the
president will deal with the problem" and offered the collective pension experience of the Legion to assist in working out
the new regulations. Budget Director Douglas drafted a series
of executive orders putting into effect the cuts he had envisaged, but congressional uproar at hardships wrought by the
reductions and total eliminations continued throughout the
hundred days that Congress remained in session, as the Legion
kept bringing individual hardship cases to the attention of
friendly senators and representatives.

The congressional protests were not only frequent, they were
often bitter. Hamilton Fish (R.-N.Y.), of all people, invoked
the rhetoric of William Jennings Bryan to depict "the war
veteran crucified on a cross of deflation and economy," but
when his colleague, Louis McFadden (R.-Pa.) managed to
find a tie-up between the Economy Act, going off the gold
standard, and an international Jewish conspiracy, Fish re-
buked him. Pointing out that the Protocols of the Elders of
Zion, which McFadden was paraphrasing, were obvious for-
geries, Fish went on to insist that "this revolution is the
product of the brain trust, practically all of whom are gentiles.
It is just another brain storm of the brain trust." On the
Democratic side, Wright Patman spoke for many who felt
that the budget director and others in the administration were
favoring Wall Street at the expense of the people. As far as
the Texan was concerned the real cause of the unbalanced
budget was the failure to tax properly the incomes and assets
of the rich.

If the tax laws are not going to be enforced against the Mellons, Morgans and Mitchells, the Federal penitentiary doors at Atlanta, Ga., should be opened and Al Capone released.

Responding to the congressional unrest and the pressure groups, the White House made a formal statement on May 11, saying that as a result of conferences between Roosevelt, Douglas and Louis Johnson, service-connected disability pensions would be revised upwards. Many of the cuts were quickly rescinded or modified, and Congress itself passed liberalizing legislation in June. The final cut was less than $300 million, with most of it coming from the total elimination of almost all non-service-connected disability pensions stemming from World War I. The veterans' advocates had certainly suffered a setback, but it was not the "rout" of the veterans' lobby that some historians have described.[13] In this climate of economy it is understandable that the immediate payment of the bonus, such a burning issue the year before, was hardly discussed. Wright Patman continued to advocate it, of course, but the bill could not muster the required signatures for a discharge petition. The only bonus vote of the session was forced by Senator Robinson (R.-Ind.), who tried to put a bonus amendment onto an agricultural relief bill, but the rider was defeated, 28 to 60.[14] Yet despite the general lack of interest, there was a bonus march in 1933, a bonus march quite different in composition, reception, and impact from that of the BEF, but a bonus march nevertheless.

A case can be made—and Republican orators often made it in the early years of the New Deal—for the proposition that the administration of Herbert Hoover was more generous to the veteran than the New Deal was. In terms of the national veterans' bill, the last Hoover year, fiscal 1933, saw a level of expenditure not again reached until 1945, except, of course, for bonus-swollen 1936. But even while he was cutting their pensions, Franklin Roosevelt remained a popular figure, while

Hoover, during the 1930s at least, remained essentially a villain. Presidential popularity is not just a matter of legislation or arithmetic; it involves style,. what we now call "image making," and above all, a sense of what the public will or will not tolerate. The American people were a mystery to Herbert Hoover; to Franklin Roosevelt they were like friends and neighbors whom he understood quite well. This difference is nowhere better illustrated than in their treatment of the bonus marchers and the bonus question generally. Each opposed the bonus, for essentially the same reasons. Yet Hoover's performance was one of tragic ineptitude while Roosevelt hardly struck a false note. It is true that Hoover's bonus march was by far the more serious and that Roosevelt was able to profit by observing Hoover's blunders. However, it is inconceivable that Roosevelt could have done as badly as Hoover had, while the Quaker President never seems to have understood what he did wrong.

The only real clues that I have found to Roosevelt's 1932 attitude—apart from his quick reactions to requests for New York State aid—are in a reminiscence by Rex Tugwell and in a letter FDR had written late in the 1932 campaign to a correspondent who had asked him about the BEF.

As Tugwell tells it, he happened to have an appointment with Franklin Roosevelt on the morning of July 29. He entered the candidate's bedroom at Hyde Park about 7:30 A.M. and found him, characteristically, in bed with the *New York Times* spread out around him. Roosevelt said that the pictures of MacArthur's troops driving the veterans from Washington looked like "scenes from a nightmare." Tugwell concluded that "if Roosevelt had had any doubts about the outcome of the election, I am certain he had none after reading *The Times* that day." It was then, according to Tugwell, that FDR decided to talk no more about Hoover, as "there was no need now." In the letter, written three months later, Roosevelt made it clear that he would have handled things differently.[15]

I was very much distressed at the unfortunate and difficult situation relative to the veterans in Washington. I think that a great deal could have been done to lessen the number that came and I feel also that a great many of them could have been employed in line with the thought that you suggest—in reforestation projects, or could have possibly have been induced to settle on subsistence farms if they had any farming experience.

In May 1933, Roosevelt's hypothetical intentions were put to the acid test: the test of reality.

The bonus march that developed that year was planned rather than semispontaneous and had a decidedly Communist origin. The key organization was the Veterans National Liaison Committee, which had at least two open Communists on its seven-man executive committee and was not at all hostile to the Communist party. Its leaders included George Alman and George D. Brady of the old BEF, and Emanuel Levin, the peacetime marine who remained the key Communist party functionary for veterans' affairs, seconded by Harold Hickerson, another open Communist. The group, formed in December 1932, had headquarters in Washington and was run on a shoestring. For its first month-and-a-half of existence, it collected only $168.59 and, at the end of January, had a working balance of just $7.68. At that time, the group envisaged a Washington convention in mid-April, but this was later postponed to mid-May. By early April the *Daily Worker* was calling for all veterans to march on Washington for an assemblage to begin on May 12. (The earlier date might have interfered with May Day parades; there was, after all, just so much Stalinist manpower to go around.) Once it was publicized, the new march was quickly disavowed, not only by the leaders of the established veterans' organizations, but also by the two most prominent BEF leaders. W. W. Waters, speaking to a businessmen's group in Omaha, insisted that there is no need for it now. The B.E.F., though it did not get the bonus, served its deeper purpose. We now have a government back there that is recognizing and attempting to improve the unemployment situation.

Similarly his rival, Royal W. Robertson, proclaimed that the veterans were standing "behind President Roosevelt though he signed the economy bill." [16]

Toward the end of April a non-Communist group whose most conspicuous leader was Harold B. Foulkrod, another old BEFer, was calling on "Colonel" Louis Howe, Roosevelt's chief secretary. The committee threatened to march on Washington in two weeks unless the administration met its demands, which included immediate cash payment, super job preferences for veterans, and the firing of Douglas MacArthur and General Hines of the VA. The canny Howe saw them, was sympathetic, but promised nothing.[17] Probably reading about this sympathetic reception, a far cry from the year previous, the Brady-Levin group wrote Howe demanding that the veterans coming in mid-May be treated "as any other group holding a Congress or Conference at the capital," and that the government foot the bill. This was not as unprecedented or far-fetched as it has seemed to some; Congress had appropriated funds for the living expenses of visiting French veterans, had subsidized American Legion conventions, and provided rifles and ammunition for target practice groups. After some haggling the administration agreed to defray most expenses and it was decided to house the veterans at Fort Hunt, Virginia, about ten miles from downtown Washington, thus putting into effect one of the suggestions Glassford and Hines had made to Hurley and Hoover. As early as May 4 planning meetings were held in General Hines' office, and two days later the Veterans Administrator suggested to the President that he use the brand new Civilian Conservation Corps to absorb some of the surplus veterans.

Both the Communist and non-Communist groups made extravagant claims about the number of veterans they could produce. Foulkrod ranted about 50,000 while the Communists, less specific, talked about many thousands. The administration was prepared to take care of about 10,000. Some unknown bureaucrat even came up with a formula of twenty "delegates" from each congressional district—that would have totaled 8,700—plus "such other independent marchers or delegates as were actually enroute May 6, 1933." [18] Although some had come as early as May 7, most of the 3,000 who finally showed up arrived on May 10, 11 and 12. Despite a great deal of talk about how tough they were going to be ("no matter how many police are in front of the White House we will walk in"—George Alman), the Communist-led veterans were quite docile. After registering at a tent set up near the site of the 1932 rioting in the federal triangle, they allowed government officials to scrutinize their discharge papers and then boarded buses to Fort Hunt. Most of them came from New York and other eastern centers by hired trucks and buses, although some did hitchhike and ride freights. A group of about 200, however, followed the leadership of Foulkrod and refused, for a time, to conform to the government's regimen. In a kind of nostalgia, they tried to bivouac where the BEF had, but the police made them keep moving, and even the weather seemed to be against them—it rained heavily every night they stayed away. Finally, on May 14, all but a handful of the right-wingers decided that dry beds and three square meals were more important than ideology and joined the others in Virginia.[19]

There had been something dramatic and quixotic about the first bonus march; the second attracted little attention. A *New York Times* reporter wrote of "a bedraggled group of unemployed ex-servicemen, attracted here by the promise of something to eat, a place to sleep, an opportunity to air their grievances at a convention."

There were those with other motives. The Communist

leaders hoped to make recruits and embarrass the administration, while some of the non-Communist promoters must have hoped, somehow, to make a good thing out of organizing veterans. At least one of the leaders of the 1933 march got a steady job; a year later George Brady was an assistant project auditor with the PWA in California. When he heard of another impending march he volunteered his services to help General Hines and Louis Howe head it off. But for most of the 3,000, who were neither Communists nor promoters, it was something to do. Many more were probably attracted by the newspaper stories than by the rather flimsy organizational apparatus.[20]

As the marchers assembled, Roosevelt solved the dispersal problem that was sure to follow. On May 11, apparently following the advice of Veterans Administrator Hines, and overriding the objections of CCC Director Robert Fechner, he signed an Executive Order which authorized the enrollment of 25,000 veterans in the newly formed Civilian Conservation Corps, which was otherwise restricted to the 16–25-year-old age bracket. Those actually in residence at Fort Hunt were to be given priority; those who enrolled received the standard CCC stipend: food, lodging, a clothing allowance, and a dollar a day. The Communists were furious and denounced what they liked to call Roosevelt's "forced labor camps," but the rank and file bonus marchers seemed to like it. As the convention broke up, 2,657 were enrolled in the forest army; the other 400 were given transportation home. In addition to his positive acts, Roosevelt was very careful not to give the wrong impression. His secretary, "Missy" Le Hand explained his refusal to make the ceremonial draw for the Davis Cup by pointing out that with the bonus marchers in town, "he thinks it wiser for him not to do things of this kind." [21]

The whole encampment—which lasted until May 22—seemed to demonstrate the essentially benevolent image the New Dealers so much wanted to foster. The men were treated as citizens rather than as a mob. The food was plain but plentiful: a typical day's menu consisted of

Breakfast:	oranges, boiled eggs, potatoes, bread, butter and coffee;
Lunch:	baked ham, boiled potatoes, green peas, rice pudding, bread, butter, coffee;
Supper:	sliced bologna, potato salad, apple butter, bread, coffee.

One newspaperman reported the following dialogue between two veterans wondering at the difference between conditions at Anacostia in 1932 and Fort Hunt in 1933: [22]

"What is this bird Roosevelt up to?"

"All I know is he's a 'hooman bein.' "

The one breach of the peace that occurred came not as a result of governmental coercion, but grew out of the animosities between the "left wing" and "right wing" groups. On May 13, before the Foulkrod group agreed to come in out of the rain, Emanuel Levin went out to speak to them. Before he could say anything he was rushed with shouts of "Kill the Red!" "Lynch him!" and "Down with Levin!" The Communist leader was quickly surrounded by protective capitalist policemen and whisked to safety.[23]

The truly dramatic event of the 1933 march was a peaceful one—the visit of the First Lady, Eleanor Roosevelt. A certain amount of myth has come to surround this event, and the record should be set straight. Professor Alfred B. Rollins, Jr., in his too-admiring biography of Louis Howe, has written that [24]

[Howe] played his master card one rainy, muddy spring afternoon. He innocently asked Eleanor Roosevelt to take him for a drive.

As they rode toward Fort Hunt, Louis explained that she was going to visit with the veterans for the afternoon. At the camp, Louis pushed her out to go it alone.

This lovely little story is another building block in the image of the innocent Eleanor Roosevelt, good at heart, but not so strong in the head, being manipulated by others—a legend Mrs. Roosevelt herself helped perpetuate. However true this may have been during World War I and the early 1920s, by 1933 she was a politically sophisticated woman who was manipulated by no one, least of all Louis Howe, who was about as subtle as a bulldozer. Howe and press secretary Steve Early had already made one inspection of Fort Hunt on May 13. In the following days, a persistent rumor sprang up and was published, to the effect that the President himself would soon pay the veterans a visit. Apparently FDR had no intention of going; yet he almost surely remembered that one of the complaints made against Hoover was that he had never even gone to see the bonus army. Probably at her husband's request, it was announced to the press on May 15 that Mrs. Roosevelt intended to visit the camp. The visit took place the next day and was a smashing success.

She and Howe drove out just before supper; she trudged through the mud that the heavy May rains had left, stuck her head into tents and her nose into pots. Then she led the men in singing "There's a Long, Long Trail," and made a short speech in which he reminisced about her canteen work and hospital visits as wife of the Assistant Secretary of the Navy during World War I. Then she concluded with an antiwar note:

I never want to see another war. I would like to see that every one had fair consideration, and I will always be grateful to those who served their country. I hope we will never have to ask such service again and I hope that you will carry on in peace times as you did in the war days, for that is the duty of every patriotic American.

This was followed by a Negro veteran's rendition of "Mother Machree," after which the First Lady returned to the White House.[25]

The veterans were so pleased with the President and his wife that FDR was elected an honorary member of their encampment. Three days later a group was permitted to march from the Washington Monument right up to the gates of the White House. Roosevelt allowed a delegation to come inside and spoke with them for twenty minutes. Even though he reiterated his opposition to paying the bonus, the meeting was friendly.[26]

There were, of course, some discordant notes. An earlier march of a dozen "right wing" irreconcilables was prevented by the police from picketing the White House, and a number of the "left" opponents of the New Deal used the occasion to try to make political hay. A Farmer-Labor Congressman, Francis H. Shoemaker of Minnesota, told one group of marchers: [27]

> You just got what you voted for. They tell you to come to Washington as often as you please, but don't come inside the city. You fought for democracy, but got influenza, prohibition and Hoover. Now you have a new deal, a raw deal I call it.

From the conservative side of the House, Hamilton Fish was upset that the administration was willing to parley with known Communists. Pointing out that 98 percent of the veterans were "loyal and patriotic," he characterized the Veterans National Liaison Committee as "inspired and led by communists" and insisted that "the great veterans organizations . . . are disgusted at the action of the White House in recognizing a red organization." Wright Patman also deplored the Communist presence, but spoke for the majority when he argued that

> we are facing a condition. . . . if the veterans want to come here, and they are coming here, I insist that it is much better for them to come as good veterans from all sections of the country . . . say their pieces—in other words get it out of their system—. . . and peaceably go back home.

Opposition was again raised in Congress in mid-June, when legislation legalizing the money already expended to pay the veterans' expenses—nearly $40,000—was pushed through just before adjournment. Congressman John Taber (R.-N.Y.), who spent a legislative lifetime opposing expenditure in almost any form, protested that it was an illegal expenditure, but most of his colleagues did not agree. With that fiscal sleight of hand that so infuriated their opponents, the New Dealers found a way to use nonappropriated funds to pay the veterans' bills: the money was taken from a "Recreation Fund" which Congress had previously set up with the profits made by the soldier newspaper, *Stars and Stripes,* during World War I.[28]

Although certainly not one of the major accomplishments of the fabulous "hundred days," the whole bonus episode shows the Roosevelt-New Deal touch at its best. It managed to maintain its basic principle (opposition to prepayment of the bonus), the public peace, and at the same time probably made "believers" out of many sincere bonus advocates. No one could reasonably charge the administration with either brutality or indifference on the one hand or extravagance on the other. Wherever it came from, the $40,000 was indeed a small expenditure. In view of the results obtained, the handling of the bonus march of 1933 must be set down as a minor victory for New Deal policy.

The bonus issue, of course, just would not die. Patman again took his case for immediate payment and currency expansion to the American Legion convention, held in Chicago in early October. He was struggling not only against the Legion hierarchy but also against the President himself. Franklin Roosevelt made an appearance before the Legionnaires, and it was a virtuoso performance. In contrast to Herbert Hoover's lackluster showing at Detroit a year earlier, the new President scored a personal triumph. The burden of his speech—Rosenman entitles it "A Call to War Veterans to Rally to the Colors in a Peacetime Sacrifice"—was a doctrine antipathetical to the very existence of the Legion. In the key passages of the speech, FDR laid down two basic principles to govern veterans' benefits. The first was, within the American experience, axiomatic: "the Government has a responsibility for and toward those who suffered injury or contracted disease while serving in its defense." The second principle, however, set definite limits on that responsibility.

> No person because he wore a uniform, must thereafter be placed in a special class of beneficiaries over and above all other citizens. The fact of wearing a uniform does not mean that he can demand and receive from his Government a benefit which no other citizen receives. It does not mean that because a person served in the defense of his country, performed a basic obligation of citizenship, he should receive a pension from his Government because of a disability incurred after his service had terminated.

To these principles, which were sound "nineteenth-century" liberal doctrine, Roosevelt added a third, which, it seems to me, is one of the first presidential endorsements, however cautious and qualified, of what we all now call the welfare state.

> The time has come, I believe, for us to add a third [principle]. There are many veterans of our wars to whom disability and sickness unconnected with war service have come. To them the

Federal Government owes the application of the same broad rule or principle which it has laid down for the relief of other cases of involuntary need or destitution.

In other words, if the individual affected can afford to pay for his own treatment he cannot call on any form of Government aid. But if he has not the wherewithal to take care of himself, it is, first of all, the duty of the community in which he lives to take care of him, and, next, it is the duty of the State in which he lives. Only if under these circumstances his own community and his own State are unable, after reasonable effort, to care for him, then, and then only, should the Federal Government offer him hospitalization and care, and the Federal Government stands ready to do that.

The bitter pill that lay at the heart of this doctrine—the veteran is, essentially, just another citizen—was sugar-coated with thick layers of presidential charm and blarney. With that casual way of his, FDR evoked memories of their common war service ("I participated with you, not only in this country but also on the North Sea, and in the Channel, and on the actual fighting front in France." "You and I who served in the World War."); their common age ("My, you are a young-looking bunch."); and their almost reflexive patriotism ("You who wore the uniform . . . I have called to the colors again. As your Commander-in-Chief and your comrade, I am confident that you will respond."). With this kind of performance, whatever chance the bonus forces might have had disappeared. The Legion convention stood by the President, even though it hurt a little, and Patman's resolution didn't even come to a vote on the floor.[29]

When Congress reconvened, in January 1934, Patman's bonus bill was still in committee. A discharge petition had been placed at the Speaker's desk the previous April by Ernest Lundeen, a Minnesota Farmer-Labor representative, but it was far short of the required 145 signatures. (As late as January 9, only 54 names had been affixed.) Few Democrats wanted to push a measure opposed by the President, who made his position quite clear in a semi-public memorandum to Speaker Henry T. Rainey: [30] "I [will] veto the bill, and I don't care to whom you tell this."

Ironically, Wright Patman himself did not sign the discharge petition for his own bill until February 20, almost ten months after Lundeen had deposited it. His was signature 128, and the last seventeen signatures were affixed that day. The pressures on House Democrats must have been almost unbearable; they all faced an election that November, and the bonus was clearly a popular issue to which many of them were individually and publicly committed. Yet the opposition stemming from the other end of Pennsylvania Avenue, from a President whose power and popularity were still waxing, was a powerful deterrent. The bill came up for debate under a most restrictive rule on March 12. The House voted discharge, 313 to 104, debated the bill and passed it, 295 to 125, within a few hours. While the debate, described by the *New York Times* as "disorderly," clearly shows the uneasiness felt by many Democrats in deserting the President, the administration wisely relaxed party discipline. Joseph W. Byrns (D.-Tenn.), the Majority Leader, made this clear to obviously relieved Democrats by saying:

> I hold no criticism of any Member of this House for whatever action he may take with reference to this bill. That is a matter upon which each individual Member must vote according to the dictates of his conscience and his judgment.

Besides, it was fairly clear that the bill had little chance in the Senate.[31]

While the bonus bill lay dormant in the Senate—and partially because it lay dormant in the Senate—the third and final bonus army moved on Washington. There had been rumors about it all year. Much of the agitation came from the special CCC camps for veterans, where the payment of the bonus must have been topic "A" in bull sessions and day-dreams. In March, Wright Patman had forestalled one such march. In a telegram which he published in the *Congressional Record,* the Texan argued that a march of any kind would be "very detrimental" to the passage of his bill. In addition, he pointed out that a march might seriously compromise not only the "rights of veterans participating but also the rights of veterans who do not participate and dependents of those who are dead." [32]

These sentimental arguments, which moved some veterans, had no effect on the Communists, who were again the chief instigators of the 1934 march, as they had been the previous year. This third bonus march was the smallest, the most Communist-dominated, and the least noticed.

Since, according to Hegel, the owl of Minerva rises only at dusk, it should come as no surprise that the arrangements were more efficient than ever before. Although Louis Howe continued to have an interest in the handling of the situation, the arrangements were supervised by Harry L. Hopkins, the Federal Relief Administrator, whose agency picked up the $30,000 tab. (At the time of the 1933 march, he was still a relief official in New York State.) Hopkins followed the prece-dents of the year before: the men were put up at Fort Hunt and allowed to run their own show. As in 1933, they were given time on a national radio network, and on May 12, three of their leaders broadcast appeals for veterans to come to Washington. Partially because Hopkins provided typewriters and a mimeograph machine and the veterans used them to put out a camp paper, we know more about the 1934 march than about that of 1933.[33]

Just under 1,500 veterans participated; 127 of them were members of the Workers' Ex-Serviceman's League, which is probably a good indicator of the incidence of Communists in

the 1934 group—about one in eleven. The leadership, however, was heavily Communist: in addition to Levin and
Hickerson who were holdovers from the year before, there
were Peter Cacchione, later one of the party's three elected
councilmen from New York City, who served as chairman of
the resolutions committee; H. E. Briggs, the "fighting vet"
of the *Daily Worker,* who ran the camp paper; and a number
of others. Honored guests included party bigwigs Israel Amter
and James W. Ford. In the fact of almost total Communist
domination of the convention proceedings, many of the veterans in residence did the one thing the party was most adamant
against—they enrolled in the CCC. ("Keep away from the
CCC camps," warned James W. Ford, "they are the forerunner
of Fascism.") Almost 600 signed up for the forest army and
some 565 were accepted.

As an exercise in agitation the 1934 march was almost a total
failure: the encampment, which lasted from May 12 to May
27, was only twice considered "fit to print," in each case in
small items on the inside pages of the *New York Times.*
Despite the standard equation of Communists with disorder,
the red-led veterans were as good as boy scouts, and much more
orderly, say, than the same number of American Legionnaires.
When original BEFer R. B. Ellison, one of the organizers of
the Khaki Shirts, called for picketing in downtown Washington, the Communist leader Cacchione denounced activism:

> When anyone advocates direct action, LOOK OUT! We have studied
> and conferred night and day on ways to get this bill out of the
> Committee, and we have good reason to believe we may be able
> to do it. Remember, Comrades, we didn't get food, shelter and
> transportation through DIRECT ACTION. . . . Remember Govern-
> ment agents are in our midst. Do nothing that would cause us to
> lose the respect of those millions back home.

A similar denunciation of militance came from Emanuel
Levin, who insisted that "we don't want to provoke a situa-

tion. No demonstration just for the sake of a demonstration." [34]

After the veterans left, some of the top administrators were fearful lest the "conventions" become a regular occurrence. Robert Fechner, a former AFL official who had little use for ex-servicemen, was particularly bitter. [35] The CCC head wrote Louis Howe:

> It is my opinion that a feeling generally prevails among War Veterans throughout the country that if a sufficient number of them congregate in Washington they can get almost anything they demand so far as the CCC is concerned.

Relief Administrator Harry Hopkins was apparently of a similar mind, but instead of writing complaining notes he set up machinery which effectively forestalled future organized gatherings. Under his new regulations, any homeless veteran who came to the capital would be shipped out to one of the decentralized transient camps of the FERA (later WPA). During late 1934, 1935, and early 1936, some 10,000 veterans were peacefully removed from Washington by that process. Wright Patman would later claim that the Roosevelt administration had shown "hospitality" to more than 18,500 bonus-seeking veterans during the first three years of the New Deal. This figure, like most crowd statistics, is somewhat swollen; 14,000 is probably a much sounder guess. Even the lower figure, however, represents a mass movement of considerable proportions. That almost all of these veterans have been ignored by historians is an eloquent tribute to the skill of New Deal bureaucrats, for the down-and-out veteran in search of his bonus was an embarrassment to the New Deal, and the less people noticed, the better the New Dealers liked it. [36]

The bonus, however, was an embarrassment that would not stay shoved out of sight. The still tractable Congress adjourned in mid-June, and the Senate, as predicted, had failed to act on Patman's measure. So once again, that fall, the fight was taken to the Legion convention, which was definitely in a bonus mood. FDR, not wishing to break a lance in a lost cause, sent a message which neither mentioned the bonus nor called for sacrifices. Former Commander Louis Johnson tried vainly to stem the tide by pointing out that the nation was "well along the road" to recovery and urged his comrades: "Don't rock the boat." But the Legion wanted the boat rocked, and Legionnaire Wright Patman was there to rock it as he made the chief speech in favor of his resolution, which recommitted the Legion to work for immediate cash payment of the bonus. It passed by an overwhelming vote of 987 to 183. The language of the resolution is of some interest:

> *Resolved,* that since the Government of the United States is now definitely committed to the policy of spending additional sums of money for the purpose of hastening recovery from the present economic crisis, the American Legion recommends the immediate cash payment . . . as a most effective means to that end.

What the Legion was saying was that since the ideal of a balanced budget was clearly out the window as far as the administration was concerned, the veterans were no longer willing to go along with the restraints which they had accepted a year before. Not unreasonably, many felt that while other segments of the population were getting more, the veterans were being asked to forego long-standing demands. However the leaders of the Legion may have felt during the crisis year of 1933, by late 1934 they were in no way willing to accept the doctrine that the veteran was just another citizen.[37]

This new mood was clearly demonstrated in the new Congress, with its lop-sided Democratic majorities—319 to 113 in the House, and 69 to 27 in the Senate—which convened in January 1935. That the mood was national is suggested by the fact that no fewer than twenty-seven state legislatures memorialized Congress to pass a bonus bill. It was very early apparent that some kind of bonus bill would pass the Congress, despite continued opposition from the White House. The questions were:

1. What kind of bonus bill would be passed?
2. Would the President veto the bill or just allow it to become law without his signature?
3. If there was a veto, would it stand up?

Although there were a number of bonus bills introduced on both sides of the Capitol, the real choice was between two House measures: the Patman bill (still, symbolically, H.R. 1) and a measure authored by a former Patman supporter, Fred M. Vinson (D.-Ky.). The Patman bill, like most of the Texan's other measures, had a double purpose that was clearly indicated in its title: "To provide for immediate cash payment . . . and for controlled expansion of the currency." The controlled expansion was to be governed by a complicated formula by which the volume of currency was tied, in good populist fashion, to commodity prices. Vinson's bill, on the other hand, merely provided for payment, although here, too, there was a certain amount of complication. Instead of cash, the veterans were to be issued negotiable bonds which, if held until 1945, would accrue interest at 3 percent. Everyone assumed, correctly as it turned out, that almost all the veterans would immediately cash in their bonds. It is not clear why the extra complication was resorted to, since it would have been easier and cheaper to issue checks. Probably the bonds were to make the method of paying the bonus look more respectable; but behind the facade of Vinson's bonds was exactly the same kind of money that would have paid the bonus had the Patman bill passed. Vinson's bill clearly offended fiscal conservatives less, and his sharp break here from the inflationist ranks seems to have been a crucial event in his career: three years later Roosevelt put him on the bench, he held a number of key administrative posts during World War II, became Secretary of the Treasury in Truman's administration, and ended by becoming the least distinguished Chief Justice of this century. It is instructive to note that Patman, with much more legislative skill and ingenuity, was debarred from such a career by his adherence to unorthodox monetary views.

The House Ways and Means Committee, naturally, approved the more conservative measure, but, in a complex and permissive parliamentary situation, the Patman bill was substituted for the Vinson bill on the floor of the House by the eyelash-close vote of 207 to 204. The vote almost defies detailed analysis, because some members who opposed the bonus voted for the motion which favored Patman's expansionist method of payment. This devious behavior was based on the correct assumption that the Texan's bill would be less likely to command the two-thirds vote necessary to override the probable veto. As Vinson warned Patman and his followers in the debate:

> I say to you, that unless you divorce currency expansion from cash payment you will have to go back and tell the boys, "Well we fought a good fight, we did the best we could, but you haven't got the money yet."

Once the House had decided between bills, the vote was a foregone conclusion. The Patman bill with its currency-expanding provisions passed on March 22 by 319 to 90, comfortably above the two-thirds required to negate a veto. More than a month passed before the Senate acted, a month in which the Legion hierarchy lobbied strenuously to dump the purely inflationist aspects and was highly critical of Legionnaire-Congressman Patman. The Texan naturally returned the compliment, and the fact that the Legion Commander that year was Frank A. Belgrano, a vice president of the Bank of America, called forth populist scorn about "Belgrano's banker bill" (i.e., the Vinson bill which the Legion chieftains preferred). But the maneuvering of the Legion and other elements of the veterans' lobby was more than matched by the counter-maneuvers of the administration leaders in the Senate. The whole issue of the Vinson bill versus the Patman bill was fought out again, with conservative Missouri Democrat Bennett Clark acting as floor manager for the Legion-backed version. Again the Patman bill won, 52 to 35. Its victory was tainted, however, by the votes of thirteen senators who voted against its enactment later that same day. Twelve of the thirteen were Democrats, and almost all of them were dyed-in-the-wool administration men, including the majority leader, Joseph T. Robinson. As *Time* magazine later analyzed it: "Leader Robinson and a little band of devoted Roosevelt followers grimly voted for what they least of all wanted—greenbacks—so that the veto could be sustained."

The Patman bill passed the Senate, 55 to 33, but there were clearly more than enough votes to sustain the veto that most expected. It is a very interesting question whether a veto of a more conservative bonus measure—like the Vinson bill—would have been sustained. While no clear answer can be given to such a hypothetical question, it is obvious that the vote would have been much closer. Bennett Clark thought, before the event, that six or eight additional Senate votes to override could have been rounded up for the Vinson bill.[38] In any event, it is quite clear that, whatever his reasons, Franklin Roosevelt wanted to make a 1935 veto of the bonus bill stick, even though he must have known that the issue would not die and that, in the following election year, the pressures on Congress would become much stronger. Perhaps he wanted the bonus paid in an election year; perhaps he wanted to improve his batting average with Congress, which had successfully overridden only one veto in the previous session (but that one involved additional benefits for veterans). Regardless of why he did it—and the President's motives were often masked from even his closest associates—Roosevelt made a real production out of his 1935 bonus veto.[39]

He asked Samuel Rosenman to come down from New York, where he sat on the state supreme court, to help draft the veto message, the first time since 1932 campaign that "Sammy the Rose" had been so employed. After the message had been drafted, he arranged not only to deliver it in person before a joint session of Congress, but also to have it broadcast from coast to coast, the first veto message thus transmitted. An examination of the message, as well as the circumstances surrounding its delivery, makes it clear that the President aimed his words not at the crowded House chamber before him, but at the nationwide radio audience.

It was a temperate, reasonable message of some four thousand words, aimed at fence-sitters and neutrals rather than at partisans. Roosevelt began by talking casually about a recent White House visit by Wright Patman and a delegation of congressmen to talk for the bill: "as I told the gentlemen . . . I have never doubted the good faith" of congressional bonus advocates. He then reviewed the history of the bonus from 1918 and insisted that "a settlement was made in 1924" and that that settlement should be left alone. The Patman bill, he argued, meant paying $1.6 billion more than the present value of the bonus certificates, and, using terms deplored by the veterans' lobby, characterized this sum as a new "gratuity or bounty."

He then examined the stated reasons for passing the bill, citing its preamble which argued that payment of the bonus would increase purchasing power, provide relief, lighten the burden of the cities, counties and states, would not create any additional debt, and would be an effective way of spending money to hasten recovery. The spending of the bonus money, FDR admitted, would "result in some expansion of retail trade," but would not, he maintained, "justify the expectations that have been raised by those who argue for it." The relief arguments the President answered by reiterating the principle he had laid down to the Legion in 1933: no "able-bodied citizen should be accorded . . . treatment different from that accorded to other citizens who did not wear a uniform." "Is it not better," he asked, "to treat every able-bodied American alike?"

The assertion that payment of the certificates would not create an additional debt, Roosevelt countered with reasonably conventional notions of "sound finance." Although he admitted that the $2.2 billion expenditure would not, of itself, bankrupt the country, he professed to believe that paying the veterans

> by this deceptively easy method of payment will raise similar demands for the payment of claims of other groups. It is easy to see the ultimate result of meeting recurring demands by issuance of Treasury notes. It invites an ultimate reckoning in uncontrollable prices and in the destruction of the value of savings, that will strike most cruelly those like the veterans who seem to be temporarily benefited. The first person injured by sky-rocketing prices is the man on a fixed income. Every disabled veteran on pension or allowance is on a fixed income. This bill favors the able-bodied veteran at the expense of the disabled veteran.

There followed a little homily against "printing-press money" and a denial that the government was obligated to pay the bonus before 1945. He then attacked at some length the final claim for the bill, that it would be an effective way of hastening recovery, even though he insisted that it was "so ill considered that little comment is necessary." The New Deal recovery program

> [had] been predicated not on the mere spending of money to hasten recovery, but on the sounder principle of preventing the

loss of homes and farms, of saving industry from bankruptcy, of safeguarding bank deposits, and most important of all—of giving relief and jobs through public work to individuals and families faced with starvation. . . . The veteran who is disabled owes his condition to the war. The healthy veteran who is unemployed owes his troubles to the depression. Each represents a separate and different problem. Any attempt to mingle the two problems is to confuse our efforts.

In his peroration the President discovered a "moral obligation" to "weigh the claims of all in the scales of equity" and to veto the bill. In so doing, he said, he was thinking of those who were in the armed forces, who worked in factories and on farms, of those who died in the war, of those in dire need today, thinking "not only of the past and the present but also of the future."

> In this future of ours it is of first importance that we yield not to the sympathy which we would extend to a single group or class by special legislation for that group or class, but that we should extend assistance to all groups and all classes who in an emergency need the helping hand of their government.
> I believe the welfare of the Nation, as well as the future welfare of the veterans, wholly justifies my disapproval of this measure.[40]

As anticipated, the veto was sustained. The unruly House overrode, 322 to 98, with only sixty Democrats standing by the President, but the Senate upheld it with a comfortable eight votes to spare, 54 to 40. The additional votes for the President's point of view came from the switches of three Democratic Senators (Coolidge of Massachusetts, Pittman of Nevada, and Pope of Indiana), and to the support of four other Democrats who had not voted earlier.

Maneuvering to get another vote on a Vinson-type bill continued throughout the unusually long session (Congress sat until nearly the end of August).[41] Royal W. Robertson showed up from California in late June, wearing his neck brace and heading a group of veterans who called themselves the Needy Veterans Bonus Association and who wanted bonus payments for all veterans who did not earn enough to pay income taxes. They were quickly shunted off to FERA camps; the administration could not have shown them "hospitality" even had it wished to, Congress having forbidden the payment of public money for the bills of any future veterans' "conventions" the previous January.[42] By early August the bonus agitation, on and off the floor, was so disruptive of the regular work of Congress that Majority Leader Robinson made private and public commitments to bring a bonus bill to a vote in the first month of the next session of Congress. Given Robinson's devotion to his party leader, it is almost inconceivable that the Senator would have made such an agreement without the advice and consent of the President.[43]

The Congress reconvened in January 1936, for the last round on the bonus battle. It was mercifully brief. Although Wright Patman and his supporters went through the motions of making a fight for an openly inflationist measure, by January 6 the Texan threw in his hand; what had been the Vinson bill became, in a bit of face-saving, the Vinson-Patman-McCormack bill on January 9, passed the House, 356 to 59, on January 10, and sailed through the Senate, 74 to 16, ten days later. President Roosevelt wrote out a brief, perfunctory veto message, and sent it to the House by the customary messenger. He noted the differences between the 1935 and 1936 measures—the current bill, despite its fiscal orthodoxy, actually would cost better than a quarter of a billion more because it forgave interest since October 1931—and referred the Congress to his 1935 message. "My convictions are as impelling today as they were then," the President concluded. "Therefore I cannot change them."

The veto was easily overridden, 326 to 61 in the House and 76 to 19 in the Senate. Only twelve Democrats joined seven

Republicans in the upper chamber in support of the President. Among the sixteen Democrats who had voted to sustain in 1935 but voted to override in 1936 were such administration paladins as Majority Leader Robinson, Joseph Guffey of Pennsylvania, Joseph O'Mahoney of Wyoming, David Walsh of Massachusetts, and Robert Wagner of New York. It was their change of position that made the bonus law. A further indication of the administration's realization that the bonus would become law that year is the fact that the Veterans Administration had the necessary application forms already printed and partially distributed to its regional offices even before the vote to override took place! [44]

Franklin Roosevelt was not always a good loser (the Supreme Court fight of 1937 is perhaps the best example of this); but in his fight over the bonus, he lost well. In fact, he probably reaped a greater immediate political reward from the bonus payment than did anyone else. The bonus payment certainly helped to make the summer of 1936 seem relatively prosperous, the most prosperous peacetime summer between 1929 and 1946. He had handled the bonus fight so that little of the animus rubbed off on him: during the second half of 1935, the Legion lobbyists had been angrier at Patman than at the President. Yet he managed, by his vetoes, both to salve his own conscience and to present himself to political moderates as a man who, despite his spending, was, after all, essentially sound on monetary matters. All these were no mean advantages in an election year. This is not to suggest that the presidential maneuverings were all political, or that his landslide triumph in 1936 was due to the settlement of the bonus issue. But politics was a factor, and the extra dollars that passed through the hands of more than 3 million potential voters didn't hurt a bit in November.[45]

10

The Bonus March
as Myth

THUS THE BONUS was paid, twelve years after it was voted,
nine years before it was due. This was a victory for the men
of the veterans' lobby, for, however reluctant some of them
had been to embrace the cause of immediate cash payment,
embrace it they did. It was also a victory for Wright Patman,
even though the bill, in its final form, was not of his choosing.
In a larger sense it was, in part, a victory for the BEF, even
though the organization no longer existed. It was one of those
rare instances of an anonymous group of powerless citizens
imposing their will on an entire society. Precisely how much
the bonus marchers contributed to the victory of 1936 can
never be measured with any degree of precision; there is no
known calculus of motives, nor are there computer programs
for the human spirit. No observer can doubt, however, that
the marchers contributed significantly to the final result; and
it was not just the march itself, as here chronicled, which
contributed, but the myths of the bonus march as well.

Every student of history knows that the effect of a historical
event is often determined not by what happened, but by what

people think happened. It is axiomatic that misconceptions may become even more significant than the reality that they distort. The mythology of the bonus march has been sharply structured by time, climate of opinion, and ideology. In the angry 1930s, the "left-liberal" interpretation which put the blame on Hoover and the army prevailed, while in the equally angry late 1940s and early 1950s a conservative anti-Communist atmosphere produced "revelations" which transferred the onus from the Quaker President to the Communists who were out to discredit him and the army. In periods of greater national unity—the era of World War II and the consensus-orientated late 1950s and early 1960s—a conciliatory myth tended to treat the whole thing as an unfortunate error regretted by all. This chronological categorization has not, of course, been exclusive: conservative interpretations were published in the early 1930s, and the most blatant left-wing distortion went to press when the star of Joseph R. McCarthy was still ascendant.

The earliest myths, of course, were created by the press, especially by liberal and Hearstian journalists with an anti-Hoover bias. As we have seen, the government overreacted, and there is much of the mythic also in many government statements and reports. But the real myths about the BEF sprang phoenixlike from the ashes of Anacostia and the other bonus camps and were multiplied as the refugees told each other horror stories on the nightmare trip to Johnstown. A week after the battle of Washington, the following myths were prevalent at the Johnstown camp and were recorded by Pennsylvania Welfare Commissioner J. Prentice Murphy: [1]

A boy received a bayonet thrust in the thigh while rushing back to get his rabbit.

Two boys, Negro and white, 11 and 12, would not leave—one bayonetted, the other struck in head with gun butt, both probably killed. . . . A marcher who returned the next morning found the white boy's body wrapped in canvas [and] remnants of the Negro boy's body, which had been burned. Only [the] heart remained over which a detective was kicking dirt.

Some "knew for a fact" that the 3d Cavalry was in the hills outside Johnstown waiting to ride into them again.

A soldier breaking the window of a closed sedan and tossing in a bomb among a sleeping mother and children.

A bomb thrown into a baby carriage where a little child was sleeping.

Tents and shacks set afire with people still in them.

A child badly crushed under a horse's feet.

As members of the BEF returned to their old communities or moved on to new ones, they spread the same kinds of stories. In late August, "Captain" Arthur Wilson, an original member of the Portland contingent, told the Willamette Society that:

Soldiers with crossed guns barred a mother attempting to reach her baby in a burning shack and that the baby was burned to death.

That mixed tear gas and mustard gas were used.

That several American flags were burned in the shacks.

That none of the BEF members were armed with "even so much as a knife."

It is almost certain that none of these things happened; the closest approximation to reality was little Bernard Myers dying in the hospital. It is not surprising, of course, that after a day and night of horror, such stories should gain wide currency and be believed. They closely approximate atrocity stories with which a whole generation was familiar—gas and babies from Belgium—and fit quite well into the old Christian tradition of the massacre of the innocents with poor Herbert Hoover badly miscast as Herod. Even the macabre detail of the buried heart strikes an authentic folk note—Hollywood or pulp horror story, out of Edgar Allan Poe.

These atrocity stories were not just localized, but truly national in scope. By August 4, just a week after the battle of Washington, Henry J. Allen, publicity director of the Republican National Committee, had received two letters from far away California protesting the ear-slicing story. In the California version, it was a young boy rather than a veteran who lost an ear to a cavalry saber. Allen remarked, in a letter to Pat Hurley, that "it reminds me of the days when we used to talk about the German atrocities." He was seriously concerned about the possible effects of these stories on Republican success in November and thought that the army should make every effort to counter them.[2] These distortions, as suggested earlier, quickly passed into the national consciousness along with the real horrors that occurred. The atrocities of the troops at Anacostia are an authentic part of the folklore of the Great Depression, along with the lemminglike suicides in Wall Street and the personal responsibility of President Hoover for most of the things that went wrong.

The myths of the bonus march were spread by word of mouth, letters, and the nation's press. In addition, a more formal literature helped perpetuate them. The two basic accounts of the bonus march, the chief sources for almost everything that has since appeared, are W. W. Waters, *B.E.F.: The Whole Story of the Bonus Army* (1933), and Jack Douglas, *Veterans on the March* (1934). Waters' volume, written with the acknowledged assistance of a professional writer, William C. White, is a personalized account with most of the flaws of the genre—overemphasis on the role of the memoirist and insufficient analysis. Waters' magnification of his part in the genesis of the bonus march has been treated earlier; his relation of the expulsion from Anacostia is lurid and suggestive, even though he admits that he abandoned his people as soon as real trouble loomed, and thus was not himself either a witness or a refugee.[3]

> The jeers and the cries of the evicted men and women rose above the crackling of the flames. The clatter of the tanks was dulled by the sirens and horns of the fire apparatus come to control the flames. The ambulance horns roared for right of way. Frightened by the noise, the cavalry horses screamed. The motorcycles of the police sounded like machine guns. Army trucks, arriving with fresh supplies of bombs, added to the uproar.
>
> The flames were mirrored in the drawn bayonets of the infantry as they advanced through the camp, driving out every individual. Some veteran called back to the advancing line, "I guess you guys will get a medal for this." Fire and gas did their work. There is no way of knowing whether, in the debacle, a few homeless men perished or not. Some poor soul may have crept into the shelter of a shack, gassed, to perish in the flames. The pungent odor of burning tar paper absorbed all other odors. The reflection of the flames was long in the sky. It could be seen from the White House.

The other book, *Veterans on the March,* written more than a year later, was a piece of Communist propaganda bearing the party imprimatur; its author was a party worker using a pseudonym. It treated both the 1932 and 1933 marches. Its chief distinction was a foreword by John Dos Passos, still in his Marxist phase. He felt that the bonus march was "one of the most instructive things" in all American history.[4]

> As time goes on, it will assume more and more importance in the history of American capitalism. . . . [The veterans] were so anxious to be considered regular hundred-percenters that they

fell a prey to all sorts of schemes and orators. . . . One thing they did accomplish. They gave the powers that be the scare of their lives. . . .

For a year the questions of veterans' relief, and the whole problem of how the ordinary working man the man who wanted to work were going to live under the regime of artificial scarcity that is necessary for the survival of the capitalist monopolies, have been hidden from the public view by the rosy democratic smoke-screen laid down by the Roosevelt Administration. In the last few months, these copious clouds, at first so fragrant to the Forgotten Man, are beginning to take on a distinct smell of tear gas and even of the vomiting gas that is the newest invention of Law 'n order. The Bonus March of 1932 offered a cross section of the ninety percent of Americans who were not in on the big money, or even the small money. Given a definite problem of action and organization they solved it brilliantly, but they were no more able to relate that problem to the general course of human affairs than a lot of children in a kindergarten. Has the Forgotten Man learned anything in the past two years? Is he learning anything now? Or is he, with the old gambler's optimism, going to let himself be led by the nose by all the disgruntled medicine salesmen and con men with fancy colored shirts to sell who are out to get him into fascist organizations where he will be used as the praetorian guard of the imperial monopolies?

In less striking prose, "Douglas" followed the regular party line; he magnified the roles of Emanuel Levin, John Pace, and the WESL, heaped scorn on Waters, Glassford, and Patman as enemies of the veterans, described the CCC as an important part of "fascist trends now developing in the United States," and professed to believe, in early 1934, that "the veterans—together with the other elements of the toiling population—are on the march." In addition to the "severed ear" and the "gassed babies" themes (including an apparently imaginary interview with Bernard Myers' mother which managed to get the family's name wrong) there were dark hints about a wide-spread conspiracy.[5]

> Stories went about of a secret service man or a . . . policeman in plain clothes who had done some shooting and then disappeared. . . . (The mysterious killing of Shinault, the policeman who had killed Hushka [sic], a few months later gave rise to stories that it was a "put-up job" because "he knew too much.")
>
> (Still another mystery was the killing, a year later, of Eddie Gosnell, official photographer of the B.E.F., who had gotten a picture of Hushka just after his murder and other "intimate" pictures, many of which later disappeared. He died after drinking acid. It was said he took it by mistake while drinking. Intimate friends of Gosnell's said he never drank intoxicants of any kind.)

Neither of these accounts, despite their prejudicial and biased nature, ever claimed that the army had killed anyone, which of course it hadn't—the two deaths occurred before the troops arrived and were the acknowledged responsibility of Glassford's police. Yet the impression was quickly transmitted to large segments, if not to a majority of the American people, that the army had fired into crowds of bonus marchers in downtown Washington. At the start of my research I interviewed a number of people in Washington who were eyewitnesses, and time and again got stories of the troops firing into crowds of people, and firing over people's heads. Sober and substantial citizens talked to me about seeing Douglas MacArthur and Dwight Eisenhower on horseback. It is undoubtedly a mistake to attribute this distortion to a planned smear or plot. While working on this book I have watched similar distortions spring up about the Watts riots of August 1965. At cocktail parties and other gatherings in the Los Angeles area, I have established to my own satisfaction that an overwhelming majority of the people whom I quizzed— who come from the best-informed segments of the population —have entirely erroneous impressions about what actually happened, even though Los Angeles' August days have been rather accurately reported. (For example, almost everyone seems to think that policemen were slaughtered by snipers firing from ambush, but the reported facts of the matter are that each of three policemen slain was killed by the guns of other policemen.) [6] I have concluded that it is almost impossible for accurate impressions of large-scale domestic violence to be transmitted. However it happened, gross inaccuracies soon became an integral part of the canon. By the end of the decade, Charles and Mary Beard, perhaps the most influential historians of their time, could write, "When a number of veterans, 'the bonus army,' poor and hungry, marched on Washington and settled there to promote 'adjusted compensation legislation,' [Hoover] employed federal troops to rout and disperse them; their tents were burned and blood was spilled." [7]

Just where this myth started, it is of course impossible to say, but in some of the contemporary press and magazine accounts the same inaccurate sequence—the shedding of blood after the troops had been called out—was put forth. In *Current History,* a magazine then put out by the *New York Times* and used a great deal by secondary school students and teachers, a September 1932 article had committed the same error. [8]

> By 4:30 P.M. the troops were out; . . . tear gas and the flat side of the sabre drove the veterans from Pennsylvania Avenue and toward their camp at Anacostia. Many were injured, but only two were killed. The troops did not stop when they reached the Potomac. Across the river, step by step, they forced the bonus marchers.

During the 1932 campaign a cabinet officer's attempts to defend the administration from exaggerated charges were laughed at. When Secretary of the Interior Ray Lyman Wilbur answered the question "Who gassed the babies in

Washington?" with the simple truth, "No one did; none were gassed," a radical Protestant journal of opinion scoffed that "this can be added to those other illusions of history—that there was a woman Pope, that Columbus first discovered America, and that Republican stump speakers from the cabinet are men of honor." [9]

Two years later, writing in Mencken's still influential *American Mercury,* Charles Angoff sneered at "Mr. Hoover's cruel and imbecile orders to the United States Army to do dirty work among their former brothers." [10] These distortions were all probably innocent errors; the worst example I have found came in a Stalinist account of the Depression written in 1940. Bruce Minton and John Stuart concluded a slanted account of the BEF with the following outright invention: [11]

> The veterans began to leave the capital. But President Hoover would not let them disband peacefully. Suddenly he announced that a violent uprising was imminent. Without warning he ordered the army forcibly to eject the B.E.F. from Washington. The soldiers charged with fixed bayonets, firing into the crowd of unarmed men, women and children. . . .

In addition, the Depression decade produced a whole panoply of tracts, pamphlets, poetry, and even a "utopian" novel about a veterans' putsch which developed out of the BEF. The poems, if they can be called that, appeared in an anonymous volume called *Ballads of the B.E.F.* (1932) and are largely attacks on President Hoover.[12]

He Fed the Kids in Belgium
   The Hoover diet is gas

The Prisoner of the White House
   In a cage that is fit for a lion
   He moves with the soul of a mouse

The Great Humanitarian
> "The starving he met with a bayonet,
> And to babies American
> 'Twas gas he fed instead of the bread"

The Battle Hymn of the B.E.F.
> I have seen the sabres gleaming as they lopped off
> veterans' ears
> And the bayonets were scarlet as they pricked us in
> the rears

> . . .

> Glory, glory Herbie Hoover, the B.E.F. lives on.

The "utopian" novel was authored by a literary figure who called himself Shaemus O'Sheel; born James Shields, he was once an office boy for S. S. McClure, and later published scholarly translations of Greek classics. His novel is perhaps the first American novel celebrating a fascist take-over, although the plotters call themselves anti-fascists. A political curiosity wholly without literary merit, which reads as if it were written in one hasty weekend from newspaper and magazine accounts, it is in the form of a memoir by General Elmer Hicks, written in 1982, of "The Veterans' Revolution of 1932." O'Sheel's BEF was headed by one Robert R. Rivers; he fades away after the Battle of Washington (which O'Sheel describes accurately). The veterans' revolution is masterminded by a civilian millionaire with a social conscience, named (naturally) Brian Barry, who seizes power and becomes president-dictator after using a rejuvenated BEF—renamed the Army of Washington—to defeat rebellions by a Communist-led red army and a big-business-financed army of gangsters. After the triumph of the veterans, the new men of power put the President, the cabinet, and Congress into a concentration camp on the Anacostia Flats.

Such spleen and fantasies were appropriate to the 1930s.

The coming of World War II and the American involvement in it produced a new atmosphere and new needs. As Franklin Roosevelt himself put it, Dr. Win-the-War replaced Dr. New Deal. National unity rather than animosity became the order of the day, and some historians, as always, were ready to use their craft in a ritualistic rather than a scholarly function. Professor Dixon Wecter produced, in 1944, a readable history of veterans in America called *When Johnny Comes Marching Home*.[13] The bonus march received 1 page out of 558, and that page error-ridden. His chief contribution was the discovery that for Douglas MacArthur, "the old hero of the Rainbow Division, it was duty, no congenial task." All sorts of people discovered this about MacArthur as he became, even in ignominious defeat, a heroic symbol of America's will to defeat Japan. A semiofficial military history, often used in ROTC courses, explained MacArthur's presence as an act of solicitude for the veterans.[14] "It has been inferred that he wanted to make certain no harm would come to any American who had served his country bravely in World War I." But the wartime consensus was a two-way affair. If the evictors of the veterans were given noble motives, the evictees were treated with sympathy, if not understanding. In the postwar years, the reputation of the bonus army became a victim of the Cold War.

Before I recount and examine the charges and counter-charges of the post–World War II years, it will be well to remember the relatively high tolerance that communism had attained in American life. Many Americans were willing to grant that it was "just another party," and for those to the left of center, an attack on any Communist tactic or leader was likely to be written off as red-baiting. During the war years, the image of Josef V. Stalin as "Good Old Uncle Joe," an essentially benevolent despot, was a part of the price of the Grand Alliance. When that alliance began to break down, when it became increasingly clear that the brave new postwar world was going to be an arena for the most intense and continuous international tension in world history, the shock was too great for many to bear with sanity. In addition, the domestic Communist movement, badly shaken by the Hitler-Stalin pact of 1939, was further jolted by the infamous Duclos letter of April 1945, and the demotion and expulsion of Earl Browder which ensued. The accommodationist, united-front Communist party of the war years ("Communism is twentieth-century Americanism"—Earl Browder) was replaced by a narrow, sectarian Stalinist clique. Under these enormous internal pressures, which were coupled with an increasingly severe domestic persecution of Communists and their allies, real and imagined, the majority of American Communists left the Communist party in the decade after 1945. Most of them drifted away quietly and remained somewhere vaguely on the left. A small minority however, including some who had been very highly placed, became themselves persecutors of their former faith. Some undoubtedly did this out of pure conviction; others out of pure opportunism; and in most, the two motives undoubtedly became strangely mixed. The result, however, was often false witness. As Professor Herbert Packer of the Stanford Law School has observed in his fascinating study of the *Ex-Communist Witnesses:* [15]

> . . . a common thread of attitude and personality runs through [their] testimony which restrains a cautious observer from giving it wholehearted credence. [They] . . . appear to have forsaken one set of absolutes for another. . . . Anyone who is not with them must necessarily be against them.

The first of the party's renegades to charge that the Communist party had really been responsible for the bonus march was Benjamin Gitlow, former general secretary of the party and its vice-presidential candidate in 1924 and 1928. In 1948 he published an autobiographical exposé called *The*

Whole of Their Lives, which included a five-page section entitled "The Communists Take Over the Bonus March." It purports to be an inside account of what went on in Washington and within the Communist party unencumbered by the embarrassing facts that Gitlow had not been on the scene and had been expelled from the party in 1929. His revelations are largely distortions and complete fabrications. His favorite verb is "to storm," and the section reads like a bad rewrite of *Ten Days That Shook the World.* In Gitlow's book, Communist-led veterans "stormed empty government buildings," "stormed the Washington court house," and "stormed the Capitol steps." It was, according to Gitlow, the Communists in Washington who dominated everything. "On July 7," he wrote, describing an event otherwise unknown to history, "the Communists seized Camp Anacostia." A board of strategy, including Emanuel Levine [sic], members of the political committee of the CP, the "C.I. Representative" [Gitlow apparently did not then know that his name was Mario Alpi], and the Communist heads of veterans delegations "met secretly in one of the fashionable hotels." Seemingly as a result of this meeting, the Battle of Washington occurred— "a fight between Communist-led veterans and police"—which was just what the party wanted.[16]

> It was what they had conspired to bring about. Now they could brand Hoover as a murderer of hungry unemployed veterans. They could charge that the United States Army was Wall Street's tool with which to crush the unemployed and that the government and the Congress of the United States were bloody fascist butchers of unarmed American workers . . . the Communist phobia [sic] against Hoover will last as long as Hoover lives.

Given what we now know about the bonus march, Gitlow's 1948 account pretty well discredits itself. *The Whole of Their Lives* was his second autobiography. Eight years previously he had published *I Confess* and given a briefer account of the party's involvement in the bonus march, which I give in its entirety.[17]

> Another issue within the ruling cliques of the Party involved the famous Bonus March during the Hoover Administration. The idea of a "Bonus March" was first formulated by the Workers Ex-Servicemen's League, an organization established by the party. But Browder rejected the idea. It was, however, taken up by the veterans' organizations and groups with which the Communists had little to do and developed into a mighty movement. When the March was actually under way, Browder instructed the Communist veterans to proceed to Washington as an independent force. In Washington the Communist veterans, upon the direct instructions of Browder, sharply denounced the non-Communist leaders and organizations who made the Bonus March a success. The Weinstone group sharply criticized Browder's for its hesitation and held him responsible for the party's failure to gain leadership and control of the movement.

The year 1948 also saw the first popular attempt to rehabilitate the reputation of Herbert Hoover, with the publication of *Our Unknown Ex-President* by Eugene Lyons, a former radical journalist turned conservative. Hoover's files had been opened to him, and the result was a semiofficial account. The bonus march depicted by Lyons was a Communist-inspired affair involving only 12,000 veterans at its peak (his 1964 version, called *Herbert Hoover*, reduced this to 11,000). Lyons correctly attributed the killings to the police—"two policemen, surrounded and endangered, began to shoot" (1948 version) and "two of the city policemen, beaten to the ground, fired in self-defense" (1964 version)—but was under the impression that the "600 troops carried no deadly weapons." His reading of the Mitchell report was faulty, so that he wrote that the criminal records were of the men remaining, rather than of a part of those who had left.[18]

In the fall of 1948, Patrick J. Hurley was trying to win a

United States Senate seat from Clinton P. Anderson in New Mexico. Naturally Hurley's role in the expulsion entered into what was a very dirty campaign, as it had two years earlier when Hurley had tried to unseat Dennis Chavez from New Mexico's other Senate seat. In the 1948 campaign Hurley asked the Republican National Committee for assistance. It not only had its own research team take a crack at it, but also arranged with Robert E. Stripling, the chief investigator of the House Committee on Un-American Activities, for a search of the committee's files for information that might be of use to Hurley. The researchers of the Republican National Committee produced an eight-page report which concluded:

> There was a considerable Communist element among the Bonus Marchers although it was probably not so extensive as was believed at the time. It is certainly true, however, that the actual number of Communists engaged in any activity has little to do with their influence and the trouble they cause. . . . Certainly the fact that certain Communist leaders were active in calling for a march on Washington and encouraged veterans throughout the country to engage in it is testimony of their part in the origin of the March. Furthermore, although no one knows absolutely, it would appear that they were prominently engaged in the riot.

It was (is?) apparently standard procedure for the House Committee on Un-American Activities to furnish information from its files to friendly persons, because the report for Hurley appears on a printed form whose letterhead reads "INFORMATION FROM THE FILES OF THE COMMITTEE ON UN-AMERICAN ACTIVITIES." An analysis of its seven pages confirms a suspicion long held by this historian, to wit, that the red hunters are not efficient researchers. They apparently did not even read open Communist periodicals thoroughly, and missed many self-incriminating statements. Hurley was not able to utilize either report, and lost both elections. The use of the bonus march against him in what he considered an unfair matter must have really gotten under the former war secretary's skin.[19]

When, a year later, *McCall's* printed an installment of Eleanor Roosevelt's autobiography which contained a typical statement of the liberal bonus march myth, the bellicose Hurley responded with a massive display of literary overkill, which, although no one had the wit to point it out, was largely off-target. The First Lady had written: [20]

The first [bonus] march, which had taken place in Mr. Hoover's administration, was still painfully fresh in everyone's mind [in 1933 when the second march occurred]. I shall never forget my feeling of horror when I realized that the army had actually been ordered to fire on the veterans. This one incident shows what fear can make people do. Mr. Hoover was a Quaker; and General MacArthur, his chief of staff, must have known how many veterans would resent the order and never forget it; he must have known too the effect it would have on public opinion. Yet they dared do nothing else in a situation which frightened them.

Hurley demanded space for a reply and found it necessary to use two full pages of the magazine to answer Mrs. Roosevelt's paragraph.[21] It has become a key document in the conservative myth of the bonus march, and as such deserves extended analysis. He began by asserting his regard for Mrs. Roosevelt and her "late and lamented" husband, but insisted that he could not ignore Mrs. Roosevelt's erroneous statements "because they do a grave injustice to former President Hoover and General MacArthur." He then pointed out that 1932 was a presidential year, and, in a coupling that was so typical of these years, wrote that "The Democratic National Committee, as well as the Soviet Comintern . . . declined to accept as true the facts pertaining to the marchers' riot in Washington. The nation was deluged with false statements." Hurley went on to point out, correctly, that no shots were fired by soldiers. But such a simple refutation of a natural error was not enough for him. He proceeded to ask three hypothetical questions "to clarify her remark."

1. Who ordered the soldiers to fire on the veterans?

2. If such an order was given, why was it that *not one shot was fired by any soldier during the riot?*

3. Since no shots were fired by the soldiers, does Mrs. Roosevelt mean to convey the idea that the soldiers would not obey what she calls *the actual orders to fire on the veterans?*

Hurley then launched into a standard Hoover administration defense of what had been done. Much of it directly followed an official statement to the press which he had issued on July 30, 1932, and which had been a reasonably brief statement. In his *McCall's* defense, Hurley began to extemporize and to rely on his memory, which played some tricks on him. "There was, and is," he insisted, "ample evidence that the Communists had gained control of the bonus marchers before the day of the riot. For instance, of the three largest camps in which the marchers lived one was called 'Camp Marx' and one 'Communist Camp.'" Hurley's "Camp Marx," of course, was really "Camp Marks," named for the Anacostia police captain rather than for the German political economist; the "Communist Camp," as such, is unknown to the bonus march canon, although there was an area where the Communists were segregated. He then quotes a passage from the wrong section of Gitlow's *The Whole of Their Lives,* inadvertently confusing the winter hunger march with the summer bonus march.

In other ways Hurley improved on his 1932 statement: then he had merely stated that "after the arrival of United States troops . . . no person was seriously injured." Now he went

further, insisting erroneously that "the Army used no weapon
other than a few tear-gas bombs."

Then, venturing out onto even thinner ice, Hurley chose
to write about the second bonus march, about which he knew
nothing firsthand. Although, as we have seen, the 1933 march
was much more Communist-dominated than the 1932 march,
it never received any attention from either red hunters or
renegades. Hurley thus assumed that there were no Communists there, and invented reasons why this should be so.

> That bonus march was unlike the first in that the marchers were
> composed entirely of veterans. . . . The second bonus march
> occurred after it was known that the new administration would
> recognize Soviet Russia . . . [which] accounts for the fact that
> there were no Communist nonveterans in the second bonus march.

Hurley's rationalizations, although built on sand—the
recognition of the USSR occurred in November 1933, six
months after the second bonus march—are quite revealing,
underscoring one of the three real fixations of the recent
American far-right: that the recognition of Russia, somehow,
was a causative factor in much that went wrong with the
mid-twentieth century world. (The other two are yearnings
for the return of the gold standard, and for the disappearance
of the income tax.)

Hurley then tried to show that New Deal benevolence was
actually more harmful than old guard repression.

> When the second bonus march arrived in Washington President
> Roosevelt used public funds to ship the bonus marchers to Florida.
> This was intended to take them far from their homes, to support
> them at government expense and to prevent agitation by them in
> a troubled period. It happened, however, that after they arrived
> in Florida they were caught in a tremendous storm. Hundreds
> of them were drowned or otherwise killed, but the press of the

period often mentioned approximately 300. I have offered no criticism of President Roosevelt's handling of the second bonus march. I have assumed that the president and his advisors acted in what they sincerely believed to be the best interests of the people.

Hurley's chronology here was askew; the hurricane disaster in the Florida Keys was on Labor Day, 1935. Few of those killed participated in the second bonus march, as the average veteran enlistment in the CCC was a little over a year; most of the veterans killed probably came into the CCC during 1934 and 1935. There were some not very successful attempts to make political capital out of the tragedy, but although antihurricane precautions on the part of local CCC and FERA administrators were deficient, no top-level negligence was established. That Hurley felt it was appropriate to dredge it up in his controversy with Mrs. Roosevelt is perhaps indicative of the extreme frustration felt by those involved in what Herbert Feis has called "the China Tangle." [23]

No one challenged Hurley's misstatements. Eleanor Roosevelt was clearly wrong, and admitted it, if somewhat lamely: [24]

> I simply stated my impressions of that day, derived from the press which I happened to read. I know others had similar impressions, but I am glad to have an authentic account published and I only wonder why it was not done much sooner.

Hurley was, of course, delighted by his triumph; he had finally beaten a Democrat. He sent a prepublication version of his piece to Tokyo to get Douglas MacArthur's approval. The general was effusive. He thought it was a "masterpiece" and "a real contribution to historical accuracy." In the same letter he apprised Hurley that John Pace, one of the Communist leaders of the BEF, was about to publish an exposé on the whole affair in the Hearst press. MacArthur knew about it because a Hearst executive had cabled for his approval; when the series appeared it carried MacArthur's imprimatur. Hurley considered rewriting his already long reply to include Pace's revelations, but decided against it.[25]

Pace's story was run in Hearst papers for three days at the end of August 1949, under the byline of Howard Rushmore, the chain's own ex-Communist. Pace, a Kentuckian, moved to Detroit in the 1920s, and, when his contracting business failed, turned to communism, joining the party in "the spring of 1931—or sometime in the winter of 1930 or 1931." He left the party in 1935, appeared as a friendly witness before the House Un-American Activities Committee in 1938 (although, as we shall see, he said little about the bonus march), acted as an expert witness on communism for the Immigration and Naturalization Service in deportation proceedings, served for two years as the chairman of the Un-American Activities Committee of the Detroit District Association of the American Legion, and, by 1949, had returned to the South (Centerville, Tennessee) where he ran a sewer contracting service, served as a deputy sheriff, and was active in the Legion and as a speaker before patriotic groups. (The week before his story appeared, Pace and another ex-Communist, Joseph Zach Kornfeder, appeared before the House Un-American Activities Committee and gave testimony that stayed secret for almost two years. Whether the Hearst people brought Pace to the attention of the Committee or vice-versa is not clear.)

It is somewhat ironic that the Hearst chain, the only major papers fully to support the BEF, should, just seventeen years later, go out of the way to defame it, but the seventeen years in question spread across one of the great watersheds of American history. In any event, the Hearst papers in 1949 made no reference to the stories they had run in 1932.[26] "RED 'SMEAR PLOT' AGAINST MACARTHUR, HOOVER EXPOSED" was the front page banner in 1949; in 1932 it had been "HOOVER'S REGIME SET BONUS ARMY RIOTING, SAYS GEN. GLASSFORD." The gist of Pace's 1949 story was contained in eight sentences published in the first installment.[27]

> I led the left-wing or Communist section of the bonus march.
>
> I was ordered by my Red superiors to provoke riots.
>
> I was told to use every trick to bring about bloodshed in the hopes that President Hoover would be forced to call out the army.
>
> The Communists didn't care how many veterans were killed.
>
> I was told that Moscow had ordered riots and bloodshed in hopes that this might set off the revolution.
>
> My Communist bosses were jumping for joy on July 28 when Washington police killed one veteran. The Army was called out the next day by President Hoover and didn't fire a shot or kill a man.
>
> General MacArthur put down a Moscow-directed revolution without bloodshed and that's why the Communists hate him even today.

The vivid language was undoubtedly Rushmore's; Pace's own verbal style in his appearances before the House Committee is dull and prolix. If the main purpose of the Communists was to provoke a riot—Pace says that there were about 400 of them in a total of 7,000 veterans—they must have been singularly inefficient, as there were two peaceful months before any real trouble started. Apart from his very fuzzy recollections about what happened—he has the troops called out the day after Huska's death—he and Rushmore produced some quite imaginative dialogue. At one point he has Emanuel Levin (whom Rushmore insists on calling "Levine") say to Pace: "Here's your chance of making a name for yourself with Stalin."

The Pace-Rushmore series received some attention in newspapers outside the Hearst chain and was inserted into the

Congressional Record, but did not get a good deal of public notice until 1951, about a year-and-a-half later. In that year, nineteen years after the event, the expulsion of the BEF from Washington received more attention from Congress than ever before. This came about because the Battle of Washington became involved in the most explosive issue of the year, President Harry S Truman's firing of General Douglas MacArthur as Supreme Commander of the war effort in Korea. It was first injected into the Congressional debate by Senator Robert S. Kerr (D.-Okla.), who was defending the President's action and questioning the general's judgment.[28]

> The worst defeat the American troops have taken in my lifetime was the result of MacArthur's erroneous conclusion that Red China would not send her armies against our forces.
>
> It may be . . . that MacArthur's present judgement that Russia would not come to the rescue of Red China if we attack her mainland is based upon the fact that if we committed this greater folly Russia would have to intervene. We would thereby seal our own doom.
>
> It may be, Mr. President, that MacArthur's conclusion about Russia's possible action is just as wrong as he was when he sat as a member of a general court martial and participated in the conviction of Gen. "Billy" Mitchell.
>
> And . . . I believe he is just as mistaken now as he was when he led the Armed Forces of this Nation down Pennsylvania Avenue and fought the battle of Anacostia Flats against the veterans of World War I, who were here to petition their Government for help.

A few days later, an opposition Senator, H. Alexander Smith of New Jersey, challenged Kerr's historical accuracy. Smith had inserted the Pace-Rushmore articles into the *Record* when they first appeared. Describing Pace as a "Tennessee farmer," Smith summarized Pace's story and added some embellishments of his own.

The Army's action was certainly not a battle; in fact it was completely bloodless and humane. . . . The facts show that the action was really directed against the acts of violence provoked by Communists, most of them not even veterans, who had taken over the bonus march, and not against the veterans themselves who were unaware of the purpose for which they were being used.

All of this was clearly news to Kerr.[29]

This is the first time I have ever heard anyone accuse the veterans who came to Washington on that march of being Communists, Communist sympathizers, Communist-inspired, or Communist led. There were in that march many veterans of World War I from Oklahoma, and there was not a Communist in that group. I do not believe that those veterans of World War I were Communists, and I believe that any charge of that sort against them is a slander upon and an insult to them.

The following day Senate Republicans returned to the subject. Someone had called Hurley's 1949 reply to Eleanor Roosevelt to Senator Smith's attention (he said he had not previously heard of it), and he read from it and had the whole thing inserted into the *Record*. Some Democrats had been doing research too. Connecticut's Brien McMahon insisted that the riot casualty list from the *New York Times* of July 29, 1932, be inserted following the Hurley account, to show that the battle had not been the innocuous affair Hurley remembered. In passing, Senator Francis H. Case (R.-S.D.), who had been a member of the House Committee on Un-American Activities before his election to the upper house, supported Smith's views by stating that "the files of the House Committee on Un-American Activities contain testimony to the effect that there was Communist leadership on the bonus march on Washington." This was the first public hint of the existence of Pace's secret 1949 testimony.[30]

That testimony was "leaked" to the *Chicago Tribune* and *Washington Times-Herald* by Congressman Harold Velde (R.-Ill.), and summarized in newspapers on June 1, 1951.[31] A little over a month later, the secret 1949 hearing was read into the record of a public hearing at which Pace reappeared.[32] The original hearing, it turns out, was a somewhat curious one. As finally printed by the committee, it appears under the heading "Communist Tactics Among Veterans' Groups," but it is the only testimony ever taken under that rubric. The original secret hearing had been held before a special subcommittee of one (Congressman John S. Wood, a Georgia Democrat) and was not considered important enough to evoke the presence of the committee's counsel or its senior investigator. Just why it was held is something of a mystery, but I suspect that someone in the Hearst organization had insisted that Pace "purge himself" with the committee before his story appeared. At the later hearing, Pace observed that "before I was just picked out of the clear sky." No one then or since chose to mention that Pace appeared before the committee in 1938. At that time the main thrust of his testimony was directed at the Communists in the Detroit labor movement. He did, however, mention the bonus march in passing in his 1938 performance. In explaining that he left the party in 1934 he then testified that he [33]

> began to change his mind during the bonus march of 1932. I had quite a few fights with the leadership of the Communist Party in connection with the bonus march. For instance I averted a couple or three riots in Washington. I had instructions not to, but I did, anyway, because I knew it was not right. It was not even right from their point of view.

He then went on to make the point that within the party, individual opinions counted for nothing. There is not a trace of the "C.I. Rep" who loomed so large in Pace's testimony from 1949 on. I strongly suspect that the "C.I. Rep" was borrowed from Gitlow's 1948 book. This is not to suggest that there were no "C.I. Reps," but that minor figures like Pace did not meet with them. After Gitlow had featured the "C.I. Rep" in his 1948 book, he appears in more and more of the apostates' testimony for the simple reason that not to have known about him was an admission of low status in what the committee usually referred to as the "International Communist Conspiracy."

Pace's testimony was in substance quite similar to the Pace-Rushmore articles, but the style, as noted earlier, was quite different. The testimony also contains one glaring historical howler. Pace remembered, in 1949, that in 1931 he had been "sent to Ann Arbor, Mich., and organized a strike of the WPA relief workers in Ann Arbor"! The WPA, of course, did not exist in 1931, and the greatest talking point the Communists had was the total lack of any kind of federal unemployment relief. If Pace's memory was deficient on a major point like this, how could his word-for-word repetitions of seventeen-year-old conversations be depended upon? He made minor slips as well. The National Provisional Bonus March Committee he consistently called "National Professional Bonus March Committee," and he got proper names wrong. In addition, he remembered a number of minor things that never happened, including a meeting between Waters (whom he considered a loyal American) and Franklin D. Roosevelt at the Chicago Democratic Convention of 1932. It was Pace's opinion, in 1949, "that had this thing gone another week, the Communists would have gained the leadership of the bonus expeditionary forces, thereby resulting in forcing the Government to take the action that they did take, at a time when the results would have been much more disastrous." In 1949 he said nothing about "averting a couple or three riots" and gave the impression that Washington was quite a turbulent place. He also revived one of the early left-wing myths, insisting that "fraternization and friendship" between Communist bonus marchers and United States Marines was responsible for the avoidance of a clash between the marines and the BEF before the Capitol. Actually the clash had been averted because Glassford got the marines called off.

Pace's testimony was, of course, played up in the Mc-Cormick–Patterson press. The *Washington Times-Herald* headlined its story: "DEMOCRATS HID HEROIC ROLE OF GENERAL MACARTHUR BONUS MARCH SMEAR ERASED BY TESTIMONY." [34] In mid-July Pace's testimony, as printed in the *Times-Herald,* came to the attention of Pelham D. Glassford, living in retirement in Laguna Beach, California. The general replied by letter to the *Times-Herald* (its publisher Eleanor "Cissy" Patterson had been one of his friends and a supporter of the BEF in 1932), but the letter apparently was never printed. Writing in "the interest of truth," Glassford avowed "the greatest respect and feeling of friendship for General Mac-Arthur, but no confidence in the veracity of John T. Pace." MacArthur, Glassford went on, accomplished the eviction "in a masterly manner," but the former police chief still denied that the eviction was necessary. To Pace's claim that his men "seized some apartment buildings," Glassford replied that they had been assigned to a single building by the police. To the general tenor of Pace's testimony, which claimed the whole march as a Communist triumph, Glassford replied at length.[35]

1. The Communist objectives were NOT successful until the eviction was ordered, and then only partially so, largely because of Gen. MacArthur's masterly handling of his troops and the support of the Metropolitan Police in keeping the thousands of spectators separate from the veterans.

2. A mass demonstration and parade advertised by the Communists for June 7 turned out to be a fizzle and was abandoned.

3. A Communist attempt to picket the White House on the night of July 16 was unsuccessful.

4. All attempts to distribute Communist literature in the camps of the bonifide [sic] veterans, and to secure membership in the Workers' Ex-Servicemen's League were thwarted by the military police of the Bonus Expeditionary Force commanded by Edward Atwell.

5. The small communist group under Pace at 13th Street was very closely watched, as was also Communist Headquarters at 905 I Street, N.W., established by the Communists at No. 1 Union Square, New York City with Emanuel Levin in charge. It was published in the newspapers that in a speech on August 1, 1932 Emanuel Levin said: "His (Glassford's) method of handling the bonus army was the best display of skill I have ever seen. He lulled Waters (Commander of the B.E.F.) and his forces to sleep with ease. He used the B.E.F. military police to combat us. He gave them full authority to club us and by this method he kept us segregated."

On July 13, 1951, Pace returned to Washington to tell his story again, this time in a public hearing. His two-year-old testimony was read into the record, and he made a few insignificant additions. Some of the right-wing press treated it like a new story; the *Washington Times-Herald,* for example, headlined it: "SECRET TESTIMONY OF COMMIE ON BONUS MARCH MADE PUBLIC HOUSE INVESTIGATORS REVEAL FACTS SUPPRESSED 21 MONTHS BY DEMOCRATS."

The charge of Democratic suppression was apparently based on the alleged opposition to the release of the testimony in 1949 by one insignificant Democratic representative from Missouri, Congressman Morgan M. Moulder, a member of the House Committee. Apparently no journalist covering the hearings spotted the obvious incongruities in Pace's testimonies, although Richard Morris of the Washington *Post* did have the wit to note that the apostate Communist did have "a remarkable faculty for recalling dates and events," and suggested that "Pace may have exaggerated the party's capabilities." [36]

Pace's testimony was given its widest dissemination by W. L. White in the fall of 1951. The son of famed Emporia, Kansas, editor William Allen White, he was an editor of the *Reader's Digest*. He "planted" an article called "The Story of a Smear" in a fairly obscure right-wing publication, *The Freeman,* so that his own mass-circulation magazine, which pretends to publish nothing original, could later rerun it. Most of the brief article was a précis of Pace's testimony, with a few quotations from Waters' book, but a few sentences were original and suggested that White had talked to some of the principals. Describing the calling out of the troops, White wrote: [37]

> The President called in his Secretary of War, Patrick J. Hurley, to discuss calling out the troops. Both men remember that Hoover suggested that the soldiers be armed, not with guns, but with "peace clubs" such as those policemen carry.
>
> "I declined," says Hurley. "There were only 600 soldiers against thousands of bonuseers. I didn't want to see the United States Army defeated by a mob!" . . .
>
> Even with the courageous confessions of Pace, Gitlow and others, the Communist smear on Hoover and MacArthur is not entirely washed away, and our Quaker ex-President can say sadly that "a large part of the veterans believe to this day that men who served their country in war were shot down in the streets of Washington at my orders."

From Laguna Beach, Glassford returned to the literary wars, but again with no real result; although the editor of *The Freeman,* John Chamberlain, answered him politely enough, he would not print the general's pointed objections.

White had written of the BEF degenerating into "a bitter
mob. There followed scenes of violence. . . ." Glassford pointed
out that there was no violence until July 28, and that quite
localized. White, following Pace, gave the impression that
there were many hundreds of Communists among the BEF,
but Glassford stuck to his police intelligence reports of about
two hundred. The former police chief also objected to the
White-Pace implication that the White House was picketed.

Glassford's major complaint was against the White-Pace
conclusion "that the Communist Party had finally achieved
the bloodshed" for which it had been working for so long.
The *"FACTS* are," he insisted, "that bloodshed was achieved
by the administration" in what he characterized as "a very
stupid attempt." It is a *"reasonable supposition,"* he countered, "that an incident involving violence was necessary in
order to justify calling out the troops which for several weeks
had been training in the use of tear gas and quelling domestic
disturbance." Annoyed by too much talk of plots on the left,
Glassford now believed that there had really been a plot on
the right! [38]

The following year Herbert Hoover spoke for himself in
that ponderous volume of his *Memoirs* subtitled *The Great
Depression, 1929–1941.* The major theme of this almost incredible book is that Hoover and his policies saved the
country and that Franklin Roosevelt and his policies ruined
it. Like everything he wrote after his 1932 rejection by the
people, the volume reeks with self-pity. Perhaps the most
infelicitous of its paragraphs deals with the street corner
apple-selling.[39]

> One incident of these times has persisted as the eternal damnation
> of Hoover. Some Oregon or Washington apple growers' association
> shrewdly appraised the sympathy of the public for the unem-
> ployed. They set up a system of selling apples on the street
> corners in many cities, thus selling their crop and raising their

prices. Many persons left their jobs for the more profitable one of selling apples.

By that standard, Hoover's pages about the bonus march are temperate. According to Hoover it was "the Bonus March on Washington in July, 1932." There were present "about 11,000 supposed veterans." He retained the impression that the Mitchell Report concerned those who stayed on after the adjournment of Congress, rather than those who accepted the federal loan against their certificates to pay their fare home. In describing the riot he blamed Glassford. "Police Commissioner [sic] Glassford failed to organize his men."

Hoover also states categorically that Glassford asked Mac-Arthur for troops. "Among the statements to the Attorney General was one from General MacArthur stating flatly that General Glassford had appealed to him directly for help." What MacArthur wrote to Attorney General Mitchell was that the "Commissioner of Police" [in other words District Commissioner Herbert Crosby] asked him to have troops "in immediate readiness." Hoover, erroneously thinking that Glassford, whom he never bothered to meet, was Police Commissioner, concluded that Glassford was a liar, and all but said so. He imagined that Dwight Eisenhower, who went along solely as MacArthur's aide and had no command functions, was "second in command" and in the process changed his major's oak leaves to colonel's eagles. He makes it very clear, however, that Hurley and MacArthur exceeded their instructions.

Certain of my instructions to the Secretary of War, however, were not carried out. Those directions limited action to seeing to it that the disturbing factions returned to their camps outside the business district. I did not wish them driven from their camps, as I proposed that the next day we would surround the camps and determine more accurately the number of Communists and ex-convicts among the marchers. Our military officers, however, having them on the move, pushed them outside the District of Columbia.

Hoover's persecution complex comes through very clearly. He remembered, falsely, that "Roosevelt use[d] the incident in the 1932 campaign," and had somehow convinced himself that Pace's testimony "shows the activities of the Communists in opposing my election in 1932," even though the election is not mentioned in any of Pace's bonus march testimony. The Communist party, of course, ran candidates of its own and insisted that there was no real difference between the parties. Hoover's narrowness of spirit is indicated by his account of the Hurley–Eleanor Roosevelt controversy.[40]

> Despite repeated refutations, Mrs. Eleanor Roosevelt as late as July, 1949, repeated the Bonus March lie in McCalls Magazine of that date. When former Secretary of War Hurley demonstrated in the December [really November] issue that it was a lie, she made no adequate apology.

In 1954 the Communist party put out a sort of festschrift for the thirtieth anniversary of its publishing house, International Publishers. It was a collection of excerpts from works in progress, many of which have not yet appeared in finished form. One of these, happily, was a fragment of a play about Peter Cacchione, the first Communist city councilman from Brooklyn, who was certainly on the second and third bonus marches, and may have been on the first, although I know of no contemporary evidence. Facts, however, never bothered the author of these play fragments, Michael Gold, who, after producing one interesting and worthwhile proletarian novel, *Jews Without Money,* became the most venomous of the party's literary hatchet men (Granville Hicks was the most benign.) One of the fragments of Gold's play, *Councilman Peter,* takes place at Anacostia during the Battle of Washington. The dialogue consists of such gems as:

ROCKY (staring off into distance): Look, Pete—they're lining up—it must be the whole army—

ORLANDO: Them kinds [sic] was in diapers while we was in France—

MIKE: That officer there—who's that?

ORLANDO: Eisenhower, I think.

MIKE: Look at the other one—dressed up like a Christmas tree—Wow—what a tailor he's got. . . .

ROCKY: That's MacArthur—Garibaldi was never dressed up so good—or General Grant.

The stage directions include much shooting, and there is an off-stage bayonetting of a sick mother by a soldier who is then disarmed by a Communist veteran.[41]

SOLDIER (whimpering): He broke my arm. I didn't mean to hurt nobody.

PETE: Then why did you stab her, damn your puny soul?

SOLDIER: It was orders. I had to. None of us likes fighting you vets.

Two years later, in 1956, Patrick J. Hurley had an authorized biography done by a right-wing journalist, Don Lohbeck. He devoted sixteen pages to the bonus march, most of it repeating what Hurley and others on the right had said previously. Lohbeck argued that "the idea of marching on Washington—of using mass pressure to coerce the government—was a direct outgrowth of the Communist Party's attempts to organize and utilize the growing masses of unemployed in the creation of a revolutionary attitude in the United States." With this as his basic attitude, most of his comments are quite predictable. The interesting material is his attempt to reconcile Hurley and MacArthur's actions with

Hoover's orders, now that Hoover's long-suffering grievance was out in the open. After quoting Hoover, Lohbeck writes:

> But, General MacArthur, having received information from Army Intelligence sources working among the bonus marchers that the Communists were in virtually complete control of the bonus army and that some elements within the camps were armed (several machine guns were found concealed in the camps), refused to merely move the rioters from the seized buildings back to their camps across the river and then keep his troops camped on the city side of the river overnight. He said bluntly, "I will not permit my men to bivouac under the guns of traitors."

Although the book is footnoted, no source is given for the above, and it must be concluded that Hurley was the source. There were of course no machine guns. In a note in the back of his book, Lohbeck quotes Hoover ("Certain of my directions to the Secretary of War were not carried out."), and then tries to get Hurley off the hook of disobedience by arguing:

> Hoover's orders to the Secretary, calling upon the Federal troops, was an oral not a written order—and Secretary Hurley has never attempted to avoid responsibility for the conduct of the troops, which, he points out, made effective the President's orders without having fired a shot or seriously injured a single person.
>
> There were, however, certain methods for suppressing the riot suggested by President Hoover which Hurley thought impracticable (and which he felt might end in the defeat of American troops by mob action on the streets of the capital). But these suggestions, with which Hurley did not comply, were not in the form of a directive or an order.

To most subordinates, "suggestions" from a President are orders; Hurley clearly felt some uneasiness about his role. Yet Hoover cannot have been too displeased with him; the frontispiece of Lohbeck's book carried a letter on Hurley from Hoover himself, which, if not gushing praise, certainly was not censure.

With the publication of the Lohbeck volume on Hurley, one key memoir was still outstanding: Douglas MacArthur's. Although the five star general's *Reminiscences* did not appear until 1964, they were clearly prefigured by some basic source documents which had long been available to friendly biographers. Sentences and even whole paragraphs are carried over from one book to another; there will be no attempt here to note the changes in the MacArthur line from volume to volume, although an analysis of the successive changes might well be instructive.

The most extravagant and presumably authoritative of MacArthur's hagiographers must be noted. Major General Courtney Whitney, for many years a key member of MacArthur's staff in Australia and Japan, published, in 1956, *MacArthur: His Rendezvous with History*. Whitney was not an observer or participant in the bonus incident; MacArthur himself must be presumed as his source.

"Strange as it may seem," Whitney wrote near the climax of the book, "the well publicized incident of the 'Bonus March' in 1932 has a definite bearing upon the recall of MacArthur from his post in Korea in 1951." Whitney concedes that the march, as originally "conceived by certain Western veterans" was "an honest and dramatic appeal," but "as the Bonus March moved east its leadership gradually became infiltrated with a hard core of Communist agitators. . . . The motley crew had no sooner arrived in Washington than its members showed, by acts of violence so severe that the civil police were unable to cope with them, that the purpose of its leadership was to flout the orderly processes of government." Despite certain unique touches, like the presumed infiltration in box cars, this is essentially the well-established right-wing myth. Then Whitney adds a new element: "In fact, a secret document which was captured later disclosed that the Communist plan covered even such details as the public trial and hanging in front of the Capitol of high government officials. At the very top of the list was the name of Army Chief of Staff MacArthur."

Whitney followed this shocker—which no one before or since has ever heard of—with a routine Hurleyesque account of the riot, with the added fillip—also nowhere confirmed— that MacArthur's report to Hurley was "prepared by then-Major Dwight D. Eisenhower." Whitney concludes this section by a denunciation of MacArthur's high-placed enemies, with a vehemence extreme even for those paranoid times: [42]

> Despite such clear refutation, the Communists and their dupes, innocent and otherwise, have continued to   parrot the falsehood that MacArthur ordered U.S. soldiers to fire upon other Americans, and to use this lie as the foundation for an equally fallacious charge that he would someday become "the man on horseback," and would attempt to become some kind of American dictator. And these same groups, noting well MacArthur's defiance of Communism everywhere, have sought continuously to discredit his every action.
>
> They found a ready, though initially innocent, ally in the "Europe-first" cliques in the War and State Departments in Washington at the time of the outbreak of World War II. Together, for their separate reasons, these two groups sought to block acceptance of MacArthur's view that Europe and Asia—the Atlantic and Pacific—were equally important in the contemplation of our national interest and security. Together they attempted to discredit MacArthur in every way and thwart even his efforts against the enemy in World War II and Korea. Together they fostered the tragic notion that appeasement instead of defiance would win in Asia. Together they were responsible for MacArthur's recall.

MacArthur's own memoirs were not so extreme. The general devoted 5 of 426 pages to what he calls the "most poignant episode" of his tenure as chief of staff. The five pages are studded with mistakes ranging from minor errors to major delusions. If Hoover felt that the bonus march was aimed primarily at his defeat, MacArthur felt that it was another attempt to disgrace him: "the beginning of a definite and ceaseless campaign that set me apart as a man to be destroyed, no matter how long the Communists and their friends and admirers had to wait, and no matter what means they might have to use. But it was to be nineteen years before the bells of Moscow pealed out their glee at my eclipse."

According to MacArthur, "the President of the United States lived in danger" during the bonus march, and "Congress shook with fear at the sight and sound of the marchers." Apparently only the chief of staff kept his cool. MacArthur remembered, erroneously, that he "issued tents and camp equipment to be set up on the Anacostia Flats" and "that Waters [was] deposed and the Communists had gained control." "As the violence increased," MacArthur wrote, "Pelham Glassford . . . twice consulted with me about calling on the Army for assistance. Both times I advised against it." About Hoover's criticism and Hurley's admissions in the Lohbeck volume MacArthur said nothing directly, but one passage seems to be his apologia.

> At Anacostia Flats I received word from the Secretary of War, as we were in the midst of crossing the river, to suspend the operation at my discretion. I halted the command as soon as we had cleared the bridge, but at that moment the rioters set fire to their own camp. This concluded the proceedings for the night.

In other words, the expulsion of men, women, and children from Camp Marks never happened! No one trudged up Good Hope Hill into Maryland that night unless they were out for a stroll. In opposition to MacArthur's somewhat evasive 1964 statement, there is, in addition to dozens of eyewitness ac-

counts, the simple statement of the official "Report of Operations Against Bonus Marchers" made to MacArthur by
Brigadier General Perry L. Miles on August 4, 1932: "At 9:00
P.M., the Brigade Commander [Miles] issued orders substantially as follows: 'This command will proceed to Anacostia
Flats and evacuate Bonus Marchers from that property.'"
MacArthur's own report, dated August 15, 1932, states that
"when the fires [at Camp Marks] started, the Brigade Commander directed his troops to proceed into the Camp." Obviously, MacArthur was not telling the truth, although, given
his egoistic personality, he may not have realized it himself.[43]

The man who served as aide that day, Major Dwight David
Eisenhower, has of course become a major figure in history,
and, after he achieved some prominence, many writers began
to "discover" his role. Actually, his name never figured in any
of the contemporary accounts, although he is prominent in
one well-known picture, seeming strangely youthful to generations that see him as a father figure, uncharacteristically in-
haling a cigarette while MacArthur wipes a sweaty neck. After
almost thirty-five years of silence, Eisenhower published a brief
account in his, *At Ease: Stories I Tell to Friends*. Less than
three pages are devoted to the bonus march, although many
times that number treat the strange relationship between
Eisenhower and MacArthur. Despite the gulf in rank that
separated them in 1932, they became military rivals during
World War II and political rivals thereafter. Early books
about Eisenhower often quoted Ike's unflattering remarks
about the older man, but in later years both the spirit of
consensus and that reluctance to criticize a fellow military
man (outsiders sometimes complain about a "West Point
Protective Association") moderated most of his comments.
Both Eisenhower's resentment and his essentially charitable
nature show through in the 1967 account.

According to Eisenhower, the bonus marchers were "quiet
and orderly," but it seemed to him that they were "pioneering
direct action against Federal legislative authority." It is typical

of Eisenhower that his account of the bonus "riot" is completely bloodless; he neglects to mention that anyone was killed. He remembers that he thought that MacArthur's decision to "go into active command in the field" was an unwise decision.

> I told him that the matter could easily become a riot and I thought it highly inappropriate for the Chief of Staff of the Army to be involved in anything like a local or street-corner embroilment. General MacArthur disagreed, saying that it was a question of Federal authority in the District of Columbia, and because of his belief that there was "incipient revolution in the air" as he called it, he paid no attention to my dissent. . . .

In his description of the Battle of Washington, Eisenhower's bland memory erased all the sticks and stones, bayonets and sabers; he remembered only that the BEF "made no more vigorous protest than a little cat-calling and jeering at the soldiers." The veterans were "guided and nudged" out of downtown Washington toward Anacostia. Then he broaches the question of MacArthur's alleged insubordination.

> Instructions were received from the Secretary of War, who said he was speaking for the President, which forbade any troops to cross the bridge into the largest encampment of veterans, on open ground beyond the bridge.
> These instructions were brought to the troops by Colonel Wright, Secretary of the General Staff, and then by General Moseley of the Assistant Secretary's office. In neither instance did General MacArthur hear these instructions. He said he was too busy and did not want either himself or his staff bothered by people coming down and pretending to bring orders.

The former President then addressed himself to the old question of who started the fires: "I know no troops started the fires; they were too far away." His judgment of the whole business, however, shows how Eisenhower differed from the typical military man. Instead of gushing about the "tactical brilliance," he thought soberly that "the whole action, from beginning to end, did nothing to alleviate the lot of the veterans or to enhance the reputation of the government and the Army." He also tells us that he tried to dissuade his chief from meeting the press, but trying to get MacArthur to hide his light under a bushel was beyond Eisenhower's or anyone else's persuasive powers.

> I suggested it would be the better part of wisdom, if not of valor, to avoid meeting them. The troop movement had not been a military idea really, but a political order and I thought that the political officials only should talk to the press.

He concludes his brief account by observing that MacArthur was only acting as an agent and that the popular impression to the contrary was "unfortunate." [44] The whole bit is vintage Eisenhower at his best and worst. His strong feeling about the subordination of the military to the civilian and his essential decency come through, along with an equally typical foggy conception and inaccuracy of detail. He even gets the military hierarchy fouled up: Wright was a lieutenant colonel, not a colonel; he says Patton was "commanding a squadron of cavalry" when he was executive officer. More important, General Moseley was not "of the Assistant Secretary's office" and thus an adjunct of a minor politician, but deputy chief of staff and therefore in charge of army headquarters during MacArthur's absence. The statement that MacArthur "did not hear" the orders and that he did not want to be "bothered by people coming down and pretending to bring orders" is simply incredible. Eisenhower follows this description of insubordination with a denial that MacArthur "was acting as something more than the agent of civilian authorities." Eisenhower always wanted to have his cake and eat it too, to be a President but no politician, to win political battles, yet remain above them.

In all of these memoirs, the bonus march was merely an incident and, for a dozen years after 1951, received little popular attention. In 1956 and 1960, two scholarly accounts were published that should have squashed all the myths: Harris G. Warren writing about Hoover and the Depression, and Irving Bernstein in his social history of the American labor movement, each devoted a chapter to the BEF, and each got most of the essential facts straight, Warren depending on secondary sources, and Bernstein using the Glassford Mss.[45] Three years later, a professional writer with unique credentials used the materials Bernstein uncovered for a colorful yet analytic article in *American Heritage*.[46]

"I was graduated from college in June 1932," John D. Weaver wrote, "and came home to Washington, D.C., to find the shabby environs of the Capitol swarming with jobless men in frayed shirts, faded jeans, and overseas caps half-covering their thinning hair." That summer he was a regular visitor to the BEF camps; the experience obviously made a strong impression upon him. In 1948 he published a novel, *Another Such Victory,* in which all the action takes place in BEF camps, culminating with the expulsion. It is probably better history than literature; it carefully follows the newspaper, memoir, and propaganda accounts, and although it overemphasizes slightly the resistance offered by the BEFers, it does less violence to the events of July 28 than most historical accounts. The *American Heritage* piece fifteen years later had the advantage of the Glassford Mss. Weaver was the first to assert that the troops were called out before the bonus marchers had been killed, but he offered no evidence.

By 1963, then, essentially accurate accounts had been published, one of them in a popular magazine of fairly wide circulation; the myths, however, would not die, and as the summer of 1963 produced its own March on Washington, organized by Bayard Rustin and led by Martin Luther King, the thirty-one-year old bonus march was trotted out again for public inspection.

"PROTEST MARCHES ARE NOTHING NEW TO THE NATION'S CAP-ITAL," the *New York Times* reminded its readers on August 25, in a six-column story clustered around a picture of the first rock-throwing melee on July 28.[47] The *Times'* account contained only minor inaccuracies. Two days later, however, the *Wall Street Journal* demonstrated the staying power of myth. Although its story was clearly slanted against the civil rights demonstration—HISTORY OFFERS LITTLE ENCOURAGEMENT TO NEGROES MARCHING ON WASHINGTON—the conservative business organ nevertheless perpetuated what Hoover had called "the Bonus March lie" and in the process discovered that there had been "violent" fighting. According to an anonymous "staff reporter," [48]

> the antics of some of the veterans got to be too much for President Hoover and local authorities. On "bloody Thursday," July 28, Gen. Douglas MacArthur moved in with infantry and cavalry to break up the camps. In the violent fighting that followed, two veterans were killed and the bonus army was driven out of the city.

Drew Pearson also got into the act with a somewhat different version. As the muckraking columnist remembered it: [49]

> the day and night picketing in front of Congress got on the nerves of congressmen, also irritated President Herbert Hoover. Finally he issued an order to Gen. Douglas MacArthur, then chief of staff, to throw the Bonus Army out.
>
> Troops advanced, their bayonets fixed. Spectators booed. The troops hurled tear gas. Veterans ran from delapidated buildings. The cavalry charged.
>
> It was all over in a few minutes. There was barely time for Gen. McArthur to pose for the photographers.

In the summer of 1965 the bonus march was again flashed before the American public: the television "obituaries" of Herbert Hoover and Douglas MacArthur often used newsreel clips of the troops expelling the bonus marchers from downtown Washington. Probably as a result of that exposure—the commentary tended to be unsure of itself as the liberal sympathies of most of the network writers conflicted with the "let us now praise famous men" approach of the obituaries—there followed a flurry of right-wing rediscoveries of the "bonus smear." Syndicated columnist Morrie Ryskind devoted half a column to "the barrage of lies" told about the bonus march. His source was a "researcher" for the California Federation of Republican Women and his targets were Eleanor Roosevelt and the *Encyclopedia Britannica*. Ryskind felt that the *Britannica's* accurate and restrained statement—"[The bonus marchers] were not dislodged until the government moved on them with bayonets and tanks"—was a classical instance of historical distortion, and passed on to his readers the false information that Mrs. Roosevelt, after being corrected by Pat Hurley, "made no correction in her subsequent book." [50] The First Lady, of course, had done no such thing. She had accurately corrected the offending statement to read, "I shall never forget my feeling of horror when I learned that the Army had actually been ordered to *evict* [my italics] the veterans from their encampment." Even though she had been technically wrong, and admitted it, Eleanor Roosevelt had correctly perceived the heart of the matter. The Battle of Washington had been a "horror," even though its excesses and casualties may seem mild indeed to a generation which sees far worse on its television screens all too regularly.

11

Epilogue

THE BONUS MARCH is already a middle-aged event, shrouded in myth, replete with heroes and villains. With the exception of Wright Patman, still a maverick, but a maverick whose seniority has been converted into power as chairman of the House committee charged with responsibility over banking legislation, all of the major protagonists are dead. Hoover and MacArthur, as major historical figures, departed with pomp, circumstance, and nostalgia; the old soldiers who led the bonus army, Robertson and Waters, just faded away without attracting any national attention, in 1938 and 1959, each returning to the obscurity from which he came. Emanuel Levin remained a loyal Communist until his death in 1956, spending most of the rest of his life as circulation manager of the *Daily Worker*. In his obituaries in the party press, his role was naturally magnified, but even so it is clear that the bonus marches were the most significant events in his life.[1]

For Pelham Glassford, too, that summer of 1932 was the crest of the wave; although he lived more than a quarter of a century more, nothing else ever seemed to click for him. There was public speculation, in the early months of the New

Deal, that some truly important public job would come his way. He was mentioned as a possible Federal Relief Administrator, a Civilian Conservation Corps chief, and, in the fall, as Fiorello La Guardia's police chief in New York (what a combination those two would have made!) and, more prosaically, as high commissioner for baseball. None of these jobs materialized. Finally, in 1934, Glassford received a federal assignment which seemed tailored to his talents; he was appointed federal conciliator for labor disputes in the rich Imperial Valley of Southern California, which had a long history of violence and misery. But Glassford had too many bosses (he had been appointed jointly by the National Labor Board, the Department of Agriculture, and the Department of Labor), and the problems of California's "factories in the field" were too deep-seated for any powerless mediator to solve or even significantly alter. Glassford served for a few months, made an intelligent report, and resigned, clearly frustrated by his impotence. He never got another civilian federal job.[2]

In 1936 he served briefly and spectacularly as police chief of Phoenix, Arizona (he demoted his predecessor to patrolman and advocated legalized prostitution) and later that year made an unsuccessful race for a congressional seat, running as an anti-New Deal Democrat. (Although he declared himself "in full accord with the humanitarian principles" of FDR, he opposed many New Deal programs, and attacked the "alien favoritism policy of Madame Perkins," Roosevelt's Labor Secretary, and "the questionable efficiency and fairness of Harry Hopkins.") By 1938 he saw "dictatorship" on the horizon, insisted that both the "present administration and the Nation's businessmen have failed," and predicted that there would be no presidential election in 1940. When that election did come, he supported Wendell Wilkie. After the election he opposed entry into the war, and when that, too, came, he returned to active duty as Chief, Internal Security Division, of the Provost Marshal General's office. As late as September

1942, he thought it necessary to warn the nation of the dangers of a Fifth Column attack. He was apparently something less than a success; on Christmas Day, 1943, in the midst of the greatest war in history, he was retired at age sixty-three. He still wore only the single star he had earned in 1918. After retirement, he settled in Laguna Beach, California, with his second wife.

When William D. Mitchell was appointed chief counsel to the postwar Pearl Harbor investigating committee, the old general issued a public protest, arguing that Mitchell's report on the bonus army disqualified him for further public service. In 1948, in his last fling at politics, he participated in the United World Federalists and organized a MacArthur for President club! He continued to paint, was a patron of a local theater group, and in 1952 was elected president of the Laguna Beach Chamber of Commerce. In comfortable circumstances all his life, he left an estate of more than $100,000 when he died in 1959. His *New York Times* obituary correctly featured the most dramatic event of his life, but the headline, BRIG. GEN. P. D. GLASSFORD DEAD; LED POLICE AGAINST BONUS MARCH, somehow missed the point.[3]

And what was the point? Although it is dangerous to draw lessons from history, most historians try to do so, explicitly or implicitly. It seems to me that there are two major lessons to be learned from the complex of events we call the bonus march and that the nation has absorbed only one of them: it has learned how to anticipate the needs of veterans—but not how to deal with demonstrators.

The World War I innovation in the treatment of veterans —the attempted switch from pensions to compensation— didn't work out, like so many other progressive experiments; yet (and this is typical of the reforms of the era of the Republican Roosevelt and Woodrow Wilson), the change was a step in the right direction. The whole system of compulsory allotments to dependents, so controversial in 1914, has become a cornerstone of military compensation, in peace and war. The pension problem does seem, as Secretary McAdoo hoped, to have been avoided. Half a century after our entry into World War I, there is still no general pension for its veterans, and none seems in sight. The whole social security system, by providing pensions for everyone, has made pensions for veterans an anachronism, although this, like so many other facts of modern life, seems to have escaped the American Legion and most other veterans' groups.

If the Wilsonians were on the right track in wanting to break the nineteenth-century mold, it is obvious that they did not disavow enough of the old tradition. Nothing better illustrates the bankruptcy of progressivism than the bungled reconstruction that followed World War I. It is a historian's cliché by now that FDR learned from Wilson's most obvious failure in the diplomatic arena. The conspicuous involvement of prominent senators of both parties in foreign policy during World War II and the wartime bipartisanship exemplified by the appointment of Henry L. Stimson and Frank Knox as service secretaries, bore fruit as the Senate approved presidential diplomacy and genuine bipartisan support developed for the United Nations and various other international organizations. Roosevelt learned economic lessons, too, lessons that paid off even more tangibly in the almost uninterrupted prosperity that has followed World War II. Long before victory was achieved, plans were being made for the reconversion that must come. The prime public blueprint was the so-called Baruch–Hancock report of February 1944, whose major theme was that [4]

> there is no need for a postwar depression. Handled with competence, our adjustment, after the war is won, should be an adventure in prosperity. Our soldiers will not be let down. They are our chief concern. No pressure group of self-seekers will take our thoughts from them.

The Baruch-Hancock report did not foresee what became the greatest single program of human reconversion, the G. I. Bill of Rights, under whose provisions millions of veterans have attended, under subsidy, high schools, trade and vocational schools, and, above all, colleges and universities. Historians have only begun to establish the genesis and evolution of this program, and this study did not directly attack that problem. Two things, though, are quite clear. Like most other American reforms, the idea of subsidized education for veterans was first tried out in the states. At least one formal proposal for a national G. I. bill involving college study was made after World War I. Congressman Florian Lambert, an obscure Wisconsin Republican, proposed, in 1920, that Congress pass a law similar to the Wisconsin statute which allowed Badger State veterans to draw $30 monthly while they attended school.[5] By 1920, Wisconsin was no longer a progressive model for the nation, and, as we have seen, even more limited plans for postwar educational benefits on a national basis were scuttled by Andrew Mellon's short-sighted fiscal policies. These abortive postwar plans of one era are almost certainly one source of fruitful programs of another. A second source was probably derived from a conscious effort to avoid following that less promising precedent, the postwar bonus. As early as August 1943, General Hines of the Veterans Administration was trying to formulate strategies which would avoid the bonus problem.[6] In part, at least, the G. I. Bill grew out of the conscious attempt to avoid repeating past error.

If the lesson of how to reconvert human beings from war to peace in a constructive manner was learned, partially as a result of the bonus fiasco, the most obvious lesson of the bonus march—how to deal with massive urban protest—has been totally ignored. No recent policy chief has even begun to learn the lessons Pelham Glassford taught about how to handle large crowds of demonstrators. The Glassford method was simple and direct. Its major assumption was that demonstrators were reasonable human beings, with whom one could conduct a dialogue. Glassford mingled with them, came to know not only their leaders and their plans, but also their hopes and aspirations. He became an umpire, an arbiter, a bridge between the BEF and the powers-that-be.

It is unrealistic to expect that every American police chief have the talent (or was it genius?) that Glassford displayed in his short tenure as Washington's police chief. But the approach which he developed is certainly more likely to insure domestic tranquility than the orthodox posture which makes law enforcement officers, ipso facto, the adversaries of protest groups. This is not to suggest that the police must become the friends of those who want to make society over, but they could at least, in Glassford's words, become "friendly enemies."

Report from the Chief of Staff, United States Army, to the Secretary of War on the Employment of Federal Troops in Civil Disturbance in the District of Columbia July 28–30, 1932

WAR DEPARTMENT
OFFICE OF THE CHIEF OF STAFF
WASHINGTON, D.C.

August 15, 1932

Dear Mr. Secretary:

On the afternoon of July 28, 1932, in response to your instructions, Federal troops entered the District of Columbia for the purpose of assisting civil officials in restoring order in certain sections of this city where considerable bodies of persons had successfully defied police authority and were then engaged in riotous activity.

Within a few hours this mission was substantially accomplished and with no loss of life or serious casualty, after the arrival of the troops, among either the civilian or military elements involved. By

291

July 30th all Federal troops were withdrawn to their proper stations and the local situation was under the complete control of the civil authorities.

I am giving below a comprehensive account of this incident, to include the sequence of events leading up to the employment of Federal forces, the authority under which the troops acted, the principal troop movements involved, and the results accomplished. Attached as appendices are copies of official communications having an immediate bearing upon the incident; a detailed report of Brigadier General Perry Miles, who was in direct command of the Federal troops; a photographic record of particular phases of the operation, and typical newspaper articles and editorials dealing with the affair.

The purpose of this report is to make of permanent record in the War Department an accurate and complete description of a particular employment of Federal troops on a type of activity in which elements of the Army have often been engaged since the founding of the Republic.

Growth and Activities of So-called Bonus Army

During late May, 1932, large groups of practically destitute World War veterans, self-styled the "Bonus Army," or "Bonus Marchers," began arriving in the City of Washington with the announced intention of conducting an aggressive lobby in favor of the immediate payment of Veterans' Adjusted Compensation Certificates, commonly called the bonus.

With no normal means of support they established themselves, with the consent of local authorities, in vacant areas and abandoned buildings, principally governmentally-owned. Subsistence and supplies were obtained through donations from local and outside sources and for the large majority the only protection from the elements were rude huts constructed from scrap material. The largest of these encampments was named CAMP MARKS, situated on an alluvial flat on the left bank of the Anacostia River, northeast of the Bolling Field area. In the same vicinity was CAMP BARTLETT, on privately-owned ground. A portion of the Bonus Army took possession of an area southwest of the Capitol where demolition activities incident to the Federal Government's building program had already begun. Smaller detachments were located in other parts of the city. The aggregate strength of the Bonus Army gradually increased until it reached an estimated maximum of some ten to twelve thousand persons, including in some cases families and dependents of the veterans.

Speaking generally, all their early activities in the city were peaceably and lawfully conducted. They organized themselves under leaders of their own choosing, and these cooperated reasonably well with the civil authorities in the preservation of order. Manifestly, however, in a large body recruited as was this one, the inclusion of a lawless element was inevitable. As the Bonus Army's increasing size gave to the members thereof a growing consciousness of their collective power and importance in the community, efforts to solve acute problems of existence often went beyond the limits of legality. Individual solicitation for material assistance was frequently couched in terms of demand rather than of request. In some cases merchants and others, when called upon for contributions, were confronted with covert threats which amounted to nothing less than a system of extortion or forced levy. But the principal and most weighty objection to the concentration of such a force in the District of Columbia was occasioned by the deplorable conditions under which these people were compelled to live, entailing an ever-present danger of disease and epidemic.

Until the end of the Congressional session the marchers used every possible influence to secure support for their project among members of Congress. Even after the proposal was decisively defeated in the Senate on June 17th, these efforts were continued, and recruits for their cause were sought throughout the United States. Meanwhile the sanitary conditions under which they lived, with the arrival of the summer heat and rains and the further crowding of the occupied areas rapidly grew from bad to worse.

After it became apparent that Congress would not favorably consider the bonus project there was of course no longer any legitimate excuse for the marchers to continue endangering the health of the whole District population by the continued occupation of these areas. From another viewpoint also the concentration in one city of so many destitute persons normally residing in other sections of the country was exceedingly unwise and undesirable. The natural outlets through which they could benefit from the resources heretofore made available for the care of the needy by the charitable instincts of the American people were the local institutions of their respective communities. In their own communities they and their relative needs were known or could be investigated, and each could receive assistance accordingly. By coming to Washington they deprived themselves individually of this assistance, while collectively they presented to the charitable resources of the District a problem of insurmountable proportions. But though the necessity for the dispersion of the Bonus Marchers daily became more evident, its accomplishment was plainly to be accompanied by many difficulties because of the destitute circumstances of the great majority. In appreciation of this fact Congress, just preceding its adjournment on July 16th, provided funds for transporting them to their homes, and some fifty-five hundred took advantage of this provision of law.

As this partial evacuation took place an influx of newcomers occurred, in many instances later arrivals being of radical tendencies and intent upon capitalizing the situation to embarrass the Government. Former leaders of the Bonus Army lost, to a considerable degree, the authority they had so far exercised over the mass, and the subversive element gradually gained in influence.

During the whole period of its stay in the city the Bonus Marchers were assisted in various ways by the local police force. Help rendered included the collection of clothing, food, and utensils; permitting the use of vacant areas and abandoned buildings; providing some medical service, and securing the loan of tentage and rolling kitchens from the District National Guard. In this matter the efforts of the police were humanitarian and more than praiseworthy. In the light of later events, however, it is likely that a portion of the marchers interpreted this attitude as an indication of timidity rather than of sympathy, and were ready to take advantage of this supposed weakness whenever it might become expedient to do so.

IMMEDIATE CAUSE OF RIOTS

In late July the evacuation of certain of the occupied areas in the vicinity of the Capitol became necessary in order that the Government's parking and building program might proceed. On July 21st the Bonus leaders were formally notified by the police of this situation and requested to make prompt arrangements for the removal of occupants from the affected areas. Although there still remained ample time for veterans to apply for Government transportation to their homes, these requests were largely ignored. Prolonged negotiations were productive of no real results.

Since the projected operations were part of the program for unemployment relief they could not be indefinitely delayed, and finally the District Commissioners directed the police to clear these areas, using force if necessary. Accordingly, on the morning of July 28th a considerable body of police went to the encampment near Pennsylvania Avenue and 4½ Street and compelled the trespassers to evacuate. Within a short time large groups of men arrived from other camps, apparently under some pre-arranged plan, and a struggle for the possession of the disputed territory ensued. The police were overwhelmingly outnumbered and were quickly involved in a serious riot. The mob, composed of veterans and others who had intermingled with them, was incited by radicals and hot-heads to a free use of bricks, clubs, and similar weapons. Several policemen were hurt, one most seriously, while another, in defending himself, was forced to shoot and kill one of the Bonus Marchers. In the pictorial supplement attached hereto are several photographs showing the desperate nature of these encounters.

Operations of Federal Troops

MESSAGE TO PRESIDENT
FROM DISTRICT COMMISSIONERS

The situation rapidly assumed such a threatening aspect that the District Commissioners reported to the President their inability longer to preserve law and order in the areas affected and requested immediate assistance of Federal forces. They gave it as their opinion and that of the Superintendent of Police that if such help failed to materialize, considerable bloodshed would ensue. A copy of the letter they sent to the President is attached hereto.

The President promptly directed the Secretary of War to cooperate with the civil authorities in restoring law and order in the District of Columbia. The issue had now become a broader one than that of the simple expulsion of recalcitrant persons from an illegally occupied area in which they were physically interfering with essential Government activity. By their open and determined defiance of the Metropolitan police the members of this mob, recruited from all or most of the bonus camps in the city, had threatened the integrity of Federal authority within the confines of the Federally-governed District of Columbia. The dispersion and expulsion from the District of the force became thus the only logical answer the Government could make to the mob's action.

At 2:55 P.M., July 28, 1932, the following order was handed me by the Secretary of War:

> To: General Douglas MacArthur, Chief of Staff,
> United States Army.
>
> The President has just now informed me that the civil government of the District of Columbia has reported to him that it is unable to maintain law and order in the District.
>
> You will have United States troops proceed immediately to the scene of disorder. Cooperate fully with the District of Columbia police force which is now in charge. Surround the affected area and clear it without delay.
>
> Turn over all prisoners to the civil authorities.
>
> In your orders insist that any women and children who may be in the affected area be accorded every consideration and kindness. Use all humanity consistent with the due execution of this order.
>
> PATRICK J. HURLEY,
> Secretary of War.

The legal sufficiency of these successive steps as authority for the employment of Federal troops in civil disturbances in the District of Columbia is clearly set forth in a memorandum from The Judge Advocate General of the Army, attached hereto.

Upon receipt of the Secretary's order I designated Brigadier General Perry Miles, Commanding the 16th Brigade, as the officer in direct charge of all elements of the Regular army to be employed. The troops selected for immediate use were:

1 Battalion 12th Infantry, stationed at Ft. Washington, Md.
1 Squadron 3rd Cavalry, stationed at Ft. Myer, Va.
1 Platoon Tanks, temporarily stationed at Ft. Myer, Va.
Headquarters Company, 16th Brigade, stationed at Washington, D. C.

Simultaneously orders were issued for the concentration of a reserve at Ft. Myer to comprise troops from Ft. Geo. G. Meade, Md., Ft. Howard, Md., and Ft. Humphreys, Va.

GENERAL PLAN FOR TROOP EMPLOYMENT

The Brigade Commander was directed to give his attention first to the requirements of the situation near Pennsylvania Avenue and 4½ Street, where, according to reports, rioting was still in progress. My general plan was to clear that area, turn then to the encampment alleged to be occupied by Communists, at 13th and C Streets, after which I intended to move against the Anacostia contingent. A point on the Ellipse a short distance south of the State, War, and Navy Building, was designated for concentration of these units so as to insure, prior to any contact with the rioting groups, complete organization of the force and proper issue of necessary instructions.

I accompanied the troops in person, anticipating the possibility of such a serious situation arising that necessary decisions might lie beyond the purview of responsibility of any subordinate commander, and with the purpose of obtaining a personal familiarity with every phase of the troops' activities.

The Cavalry Squadron and Tank Platoon arrived at the Ellipse about 3:00 P.M., and the Infantry Battalion about 4:20 P.M. The Brigade Commander issued necessary instructions, particularly cautioning subordinate commanders to avoid rushing tactics and undue haste as likely to provoke useless conflict with the rioters. General Miles proceeded correctly on the theory that a demonstration of overpowering force, accompanied by sufficient time to permit dispersion of the rioters, promised the surest, simplest, and safest results in this situation. Necessary special equipment was issued to the troops, particularly tear gas bombs.

UNDERSTANDING WITH CIVIL POLICE

While essential preparations were in progress I was in receipt of several messages from members of the police force concerning the existing situation. About 3:45 P.M. General P. D. Glassford, Superintendent of the Metropolitan Police, contacted me, and the projected troop movement was discussed. At my request he undertook the special and immediate mission of notifying leaders of all bonus groups that Federal property in the District would have to be evacuated before nightfall. This I considered important, since in the chaotic conditions then prevailing there was grave danger of many innocent or neutral persons becoming involved in difficulties because of lack of understanding of the orders under which the troops were operating.

Unfortunately, the leader of the bonus movement had apparently lost all control of the situation. According to reports made to me he had stated he was no longer able to handle his men and had withdrawn from the scene of operations. I vainly sought him during the entire operation so that I might utilize his influence towards pacification of the situation.

At this conference General Glassford also reported that his men were exhausted by long hours of continuous duty and by their strenuous efforts of that day in the riot on lower Pennsylvania Avenue. It was apparent to me that unless assistance was quickly forthcoming there would probably be permitted a situation to develop involving the gravest consequences.

Promptly at 4:30 P.M. the troops began moving east on Pennsylvania Avenue, the Cavalry and Tanks leading; the Infantry following in extended formation.

The march to the Capitol area was made without incident. Upon arrival there, and while troops were taking up designated positions, repeated warnings to disperse were given to a large crowd of spectators on the north side of the Avenue. These people were in no sense law-breakers and their dispersion was desired only to safeguard innocent bystanders from accident incident to subsequent activity. These warnings were temporarily ignored, but later when it became necessary to release tear bombs against the rioters, the prevailing wind carried a light gas concentration into the crowd of spectators and the area was quickly cleared.

TROOP EMPLOYMENT

The rioting elements were immediately ordered to evacuate the area south of the Avenue, which order they ignored. In line with my determination to give a reasonable time to any and all groups to disperse, no troop movement was initiated against them until 5:30 P.M. At that moment they were still apparently determined to hold their ground.

It is to be remembered that for many weeks members of the Bonus Army had seen all their wishes and desires, as far as the local situation was concerned, acceded to by civil officials, and more recently they had successfully defied constituted authority and withstood police efforts to evict them. It is doubtful, therefore, that when the Regular troops were deployed in their front the rioters really believed that the eviction order was to be definitely enforced. At least it is a fact that as the troops started to move forward the mob showed a surly and obstinate temper and gave no immediate signs of retreating. As the soldiers approached more closely a few brickbats, stones, and clubs were thrown, and it became apparent that some hint must be given of the determination underlying the employment of Federal troops in this contingency. This hint was given through the medium of harmless tear gas bombs. A number of these were thrown by the soldiers among the foremost ranks of the rioters, and from that moment little organized defiance was encountered.

Troop operations were strictly confined to evacuation of Governmentally-owned tracts. A short distance south of Pennsylvania Avenue was a bonus detachment reported by the police to be occupying leased property. These men were not molested. For the same reason no action was taken against a small group of bonus seekers on the 7th Street Wharves—a detachment brought to my attention by General Glassford in person.

The program previously outlined for the day's activities was carried out expeditiously, albeit with a leisureliness that permitted every member of the Bonus Army ample time to make his unhindered way, if he was so minded, out of the path of the troops. I was particularly desirous that the drift of the dispersed groups be toward the Anacostia encampment and away from the principal business and residence sections of the city. This was accomplished through appropriate dispositions and movements of the troops.

That ample time was accorded everyone to remove himself and his belongings from affected areas before the arrival of the troops is evidenced by the general time schedule of the movement. At 3:45 P.M. word had been sent to all detachments of the Bonus Army to evacuate Governmentally-owned ground. It was 5:30 P.M. before the first movement started against the occupants of the area in which rioting had taken place during the day. It was another hour before the so-called Communist area at 13th and C Streets was reached. This, incidentally, had already been evacuated.

Here the troops were rested and fed, affording the CAMP MARKS occupants additional time for evacuation. I held personal conferences with subordinates and with representatives of the police. At this point General Glassford called my attention to one group of Government buildings occupied by women and children and asked my instructions concerning them. I informed him that not only would they be unmolested, but that I was prepared to furnish a guard for their protection if he so desired. He replied that the police could take care of this activity, and stated that the Red Cross had volunteered assistance in caring for these groups.

The march toward Anacostia was resumed about 9:10 P.M. Upon arriving at that camp half an hour later the eastern end was found vacant. Almost immediately there reported to me a man who gave his name as Atwell and his position as commander of CAMP MARKS. He asked for an additional delay of an hour to complete the evacuation of that encampment, to which request I promptly acceded and directed the troops to halt and bivouac for the night.

Bonus detachments at CAMP MEIGS, CAMP SIMS, and near the Congressional Library were not evacuated that night, although I was in receipt of several specific requests from the District Commissioners to clear out these places. I did, however, send the occupants of those camps a message to the effect that the troops would move against them the following day if not previously evacuated.

Because of the relative slowness of their general advance, and their calm and unhurried demeanor at all times, the troops largely avoided actual physical contact and conflict with rioting elements. In isolated instances it was necessary to threaten individual members of the mob, and upon several occasions troops were subjected to showers of bricks and stones. The report of the Brigade Commander gives the details of these incidents.

BURNING OF ENCAMPMENTS

Invariably, as each area was evacuated during the afternoon and evening, fires broke out among the shacks previously occupied by the marchers. Constructed of highly inflammable materials, these structures stood so close together that the spread of the flames was extremely rapid. In each instance, however, the troops and the Fire Department prevented any damage to permanent buildings in the vicinity. Considerable argument was obtained concerning the origin of these fires, and I therefore give below the facts, as far as I have been able to determine them.

At no time did I give orders to subordinate commanders that could have been construed as authorization for initiating the destruction of the encampments, and investigation has failed to reveal a single instance where a subordinate gave any such instructions. The first of these fires came to my notice within a few moments after the troops began their initial advance against the rioters on lower Pennsylvania Avenue. Personally stationed at that time within a few yards of the spot where this occurred, I was under the distinct impression that, in view of the proportions the fire quickly attained, it must have been ignited at least several minutes before the foremost troops reached it. The District Fire Department came immediately to the scene, and a considerable number of shacks in that general vicinity were not harmed by fire on the evening of July 28th.

My arrival at the encampment at 13th and C Streets was almost simultaneous with that of the leading troops. The area was practically deserted and already dotted with fires, started, in my opinion, by the former occupants. Under the circumstances the only feasible action was to hasten the spread of the flames so that danger to neighboring areas would be minimized and personnel relieved from the necessity of standing guard. This the troops did.

At CAMP MARKS, by far the largest of the encampments, responsibility for firing the main camp lay definitely with the Bonus Marchers. The troops entered the area at the eastern tip, descending onto the flats through a steep, poorly conditioned road. This portion of the area was completely deserted, and one or two abandoned and partially demolished shacks in the vicinity of the Anacostia Bridge were fired to illuminate the immediate surroundings and permit orderly disposition of the troops. It was in this area, completely outside of the main part of the camp, that the troops were halted by my order to afford more time for evacuation. During this period of inaction the firing of CAMP MARKS began, apparently by concerted action of its occupants, for within a few minutes the blaze was general throughout the area.

In this area was a considerable amount of Government property, previously loaned to the veterans by the National Guard, which we had contracted to recover. Consequently, when the fires started the Brigade Commander directed his troops to proceed into the camp, now obviously abandoned, to save as much of this property as possible, and to clear the area of possible stragglers. Reported subsequent burning of individual shacks by soldiers, if authentic, was for the purpose only of hastening the destruction of a camp already doomed by the action of the Bonus Marchers themselves.

In the process of mopping up the various areas the following day the troops discovered here and there various partially burned or destroyed hovels. The destruction of all these was completed with a view of facilitating the clearing up process which must inevitably follow.

During the night of July 28–29 groups of rioters on the heights east and south of CAMP MARKS attempted to initiate attacks against isolated detachments of soldiers. They were dispersed with a few tear gas bombs, and no further trouble was experienced. Searchlights provided by the District Fire Department and by the National Guard were helpful in maintaining proper outposts. Troops were placed at critical points to prevent the return of Bonus Marchers, either individually or collectively, toward the business centers of the District.

In employing Federal troops for reestablishing law and order, there had been no occasion for a declaration of martial law, so that responsibility for general control of traffic and spectators remained with the police. Congestion of the most serious kind occurred in the streets and areas around the Anacostia Bridge—a condition that kept the police extremely busy until a late hour at night. In some instances they were forced to use tear gas bombs, but by morning approximately normal conditions in this respect were restored.

During the day of July 29th the troops completed the task laid out for them. Stragglers near the Capitol and in other areas were evacuated and order restored throughout the city. The details of these movements, all of which were accomplished without unusual incident, are given in General Miles' report. Isolated shacks were demolished, and the troops, as a precautionary measure, remained on guard that night.

The following day, July 30th, all troops were withdrawn. The mission given them had been performed loyally and efficiently and in accordance with your personal injunction to "use all humanity consistent with the execution of this order." They had neither suffered nor inflicted a serious casualty. They had not fired a shot, and had actually employed no more dangerous weapons than harmless tear gas bombs. Even these were not used in heavy concentrations, or over periods more than a few minutes each, and any contention that injury to individuals was caused by them is entirely without foundation. This is evidenced by the fact that in several instances individual officers and soldiers remained, without masks, in the midst of gas concentrations throughout their duration.

COOPERATION WITH CIVIL AGENCIES

At every stage of this operation the cooperation received from the Police and Fire Departments of the District of Columbia was all that could be desired. Their help in transmitting messages, controlling fires, providing transportation, furnishing searchlights, and in similar activity was freely given and deeply appreciated. The Commanding General of the 16th Brigade has written letters of appreciation to them as he did also to the Commanding Officer of the National Guard of the District of Columbia, who assisted by furnishing searchlight service on the night of July 28–29.

General Observations

VALUE OF DISCIPLINE

From the standpoint of the Army one of the outstanding features of this entire incident was the exemplary conduct of the rank and file of the units employed. Compelled often to act entirely on their own responsibility, and frequently under extreme provocation, the enlisted men exhibited a patience, a forebearance, and a sympathetic though determined attitude that won the praise of every impartial observer. The value of obedience, cohesion and discipline, all products of intelligent and thorough training, was again exemplified and emphasized. This leads to a reiteration of the axiom, so well understood by military men, that whenever necessity arises for employment of Federal troops in civil disturbance, only such units should be used as are known to have attained a high degree of excellence in training and discipline.

Noticeable also were the efficiency, good judgment, and tireless devotion to duty displayed by commissioned personnel. From officers we expect, as a matter of course, the utmost in loyal and intelligent service. Yet situations of this kind invariably present to all unit commanders problems of extreme delicacy, characterized more by rapid and kaleidoscopic change than by predictable detail. The possibility of errors in judgment, with far-reaching and serious consequences, is always present. I report with real gratification that during this whole affair there came to my attention no instance warranting the slightest criticism of the action of any officer, from the Brigadier General commanding to the Second Lieutenant latest commissioned.

ADEQUATE FORCE MINIMIZES CASUALTIES

It is almost superfluous to say that in employing troops to quell civil disorder the prevention of casualties among civilians and soldiers alike is a consideration of the utmost importance. This end is best attained through the concentration of a force strong in apparent as well as in actual power. Suspected weakness on the side of law and order encourages riotous elements to resist, usually resulting in open conflict, while obvious strength gains a moral ascendancy that is normally all-sufficient.

These truths were strikingly illustrated in the events of July 28th on lower Pennsulvania [sic] Avenue. By 3:00 P.M. of that day the police were almost exhausted after hours of failure to make headway against a mob of overwhelming numbers. This was not due to any fault of the police force, for the members of which I have nothing but praise. The real cause for failure lay in the great disparity in apparent power—a disparity that could be made good only by the use of deadly weapons. This, obviously, was a method of last resort—a circumstance of which the rioters advantaged themselves in refusing to evacuate disputed territory. Even so, casualties were serious on both sides, resulting in the immediate death of one man and the subsequent death of another.

But within a few minutes of the first definite advance by Regular troops this area was hastily vacated and with no casualty worth the name. The rioters lost heart in the face of a power they could recognize as overwhelming, even though numerically their advantage was still some five or six to one. But the combination of sufficient numbers, proper equipment, concerted action, and solid discipline are not to be withstood by any mob.

For the reasons I have been discussing, tanks are particularly valuable in quelling civil disorder. They create an impression of irresistible and inexorable power, and being visible from some distance they create apprehension in the rear as well as in the front elements of a mob. This is important, for thus is avoided any tendency of a mob to force its forward elements into a fight because of physical pressure from those who imagine themselves to be in an area of comparative safety in the rear. Cavalry also, aside from its mobility, is useful for similar reasons.

Most efficacious of all weapons in such circumstances is the tear gas bomb. In the hands of well trained infantry, advancing with an evident determination, this harmless instrument quickly saps the will to resist of unorganized and unprepared bodies. Its small smoke cloud is visible from some distance, and its moral suasion thus extends over a far greater area than does its actual effects. It creates an irresistible desire to run from rather than toward the scene of its use.

We are led then to a second observation applicable in situations of this kind. Having selected well disciplined troops, it is desirable and necessary that they be concentrated in sufficient strength to awe the opposition, and that they be equipped with such weapons as tend to increase the impression of irresistible power. The greater the real and apparent strength of the force on the side of law and order, the smaller will be the casualties among the disaffected elements.

NEWSPAPER REPRESENTATIVES

Finally, I desire to invite attention to the handling of representatives of the public press during this affair. Employment of Federal troops on an occasion of this kind is essentially disagreeable and repugnant to the units involved, and the natural impulse is to attempt to hold newspapermen at a distance. Any such attempt is a fundamental error. Incidents of this character are of intense interest to the public, and accurate information concerning them should appear in the columns of the daily newspapers.

The conduct of military units must be such that when accurately reported no fair-minded person can justly criticize them. The logical answer therefore is to accord to representatives of the press the utmost freedom consistent with the requirements of the military task to be accomplished. In this instance this procedure was used. All reporters were invited to go to any spot at any time they desired, and to see everything they possibly could. Arrangements were made to assist in their transportation during moves of considerable length, and no attempt was made to confuse or deceive them as to the details of any phase of the operation. As a result there appeared in the daily press, except for a few obviously prejudiced accounts, a very fair presentation of the facts as they were seen and interpreted by the reporters.

Occasion for the necessitous employment of the Army in service of this character must be universally deplored. It is indicative of a temporarily unhealthy condition in the body politic, no matter how localized may be the inciting cause. For the Army itself there is involved a task of the most unwelcome sort. It nevertheless constitutes a duty that must be performed with loyal determination, but without harshness or brutality. The objective to be attained is prompt restoration of law and order, with a minimum of physical violence and with the least possible interference in the normal activities of the civil community. By adhering firmly to these methods military units will not only serve best the public interest, but will win for themselves the renewed respect and appreciation of public-spirited citizens.

In the case at hand these standards of conduct were rigidly observed by the Army. Its allotted tasks were performed rapidly and efficiently, but with the maximum consideration for the members of the riotous groups consistent with their compulsory eviction. The results speak for themselves. Within a few hours a riot rapidly assuming alarming proportions was completely quelled, and from the moment the troops arrived at the scene of the disorder no soldier or civilian received a permanent or dangerous injury. Thus a most disagreeable task was performed in such a way as to leave behind it a minimum of unpleasant aftermath and legitimate resentment.

DOUGLAS MACARTHUR
General
Chief of Staff.

Notes

Chapter 1

1. Amelia C. Ford, *Colonial Precedents for Our National Land System as It Existed in 1800* (Madison, Wis., 1910), pp. 103–107.
2. Jerry A. O'Callaghan, "The War Veteran and the Public Lands," and Rudolph Freund, "Military Bounty Lands and the Origins of the Public Domain," in Vernon Carstensen, ed., *The Public Lands* (Madison, Wis., 1963). A typically mugwump evaluation of these policies was that "as an example of how not to dispose of public land [military bounties were] excellent." (See n. 22 for enlargement on "mugwump.") Benjamin Horace Hibbard, *A History of the Public Land Policies* (New York, 1924), p. 129.
3. William H. Glasson, *History of the Military Pension Legislation in the United States* (New York, 1900), pp. 23–51.
4. John William Oliver, *History of the Civil War Military Pensions* (Madison, Wis., 1915), p. 5.
5. Wallace E. Davies, *Patriotism on Parade: The Story of Veterans' and Hereditary Organizations in America, 1783–1900* (Cambridge, Mass., 1955), p. 27, writes of earlier groups as scattered "precedents [for] the post–Civil War epidemic of associational activity."
6. Mary R. Dearing, *Veterans in Politics* (Baton Rouge, 1952), p. 106.
7. Figures from Davies, *Patriotism on Parade*, pp. 74–75.
8. Ibid., p. 147.
9. U.S., Congress, Senate, *Homesteads for Soldiers and Sailors*, Report 482, 42d Cong., 3d sess., 1872, p. 17.
10. O'Callaghan, "The War Veteran."

11. Glasson, *Military Pension Legislation,* pp. 60–64.

12. Oliver, *Civil War Military Pensions,* pp. 51–62.

13. Glasson, *Military Pension Legislation,* pp. 106–107.

14. Ibid., pp. 66–69.

15. James D. Richardson, ed., *Messages and Papers of the Presidents* (Washington, D.C., 1911), VIII, pp. 549–557.

16. Robert McElroy, *Grover Cleveland* (New York, 1923), I, pp. 189–217.

17. Kirk H. Porter and Donald B. Johnson, eds., *National Party Platforms, 1840–1960* (Urbana, Ill., 1961), p. 82.

18. Grand Army of the Republic, *Journal of the National Encampment . . . 1888* (Cincinnati, 1888), p. 190.

19. Glasson, *Military Pension Legislation,* pp. 116–117. McKinley, even after his elevation to the presidency, usually deferred to the GAR. In 1899, for example, he prefaced a recommendation to Congress for a modification of the pension laws with the remark: "The Grand Army of the Republic at its recent National Encampment . . . has brought to my attention." Richardson, ed., *Messages and Papers,* X, p. 163.

20. Tanner to General W. T. Sherman, January 5, 1899, cited in Dearing, *Veterans in Politics,* p. 393.

21. Computed from U.S., Department of Commerce, Bureau of the Census, *Historical Statistics of the United States: Colonial Times to 1957* (Washington, D.C., 1960), Series Y350–356, Y801–811, pp. 718–719, 739.

22. A mugwump was, in the first instance, one of those genteel GOPers who couldn't "hold their nose and vote for Blaine" in 1884 and so voted for Cleveland. By extension, the mugwump type has come to mean the upper-class, WASP, genteel, well-educated reformer, dedicated to laissez-faire, low taxes, good government, etc.

23. Carl Schurz, "The Pension Scandal," *Harper's Weekly* (May 5, 1894).

24. McElroy, *Cleveland,* I, p. 200.

25. Senator Robert Taylor of Tennessee in *Proceedings of the Democratic National Convention, 1908* (Denver, 1908), p. 46.

26. Davies, *Patriotism on Parade,* pp. 162–163.

27. William H. Glasson, *Federal Military Pensions in the United States* (New York, 1918), pp. 246–261. Fiscal 1921 was the most expensive year for Civil War pensions. Just over a quarter billion dollars was spent. Bureau of the Census, *Historical Statistics,* Series Y801–811, p. 739.

28. *Congressional Record,* 59th Cong., 2d sess. (January 9, 1907), p. 805.

29. Although Georgia-born McAdoo was a New York attorney at the time of his cabinet appointment, he was recognized as a leading spokesman for the dry, Protestant, and largely southern wing of the party; in 1924, his supporters helped to wreck the Democratic convention by refusing to condemn the Ku Klux Klan.

30. McAdoo to Wilson, June 23, 1917, cited in William G. McAdoo, *Crowded Years* (New York, 1931), pp. 428–429. McAdoo's colleague, Canadian-born Franklin K. Lane, who came to the Interior Secretaryship from California, agreed that there had been "a great deal of fraud" in the

pension system. Franklin K. Lane, *The American Spirit* (New York, 1918), p. 55.

31. McAdoo, *Crowded Years*, p. 428. A good, contemporary, popular analysis is Samuel McCune Lindsay, "Soldiers' Insurance Versus Pensions," *Review of Reviews* (October 1917); the most detailed treatment is William F. Gephart, *Effects of the War Upon Insurance with Special Reference to the Substitution of Insurance for Pensions* (New York, 1918).

32. Baker to FDR, May 23, 1935, PPF 1820, Franklin D. Roosevelt Library, Hyde Park. The letter praised the President for his veto of the 1935 bonus bill (see Chapter 9). In his memoirs, Gompers says not that he thought up the whole measure, but that it was he who suggested that the principle of workmen's compensation should be employed in place of the Pension Bureau schedules; he may, however, have been understating his role. It is revealing that his fetish for voluntarism was so great that his account of the legislation fails to mention the compulsory aspects of the scheme. Samuel Gompers, *Seventy Years of Life and Labor* (New York, 1925), II, pp. 370–372. For a brief account of Judge Mack's career, see his obituary in the *New York Times*, September 6, 1943.

33. It is not discussed, for example, in Seward Livermore, *Politics is Adjourned: Woodrow Wilson and the War Congress, 1916–1918* (Middletown, Conn., 1966), or in any of the several books on Baker. The latest of these, Daniel R. Beaver, *Newton D. Baker and the American War Effort, 1917–1919* (Lincoln, Neb., 1966), p. 215, has a passage on the persistence of progressivism during the war and discusses several statutes, but not the veterans' legislation.

34. Mary Synon, *McAdoo* (New York, 1924), pp. 302–303. For examples of insurance industry opinion, see *Congressional Record*, 64th Cong., 2d sess. (September 7, 1917), pp. 6769–6770.

35. McAdoo to Wilson, July 31, 1917, in *Congressional Record*, 65th Cong., 1st sess. (September 10, 1917), pp. 6900–6901.

36. For Rayburn's remarks, see *Congressional Record*, 65th Cong., 1st sess. (September 7, 1917), pp. 6753–6760; for London's comments, see ibid., p. 6924; for the annoyance of pension forces, see remarks of Key of Ohio, ibid., p. 6753, and his letter to Congressman Adamson, ibid., p. 6828. For a conservative view, see Hershey of Maine, ibid., p. 6909. Theodore Roosevelt's support is in a letter to Judge Mack, August 21, 1917, in ibid., p. 6835. The ex-President was particularly pleased that the bill put the emphasis on "the family instead of . . . the man" and wanted "the compensation for the family so arranged as to put a premium on the soldier having a considerable number of children; his is the stock which the Nation cannot permit to die out." Woodrow Wilson wrote Congressman Adamson that the bill was "one of the most admirable pieces of legislation that has been proposed in connection with the war." He noted with approval that it encompassed "justice and humanity both to the soldier and to his family." For other views see U.S., Congress, Senate, *Bureau of War Risk Insurance*, Report 130, 65th Cong., 1st sess., 1917.

37. The statute is Public Law 90 and was amended by Public Law 175, 65th Cong. The data on costs are from William Pyrle Dillingham, *Federal Aid to Veterans, 1917–1941* (Gainesville, Fla., 1952). Smoot had declared that no matter what kind of legislation was passed "just as sure as I live . . . there will be special pension legislation." *Congressional Record,* 65th Cong., 1st sess. (October 4, 1917), p. 7739.

38. Nor was it insurance against McAdoo himself; by 1935, Senator McAdoo voted to override President Roosevelt's veto of a bonus bill (see Chapter 9) and, on Armistice Day of that year, demagogically advised a gathering of 1,500 Los Angeles veterans to march on Washington to get their bonus, even though he must have known that a "deal" had already been made by congressional leaders to pass the bill in January. See J. F. T. O'Connor to Marvin McIntyre, with enclosed clipping, December 2, 1935, OF 391, FDRL.

Chapter 2

1. Lane to Congressman Henry Z. Osborne (R.-Cal.), in *Congressional Record,* 65th Cong., 2d sess. (October 19, 1918), pp. 11387–11388. For an even earlier version of Lane's plan, see also U.S., Department of the Interior, *Annual Report, 1918* (Washington, D.C., 1918), and U.S., Congress, House, *Farms for Soldiers,* Document 173, 66th Cong., 1st sess., 1919.

2. Joy MacAskill, "The Chartist Land Plan," in Asa Briggs, ed., *Chartist Studies* (London, 1957).

3. The proposals are conveniently summarized in U.S., Congress, House, *National Soldier Settlement Act,* Report 216, 66th Cong., 1st sess., 1919. See also U.S., Congress, Senate, *Work and Homes for Returning Soldiers, Sailors, and Marines,* Report 780, 65th Cong., 3d sess., 1919. The best scholarly accounts of twentieth-century back-to-the-landism are Bill G. Reid, "Propaganda for Soldier Settlement during World War I," *Mid-America* (July 1964), and his, "Franklin K. Lane's Idea for Veterans Colonization," *Pacific Historical Review* (November 1964), both of which derive from his Ph.D. dissertation, "American Proposals for Soldier Settlement During the World War I Period" (University of Oklahoma, 1963), and Paul G. Conkin, *Tomorrow a New World: The New Deal Community Program* (Ithaca, N.Y., 1961). Neither seems to be aware of the amount of continuing interest by western legislators in getting massive reclamation–resettlement projects going during the 1920s. See, for example, Senator McNary's proposed amendment to the 1922 bonus bill in *Congressional Record,* 67th Cong., 2d sess. (August 26, 1922), p. 11816. For administration opposition, see David F. Houston, *Eight Years With Wilson's Cabinet* (New York, 1926), I, p. 351. The Mondell plan received a great deal of favorable publicity, as demonstrated by press clippings in the Mondell Mss., University of Wyoming.

4. Huddleston's remarks in *Congressional Record*, 68th Cong., 1st sess. (January 24, 1924), p. 1397. Alex M. Arnett, *Claude Kitchin* (Boston, 1937), makes no mention of the alleged incident. The mustering-out bonus—sometimes called the "suit of clothes" bonus—was effected by Section 1406, Public Law 1254, 65th Cong. See also House, *National Soldier Settlement Act*, Report 216, 1919.

5. There is no reliable history of the Legion. Marquis James, *A History of the American Legion* (New York, 1923), Richard Seelye Jones, *A History of the American Legion* (Indianapolis, 1946), and Raymond Moley, Jr., *The American Legion Story* (New York, 1966), are essentially press agentry, while William Gellerman, *The American Legion as Educator* (New York, 1938), and Justin Gray, *The Inside Story of the Legion* (New York, 1948), are muckracking attacks from the left. Rodney Minott, *Professional Patriots: Organized Veterans and the Spirit of Americanism* (Washington, 1962), is quite specialized and superficial. The best work, despite its obvious limitations, is the hostile journalistic account, Marcus Duffield, *King Legion* (New York, 1931). For examples of surreptitious federal aid to the Legion, see Correspondence of the Secretary of the Treasury, Individual Correspondents—"American Legion," Record Group 56, National Archives (hereafter cited as RG, NA).

6. James, *American Legion*, p. 59.

7. American Legion, *Committee Reports and Resolutions . . . 1st National Convention of the American Legion* (n.p., n.d.), p. 35.

8. The bill is printed in *Congressional Record*, 66th Cong., 2d sess. (May 29, 1920), pp. 7930–7934; Houston's remarks, along with other comments, are in U.S., Congress, House, *World War Adjusted Compensation*, Report 1020, 66th Cong., 2d sess., 1920; Rainey's are in *Congressional Record*, 66th Cong., 2d sess. (May 29, 1920), p. 7940; the House vote is in ibid., p. 7941. See also David F. Houston, *Eight Years with Wilson's Cabinet* (New York, 1926), II, p. 100.

9. *The Commoner* (April 1920): 1.

10. Wesley M. Bagby, *The Road to Normalcy* (Baltimore, 1962), p. 105.

11. Kirk H. Porter and Donald B. Johnson, eds., *National Party Platforms, 1840–1960* (Urbana, Ill., 1961), pp. 249, 264.

12. American Legion, *Committee Reports and Resolutions . . . 2nd Convention* (n.p., n.d.), p. 16.

13. James, *American Legion*, p. 259.

14. After the election, lame-duck Senator C. S. Thomas (D.-Colo.) authored a minority report insisting that it was "not too extravagant to assert that if the American Nation has been preserved from German aggression only to loose the floodgates of its Treasury upon its returning soldiers, it is a serious question whether it is worth while to safeguard a country from its enemies only to be plundered by its own Citizens." U.S., Congress, Senate, *Soldier Bonus*, Report 821, 66th Cong., 3d sess., 1921, pt. 2, pp. 5–6.

15. Details of the 1921 measure are found in U.S., Congress, Senate,

Veterans' Adjusted Compensation Bill, Report 133, 67th Cong., 1st sess., 1921.

16. Mellon to Senator Joseph S. Frelinghuysen (R.-N.J.), July 2, 1921, in U.S., Congress, Senate, *Compensation for the Veterans of the World War,* Document 45, 67th Cong., 1st sess., 1921.

17. The President's speech is in U.S., Congress, Senate, *Soldiers' Adjusted Compensation Bill,* Document 48, 67th Cong., 1st sess. Two of Harding's biographers have reported this incident inaccurately. Cf. Samuel Hopkins Adams, *Incredible Era* (Boston, 1939), p. 229, and Andrew Sinclair, *The Available Man* (New York, 1965), pp. 212–213. Reflecting their own very different eras, the first finds Harding's antibonus actions one of the few marks on the credit side of the President's ledger, while the second concludes that he was "in favor of the wealthy at the expense of the brave." The more authoritative Robert K. Murray, *The Harding Era: Warren G. Harding and His Administration* (Minneapolis, 1969), pp. 186–188, 308–314, gets the facts right. His attitude toward the bonus echoes Adams'. He ignores Harding's campaign statement favoring a bonus. Chief Justice William Howard Taft claimed that he had strengthened Harding's antibonus position and otherwise "improved" the veto message in 1922. See A. T. Mason, *William Howard Taft: Chief Justice* (New York, 1964), p. 139.

18. The vote is in *Congressional Record,* 67th Cong., 1st sess. (July 15, 1921), p. 3875. Pairs are included in my analysis. Watson in ibid., p. 3654. See ibid., 68th Cong., 2d sess. (January 9, 1925), for comments on such a coalition by Senator Norris. James T. Patterson, "A Conservative Coalition Forms in Congress," *Journal of American History* (March 1966), reviews what historians have said about such coalitions.

19. James, *American Legion,* pp. 233–235.

20. U.S., Congress, House, *Soldiers' Adjusted Compensation,* Report 804, 67th Cong., 1st sess., 1921.

21. *Congressional Record,* 67th Cong., 2d sess. (February 16, 1922), p. 2655.

22. Ibid. (March 23, 1922), p. 4409.

23. Ibid., p. 4416.

24. Byrnes in ibid. (April 12, 1922), p. 5420; vote in ibid. (March 23, 1922), pp. 4447–4448.

25. Ibid. (June 17, 1922), p. 8911.

26. *New York World,* cited in ibid. (June 16, 1922), p. 8905.

27. Senate vote in ibid. (August 31, 1922), p. 12033; Senator McCumber in ibid. (September 15, 1922), p. 12690; for Conference Report, see ibid. (September 14, 1922), pp. 12607, 12697.

28. Harding's veto is U.S., Congress, Senate, *Soldiers' Adjusted Compensation,* Document 396, 67th Cong., 2d sess., 1922.

29. Actually only one Senator, Arizona Republican Ralph H. Cameron, switched from aye to nay; ten Senators who had not voted previously participated, and seven of these sustained the President; seven Senators

who had voted earlier did not participate, and five of these had been bonus adherents. Without the support of seven Democratic Senators, six of them Southerners, Harding would have suffered a defeat.

30. James, *American Legion,* pp. 280–283. For Democratic use of the bonus issue, see Antoinette Funk, "Why Women Are Joining the Democratic Party," *Congressional Digest* (August 1922): 21.

31. William Larimer Mellon and Boyden Sparkes, *Judge Mellon's Sons* (privately printed, 1948), pp. 430–431. For another admiring account, see Philip H. Love, *Andrew W. Mellon: The Man and His Work* (Baltimore, 1929). Harvey O'Connor, *Mellon's Millions* (New York, 1933), is a muckraking attack. A perceptive contemporary evaluation is found in Walter Lippmann, "The Greatness of Mr. Mellon," in his, *Men of Destiny* (New York, 1927). There is a real need for a scholarly account of Mellon's stewardship of the Treasury. The Anti-Bonus League is from the *Christian Science Monitor,* cited in *Literary Digest* (November 3, 1923): 14.

32. National Industrial Conference Board, *The Soldier's Bonus or Adjusted Compensation for Soldiers* (New York, 1923), p. 36. For similar views, see Chamber of Commerce of the United States, *Referendum No. 38 on Legislation for Veterans of the World War* (Washington, D.C., 1922). A useful compilation is Julia E. Johnson, comp., *Soldiers' Bonus* (New York, 1924), a debate handbook. See also *Congressional Digest* (June 1922).

33. Both quoted in *Literary Digest* (December 8, 1923): 7.

34. This was the conclusion of *Literary Digest* (November 3, 1923): 14.

35. *Literary Digest* (December 8, 1923). Other "progressives" who spoke for some kind of bonus included Hiram Johnson of California, George Norris of Nebraska, and Burton K. Wheeler of Montana. It formed an early plank of Robert M. La Follette's 1924 platform. The leading voice of eastern progressivism, the *New York World,* opposed the bonus on "mugwumpish" grounds. See also James H. Shideler, "The Neo-Progressives: Reform Politics in the United States, 1920–1925" (Ph.D. diss., University of California, Berkeley, 1945), pp. 132, 212.

36. *Washington Post,* December 30, 1923.

37. *Congressional Record,* 68th Cong., 1st sess. (December 6, 1923), p. 99.

38. Ibid. (February 6, 1924), p. 2338.

39. "Political Aspects of the Bonus," *Chicago Tribune,* January 1, 1924.

40. *Washington Daily News,* January 4, 1924.

41. *Congressional Record,* 68th Cong., 1st sess. (December 20, 1923), p. 456 (Senate Resolution No. 107). Senator Harry F. Ashurst (D.-Ariz.) wrote to John R. Quinn, National Commander of the Legion: "a well organized lobby is working by day and by night here in Washington in opposition to a bonus for poor soldiers, and I might add that this same lobby is also working . . . in behalf of a bonus for a large number of millionaires whose hides and fortunes in the World War were saved by the valor of the American doughboy." Ibid. (January 7, 1924), p. 578.

42. Ibid. (January 11, 1923), p. 856. This was also an article in the Hearst press.

43. Ibid. (March 18, 1924), p. 4440.
44. Ibid. (April 22, 1924), p. 6873.
45. As cited, ibid. (March 14, 1924), p. 4183.
46. See, for example, ibid. (June 5, 1924), p. 10762.
47. Ibid. (January 8, 1924), pp. 689–690, for Copeland; ibid. (February 19, 1924), p. 2749, for Caraway.
48. Shapiro to Senator Joseph T. Robinson (D.-Ark.), telegram, in ibid. (April 19, 1924), p. 6703.
49. Ibid. (March 18, 1924), p. 4444, for House vote; ibid. (April 23, 1924), p. 6971, for Senate vote. In the House, a special "gag" rule was again resorted to, with a total of forty minutes of debate and no amendments allowed. The fight over the cash option was essentially probonus Republicans against and probonus Democrats for. See U.S., Congress, Senate, *Adjusted Service Compensation,* Report 402, 68th Cong., 1st sess., 1924, pts. 1–2.
50. For example, the discussion in *Congressional Record,* 68th Cong., 1st sess. (April 18, 1924), pp. 6650–6651.
51. Coolidge's veto is in U.S., Congress, House, *Soldiers' Adjusted Compensation,* Document 281, 68th Cong., 1st sess., 1924. The text of the bill is appended. Coolidge's biographer feels that the President showed courage in his attempt to fend off "a raid on the Treasury." Donald McCoy, *Calvin Coolidge: The Quiet President* (New York, 1967), pp. 232–234.
52. *Congressional Record,* 68th Cong., 1st sess. (May 17, 1924), p. 8812.
53. Ibid., pp. 8813–8814.
54. The Senate vote in ibid. (May 19, 1924), p. 8871. The five who switched, all Republicans, were Colt (R.I.), Keyes (N.H.), McKinley (Ill.), Phipps (Colo.), and Sterling (S.D.). American Legion boasts that they played havoc with the careers of those who opposed the bonus issue just do not stand up. Of the five who switched, for example, Colt died that year, Phipps and Keyes were reelected that year, while Sterling and McKinley were defeated in primaries in 1924 and 1926 respectively. In the two defeats, there were factors other than the bonus involved. For the anxiety of bonus supporters, see *Washington Post,* "Bonus Advocates, Keep Your Eye on These 10 Senators," May 19, 1924.

Chapter 3

1. *Congressional Record,* 71st Cong., 1st sess., pp. 1694, 2145–46, 2479ff. The bills were S. 1222, H.R. 3490, 3493.
2. *Proceedings of the American Legion,* 12th Annual Convention (Washington, D.C., 1931), p. 58.
3. *Congressional Record,* 71st Cong., 3rd sess., bills S. 5060, 5811, 5882; H.R. 13557, 13561, 14052, 14808, 14809, 14910, 14994, 15272, 15563, 15565, 15567, 15589, 15687, 15993, 16472, 16699, 16832, 17027.

4. *Washington Daily News,* January 21, 1931. This is from one of the scrapbooks of Congressman Wright Patman, in his possession (hereafter cited as Patman Scrapbooks).

5. For amplification of this action, see the explanations made at the Detroit convention in *Proceedings of the American Legion,* 13th Annual Convention (Washington, 1932), pp. 86ff, 162ff.

6. U.S., Congress, House, Committee on Ways and Means, *Payment of Adjusted Compensation Certificates, Hearings* on H.R. 3490 and Other Bills, 71st Cong., 3d sess., 1931. For Young, see Ida M. Tarbell, *Owen D. Young* (New York, 1932), pp. 288–291.

7. Mellon's letter in *Congressional Record,* 71st Cong., 3d sess. (January 21, 1931), p. 2826; Fish on p. 903.

8. Votes in ibid. (February 16, 19, 1931), pp. 5082, 5386.

9. *New York Times,* February 19, 1931.

10. Hoover's veto is U.S. Congress, House, *Message from the President of the United States,* Document 790, 71st Cong., 3d sess., 1931. See also his message vetoing an increase in disability pensions in 1930 in U.S., Congress, House, *Veto Message Relating to Amendment of World War Veterans Act,* Document 495, 71st Cong., 2d sess., 1930. This was also overridden.

11. *Congressional Record,* 71st Cong., 3d sess. (February 26, 27, 1931), pp. 6171, 6230.

12. Ibid., p. 6299.

13. Clippings and speeches, 1928, Patman Mss.

14. For a critical review of this literature, see Theodore Saloutos, "The Professors and the Populists," *Agricultural History* (October 1966).

15. The only work that talks about Patman's monetary views at any length is Joseph E. Reeve, *Monetary Reform Movements* (Washington, D.C., 1943), pp. 99–103 and passim; it is a hostile and not wholly accurate account. Economic historians have all but ignored Patman and other non-academic inflationists. The most perceptive essay on an unorthodox monetary reformer is Richard Hofstadter, "Free Silver and the Mind of 'Coin' Harvey," in his, *The Paranoid Style in American Politics* (New York, 1965), pp. 238–315. It is marred, however, by mugwumpish bias, that is, he writes off the federal silver purchase program of the 1930s as "pointless" (p. 238) without even a trace of an analysis of its economic effect.

16. Text of bill in Patman Mss.; *Congressional Record,* 71st Cong., 1st sess. (June 6, 1929), pp. 2479ff.

17. Patman to "My Dear Colleague," March 24, 1930, Patman Mss.; *Proceedings of the Veterans of Foreign Wars,* 33d National Encampment (Washington, D.C., 1933), p. 192.

18. Annotation of speech delivered April 3, 1930, Patman Scrapbooks.

19. Patman to "Dear Friend," October 14, 1930, Patman Mss.

20. Patman in *Congressional Record,* 71st Cong., 3d sess., pp. 157–159, 897–902; Rankin in *Proceedings of the Disabled American Veterans,* 11th National Convention (Washington, D.C., 1931), p. 16.

21. *New York Times,* February 3, 10, 1931.

22. *Pay the Bonus in Full Now* (Chicago, 1931), four-page pamphlet in my possession.

23. To cite only four examples, there is 1931 correspondence in the Patman Mss. with a Veterans' Political Association of America, Inc. (Detroit), Rank and File Veterans Association (Chicago), Pay Bonus Now Organization (Houston), and American Federation of World War Veterans (Asheville).

24. *Proceedings of the American Legion,* 14th Annual Convention (Washington, D.C., 1932), p. 4. Murphy had supported cash payment as early as January 30, 1931, according to the *Detroit News* of that date.

25. For the details surrounding the President's visit, I rely on J. F. Essary of the *Baltimore Sun,* cited in *Literary Digest* (October 3, 1931): 7.

26. *Proceedings of the American Legion,* 14th Annual Convention, pp. 86ff.

27. For the VFW, see the proceedings of their 1931, 1932, and 1933 national encampments, especially the officers' reports on the bonus campaign. The ACLU resolution is on p. 262 of the volume for 1933.

28. Patman to William Randolph Hearst, October 23, 1931, Patman Mss.

29. Herbert Hoover, *The State Papers and Other Public Writings of Herbert Hoover,* ed. William Starr Myers (New York, 1934), II, p. 53.

30. The bills were S. 272, 1251, 1799, 3874, 4350; H.R. 1, 27, 94, 4493, 4535, 4539, 5331, 5461, 5634, 6158, 6180, 6584, 6693, 7726, 8016, 8562, 9593, 9694, 9929, 10096, 10367, 11117, 11300, 11674, 11987, 11992, 12408, 12590, 12957, 12978, 12979. For comments see House Reports 1242 through 1261, and 1565; and Senate Report 488. All 72d Cong., 1st sess. The bill in *Congressional Digest* (November 1932): 267, is the unamended committee bill, not the measure that was actually voted upon.

31. There is also an increasing sophistication in terminology; earlier speeches were couched in the old Greenback-Populist rhetoric about circulation per capita; by early 1932, more modern concepts like "the velocity of money" began to be used. See, for example, *Congressional Record,* 72d Cong., 1st sess. (March 26, 1932), p. 6886.

32. Speaking itinerary and handbills in Patman Scrapbooks. Patman to FDR, telegrams, n.d., but ca. April 3/4, 1932; FDR to Patman, telegram, April 4, 1932; Patman to FDR, telegram, April 5, 1932: all Patman Mss.

33. Patman's impeachment of Mellon has been all but ignored by historians; only Harvey O'Connor, *Mellon's Millions* (New York, 1933), treats it at any length. It is entirely possible that the impeachment might have been voted by the Democratic House, but certainly the Senate would never have convicted. Extended discussion in Congress would not have been helpful to the administration, and surely this possibility was a factor in the shake-up that sent Mellon to London and promoted Ogden Mills to top spot in the Treasury. In addition, relations between Mellon and Hoover were strained, to say the least, while Mills was a member of the so-called medicine-ball cabinet which formed the inner circle of the administration.

34. *Congressional Record,* 72d Cong., 1st sess., pp. 350–61, 1144–45, 2566–67, 4290–99, 5224, 7983–84, 10720, 15163–64.

35. Ibid., pp. 7969–70 for Rankin; Vinson at p. 12912; Thomas at 13247–48.

36. Mills quoted in ibid., p. 547; Fish, p. 8739–40; Norris, p. 13255; La Guardia, p. 12847; La Follette, p. 13259–60.

37. Congressman Emanuel Celler (D.-N. Y.) and Senators David I. Walsh, (D.-Mass.), Marcus A. Coolidge (D.-Mass.), Royal S. Copeland (D.-N.Y.), and Robert F. Wagner (D.-N.Y.), all took such a position. Ibid., pp. 12922, 13268.

38. Cited in ibid., p. 13145.

39. John M. Blum, *From the Morgenthau Diaries: Years of Crisis, 1928–1938* (New York, 1959), p. 249.

40. Douglas C. North, *Growth and Welfare in the American Past* (Englewood Cliffs, N.J., 1966), p. 175. Marriner Eccles, sometimes called the New Deal's leading Keynesian, judged the 1936 bonus payment improper and inflationary. See material in file, "Eccles, M.," Harry Hopkins Mss., FDRL. The current respectability of once-heretical economic doctrines has its ironic aspects. In one sense, Milton Friedman is perhaps closer to what I have called neo-populist monetary doctrine than any other prominent contemporary economist. Economics, like politics, makes strange bedfellows; the neo-populists, like their ancestors, saw monetary expansion as *one* of the things they wanted government to do to advance the general welfare; Friedman would give the government great, though rigidly prescribed, monetary powers, but feels that the general welfare would be best advanced if most of the other powers of the federal government were severely limited. His views may be best sampled in his, *Capitalism and Freedom* (Chicago, 1962).

41. Hoover, *State Papers,* II, p. 151.

42. *Portland Oregonian,* April 5, 9, 1932.

43. Committee on Ways and Means, *Payment of Adjusted Compensation Certificates, Hearings.* Coughlin had stressed the bonus issue as early as November 30, 1930, when, in advocating payment of the bonus, he compared Mellon to Judas Iscariot saying: "Have we forgotten that it was to a soldier, a Roman centurion, to whom it was said: 'Such have I not found, no not in Israel'? . . . It was no soldier who betrayed the Man of Galilee, but as usual, the Keeper of Silver. History is repeating itself." Cited in Louis B. Ward, *Father Coughlin: An Authorized Biography* (Detroit, 1933), pp. 80–81. See also Ruth Mugglebee, *Father Coughlin* (Garden City, N.Y., 1933), pp. 225–226.

44. U.S., Congress, House, *Payment of Adjusted Service Certificates,* Report 1252, 72d Cong., 1st sess., 1932, pts. 1–2.

45. For the change in rules, see Edward C. Blackorby, *Prairie Radical* (Lincoln, Neb., 1963), p. 207.

Chapter 4

1. For Coughlin, see Charles J. Tull, *Father Coughlin and the New Deal* (Syracuse, N.Y., 1965). For Brinkley, Gerald Carson, *The Roughish World of Doctor Brinkley* (New York, 1960), is a popular account, but see also Francis W. Schruben, *Kansas in Turmoil* (Columbia, Mo., 1969). For Schuler, see Duncan Aikman, "Savonarola in Los Angeles," *American Mercury* (December 1930).

2. Louis Adamic, "The Papers Print the Riots," *Scribner's* (February 1932).

3. The best account of how the workingman fared during the Depression is Irving Bernstein, *The Lean Years* (Boston, 1960). There is much information in James J. Hannah, "Urban Reaction to the Great Depression in the United States, 1929–1933" (Ph.D. diss., University of California, Berkeley, 1956). There is no full account of Father Cox. For hostile views, see Felix Morrow's letter to the *Nation* (February 3, 1932): 144, and *Daily Worker,* July 13, 14, 1932. There are good pictures of him in action in Stefan Lorant, *Pittsburgh* (New York, 1964), pp. 340–341. Broun is cited in Francis Chase, Jr., *Sound and Fury* (New York, 1942), p. 237.

4. Arthur M. Schlesinger, Jr., *The Crisis of the Old Order* (New York, 1957), p. 519.

5. *Daily Worker,* May 10, 17, 1932 passim. Felix Morrow, *Bonus March* (New York, 1932), and Jack Douglas [pseud.], *Veterans on the March* (New York, 1934), are two Communist accounts. By early July, Earl Browder was giving the WESL credit for the whole bonus march; see his, "The Impending Financial Crisis and the Bonus Expeditionary Force," *Daily Worker,* July 5, 1932. The WESL, which changed its name to the American League of Ex-Servicemen in 1934, published at least three pamphlets—*Veterans Close Ranks* (New York, 1932), H. E. Briggs, *New Deal for the Vets* (New York, 1933), and H. E. Briggs, *The Veterans Fight for Unity* (New York, 1935)—and a "newspaper" variously titled *The Fighting Vet* and *The Veterans News,* one issue of which, dated October 15, 1932, is in Box VII, Glassford Mss., UCLA. WESL activities are chronicled in Briggs's 1935 pamphlet cited above and in his periodic column in the *Daily Worker,* "The Fighting Vet." Harry Raymond, "The Siege of the Capitol," *New Masses* (August 1932), and his review of Waters's book in *New Masses* (May 1933): 26–28, where he argues that "no recent political event has so exemplified the bankruptcy of Socialists and Liberals as their opposition to the veterans' struggles." Emanuel Levin contributed two articles to *The Communist:* "The Veterans and the United Front" (July 1933) and "The Veterans in the Struggle Against Fascism and Imperialist War" (August 1934). In July 1935 the Veterans Administrator Hines furnished the White House with information on a number of Communists and others active in the bonus struggle. Hines to Stephen Early, with enclosure, July 12, 1935, OF 95, Franklin D. Roosevelt Library.

6. *Philadelphia Public Ledger,* January 25, 26, 28, February 8, 13, 1931. Unidentified clipping, January 1931, Patman Scrapbooks. See also *Daily Worker,* January 26, 1931.

7. See *Portland Oregonian,* December 11, 18, 1931, January 20, June 5, 1932. In January 1935 Hazen wrote to President Roosevelt claiming that he had "organized the Bonus March in 1932" and that "Hoover Regime and the American Legion" were responsible for his deposition by Waters. Claiming to have great influence among veterans, he offered to come to Washington to lobby against the bonus. According to the information furnished the White House by VA Administrator Hines, Hazen had served sixteen months in the army, had achieved the rank of sergeant, and had contracted bronchial asthma for which he was rated as 10 percent disabled. Chester A. Hazen to Roosevelt, January 7, 1935, Hines to Howe, January 24, 1935, OF 95-C, Franklin D. Roosevelt Library, Hyde Park.

8. Historians of the Pacific Northwest have ignored this question. Farley quoted in John Gunther, *Inside U.S.A.* (New York, 1948), p. 87.

9. *Portland Oregonian,* February 11, 19, 1932; *Oregon Journal,* April 25, 1932.

10. *Oregon Journal,* May 29, 1932; Veterans Administration, *Annual Report* (Washington, D.C., 1932), p. 37.

11. For conditions in Oregon during these years, see Harold Ahrendt, "The History of Work Relief in Multnomah County, Oregon, 1930–1933" (Master's thesis, State College of Washington, 1944), and Portland newspapers. Most of the data cited come from the *Portland Oregonian,* January 6, 8, February 5, March 18, April 3, 24, 28, May 2, 13, August 28, 1932. Joanna C. Colcord, "The West is Different," *Survey* (June 1, 1932), treats Pacific slope conditions generally. In June 1932, Governor Julius L. Meier informed Congress that "Federal aid is essential if we are to avert hunger and suffering." *Congressional Record,* 72d Cong., 1st sess. (June 21, 1932), p. 13552.

12. John Kelly in *Portland Oregonian,* June 10, 1932.

13. *Washington Star,* June 6, 1932.

14. Ibid., June 13, 1932.

15. *Portland Oregonian,* April 29, 30, May 1, 7, 11, June 15, 1932; *Oregon Journal,* May 7–10, 14, 1932. W. W. Waters, *B.E.F.: The Whole Story of the Bonus Army* (New York, 1933), pp. 17, 19–26. There is an obviously incomplete roster containing 255 names of the "Portland Oregon on to Washington Bonus March" in the Kleinholz Mss., University of Oregon.

16. Waters, *B.E.F.,* pp. 4–6; Jack Douglas [pseud.], *Veterans on the March* (New York, 1934), pp. 26–29; "Memorandum for the Chief of Staff," June 12, 1932, RG 94, NA.

17. Lawrence F. Bamber in *Portland Oregonian,* July 4, 1932. He may have been influenced by his paper's maudlin editorial, "Waters of Portland," three days earlier, which concluded that "Waters was an executive before hard times took his job away. He must have been a competent

executive. The qualities of leadership are no mushroom growth in any man. For only an executive of personality and power could administer the affairs of the veterans encamped in Washington, and hold them to heel while retaining their confidence, respect and affection. Nobody knows how long the siege of the capital will continue, not even the veterans themselves, but it is fairly predictable that Walter W. Waters of Portland, Oregon, will never again be stationed in obscurity. Such men usually go far. It is as if fate intended they should."

18. My account of the cross-country trips is drawn from Waters, *B.E.F.;* Douglas, *Veterans on the March;* George Kleinholz Mss., University of Oregon; George Kleinholz, *The Battle of Washington* (New York, 1932); Henry O. Meisel, *Bonus Expeditionary Forces . . . The True Facts* (Clintonville, Wis., 1932); Edward F. Atwell, *Washington, The Battle Ground* (Washington, D.C., n.d. [1933]); Ozen Gunn, *Psychology of the Bonus March* (n.p., n.d.); Thomas W. Saling, *History of the Bonus Expeditionary Force and the Battle of Washington* (n.p., 1932); and the following newspapers: *Portland Oregonian, Oregon Journal, Washington Star, New York Times, Daily Worker,* and *BEF News.*

19. For the overestimate and variations thereof, see Constance M. Green, *Washington: Capital City* (Princeton, 1959), p. 373, *The Rise of Urban America* (New York, 1965), p. 155, and *The Secret City* (Princeton, 1967), p. 220. Waters' data is from his, *B.E.F.,* pp. 257–259. Chief of Staff Douglas MacArthur estimated, on June 28, that there were 11,412, in a memorandum to Lawrence Richey, June 28, 1932, Herbert Hoover Presidential Library. An undated, unsigned memorandum in HHPL, probably from General Hines of the VA, puts the figure for June 22 at "less than 7,500." A recent scholar has discovered, somehow, that "94 percent" of the BEF or "approximately 20,000" were veterans. Davis R. B. Ross, *Preparing for Ulysses* (New York, 1969), p. 18.

20. General Frank Hines to Hoover, August 2, 1932, RG 94, NA, contains the VA data.

21. Roy Wilkins, "The Bonuseers Ban Jim Crow," *Crisis* (October 1932). Green, *The Secret City,* p. 220, cites Wilkins' article, but finds "not a trace of Jim Crow in the entire Bonus Army." Her estimate of 2,000 Negroes is far too high. Washington's Negro community did not ignore this phenomenon; one of the largest contributions Glassford received was $206.84, taken up in a collection for the BEF by Elder Lightfoot Michaux, a Negro evangelist. Glassford to Michaux, June 14, 1932, Glassford Mss., UCLA.

22. My account of the Southern California march is drawn from a senior thesis by David Disco, "The California Contingent and the Bonus March of 1932" (University of California, Los Angeles, 1964), in my possession. His sources were the Glassford collections and local newspapers.

Chapter 5

1. Much of this chapter and the next two is based on the collected papers of Pelham D. Glassford, located at this writing (1970) in two separate library buildings at the University of California, Los Angeles. The larger and more important is in the Social Sciences Materials Center, Research Library, and will simply be cited as Glassford Mss. The other, in Special Collections, Powell Library, UCLA, will be cited as Glassford Mss., Special Collections. Among the most useful of these papers are typed summaries of events written by Glassford roughly contemporaneous with the events they describe, in the Glassford Mss. They are variously headed "Chronology of the Bonus Army Invasion," "Memorandum," "Memorandum for Record," "Diary," and "Events of the Day." Glassford later referred to these sheets as his "diary," but they are not a diary in the ordinary sense. There are many days for which no account exists. With all of their lacunae and bias, they form the best single record of events between late May and the day of the Battle of Washington. They will be cited here as Glassford's Account. In late October, Glassford produced a series of eight articles, which appeared in the Hearst newspapers from October 8 to November 6, 1932 (November 8 was Election Day). They are cited as Glassford's Newspaper Article.

2. Glassford's Account, May 22, 1932. There was an earlier item in the *Washington Post*, May 18, but apparently Glassford didn't read the *Post*, which was not then the first-class paper it is today.

3. Information from various sources, Glassford Mss., and Glassford Mss., Special Collections. See also Drew Pearson and Robert S. Allen, *More Merry-Go-Round* (New York, 1932), pp. 27–28. Cf. Irving Bernstein, *The Lean Years* (Boston, 1960), pp. 441–443, and Constance McLaughlin Green, *Washington, Capital City, 1879–1950* (Princeton, 1963), pp. 365–366.

4. Glassford to Adjutant General, April 29, 1911, Glassford, Mss., Special Collections.

5. Pearson and Allen, *More Merry-Go-Round*, pp. 27–28.

6. Bernstein, *The Lean Years*, pp. 430–431.

7. Glassford's Account, May 24, 1932. Apart from providing for Legion conventions and the like, the army was willing to have its surplus equipment used to help feed the unemployed. In November 1930, for instance, at the request of Senator Robert F. Wagner, Hurley sent a rolling kitchen to New York City to help feed the unemployed. See Robert F. Wagner to Herbert Lehman, November 20, 1930, Lt. Gov. Mss., FDRL, Hyde Park.

8. Glassford's Account, May 25, 1932.

9. This is from an undated typed draft of a speech Glassford used frequently in late 1932 and 1933, in Glassford Mss., Special Collections. Hereafter cited as Glassford's Basic Speech.

10. Ibid.

11. *Washington Star,* May 26, 1932.

12. J. J. Hannah, "Urban Reaction to the Great Depression, 1929–1933" (Ph.D. diss., University of California, Berkeley, 1956); Green, *Capital City,* pp. 378–389; *Washington Star,* May 27, June 23, 1932; *Washington Post,* May 22, 1932; *Business Week,* cited in *Literary Digest* (May 7, 1932): 17; the waybill in Glassford Mss.

13. Glassford's Account, May 26; Glassford's Basic Speech; *Washington Star,* May 27, 1932.

14. Glassford's Account, May 28, 29, 1932; *Washington Star,* May 28, 29, 1932. Glassford, "Information [for the press] Concerning Visiting Veterans," May 29, 1932, "Memorandum" [of a telephone conversation with Major Don Knowlton], June 3, 1932, both Glassford Mss.

15. Patrolman J. E. Bennett to Glassford, holograph report, 6 pp., May 30, 1932, Glassford Mss.; *Washington Star,* May 30, 1932.

16. *Portland Oregonian,* June 23, 1932.

17. Glassford, "Visiting Veterans" [press statement], May 30, 1932, Glassford Mss.

18. Glassford, "Information Bulletin" [for press], May 31, 1932, Glassford Mss.

19. According to the Minutes of the Board of Commissioners, District of Columbia, LIII, p. 954, $719.76 was spent on toilets. U. S. Grant III to Commissioner Reichelderfer, July 21, 1932, Glassford Mss., Special Collections; Harold B. Foulkrod to Glassford, August 4, 1932, Glassford, Mss.

20. Glassford to Commissioners, "Assembly of Out-of-Town Veterans in this City," June 3, 1932 (SECRET), Glassford Mss.

21. District Commissioners to "All Governors," telegrams with replies, June 10, 1932, Files of the District Commissioners (in their possession). See also telegrams in FDR, Gov. Mss., FDRL. Roosevelt had Harry L. Hopkins, then running New York's Temporary Emergency Relief Administration, handle the matter. Using some nonappropriated funds at his disposal, Hopkins sent sociologist Nels Andersen of Columbia, an authority on transients, to Washington to bring the men back, with meager results. See *New York Times,* June 11, 1932. For cooperation between the Commissioners and the railroads, see R. H. Aishton to Reichelderfer, letter and telegram, Aishton to Executives of Member Roads, both June 10, Association of American Railroads files, courtesy of L. I. McDougle, Asst. Manager, Educational and Group Relations.

22. Accounting in "Press Release #2," June 20, 1932; various bills and receipts: Glassford Mss. Coughlin's contribution was made by his regular Washington attorney (why did a Michigan priest need a Washington lawyer?). See Robert W. Burton to Glassford, with enclosures, June 10, 1932, Glassford Mss. Accounts of the BEF are many. I have drawn from all the sources cited in n. 14, Chapter 4, plus John Henry Bartlett, *The Bonus March and the New Deal* (Chicago, 1937); John Dos Passos, "The Veterans Come Home to Roost," *New Republic* (July 29, 1932); Mauritz

Hallgren, "The Bonus Army Scares Mr. Hoover," *Nation* (July 27, 1932); Gardner Jackson, "Unknown Soldiers," *Survey* (August 1, 1932); Fleta Campbell Springer, "Glassford and the Siege of Washington," *Harper's* (November 1932); John D. Weaver, "Bonus March," *American Heritage* (July 1963); and Owen P. White, "General Glassford's Story," *Collier's* (October 29, 1932).

23. Waters, *B.E.F.;* Douglas, *Veterans on the March;* Glassford's Newspaper Article.

24. *Portland Oregonian,* July 11, 1932. See also *Oregon Journal,* June 27, 1932.

25. For this and other Communist complaints, see *Daily Worker,* June 24, 27, 1932.

26. Glassford's Newspaper Article.

27. *Daily Worker,* July 5, 1932.

28. See Chapter 10 for details.

29. Ralph Glassford [no relation] to Glassford, July 30, 1932, Glassford Mss.; Report, "WATKINS, Marion—Arrest and detention of," June 29, 1932, by Precinct Detective Paul E. Ambrose, Glassford Mss.

30. WESL Leaflet, Glassford Mss.; *Literary Digest* (June 18, 1932).

31. *Washington Star,* June 4–9, 1932; *Literary Digest* (June 18, 1932).

32. Father Cox quoted from Arthur L. Hennessy, Jr., "The Bonus Army: Its Roots, Growth and Demise" (Ph.D. diss., Georgetown University, 1957); Murray from *Nation* (June 15, 1932): 664; for other visitors, see *Washington Star.* See also Simpson's speech, "Economic Righteousness," *Congressional Record,* 72d Cong., 1st sess. (June 15, 1932), pp. 13941–13944.

33. Rainey and Rankin quoted from *Washington Star,* June 4, 1932; Blanton from *Congressional Record,* 72d Cong., 1st sess. (June 6, 1932), p. 12105 (he had been the third man to sign the discharge petition); Fish from ibid. (June 13, 1932), p. 12845.

34. *Washington Star,* June 4, 1932.

35. *Congressional Record,* 72d Cong., 1st sess. (May 30, 1932), p. 11523.

36. The names of the signatories and the order in which they signed is in ibid. (June 4, 1932), p. 12042.

37. Ibid. (June 13, 1932), p. 12853; House Resolution 220 in ibid., p. 12854. Discharge passed 226 to 175 and the resolution by 225 to 170.

38. The text is printed in ibid. (June 15, 1932), p. 13043. Joseph Reeve, *Monetary Reform Movements* (Washington, D.C., 1943), pp. 20–30, does not indicate the nature of this change.

39. For the debate, see *Congressional Record,* 72d Cong., 1st sess. (June 14, 15, 1932). The vote is in ibid. (June 15, 1932), pp. 13053–13054. Two-thirds of the Republicans deserting the President were from the Midwest and Far West; most of the rest were from the Pennsylvania delegation. LaGuardia quoted from ibid. (June 13, 1932), p. 12847.

40. Ibid. (June 15, 1932), p. 13001.

41. "H" [a police clerk] to General Glassford, memorandum, June 15, 1932, Glassford Mss.

42. *Congressional Record,* 72d Cong., 1st sess. (June 16, 1932), p. 14268.

43. Ibid., pp. 13256, 13259–13260, 13264.

44. Hiram W. Johnson to "Jack," June 18, 1932, Johnson Mss., pt. VI, Bancroft Library. I am indebted to Professor Spencer Olin, Jr., for unearthing this letter for me. Similarly, Arthur Vandenberg, Republican Senator from Michigan, wrote that the BEF represented "the most amazing, colorful, ominous, tragic and yet thrilling experience of a lifetime." Vandenberg Mss., cited by Jordon A. Schwartz, *The Interregnum of Despair: Hoover, Congress and the Depression* (Urbana, Ill., 1970), pp. 174–175.

45. *Congressional Record,* 72d Cong., 1st sess. (June 17, 1932), p. 13274.

46. Waters, *B.E.F.,* p. 151–152.

47. *Portland Oregonian,* June 24, 1932.

48. *Washington Star,* June 19, 1932; Waters, *B.E.F.,* pp. 151–153.

49. *Congressional Record,* 72d Cong., 1st sess. (June 17, 1932), p. 12441.

50. Professor Nels Andersen of Columbia University, FDR's and Harry Hopkins' emissary to bring New Yorkers back home, as quoted in *Washington Star,* June 13, 1932.

Chapter 6

1. *Washington Star,* June 16, 1932; Glassford's Newspaper Article; Aldace Walker, memorandum, "A Resume of My Activities in Connection with the Bonus Army in Washington," August 11, 1932, typescript, 8 pp., with 12 exhibits, hereafter cited as Walker's Resume, Glassford Mss. There is also a shorter version of this report.

2. Bartlett to Glassford, July 28, 1932, Glassford Mss.; John Henry Bartlett, *The Bonus March and the New Deal* (Chicago, 1937), pp. 55–56. At the time of the bonus march, Bartlett was a member of the International Joint Commission, a sinecure worth $10,000 a year.

3. Glassford to Pennsylvania Railroad Company [and five other railroads], June 21, 1932; Walker's Resume; Glassford to Senator James E. Watson, June 23, 1932; press release, June 25, 1932; Glassford's Account, June 25: Glassford Mss.

4. Glassford to Commissioners, memorandum, June 25, 1932; Glassford's Account, June 27, 1932: Glassford Mss.

5. *Portland Oregonian,* June 27, 1932; *Washington Star,* June 23–29, 1932. The *Daily Worker* contains almost daily abuse of Waters.

6. Glassford, "Memorandum [for the Press]: Re the Bonus," June 15, 1932, Glassford Mss.

7. There were actually two joint resolutions, House Joint Resolutions 462 and 473. I have described the second, which partially superseded and liberalized the first. *Congressional Record,* 72d Cong., 1st sess. (July 14, 1932), pp. 15343, 15351. Accounting is in Veterans Administration, *Annual Report,* 1933, p. 68. In a memorandum for President Hoover, Hines gave the following data on returnees:

Transportation:	
railroad (men)	4,344
Transportation:	
automobile (men)	939
Transportation	
furnished by Red Cross:	
Women	221
Children	247
Total persons transported	5,751

Hines, "Memorandum for the President," July 26, 1932, Records of the Justice Department, RG 60, NA. Foster Rhea Dulles, *The American Red Cross* (New York, 1950), pp. 316–317, mentions the bonus march but refers neither to the constant refusal of the semiofficial organization to do anything for the men in Washington nor to the aid it furnished the returning women and children. Similarly lacking in Christian charity was William Hirst Heigham, D.D., Rector of a Maryland Episcopal church just over the District line. He protested to the Commissioners about the proposed move to Camp Bartlett and feared that the BEFers would constitute "a danger to all in this community. . . . Is there nothing at all that can be done to persuade or FORCE these men to return to their own States? If not, I can clearly foresee as the alternative, written in big, lurid letters, ANARCHY and PESTILENCE." Heigham to Commissioners, July 28, 1932, Files of the District Commissioners. On the other hand, the Salvation Army wanted to do all it could, and the rector of Catholic University supplied fifteen gallons of milk daily for the bonus army's children. The Salvation Army's offer in James Asher to Commissioners, June 16, 1932, Glassford Mss.

8. *Congressional Record*, 72d Cong., 1st sess. (July 15, 1932), pp. 15495–15498.

9. David Disco, "The California Contingent and the Bonus March of 1932" (Senior thesis, University of California, Los Angeles, 1964); *BEF News*, July 23, 1932.

10. Glassford's Account, July 12–15, 1932; Glassford's Newspaper Article; *Washington Star*, July 12–16, 1932. For Curtis, see Marvin Ewy, *Charles Curtis of Kansas: Vice President of the United States, 1929–1933* (Emporia, Kan., 1961), p. 43.

11. Their conflicting press statements of July 15 are in Glassford Mss. See also *Washington Star*, July 15, 16, 1932.

12. Glassford's Account, July 16, 1932; Glassford to Senator Hiram Bingham, July 16, 1932; Glassford to Commissioners, memorandum, "Prohibiting Picketing in the Vicinity of the White House," July 16, 1932 (two separate items); typed copy of Crosby's instructions with Glassford's annotations: Glassford Mss. Glassford's Newspaper Article; W. W. Waters, *B.E.F.: The Whole Story of the Bonus Army* (New York, 1933), pp. 145–171; *Washington Star*, July 15–18, 1932.

13. *Washington Star,* July 18, 1932; *Congressional Record,* 72d Cong., 1st sess. (July 15, 1932), p. 15497; letter from A. Johnson in *Washington Star,* July 13, 1932; Glassford's Newspaper Article.

14. *Washington Star,* July 13, 23, 1932; *Portland Oregonian,* July 18, 1932; *BEF News,* July 27, 1932. There is a typescript in the Glassford Mss., apparently by Louis Walde, who helped put out the *BEF News* and who was a founder of the Khaki Shirts, which sheds some light on the journalistic enterprises.

15. Waters, *B.E.F.,* pp. 178–179.

16. Butler quoted from a report by Private John Auffenberg, Glassford's man at Anacostia, July 19, 1932, Glassford Mss.

17. The documentation of the inner history of the expulsion of the bonus army has been made difficult by the absence of many key documents —and in some instances parts of key documents—from the National Archives. Many of the missing papers were found in the recently opened manuscripts of President Hoover. A basic source for the rest of this chapter is a seven-page typed memorandum by Glassford, "Circumstances Leading Up to the Use of Federal Forces Against the Bonus Army," July 31, 1932. Attached are eight exhibits: Directive, Commissioners to Glassford, July 21, 1932; Glassford to Commissioners, July 22, 1932; Commissioners to Glassford, July 22, 1932; Ferry K. Heath to Glassford, June 10, 1932; District Commissioners to Glassford, July 27, 1932; Heath to District Commissioners, July 25, 27, 1932; and a memorandum, July 31, 1932, on the topography of the riot area. See also Heath to Glassford, July 20, 1932; Glassford to Seymour Lowman, Assistant Secretary of the Treasury, July 21, 1932; Glassford to Heath, July 21, 1932; and A. J. Brylawski to Glassford, July 21, 1932, cited in Glassford to Waters, July 22, 1932: all Glassford Mss. U. S. Grant III to Reichelderfer, July 21, 1932, Glassford Mss., Special Collections. Copies of many of these documents are in the files of the District Commissioners. I could locate none in the files of the Treasury in the National Archives. Many documents one would normally expect to find there are in Hoover's papers. The following are found *only* in HHPL, Container No. 1–E/300: Glassford to Heath, June 10, 1932; Heath to Rhine & Company, July 20, 1932; Heath to Crosby, July 20, 1932; Lowman to Glassford, July 21, 1932; Lowman to Crosby, July 21, 1932. For the history of the area, see Works Progress Administration, Federal Writers Project, *Washington: City and Capital* (Washington, D.C., 1937), p. 634.

18. Glassford to Commissioners, July 22, 1932, Glassford Mss.

19. See a letter by Ward in *New Republic* (November 9, 1932): 359.

20. The above is based on the following documents found only in HHPL: Assistant Chief Law and Records [Treasury Dept.] for Ferry K. Heath, memorandum, July 25, 1932; "Memorandum to the Attorney General: from Nugent Dodds, July 27, 1932 (two on this date, one of which has nine enclosures); E. N. Chisolm to Edgar C. Snyder [U.S. Marshall for District of Columbia], July 28, 1932; David D. Caldwell to

the Attorney General, memorandum, July 28, 1932; W[illiam] D. M[itchell] to David D. Caldwell, memorandum, July 28, 1932; E. N. Chisolm to William D. Mitchell, July 28, 1932; Ferry K. Heath to William D. Mitchell, memorandum with two enclosures, July 28, 1932; Major General Blanton Winship [Judge Advocate General] to Chief of Staff [Douglas MacArthur], two memoranda, "Dispersion of the So-Called Bonus Expeditionary Force by the Executive Power with the Employment of Military Force," 5 pp., and "Bonus Expeditionary Force," 4 pp., July 28, 1932 (the latter memo refers to a previous memorandum of July 26, 1932, on the same subject, which has not been found); Patrick J. Hurley to Mr. President, July 28, 1932, enclosing a draft proclamation calling out troops. It appears that all the above dated July 28 were prepared in the morning, before any of the rioting began. Hurley's letter, for example speaks of "use by you in the event of an emergency."

21. Waters, *B.E.F.*, p. 203. Easby-Smith was eventually investigated by the FBI. He was attorney for a number of labor unions and taught at Georgetown Law School. The Bureau thought it pertinent to pass on the following to the President: "The Bureau files further reflect that in May of 1918, an unknown woman who was allegedly a German Agent stopped with Mrs. J. Easby-Smith, wife of Lieutenant Colonel J. Easby-Smith, who was then living at 1721 S Street, N.W., Washington, D.C. Investigation in this matter is not complete." "Memorandum for the Director," August 29, 1932, enclosed in J[ohn] E[dgar] H[oover] to Lawrence Richey, September 2, 1932, HHPL. Smith, himself, had complained in 1917 that his telephone had been tapped; see Joan M. Jensen, *The Price of Vigilance* (Chicago, 1968), p. 150.

22. "Report of Private J. O. Patton, M.P., Crime Prevention Division, Relative to Activities at Third Street and Pennsylvania Avenue, N.W., on July 28, 1932," typescript, 3 pp., July 29, 1932, Glassford Mss.; Walker's Resume; Waters, *B.E.F.*, pp. 207–210.

23. Glassford, memorandum, "Circumstances Leading Up to the Use of Federal Troops"; Glassford's Newspaper Article; J. W. Wilford [Camp Glassford Commander], statement, typescript, 2 pp., August 9, 1932, Glassford Mss.; Inspector Lewis I. H. Edwards, statement, typescript, 3 pp., August 3, 1932, Files of the District Commissioners.

24. "Report of Private J. O. Patton," Glassford Mss. In a chit dated August 4, 1932, Glassford wrote Inspector Davis, Patton's chief, that he was removing "Patton's excellent report" for his own files. Glassford's version, given to the Grand Jury on August 1, 1932, was as follows:

It was at this time that I received a report from police officers that Commander Waters had gone to Anacostia and held a meeting at Camp Marks and Camp Bartlett, telling the veterans what was being done at the Pennsylvania Avenue area and advising them that he could not prevent them from going over there. Almost simultaneously with this report the veterans began to arrive. Most of them assembled in a park immediately south of [the] Pennsylvania Avenue billets between Missouri Avenue and Maryland Avenue. I watched this assemblage very closely. Suddenly, somewhere around noon, I saw them start toward the repossessed area. The[y] came over in a wedge. I ran to the edge of the repossessed area where the point of this wedge was headed for, yelling to the police, "Hold the line." The police along this south face of the area were reinforced, and as the veterans came up they began to spread out. One of the veterans threw a brick, and this started a brick battle which was participated in by both veterans and the police. Seeing the danger of the situation, I jumped out from behind a little shelter at every opportunity that presented itself, waving my hands and calling for a cessation of the fight. Bricks were flying so fast that I was forced to take shelter several times. Then there was one particular veteran [McCoy] who had the range of about twenty-five feet who was attempting to pelt me with bricks. . . . As soon as I was able to get out in that position without the necessity of dodging behind this shelter, the brick battle subsided, and I made the veterans a little talk, stating that we did not want to have this fight, and it was time to declare an armistice and for everybody to go to lunch. The veterans were in an ugly mood before the agitation gradually subsided. [Moments later] Commander Waters told me that he had lost control of the veterans."

Glassford testimony, Washington Grand Jury, August 1, 1932, HHPL. Glassford's testimony has been removed from the set in RG 60, NA.

25. Glassford's Newspaper Article. Glassford, "Circumstances Leading Up to the Use of Federal Troops"; Glassford to Commissioners, July 29, 1932 [marked "Not Sent"]; Walker's Resume: Glassford Mss. Police Lieutenant Ira E. Keck, statement, typescript, 4 pp.; Reichelderfer to the Attorney General, August 2, 1932; Reichelderfer to the President of the United States, July 28, 1932: all Files of the District Commissioners.

26. Glassford Grand Jury testimony, HHPL.

27. Bruce E. Clark to Glassford, August 1, 1932, Glassford Mss. Clark sent along a sketch map and indicated that he had been "about thirty feet" from the disputed building. I have corrected typographical errors and made minor editorial changes in Clark's narrative.

Chapter 7

1. Glassford to the Secretary of War, May 28, 1932; Lieutenant Colonel Clement H. Wright, "Memorandum for the Chief of Staff," May 31, 1932; Hines to General Douglas MacArthur, August 18, 1932: RG 94, NA. (This is the basic source on the army and the bonus march, filed under WD AGO 240 [5-28-32], Sec. I, II, III.) Major General H. W. Blakeley, "When the Army Was Smeared," *Combat Forces Journal* (February 1952).

2. Major General Samuel Hof to Commanding Officer, Aberdeen Proving Ground, June 4, 1932, RG 98, NA. (This is the file on the opera-

tional aspects of the bonus march and is filed under "Military District of Washington, Report of Operations Against Bonus Marchers, 1932.")

3. Brigadier General Perry L. Miles to Chief of Staff, memorandum, "White Plan for the District of Columbia," June 4, 1932, RG 98, NA.

4. Colonel Alfred T. Smith to Chief of Staff, memorandum of radiogram with replies; Lieutenant Colonel Robert Morris to Major Alexander M. Weyand, August 1, 1932; Colonel J. T. Conrad to the Adjutant General, memorandum, "Subversive Influence Reported in the Veterans' Bonus Marches," June 15, 1932; Major F. M. Armstrong to Commanding General, Eighth Corps Area, memorandum, "Intelligence Report (B.E.F.)," November 4, 1932: RG 98, NA. The one historian who has published from these materials has systematically avoided items which reflect badly on the army. See John W. Killigrew, "The Army and the Bonus Incident," *Military Affairs* (Summer 1962).

5. W. W. Waters, *B.E.F.: The Whole Story of the Bonus Army* (New York, 1933), p. 199; Glassford, "MacArthur and the Bonus Army," typescript, 12 pp. [1948?], Glassford Mss., Special Collection; Douglas MacArthur, *Reminiscences* (New York, 1964), pp. 93ff.

6. The draft proclamation is enclosed in Hurley to the President, July 28, 1932, Hoover Mss. It is not certain that it was in Hoover's hands by that afternoon. Bennett Milton Rich, *The Presidents and Civil Disorder* (Washington, D.C., 1941), p. 174, notes the absence of a proclamation. On pages 189–211 he discusses in detail the constitutional and statutory sources of presidential authority. Assuming that Hoover had the draft proclamation before him, a possible reason for his not using it was that he, as we shall see, envisaged keeping the BEF for examination rather than dispersing it. Donald J. Lisio, "A Blunder Becomes Catastrophe: Hoover, the Legion and the Bonus Army," *Wisconsin Magazine of History* (August 1967), is surer of Hoover's motives than the evidence entitles him to be; see, for example, pp. 40–41.

7. Major General Blanton Winship [Judge Advocate General], "Memorandum for the Chief of Staff, Subject: Bonus Expeditionary Force, July 28, 1932," Hoover Mss. Winship, who had been the law member of General "Billy" Mitchell's court-martial and was from 1934 to 1939 a disastrous governor of Puerto Rico, was much concerned lest, once the deportation got underway, the soldiers in charge of the various truckloads of bonus marchers would be served writs of habeas corpus en route.

8. "Report from the Chief of Staff, United States Army, to the Secretary of War on the Employment of Federal Troops in Civil Disturbance in the District of Columbia, July 28–30, 1932," August 15, 1932, Hoover Mss. This report cannot be found in the National Archives. It was quoted in part (corruptly) in Theodore Joslin, *Hoover Off the Record* (New York, 1934), pp. 269–275. For the full text of MacArthur's report, see p. 291 above.

9. The original order is in RG 94, NA. The timetable is best established in a three-page typed document on the letterhead, "Headquarters,

Sixteenth Brigade, Office of the Brigade Commander" and dated July 28, 1932. An inked title reads "Mr. Alf's Record at Message Center, Room 1032, Munitions Building." After an introduction, "The following is a record of events in connection with the evacuation of government buildings and grounds by the B.E.F." The first six entries read:

1:35 P.M. General MacArthur called by telephone and directed General Miles to alert the troops at Fort Washington and Fort Myer.

1:40 P.M. General MacArthur directed General Miles to order the troops at Fort Myer and Fort Washington to assemble on the ellipse at once.

2:15 P.M. The Adjutant, Second Squadron, 3rd Cavalry reported to General Miles in his office.

2:20 P.M. General MacArthur directed General Miles to report to him at his office in the State-War and Navy Building as soon as the troops had assembled on the ellipse.

2:22 P.M. The Adjutant at Fort Myer reported by telephone that the Cavalry had started for the ellipse and that the Tanks were loading preparatory to start for the ellipse.

2:40 P.M. Commanding Officer, Fort Myer, reported that the Machine-Gun Troop and Tanks were leaving Post for Washington.

This chronology is confirmed in General Perry L. Miles' "Report of Operations against Bonus Marchers," RG 98, NA, which begins:

1. At 1:35 P.M., July 28, 1932, General Douglas MacArthur called by telephone and directed the Commanding General, Sixteenth Brigade, to alert troops at Fort Washington, Md., and Fort Myer, Va., to prepare to assemble in Washington with a view to going into action against Bonus Marchers who were occupying Government property and resisting police who sought to eject them.

2. At 1:40 P.M., General MacArthur directed General Miles to order troops from Fort Myer and Fort Washington to assemble on the Ellipse at once and to report to him at his office as soon as troops had assembled. Troops were ordered to assemble and the 2nd Squadron, 3rd Cavalry, with a platoon of tanks attacked, arrived at the Ellipse at 3:50 P.M.

It is possible to put forth the hypothesis that MacArthur gave these orders without official sanction and that in fact Hurley gave him no order until 2:55 P.M., but that is pretty far-fetched. The chronology put forth in MacArthur's report (see p. 291) would have us believe that troops began arriving at the Ellipse from Fort Myer five minutes after being summoned. Reichelderfer to the President of the United States, July 28, 1932, Files of the District Commissioners. This letter and Hoover's press release were printed in contemporary newspapers and in William

Starr Myers and Walter H. Newton, *The Hoover Administration* (New York, 1936), pp. 478–479. MacArthur's scholarly biographer pierces some, but not all, of the confusion. In a critical chapter, curiously titled "Prophet Without Honor," Professor James makes it clear that the troops started at 1:40 P.M. rather than at 2:55 P.M., but he draws no inferences from the discrepancy and does not critically examine MacArthur's report. D. Clayton James, *The Years of MacArthur*, Vol. I, *1880–1941* (Boston, 1970), pp. 382–414.

10. Much of the rest of this chapter is based on Miles, "Report of Operations," and the reports of subordinate unit commanders and specialists upon which it is based, RG 98, NA.

11. Thomas L. Stokes, *Chip Off My Shoulder* (Princeton, 1940), pp. 300–304; Arthur M. Schlesinger, *The Crisis of the Old Order* (Boston, 1957), p. 262. The MacArthur-on-a-horse image is persistent. One of Studs Terkel's interviewees told him: "The picture I'll always remember . . . here is MacArthur coming down Pennsylvania Avenue. And, believe me, ladies and gentlemen, he came on a white horse. He was riding a white horse. Behind him were tanks, troops of the regular army." Studs Terkel, *Hard Times: An Oral History of the Great Depression* (New York, 1970). This illustrates nicely one of the pitfalls of oral history.

12. Glassford, "Speech to Veterans Rally, Philadelphia, November 3, 1932," Glassford Mss., Special Collections.

13. Miles, "Report of Operations"; Lieutenant L. M. Grener, report, "Disposition of C.W. [Chemical Warfare] Supplies," August 10, 1932, RG 98, NA.

14. Herbert Hoover, *The Memoirs of Herbert Hoover: The Great Depression, 1929–1941* (New York, 1952), pp. 226–227.

15. Theodore Joslin, *Hoover Off the Record* (New York, 1934), p. 268.

16. Major General George Van Horn Moseley, "The Bonus March," typescript, 15 pp., January 24, 1938, Moseley Mss., Library of Congress. Moseley's statement was first reported in Maurice P. Sneller, Jr., "The Bonus March of 1932: A Study of Depression Leadership" (Ph.D. diss., University of Virginia, 1960). It was "rediscovered" by James F. and Jean H. Vivian, "The Bonus March of 1932: The Role of General George Van Horn Moseley," *Wisconsin Magazine of History* (August 1967). For a good characterization of Moseley, see John J. Saalberg, "Roosevelt, Fechner and the CCC—A Study in Executive Leadership" (Ph.D. diss., Cornell University, 1963), p. 45.

17. Paul Y. Anderson, "Tear-Gas, Bayonets, and Votes: The President Opens His Reelection Campaign," *Nation* (August 17, 1932).

18. Miles, "Report of Operations"; HQ, 3d U.S. Cavalry, Gen. Orders #6, August 9, 1932, RG 98, NA; MacArthur, "Report," Hoover Mss.

19. War Department, Press Section, "Interview with Secretary of War by the Press at 11:00 P.M., July 28, 1932," RG 94, NA. Despite the title, MacArthur did almost all the talking. For an astute analysis of MacArthur's rhetoric generally, see Stephen Robb, "Fifty Years of Farewell: Douglas MacArthur's Commemorative and Deliberative Speaking" (Ph.D.

diss., Indiana University, 1967). I am indebted to Professor Martin Ridge for this last reference.

20. *Baltimore Sun,* editorial, July 31, 1932.

21. Myers and Newton, *The Hoover Administration,* p. 499.

22. Hoover to Reichelderfer, July 29, 1932, Files of the District Commissioners, printed in part in Myers and Newton, *The Hoover Administration,* p. 500.

23. Hurley, press statement, August 3, 1932, RG 319, NA.

24. *Washington Star,* July 30, 31, August 1, 2, 8, 1932.

25. Anderson, "Tear-Gas"; for something of the impact of gas, see W. L. Langer, *Gas and Flame in World War I* (New York, 1965).

26. Blakeley, "When the Army was Smeared."

27. Lieutenant Colonel H. L. Gilchrist to the Adjutant General, August 2, 1932, RG 94, NA. See also J. E. Hoover to Nugent Dodds, memorandum with enclosure, September 12, 1932, HHPL.

28. Press conference, July 28, 1932, RG 94, NA; Press statement, August 3, 1932, RG 319, NA.

29. *New Yorker* (September 24, 1932):18. For shack burning, see Miles to Moseley, memorandum, "Firing of Shacks Occupied by Bonus Marchers," September 23, 1932, RG 98, NA; for the chemical warfare equipment, see Lieutenant Colonel James M. Lockett to C.O., 3d Bn., 12th Infantry, with 1st endorsement, August 4, 8, 1932, RG 98, NA. Hurley to Congressman Hatton W. Summers, February 28, 1933, RG 94, NA; Hurley to Congressman J. J. McSwain, December 29, 1932, RG 94, NA. The nature of the few army casualties shows clearly the defective nature of the gas equipment: the 3d Bn., 12th Infantry reported six minor burns, all from gas equipment; the 3d Cavalry also had six casualties, four from thrown missiles, two from their own gas. One of the latter was Lucian K. Truscott, later a World War II general of some note. One horse soldier, a Corporal Kermit Quick, struck in the cheek by a brick, needed minor surgery and was not returned to duty until August 18. He seems to be the major military victim of the bonus march. Captain H. B. Smith, reports, September 8, 1932 (2), RG 98, NA.

Chapter 8

1. *Philadelphia Ledger,* July 31, 1932; *New York Times,* August 1–8, 1932; *Oregon Journal,* August 4, 1932; *Portland Oregonian,* August 7, 1932; Malcolm Cowley, "The Flight of the Bonus Army," *New Republic* (August 17, 1932).

2. J. Prentice Murphy, "Report on the Bonus Expeditionary Force Emergency Camp at Johnstown, Penna., and Also Other Kindred Matters and Visits," typescript, 22 pp., August 10, 1932, Glassford Mss.

3. *New York Times,* August 3–7, 1932; *Washington Star,* August 4–12, 1932; *Portland Oregonian,* August 7, 1932.

4. *Oregon Journal,* August 10, 1932; *Portland Oregonian,* August 11, 17, 1932.

5. Patman Mss., passim.; John L. Shover, *Cornbelt Rebellion* (Urbana, Ill., 1965), p. 49. One commentator wrote: "A few [BEFers] may drift into revolutionary parties. Many more might affiliate with a fascist organization if one should materialize sufficiently plausible and sufficiently glamorous. But the vast majority of these men have failed to accumulate a potential of revolution because they feel that they left Washington, not under the compulsion of a brutal and tyrannous government, but as ghosts fleeing before their real selves of fifteen years ago." John Forell, "The Bonus Crusade," *Virginia Quarterly Review* (January 1933). See also Gertrude Springer, "What Became of the B.E.F.?" *Survey* (December 1, 1932). Waters made a number of speaking engagements around the country and put out at least one issue of a tabloid, *B.E.F. Crusader,* modeled after the *B.E.F. News.* Vol. 1, no. 1 [all published?], n.d., but mid-August 1932, is in the Kleinholz Mss., University of Oregon.

6. "Memorandum of the Testimony Presented to the Grand Jury, District of Columbia," typescript, 198 pp., August 4, 8, 10, 15, 1932, transcript of shorthand notes by Talma L. Smith of the Department of Justice, RG 60, NA. For coroner's jury, see *Washington Star,* August 2, 1932. The officer responsible for the deaths, Patrolman George Shinault, was slain a few days later in the line of duty in an entirely unrelated matter.

7. Glassford to Leo A. Rover [U.S. Attorney], August 20 [1932], Glassford Mss.

8. Hurley and Mellon quoted in *Congressional Record,* 72d Cong., 1st sess. (May 30, July 15, 1932), pp. 11535, 15418.

9. Hoover statements in William Starr Myers and Walter H. Newton, *The Hoover Administration* (New York, 1936), pp. 498–500.

10. Dr. [initials illegible] Fowler, "Health Report," annotated "To Commissioner Reichelderfer: For His Information," July 4, 1932, Files of the District Commissioners; Fowler to the Attorney General, September 9, 1932, RG 60, NA.

11. The report and some of the working papers used to assemble it are in RG 60, NA, as is Hines to Hoover, June 15, 1932, with enclosures.

12. H. L. Mencken, "Commentary," *American Mercury* (November 1932): 382.

13. Henry J. Allen to Hurley, August 4, 1932, RG 60, NA. For an example of administration concern about the Legion, see Lawrence Richey to Mark L. Requa [a Hoover intimate], telegram, August 13, 1932, HHPL. *Inter alia,* Richey assured Requa that "except for the Communist group the socalled bonus marchers were not driven out of the District by troops. They all fled because of the announcement of the appointment of a grand jury to investigate and determine the identity of every person engaged in these riots."

14. *Portland Oregonian,* August 11, 1932.

15. MacArthur to Richey, August 12, 1932, RG 94, NA.

16. *New York Times,* September 12, 1932.

17. Glassford to Morris A. Beale, editor of *Plain Talk,* August 22, 1932, Glassford Mss.

18. *New York Times,* September 13, 1932.

19. *Editor and Publisher,* editorial, September 24, 1932.

20. Patman to Morris A. Beale, August 23, 25, 1932, Patman Mss.; *Oregon Journal,* September 10, 1932.

21. *Proceedings of the American Legion,* 1932, passim; undated Rogers column, Glassford Mss.; Hurley's statement in *Portland Oregonian,* September 17, 1932. Cf. the version in Don Lohbeck, *Patrick J. Hurley* (Chicago, 1956), pp. 115–118.

22. Herbert Hoover, *The Memoirs of Herbert Hoover: The Great Depression, 1929–1941* (New York, 1952), pp. 229–230. For an example of the use of the bonus incident by Democrats, see Erwin L. Levine, *Theodore Francis Green* (Providence, R.I., 1963), p. 142.

23. Walter H. Newton to the Commissioners, October 13, 1932, with enclosures, Files of the District Commissioners. See Minutes of the Board of Commissioners, October 20, 1932, for the resignation.

24. Glassford's Newspaper Article; headlines from *Washington Times-Herald,* October 30–November 6, 1932.

25. "Speech by Brig. Gen. Pelham D. Glassford at Veterans' Rally, Philadelphia, Pa., November 3, 1932," mimeographed, 6pp., Glassford Mss., Special Collections. Just after the election, the possibility of having Glassford court-martialed was discussed at the highest military levels. See statement, November 9, 1932, Moseley Mss., LC.

Chapter 9

1. Howard Zinn, *LaGuardia in Congress* (Ithaca, N.Y., 1958), pp. 205–206; cf. Arthur Mann, *LaGuardia, A Fighter Against His Times* (Philadelphia, 1959), p. 305. See also Adolph J. Sabath to Hoover, July 30, 1932, HHPL.

2. *Congressional Record,* 72d Cong., 2d sess. (December 12, 14, 1932), pp. 304–305, 367, 422.

3. Ibid. (December 27, 1932), p. 995.

4. Speech on NBC, December 14, 1932, printed in ibid. (December 15, 1932), pp. 552–553. Actually, four bills to pay the bonus were introduced in the lame-duck session, but none got out of committee.

5. Slater Brown and Malcolm Cowley, "Red Day in Washington," *New Republic* (December 21, 1932): 153–155.

6. "Campaign Address on the Federal Budget at Pittsburgh, Pa., October 14, 1932," in Franklin D. Roosevelt, *The Public Papers and Addresses of Franklin D. Roosevelt,* ed. Samuel I. Rosenman (New York, 1938), I, pp. 795–812. This speech did contain a wonderful Rooseveltian hedge:

"The above two categorical statements are aimed at a definite balancing of the budget. At the same time, let me repeat from now to election day so that every man, woman and child in the United States will know what I mean: If starvation and dire need on the part of any of our citizens make necessary the appropriation of additional funds which would keep the budget out of balance, I shall not hesitate to tell the American people the full truth and ask them to authorize the expenditure of that additional amount." Ibid., p. 810. For an extreme example of the casuistry of which FDR was capable, see the note following this speech in ibid. Writing in 1937 or 1938, he argues that the "regular expenses" of government were, in fact, reduced. For indications of Hopkins' hostility to special benefits for able-bodied veterans, see transcripts of his press conferences, January 9, 30, 1936, Hopkins Mss., FDRL.

7. "A Radio Invitation to All Veterans for Cooperation, March 5, 1933," Roosevelt, *Papers,* II, pp. 17–18.

8. "A Request to Congress for Authority to Effect Drastic Economies in Government, March 10, 1933," ibid., pp. 49–51. This statement contains a typical FDR use of "history" to support his point of view: "Too often in recent history liberal governments have been wrecked on the rocks of loose fiscal policy. We must avoid that danger." There are no known examples of this phenomenon in United States history; in the history of Europe, perhaps the Weimar Republic could be cited to support the generalization, but in fact the converse has more often been true. Liberal governments, including the New Deal, have been inhibited by the inheritance of orthodox fiscal policies from the discredited regimes they superseded. In all the Democratic administrations since World War I, the Secretary of the Treasury has been a fiscal conservative. See also George E. Mowry, "The Uses of History by Recent Presidents," *Journal of American History* (June 1966): 1–18.

9. *Proceedings of the American Legion,* 1933, pp. 209ff., contains a convenient summary of much of this.

10. *Congressional Record,* 73d Cong., 1st sess. (March 11, 1933), pp. 198–238. For the caucus, see ibid., p. 211; for the vote, see ibid., pp. 217–218. While 92 Democrats, 41 Republicans, and all 5 Farmer-Labor Representatives opposed the bill, 197 Democrats and 69 Republicans favored it.

11. Ashurst telegram in ibid., p. 177.

12. Ibid. (March 15, 1933), pp. 467, 471. On the Connally amendment, 17 Democrats and 11 Republicans supported the limitation, while 22 Democrats and 18 Republicans opposed. On the bill itself, only 4 Democrats and 9 Republicans voted no. (Two Republicans, 1 Democrat, and 1 Farmer-Laborite were paired against.) Although many of the Senate opponents could be labeled "progressives" (Borah, Frazier, Nye, Cutting, and La Follette), the short list also included conservatives like Clark, McCarran, Dickinson, and Steiwer.

13. *Proceedings of the American Legion,* 1933, pp. 209ff.; *Congressional Record,* 73d Cong., 1st sess. (May 11, 1933), p. 3227; (May 29, 1933), pp. 4538–4543; (June 10, 1933), pp. 5662, 5664. Veterans Administration, *Annual*

Report, 1933, pp. 1–10; Veterans Administration, *Annual Report,* 1934, p. 50, table 12; Roosevelt, *Papers,* II, pp. 51–54. For previous treatments, cf. Basil Rauch, *A History of the New Deal* (New York, 1944), p. 63; James M. Burns, *Roosevelt: The Lion and the Fox* (New York, 1956), p. 167; Arthur M. Schlesinger, Jr., *The Coming of the New Deal* (Boston, 1959), pp. 10–11; William Leuchtenberg, *Franklin D. Roosevelt and the New Deal* (New York, 1963), p. 45. Contemporary officialdom contributed to the confusion by making many conflicting statements about the size and effect of the cuts. I followed the VA reports and the figures cited in U.S., Department of Commerce, Bureau of the Census, *Historical Statistics of the United States from Colonial Times to 1957* (Washington, D.C., 1960), Series Y812–825, p. 740. In fiscal 1933—that is, before the Economy Act took effect—412,482 World War I veterans drew non-service-connected disability stipends. The Economy Act orders cut that figure to 29,903.

14. *Congressional Record,* 73d Cong., 1st sess. (March 9, 1933), p. 85; (April 28, 1933), p. 2531. Thirteen other bonus measures of some type were introduced, but none got out of committee. See H.R. 141, 1641, 1687, 1717, 2848, 3652, 3655, 4348, 5682, 5802, and 5997, and S.B. 72 and 1387.

15. Rexford G. Tugwell, *The Brains Trust* (New York, 1968), pp. 357–359. Franklin D. Roosevelt to "Dear Sir," October 29, 1932, PPF, Box 67, FDRL. Other material on the bonus appears in OF 391 and 1820; his concern while governor of New York can be seen in FDR, Gubernatorial Mss., Box 184, folder "TERA:A-C," and Box 185, folders "TERA-Misc.," FDRL.

16. *Daily Worker,* April 3, 1933, p. 3. The Communist line on veterans' affairs can most conveniently be seen in the column "The Fighting Vet" or "Fighting Vet" by H. E. Briggs, which appeared irregularly but frequently in the *Daily Worker* during the early New Deal years. On April 10, the *New York Times* had a detailed story on the impending march. Data on the front group is from Bulletin No. 3, Veterans National Liaison Committee, Washington, D.C., January 31, 1933 (mimeographed), Emanuel Levin Mss., UCLA. For Waters and Robertson, see *New York Times,* April 23, 1933, sec. IV, p. 6, and *Daily Worker,* April 18, 1933.

17. *New York Times,* April 28, 1933. Alfred B. Rollins, *Roosevelt and Howe* (New York 1962), fails to mention this meeting.

18. Rollins, *Roosevelt and Howe,* pp. 386–388; Veterans Administration, *Annual Report,* 1933, pp. 4–5. Hines' activity is traced in James Russell Woods, "The Legend and the Legacy of FDR and the CCC" (Ph.D. diss., Syracuse University, 1964), pp. 154–169.

19. Assorted clippings in a scrapbook compiled by Emanuel Levin, Levin Mss., UCLA. The march can be best followed in the *New York Times, Daily Worker,* and *Washington Star.*

20. Brady to Hines, May 3, 1934, enclosed in Hines to Howe, May 10, 1932, OF 391, FDR Mss., FDRL.

21. See Hines to FDR, May 6, 1933, OF 268, FDRL, and Hines to S. Early for FDR, memorandum of telephone call, May 23, 1933, both cited

in John J. Saalberg, "Roosevelt, Fechner and the CCC—A Study in Executive Leadership" (Ph.D. diss., Cornell University, 1963), pp. 42–43. This dissertation is superior to most published monographs on the New Deal. Veterans Administration, *Annual Report,* 1933, pp. 4–5. For Fechner's objections, see Woods, "Legend of the CCC," p. 155 passim. Executive Order No. 6129 (May 11, 1933) authorized the enrollment of 25,000 World War I veterans, while No. 6144 (May 24, 1933) allowed the enrollment of veterans of other wars. Veterans, an afterthought, thus comprised about 10 percent of the authorized strength of the CCC. By 1940, nearly 200,000 veterans had passed through it. See Veterans Administration, *Annual Report,* 1941, p. 3. Marguerite Le Hand to James Roosevelt, May 11, 1933, OF 189—"Sports, 1933," FDRL.

22. *New York Times,* May 15, 1933.

23. *Washington Herald,* May 13, 1933. For other material on the "right wing," see *Congressional Record,* 73d Cong., 1st sess. (May 24, 1933), pp. 4093–4094; (June 10, 1933), p. 5609.

24. Rollins, *Roosevelt and Howe,* p. 387. Insofar as the bonus marchers are concerned, Rollins gives Howe credit for measures that came from General Hines and others. Howe was certainly *an* architect of the successful tactics, but his biographer makes him *the* architect.

25. Howe and Early's visit is in the *New York Times,* May 14, 1933; Mrs. Roosevelt's visit is in ibid., May 17, 1933. The announcement that she would visit is found deep in the *Times'* story on the camps for May 16, p. 5, but it was not listed in the *New York Times Index,* which helps explain why it has not been noted previously. Mrs. Roosevelt's account is in *This I Remember* (New York, 1949), pp. 112–113. See also Lela Stiles, *The Man Behind Roosevelt* (Cleveland, 1954), pp. 264–266. A standard device of historians has been to quote a remark allegedly made by an admiring veteran: "Hoover sent the Army; Roosevelt sent his wife." I can find no contemporary citation. It seems to appear first in the Stalinist account by Jack Douglas [pseud.], *Veterans on the March* (New York, 1934), p. 324: "To confuse the convention and to strengthen the influence of the Administration among the vets . . . Mrs. Roosevelt visited the camp. There was an informal program. Mrs. Roosevelt asked them to sing, 'There's a Long, Long Trail,' and led the singing herself. An unappreciative vet remarked, 'Hoover sent the army; Roosevelt sent his wife.'" Intended as a sneer, this has been turned into praise by deft historianship.

26. *New York Times,* May 20, 1933; *Washington Daily News,* May 20, 1933.

27. *New York Times,* May 12, 1933.

28. *Congressional Record,* 73d Cong., 1st sess. (May 9, 1933), pp. 3098–3099, 3101; (June 15, 1933), pp. 6148–6149. Veterans Administration, *Annual Report,* 1933, p. 5.

29. *New York Times,* September 30–October 6, 1933, has a contemporary account of the convention. The official proceedings, in this instance, mask more than they reveal; the only trace of the bonus fight is the title of

Patman's resolution, which was voted down in committee. See *Proceedings of the American Legion*, 1933, p. 62. For Roosevelt's speech, see Roosevelt, *Papers*, II, pp. 373–378. For repeated use of the "war emergency" theme, see William Leuchtenberg, "The New Deal and the Analogue of War," in John Braeman et al., *Change and Continuity in Twentieth Century America* (Columbus, Ohio, 1964).

30. *Congressional Record*, 73d Cong., 2d sess. (January 10, 1934), pp. 363–364. FDR's memo was eventually inserted into the record by economy advocate Alan T. Treadway (R.-Mass.). Ibid. (March 12, 1934), p. 4294. Lundeen's action in pushing for the bill was characteristic of wheat belt agrarians, regardless of party. William Lemke, the maverick agrarian from North Dakota, characterized those who opposed the bonus as a "bunch of coupon-clipping international bankers." Ibid. (June 16, 1934), p. 12272.

31. Ibid. (February 20, 1934), pp. 2938–2939, for discharge petition signatories. The debate in the House is in ibid. (May 12, 1934), pp. 4287–4358, the roll call on discharge is on pp. 4298–4299, and Congressman Byrns is quoted on p. 4237. *New York Times*, May 13, 1934.

32. Telegrams between Patman and George Koryski, CCC Camp Wilson, East Barre, Vermont, are in *Congressional Record*, 73d Cong., 2d sess. (March 21, 1934), p. 5078. For continuing concern over bonus march agitation in the veterans' CCC camps, see the material in War Department File AGO 240 Bonus, RG 94, NA.

33. Hopkins' role can be pieced together from various letters and reports in Box 64, Folder "BO-BY," Hopkins Mss., and OF 391, Folders 1934 and 1935, FDR Mss., both FDRL. See also Veterans Administration, *Annual Report*, 1935, pp. 4–5; Veterans Administration, *Annual Report*, 1936, p. 4. A bound set of the mimeographed Fort Hunt paper for the 1934 convention, *The Rank and File Vet* (eleven issues between May 11 and May 27, 1934), is in the Emanuel Levin Mss., UCLA.

34. *The Rank and File Vet*, passim. According to figures published there, 1,429 veterans from 45 states registered; 270 were Negroes. The average age was 41; 396 had been enrolled in CCC camps.

35. Fechner to Howe, July 7, 1934, cited by Woods, "Legend of the CCC," p. 165.

36. This policy can be pieced together from a number of official reports (see n. 33, above), but the best single account is in a letter from VA Administrator Hines to the President's secretary, Marvin McIntyre, December 10, 1935, OF 391, Folder 1935, FDR Mss., FDRL. For Patman, see *Congressional Record*, 74th Cong., 2d sess. (June 19, 1936), p. 10187.

37. *Proceedings of the American Legion*, 1934, pp. 7, 44, 72–73, 76.

38. Ibid., 1935, pp. 211–253, contains a good account of legislative maneuvering that year. See also *Congressional Record*, 74th Cong., 1st sess. (March 14, 1935), pp. 3940–3988, for the texts of the competing measures. The key House votes are in ibid. (March 22, 1935), pp. 4309, 4313–4314; the Senate votes in ibid. (May 7, 1935), p. 7068. *Time* (July 15, 1935): 7.

39. New Deal historians have been misled about Roosevelt's position and action on the bonus by relying far too much on the "diary" of Henry Morgenthau, Jr., Secretary of the Treasury, who described a meeting on May 16 at the White House in which he "convinced" the President to make a real fight on the bonus veto. Since this was after Majority Leader Robinson's moves in the Senate, FDR's mind was clearly already made up. Morgenthau and the historians who rely upon him are oblivious to what happened in the Senate. Morgenthau, personally devoted to the President, was unusually dense even for a Secretary of the Treasury, and the complicated legislative tactics the President often employed were a closed book to him. Morgenthau thought that the President dictated his veto message during that May 16 meeting, but an examination of the message shows clearly that it was a staff production. Anyway, Samuel Rosenman has written that he helped draft the message on the yacht *Sequoia.* Amusingly, Morgenthau was a nonworking passenger on that cruise. See John M. Blum, *From the Morgenthau Diaries: Years of Crisis, 1928–1938* (Boston, 1959), pp. 249–259; Samuel I. Rosenman, *Working With Roosevelt* (New York, 1952), p. 94; Arthur M. Schlesinger, Jr., *The Politics of Upheaval* (Boston, 1960), pp. 10–11; Samuel Burton Hand, "Samuel I. Rosenman: His Public Career" (Ph.D. diss., Syracuse University, 1960), pp. 135–136. For an example of how FDR delighted in keeping his subordinates in the dark (in this case on whether he would veto the 1936 bill), see Harold L. Ickes, *The Secret Diary of Harold Ickes* (New York, 1954), I, p. 525.

40. "The President Vetoes the Bonus Bill. May 22, 1935," Roosevelt, *Papers,* IV, pp. 182–193. In the best single volume on the New Deal, William Leuchtenberg, *Franklin D. Roosevelt and the New Deal* (New York, 1963), this message is described as part of a conservative trend that "left his progressive followers in a quandary"; Leuchtenberg thinks that in it FDR "sounded for all the world like Grover Cleveland venting his indignation at the Silver Purchase Act." Ibid., p. 147. Since Roosevelt was thoroughly consistent on the bonus bill from the 1920s, I fail to see the quandary, nor do I find the message Clevelandesque. The idea of extending "assistance to all groups and all classes who in an emergency need the helping hand of the government" is the antithesis of Cleveland's nineteenth-century mugwumpery. Cleveland's ideas about the role of government are best seen in his 1887 veto of a $10,000 drought-relief appropriation: "though the people support the Government the Government should not support the people." James D. Richardson, ed., *The Messages and Papers of the President* (Washington, D.C., 1911), VIII, pp. 557–558. Conversely, James M. Burns, *Roosevelt: The Lion and the Fox* (New York, 1956), p. 324, calls it "a brilliant message," but thinks that Congress sustained it "by a hair."

41. *Congressional Record,* 74th Cong., 1st sess. (May 22, 1935), pp. 7996–7997; (May 23, 1935), pp. 8066–8067.

42. *New York Times,* June 28, 1936; *Congressional Record,* 74th Cong., 1st sess. (January 21, 1935), pp. 709–711 (January 29, 1935), p. 1109. It was

introduced by Hamilton Fish, who was in a tizzy when he discovered that a few minor government officials, including Gardner Jackson of the AAA, had made monetary contributions to the Communist-dominated Veterans National Liaison Committee the year before.

43. *New York Times,* August 7, 1935; *Proceedings of the American Legion,* 1935, p. 253.

44. *Congressional Record,* 74th Cong., 2d sess. (January 9, 1936), pp. 218–236; (January 10, 1936), pp. 291–292; (January 20, 1936), p. 793; (January 24, 1936), pp. 975–976; (January 27, 1936), p. 105, "The President Vetoes for a Second Time the Soldiers' Bonus. A Message in Longhand. January 24, 1936," Roosevelt, *Papers,* V, p. 67. Cf. Carlton Jackson, *Presidential Vetoes* (Athens, Ga., 1967), pp. 208–213.

45. For an example of how the Democrats used the bonus issue in 1936, a six-page flyer distributed by the Veterans Advisory Committee of the Democratic National Committee was headed "Veterans have won *Full Recognition under the New Deal*" and, after asking its readers to "recall the veterans' plight under Hoover in 1932," listed twelve New Deal accomplishments, the first of which was "bonus enacted and promptly paid." Elsewhere it argued: "The Adjusted Compensation Act became a law on January 27, 1936, bringing to a close a controversy which had been waged for sixteen years. President Roosevelt, like his predecessors, Presidents Harding, Coolidge, and Hoover, vetoed the Bonus, but when the DEMOCRATIC Congress overrode the veto, President Roosevelt did not delay the payment of the Bonus but with prodigious energy organized and set in motion the vast machinery necessary to pay off the Adjusted Service Certificates, and the Treasury and Post Office Departments functioned so efficiently that more than 3,000,000 veterans were paid the amounts due them over a period of a very few days." Copy of flyer, New Deal Pamphlet Collection, University of Wyoming.

Chapter 10

1. See his typewritten report, Box VII, IIR, Glassford Mss.

2. *Portland Journal,* August 27, 1932; Henry J. Allen to Hurley, August 4, 1932, RG 94, NA.

3. W. W. Waters, *B.E.F.: The Whole Story of the Bonus Army* (New York, 1933), p. 235. For other views, see Talcott Powell, *Tattered Banners* (New York, 1933), and Katherine Mayo, *Soldiers What Next!* (Boston 1934).

4. Jack Douglas [pseud.], *Veterans on the March* (New York, 1934), pp. v–vi.

5. Ibid., pp. 366, 370, 228–253 passim.

6. See my review of the official report on the Watts riots in *Pacific Historical Review* (May 1966): 239–240.

7. Charles A. Beard and Mary R. Beard, *American in Midpassage* (New York, 1939), I, p. 93. It could be quite amusing and exhausting to compile a syllabus of errors from textbooks and general treatments by historians, but since here I am concerned with the popular mind, these are of little relevance. Significant errors by historians have been mentioned in passing in the notes.

8. E. Francis Brown, "The Bonus Army Marches to Defeat," *Current History* (September 1932): 688.

9. *World Tomorrow* (November 9, 1932): 455.

10. Charles Angoff, "Blubbering From the Graveyard," review of *The Challenge to Liberty* by Herbert Hoover, *American Mercury* (December 1934):500.

11. Bruce Minton and John Stuart, *The Fat Years and the Lean* (New York, 1940), pp. 259–260. An earlier Communist work had said: "Hoover blasted the ex-soldiers out of Anacostia with the gunfire, tear gas and bayonets of the United States Army." A. B. Magil and Henry Stevens, *The Peril of Fascism* (New York, 1938), p. 248.

12. *Ballads of the B.E.F.* (New York, 1932); Shaemus O'Sheel, *It Could Never Happen* (New York, 1932). For O'Sheel's background, see Peter Lyon, *Success Story* (New York, 1963), p. 260, and "He Went Forth to Battle . . . In Memoriam Shaemus O'Sheel," pp. 7–10, in O'Sheel, *Antigone and Selected Poems* (Philadelphia, 1961).

13. Dixon Wecter, *When Johnny Comes Marching Home* (Boston, 1944), pp. 447–448. He gave about as much space to describing the minority of veterans who opposed the bonus. The only source he cited was Brown, "The Bonus Army," which contains no comment on MacArthur's attitudes, real or imagined. Four years later, Wecter was more accurate in his, *The Age of the Great Depression* (New York, 1948), basing his account on Waters' book, but still giving it only a single page. A lesser known wartime book, Willard Waller, *The Veteran Comes Back* (New York, 1944), pp. 240–245, contains an essentially accurate account.

14. William Addleman Ganoe, *The History of the United States Army*, rev. ed. (New York, 1942), pp. 500–501.

15. Herbert Packer, *Ex-Communist Witnesses* (Stanford, Calif., 1962), p. 225.

16. Benjamin Gitlow, *The Whole of Their Lives* (New York, 1948), pp. 226–230. For another analysis of Gitlow, see Arthur M. Schlesinger, Jr., *The Crisis of the Old Order* (Boston, 1956), pp. 518–519. He quotes a Gitlow article of September 1933, in which the former Communist, still a Marxist, wrote: "When the Communist Party tried to inject itself into the Veterans' Bonus March, the mass of the veterans resented it as interference and looked upon the Communists as a foreign, hostile source." Benjamin Gitlow, "A Labor Party for America," *Modern Monthly* (September 1933).

17. Benjamin Gitlow, *I Confess* (New York, 1940), p. 328.

18. Eugene Lyons, *Our Un-Known Ex-President* (New York 1948), pp. 288–289; Eugene Lyons, *Herbert Hoover* (New York, 1964), pp. 240–243.

There are other minor, but interesting, differences. The later edition notes the presence of Colonel [sic] Dwight D. Eisenhower serving as "second in command" and suppresses an accurate, critical account of the Hearst reporting of the bonus march. In using the testimony of John Pace (see below), Lyons mistakenly quotes the more colorful Pace-Rushmore from the Hearst papers rather than his slightly different sworn statements.

19. Floyd E. McCaffree [Director of Research, Republican National Committee] to Hurley, September 28, 1948, enclosing two typed memoranda, "Communist Influence in the Bonus March of 1932," 8 pp., and "Information from the Files of the Committee on Un-American Activities for Mr. Floyd E. McCaffree," September 18, 1948, 7 pp. On October 28, 1946, Hurley had issued a four-page statement on the bonus march to counter an attack made by the Chavez forces. In it he stated something he would not claim later, that the police were subjected to "a definite, organized attack." All are from Hurley Mss., University of Oklahoma, Norman, Oklahoma. For access to this material, I am indebted to Mr. Jack Haley of the University Archives and Professor Gilbert Fite.

20. *McCall's* (July 1949).

21. Ibid. (November 1949), reprinted in *Congressional Record*, 82d Cong., 1st sess. (April 18, 1951), pp. 4056–4058.

22. See Gitlow, *The Whole of Their Lives,* pp. 220–221. As rendered by Hurley, the quotation is slightly corrupt.

23. *Washington Times-Herald,* November 1, 1949, published a long editorial entitled "Eleanor Set Right," which went even further. Starting "Patrick J. Hurley, using the language of a cavalier," it ended: "President Hoover did not cause the death of a single bonus marcher. On the other hand, Mrs. Roosevelt's husband bears the responsibility for the deaths of 256 of them." According to a 1936 report by VA Administrator Hines, this is the number of veterans killed. See *Congressional Record,* 82d Cong., 1st sess. (June 4, 1951), p. 6045.

24. *McCall's* (November 1949).

25. MacArthur to Hurley, August 27, 1949; Hurley to Otis Lee Weise [editor and publisher, *McCall's*], September 9, 1949: Hurley Mss.

26. Information on Pace comes from his articles and testimony listed below, and from Jacob Spolansky, *The Communist Trail in America* (New York, 1951), pp. 48–52. Spolansky was perhaps the original "Communist for the F.B.I."

27. The story appeared in afternoon Hearst papers of August 28, 29, 30, 1949. I quote from the *Los Angeles Herald-Examiner.*

28. *Congressional Record,* 82d Cong., 1st sess. (April 11, 1951), p. 3647.

29. Ibid. (April 17, 1951), pp. 3978–3979.

30. Ibid. (April 18, 1951), pp. 4056–4058. There were several other insertions in the record, including six pages of documents on the 1935 Labor Day hurricane disaster put in by Senator Owen J. Brewster (R.-Me.). Ibid. (June 4, 1951), pp. 6043–6048. Congressman Wint Smith (R.-Kan.) contributed a unique detail. According to the Kansan, Lieutenant Colonel [sic] George S. Patton did all the planning for MacArthur in the bonus

march affair. Smith served overseas under Patton, and probably picked up this fabrication from its source. See *Congressional Record*, 1951, page A2035.

31. *Washington Times-Herald*, June 1, 1951; *Congressional Record*, 82d Cong., 1st sess. (June 4, 1951), pp. 6042–6043.

32. The testimony comprises pp. 1925–1964 of the committee's eccentrically assembled hearing for 1951. U.S., Congress, House, Committee on Un-American Activities, *Communist Tactics Among Veterans' Groups, Hearings*, 82d Cong., 1st sess., 1951. This is often cited by the date of the secret hearing, August 23, 1949, but that hearing appears in print only as a part of the 1951 public hearing. The invaluable Fund for the Republic, *Digest to the Public Record of Communism in the United States* (New York, 1955), would be much more useful if it gave page references to the annual bound volumes, to which there are no indexes.

33. U.S., Congress, House, Committee on Un-American Activities, *Hearings*, before the Special Committee on Un-American Activities, 75th Cong., 3d sess., 1938, pp. 2266–2287. Fund for the Republic, *Digest*, p. 591, did not consider the bonus march worthy of recording.

34. *Washington Times-Herald*, June 1, 1951.

35. Glassford to *Times-Herald*, July 12, 1951, Glassford Mss., Special Collections.

36. *Washington Times-Herald*, July 14, 1951; *Washington Post*, July 22, 1951.

37. W. L. White, "The Story of a Smear," *The Freeman* (October 22, 1951). See also Major General H. W. Blakeley, "When the Army was Smeared," *Combat Forces Journal* (February 1952).

38. Glassford to John Chamberlain, January 25, 1932, Glassford Mss., Special Collections.

39. Herbert Hoover, *The Memoirs of Herbert Hoover: The Great Depression, 1929–1941* (New York, 1952), p. 195.

40. Ibid., pp. 225, 232. The MacArthur letter to the Attorney General, August 2, 1932, is in RG 94, NA.

41. Michael Gold, "Councilman Pete," in International Publishers, *Looking Forward* (New York, 1954), pp. 143–152.

42. Don Lohbeck, *Patrick J. Hurley* (Chicago, 1956), pp. 102–118, 486–488; Courtney Whitney, *MacArthur: His Rendezvous with History* (New York, 1956), pp. 513–515.

43. Douglas MacArthur, *Reminiscences* (New York, 1964), pp. 92–97. The "Report of Operations" is in RG 98, NA. MacArthur's "Report" is in HHPL.

44. Dwight D. Eisenhower, *At Ease* (New York, 1967), pp. 215–218.

45. Harris G. Warren, *Herbert Hoover and the Great Depression* (New York, 1959), pp. 224–236; Irving Bernstein, *The Lean Years* (Boston, 1960), pp. 437–455. Yet wildly erroneous accounts continue to appear. The latest of these, Gene Smith, *The Shattered Dream* (New York, 1970), devotes forty-two pages to the bonus march. Despite a citation of Warren, he gets many facts wrong, conflates the two incidents on July 28 into one, per-

petuates old myths, and produces new ones. He used the Hoover and Moseley Mss. (but gets Moseley's name wrong) and fails to acknowledge the prior use of the latter papers. After describing Mrs. Roosevelt's 1933 visit, he writes: "from that day on the bonus was dead." See ibid., pp. 126–166, 233–234.

46. John D. Weaver, *Another Such Victory* (New York, 1948), and his, "The Bonus March," *American Heritage* (June 1963).

47. *New York Times*, August 1963.

48. *Wall Street Journal*, August 27, 1963; see also *National Observer*, April 29, 1968.

49. Drew Pearson in *Los Angeles Times*, August 28, 1963.

50. Morrie Ryskind in *Los Angeles Times*, April 16, 1967.

51. Eleanor Roosevelt, *This I Remember* (New York, 1949), p. 112.

Chapter 11

1. Robertson's death from David Disco, "The California Contingent and the Bonus March of 1932" (Senior thesis, University of California, Los Angeles, 1964); Waters' from *Walla Walla* (Washington) *Union Bulletin*, April 23, 1959. Levin obituaries are in *Daily Worker* and *People's World* (San Francisco), April 23–24, 1956. A telegram of condolence from William Z. Foster to his widow said in part: "his name is imperishably connected with one of the grandest traditions of the Communists in the United States for it was he who in April, 1932, first issued the call for national march on Washington to win the soldier's bonus and the following year he was one of the leaders of the great veterans' movement which conducted the bonus march on Washington." Foster to Mrs. Anna Levin, telegram, April 23, 1956, Levin Mss., UCLA.

2. Material on Glassford from clipping scrapbooks, Glassford Mss., Special Collections, and Mary Griset, "Pelham D. Glassford and the Imperial Valley," seminar paper in my possession. For the Imperial Valley labor history, see Stuart Jamison, *Labor Unionism in American Agriculture* (Washington, D.C., 1945), pp. 70–78, 105–115.

3. Glassford's 1936 political views from a four-page campaign throwaway, Glassford Mss., Special Collections; obituary, *New York Times*, August 10, 1959.

4. U.S., Office of War Mobilization, *Report on War and Post-War Adjustment Policies* (Washington, D.C., 1944), p. 3.

5. U.S., Congress, House, Committee on Ways and Means, *Soldier's Adjusted Compensation, Hearings*, 66th Cong., 2d sess., 1920, pp. 496–511.

6. Hines to FDR, August 6, 1943, OF 1820, FDRL. For an interesting although incomplete account of the genesis of the G.I. Bill, see Davis R. B. Ross, *Preparing for Ulysses* (New York, 1969), pp. 89–124.

Bibliography

Manuscripts

In the National Archives, Washington, D.C.
Record Group 56, General Records of the Department of the Treasury
Record Group 60, General Records of the Department of Justice
Record Group 94, Records of the Adjutant General's Office
Record Group 98, Records of the United States Army Commands
Record Group 319, Records of the Army Staff
In the Library of Congress
Major General George Van Horn Moseley Mss.
In the Franklin D. Roosevelt Library, Hyde Park, New York
Harry L. Hopkins Mss.
Herbert Lehman Mss.
Franklin D. Roosevelt Mss.
In the Herbert Hoover Presidential Library, West Branch, Iowa
Herbert Hoover Mss.
In the University of Oklahoma
Patrick J. Hurley Mss.
In the University of Wyoming
Frank Mondell Mss.

347

In the University of Oregon
  George Kleinholz Mss.
In the University of California, Berkeley
  Hiram W. Johnson Mss., The Bancroft Library
In the University of California, Los Angeles
  Pelham D. Glassford Mss. (two collections)
  Emanuel Levin Mss.

Collections Not in Libraries

Papers of the Association of American Railroads, Washington, D.C.
Papers of the District Commissioners, Washington, D.C.
Papers of Wright Patman, Washington, D.C.

Newspapers

BEF News (Washington, D.C.) (two separate papers)
Daily Worker (New York City)
New York Times
Portland Oregonian
Oregon Journal (Portland)
Washington Star

Books, Pamphlets, Magazine Articles, and Theses

ADAMIC, LOUIS. "The Papers Print the Riots." *Scribner's* (February 1932).

ADAMS, SAMUEL HOPKINS. *Incredible Era: The Life and Times of Warren Gamaliel Harding*. Boston, 1939.

AHRENDT, HAROLD. "The History of Work Relief in Multnomah County, Oregon, 1930–1933." Master's thesis, State College of Washington, 1944.

AIKMAN, DUNCAN. "Savonarola in Los Angeles." *American Mercury* (December 1930).

ALLEN, ROBERT S., and PEARSON, DREW. *More Merry-Go-Round.* New York, 1932.

AMERICAN LEGION. *Committee Reports.* 1919–1936.

AMTER, I[SRAEL]. *The March Against Hunger.* New York, 1932.

ANDERSON, PAUL Y. "Cowardice and Folly in Washington." *Nation* (August 10, 1932).

———. "Glassford Sees It Through." *Nation* (September 28, 1932).

———. "Republican Handsprings." *Nation* (August 31, 1932).

———. "Tear-Gas, Bayonets, and Votes," *Nation* (August 17, 1932).

ANGOFF, CHARLES. "Blubbering in the Graveyard." Review of *The Challenge to Liberty,* by Herbert Hoover. *American Mercury* (December 1934).

ARNETT, ALEX M. *Claude Kitchin.* Boston, 1937.

ATWELL, EDWARD F. *The Battle Ground: The Truth About the Bonus Riots.* Washington, n.d. [1933].

BAGBY, WESLEY M. *The Road to Normalcy: The Presidential Campaign of 1920.* Baltimore, 1962.

Ballads of the B.E.F. New York, 1932.

BARTLETT, JOHN HENRY. *The Bonus March and the New Deal.* Chicago and New York, 1937.

BEARD, CHARLES A., and BEARD, MARY R. *America in Midpassage.* 2 vols. New York, 1939.

BEAVER, DANIEL R. *Newton D. Baker and the American War Effort, 1917–1919.* Lincoln, Neb., 1966.

BERNSTEIN, IRVING. *The Lean Years.* Boston, 1960.

BLACKORBY, EDWARD C. *Prairie Rebel.* Lincoln, Neb., 1963.

BLAKELEY, H. W. "When the Army Was Smeared." *Combat Forces Journal* (February 1952).

BLUM, JOHN MORTON. *From the Morgenthau Diaries: Years of Crisis, 1928–1938.* New York, 1959.

BRIGGS, ASA, ed. *Chartist Studies.* London, 1957.

BRIGGS, H. E. *New Deal for the Vets.* New York, 1933.

———. *The Veterans Fight for Unity.* New York, 1935.

BROWDER, EARL. "The Impending Financial Crisis and the Bonus Expeditionary Force." *Daily Worker,* July 5, 1932.

BROWN, E. FRANCIS. "The Bonus Army Marches to Defeat." *Current History* (September 1932).

BROWN, SLATER, and COWLEY, MALCOLM. "Bad Day in Washington." *New Republic* (December 21, 1932).

"Bullets for the B.E.F.: Hoover Relief, New Style." *New Republic* (August 10, 1932).

BURLINGAME, ROGER. *Peace Veterans: The Story of a Racket and a Plea for Economy.* New York, 1932.

BURNS, JAMES M. *Roosevelt: The Lion and the Fox.* New York, 1956.

CANNON, JOHN S. *Billions for Boondoggling, Vetoes for Veterans.* Kansas City, 1936.

CARSON, GERALD. *The Roughish World of Doctor Brinkley.* New York, 1960.

CARSTENSEN, VERNON, ed. *The Public Lands.* Madison, 1963.

CHAMBER OF COMMERCE OF THE UNITED STATES. *Referendum No. 38 on Legislation for Veterans of the World War.* Washington, D.C., January 7, 1922.

CHASE, FRANCIS, JR. *Sound and Fury: An Informal History of Broadcasting.* New York, 1942.

COLCORD, JOANNA C. "The West is Different." *Survey* (June 1, 1932).

CONKIN, PAUL K. *Tomorrow a New World: The New Deal Community Program.* Ithaca, N.Y., 1959.

COWLEY, MALCOLM. "The Flight of the Bonus Army." *New Republic* (August 17, 1932).

DANIELS, ROGER. Book review. *Pacific Historical Review* (May 1966).

DAVIES, WALLACE E. *Patriotism on Parade: The Story of Veterans and Heredity Organizations in America, 1783–1900.* Cambridge, Mass., 1955.

DEARING, MARY R. *Veterans in Politics: The Story of the G.A.R.* Baton Rouge, La. 1952.

DEMOCRATIC NATIONAL COMMITTEE. *Proceedings of the Democratic National Convention.* Denver, 1908.

DILLINGHAM, WILLIAM PYRLE. *Federal Aid to Veterans, 1917–1941.* Gainesville, Fla., 1952.

DISCO, DAVID. "The California Contingent and the Bonus March of 1932." Senior thesis, University of California, Los Angeles, 1964.

DOS PASSOS, JOHN. "The Veterans Come Home to Roost." *New Republic* (July 29, 1932).

DOUGLAS, JACK [pseud.]. *Veterans on the March*. New York, 1934.

DUFFIELD, MARCUS. *King Legion*. New York, 1931.

DURHAM, KNOWLTON. *Billions for Veterans*. New York, 1932.

EISENHOWER, DWIGHT D. *At Ease*. New York, 1967.

EVERETT, E. F. "Khaki Shirts and Fascism" (letter to the editor). *New Republic* (October 19, 1932).

EWY, MARVIN. *Charles Curtis of Kansas: Vice President of the United States, 1929–1933*. Emporia State Research Studies, vol. 10, no. 2. Emporia, Kan., 1961.

FORD, AMELIA C. *Colonial Precedents of Our National Land System as It Existed in 1800*. Madison, 1910.

FORELL, JOHN. "The Bonus Crusade." *Virginia Quarterly Review* (January 1933).

FOSTER, WILLIAM Z. *History of the Communist Party of the United States*. New York, 1952.

FRIEDMAN, MILTON. *Capitalism and Freedom*. Chicago, 1962.

FREUD, RUDOLPH. "Military Bounty Lands and the Orgins of the Public Domain." *Agricultural History* (1946).

FUND FOR THE REPUBLIC. *Digest of the Public Record of Communism in the United States*. New York, 1955.

FUNK, ANTOINETTE. "Why Women Are Joining the Democratic Party." *Congressional Digest* (August 1922).

GANOE, WILLIAM ADDLEMAN. *The History of the United States Army*. Rev. ed. New York, 1942.

GATES, JOHN. *The Story of an American Communist*. New York, 1958.

GELLERMAN, WILLIAM. *The American Legion as Educator*. New York, 1938.

GEPHART, WILLIAM F. *Effects of the War Upon Insurance with Special Reference to the Substitution of Insurance for Pensions*. New York, 1918.

GILTINIAN, CHARLOTTE. "An Eye-Witness on the Rout of the B.E.F. in Washington." *Fortnightly Review* (September 1932).

GITLOW, BENJAMIN. *I Confess*. New York, 1940.

———. "A Labor Party for Modern America." *Modern Monthly* (September 1933).

———. *The Whole of Their Lives*. New York, 1948.

GLASSON, WILLIAM H. *Federal Military Pensions in the United States*. New York, 1918.

———. *History of the Military Pension System in the United States*. New York, 1900.

GOLD, MIKE. "Councilman Pete." In International Publishers, *Looking Forward*. New York, 1954.

GOMPERS, SAMUEL. *Seventy Years of Life and Labor*. New York, 1925.

GRANT, LOUIS T. *The Taxpayer and the War Veteran*. San Francisco, 1934.

GRAY, JUSTIN. *The Inside Story of the Legion*. New York, 1948.

GREEN, CONSTANCE MCLAUGHLIN. *The Rise of Urban America*. New York, 1965.

———. *The Secret City*. Princeton, 1967.

———. *Washington, Capital City, 1879–1950*. Princeton, 1963.

GRISET, MARY. "Pelham D. Glassford and the Imperial Valley." Seminar paper, University of California, Los Angeles, 1964.

GUNN, OZEN. *Psychology of the Bonus March: Its Relation to People and Government*. n.p., n.d. [1932–1933].

GUNTHER, JOHN. *Inside U.S.A.* New York, 1947.

HALLGREN, MAURITZ. "The Bonus Army Scares Mr. Hoover." *Nation* (July 27, 1932).

HAND, SAMUEL BURTON. "Samuel I. Rosenman: His Public Career." Ph.D. dissertation, Syracuse University, 1960.

HANNAH, JAMES J. "Urban Reaction to the Great Depression in the United States, 1929–1933." Ph.D. dissertation, University of California, Berkeley, 1956.

HENNESSY, ARTHUR L., JR. "The Bonus March: Its Roots, Growth and Demise." Ph.D. dissertation, Georgetown University, 1957.

HIBBARD, BENJAMIN HORACE. *A History of the Public Land Policies*. New York, 1924.

HOFSTADTER, RICHARD. *The Paranoid Style in American Politics*. New York, 1965.

HOOVER, HERBERT C. *The Memoirs of Herbert Hoover: The Great Depression, 1929–1941*. New York, 1952.

———. *The State Papers and Other Public Writings of Herbert Hoover*. Edited by William Starr Myers. 2 vols. New York, 1934.

HOUSTON, DAVID F. *Eight Years with Wilson's Cabinet*. 2 vols. New York, 1926.

HOWE, IRVING, and COSER, LEWIS. *The American Communist Party*. Boston, 1957.

HURLEY, PATRICK J. "Letter to the Editor." *McCall's* (November 1949).

ICKES, HAROLD L. *The Secret Diary of Harold Ickes*. 3 vols. New York, 1954.

JACKSON, CARLTON. *Presidential Vetoes, 1792–1945*. Athens, Ga., 1967.

JACKSON, GARDNER. "Khaki Shirts and Fascism." *New Republic* (October 19, 1932).

———. "Unknown Soldiers." *Survey* (August 1, 1932).

JAMES, D. CLAYTON. *The Years of MacArthur*. Vol. 1: *1880–1941*. Boston, 1970.

JAMES, MARQUIS. *A History of the American Legion*. New York, 1923.

JAMISON, STUART. *Labor Unionism in American Agriculture*. Washington, 1945.

JESSUP, MARY FROST. "Public Attitude Toward Ex-Servicemen After World War I." *Monthly Labor Review* (December 1943).

JOHNSON, JULIA E., comp. *Soldiers' Bonus*. New York, 1924.

JONES, RICHARD SEELYE. *A History of the American Legion*. Indianapolis, 1946.

JOSLIN, THEODORE. *Hoover Off the Record*. New York, 1934.

KEMPTON, MURRAY. *Part of Our Time: Some Ruins and Monuments of the Thirties*. New York, 1955.

KILLIGREW, JOHN W. "The Army and the Bonus Incident." *Military Affairs* (Summer 1962).

———. "The Impact of the Great Depression on the Army, 1929–1936." Ph.D. dissertation, Indiana University, 1960.

KLEINHOLZ, GEORGE. *The Battle of Washington: A National Disgrace*. New York, 1932.

LANE, FRANKLIN K. *The American Spirit*. New York, 1918.

LANGER, WILLIAM L. *Gas and Flame in World War I*. New York, 1965.

LEUCHTENBERG, WILLIAM. *Franklin D. Roosevelt and the New Deal*. New York, 1963.

———. "The New Deal and the Analogue of War." In John Braeman et al. *Change and Continuity in Twentieth Century America*. Columbus, Ohio, 1964.

LEVIN, EMANUEL. "The Veterans and the United Front." *The Communist* (July 1933).

————. "The Veterans in the Struggle Against Fascism and Imperialist War." *The Communist* (August 1934).

LEVINE, ERWIN L. *Theodore Francis Green*. Providence, R. I., 1963.

LINDSAY, SAMUEL MCCUNE. "Soldiers' Insurance versus Pensions." *American Review of Reviews* (October 1917).

LIPPMANN, WALTER. *Men of Destiny*. New York, 1927.

LIVERMORE, SEWARD W. *Politics Is Adjourned: Woodrow Wilson and the War Congress, 1916–1918*. Middletown, Conn., 1966

LOHBECK, DON. *Patrick J. Hurley*. Chicago, 1956.

LORANT, STEPHEN. *Pittsburgh*. New York, 1964.

LOVE, PHILIP H. *Andrew W. Mellon: The Man and His Work*. Baltimore, 1929.

LYON, PETER. *Success Story*. New York, 1963.

LYONS, EUGENE. *Herbert Hoover*. New York, 1964.

————. *Our Un-Known Ex-President*. New York, 1948.

MACADOO, WILLIAM GIBBS. *Crowded Years*. New York, 1931.

MACARTHUR, DOUGLAS. *Reminiscences*. New York, 1964.

MCCOY, DONALD. *Calvin Coolidge: The Quiet President*. New York, 1967.

MCELROY, ROBERT. *Grover Cleveland: The Man and the Statesman*. New York, 1923.

MCMURRY, DONALD L. *Coxey's Army*. Boston, 1929.

MAGIL, A. B., and STEVENS, HENRY. *The Peril of Fascism*. New York, 1938.

MANN, ARTHUR. *LaGuardia: A Fighter Against His Times*. Philadelphia, 1959.

MASON, ALPHEUS THOMAS. *William Howard Taft: Chief Justice*. New York, 1964.

MAYO, KATHERINE. *Soldiers What Next!* Boston, 1934.

MEISEL, HENRY O. . . . *Bonus Expeditionary Forces . . . The True Facts*. Clintonville, Wis., 1932.

————. *Second "Bonus Army" 1933*. Shawano, Wis., 1934.

MELLON, WILLIAM LARIMER, and SPARKES, BOYDEN. *Judge Mellon's Sons*. n.p., 1948.

MENCKEN, H. L. "Commentary." *American Mercury* (November 1932).

MINOTT, RODNEY C. *Peerless Patriots: Organized Veterans and the Spirit of Americanism.* Washington, 1962.

MINTON, BRUCE, and STUART, JOHN. *The Fat Years and the Lean.* New York, 1940.

MOCK, JAMES R., and THURBER, EVANGELINE. *Report on Demobilization.* Norman, Okla., 1944.

MOLEY, RAYMOND, JR. *The American Legion Story.* New York, 1966.

MORROW, FELIX. *Bonus March.* New York, 1932.

————. "Letter to the Editor." *Nation* (February 2, 1932).

MOWRY, GEORGE E. "The Uses of History by Recent Presidents." *Journal of American History* (June 1966).

MUGGLEBEE, RUTH. *Father Coughlin: The Radio Priest of the Shrine of the Little Flower, An Account of the Life, Work and Message of Reverend Charles E. Coughlin.* Garden City, N.Y., 1933.

MURRAY, ROBERT K. *The Harding Era: Warren G. Harding and His Administration.* Minneapolis, 1969.

MYERS, WILLIAM STARR, and NEWTON, WALTER H. *The Hoover Administration: A Documented Narrative.* New York, 1936.

NATIONAL INDUSTRIAL CONFERENCE BOARD. *The Soldier's Bonus or Adjusted Compensation for Soldiers.* New York, 1923.

————. *The World War Veterans and the Federal Treasury.* New York, 1932.

NORTH, DOUGLAS C. *Growth and Welfare in the American Past.* Englewood Cliffs, N.J., 1966.

O'CALLAGHAN, JERRY A. "The War Veteran and the Public Lands." *Agricultural History* (1954).

O'CONNOR, HARVEY. *Mellon's Millions.* New York, 1933.

OLIVER, JOHN WILLIAM. *History of the Civil War Military Pensions.* Madison, 1915.

PACKER, HERBERT L. *Ex-Communist Witnesses.* Stanford, 1962.

PADELFORD, NORMAN J. "The Veterans' Bonus and the Constitution." *American Political Science Review* (December 1933).

PATMAN, WRIGHT. "Behind the Scenes of the Bonus Fight." *Plain Talk* (November 1935).

PATTERSON, JAMES T. "A Conservative Coalition Forms in Congress." *Journal of American History* (March 1966).

PAXSON, FREDERIC L. *American Democracy and the World War*. Vol. 3: *Postwar Years: Normalcy, 1918–1923*. Berkeley, 1948.

Pay the Bonus in Full Now. Chicago, 1931.

PINCHOT, AMOS. *General Goober at the Battle of Anacostia*. New York, 1932.

PORTER, KIRK H., and JOHNSON, DONALD B. *National Party Platforms, 1840–1960*. Urbana, Ill., 1961.

POWELL, TALCOTT. *Tattered Banners*. New York, 1933.

Proceedings of the American Legion. Washington, D.C., 1919–1936.

Proceedings of the Disabled American Veterans. Washington, D.C., 1920–1936.

Proceedings of the Veterans of Foreign Wars. Washington, D.C., 1919–1936.

RAUCH, BASIL. *A History of the New Deal*. New York, 1944.

RAYMOND, HARRY. "The Siege of the Capitol." *New Masses* (August 1932).

REEVE, JOSEPH E. *Monetary Reform Movements*. Washington, 1943.

REID, BILL G. "American Proposals for Soldier Settlement During the World War I Period." Ph.D. dissertation, University of Oklahoma, 1963.

———. "Franklin K. Lane's Idea for Veterans' Colonization." *Pacific Historical Review* (November 1964).

———. "Proposals for Soldier Settlement During World War I." *Mid-America* (July 1964).

RICH, BENNETT MILTON. *The Presidents and Civil Disorder*. Washington, D.C., 1941.

RICHARDSON, JAMES D., ed. *The Messages and Papers of the Presidents*. Washington, D.C., 1911.

RIKER, WILLIAM H. *The Firing of Pat Jackson*. Washington, 1951.

ROBB, STEPHEN. "Fifty Years of Farewell: Douglas MacArthur's Commemorative and Deliberative Speaking." Ph.D. dissertation, Indiana University, 1967.

ROBINSON, HENRY MORTON. *Fantastic Interlude*. New York, 1943.

ROLLINS, ALFRED H. *Roosevelt and Howe*. New York, 1962.

ROOSEVELT, ELEANOR. "Autobiography." *McCall's* (July 1949).

———. "Letter to the Editor." *McCall's* (November 1949).

———. *This I Remember*. New York, 1949.

ROOSEVELT, FRANKLIN D. *The Public Papers and Addresses of Franklin Delano Roosevelt.* Edited by Samuel I. Rosenman. New York, 1939–1950.

ROSENMAN, SAMUEL I. *Working With Roosevelt.* New York, 1952.

ROSENWASSER, HERMAN, and RASMUSSEN, WILFORD. *The Crucifixion of the Bonus Army.* n.p., 1932.

ROSS, DAVIS R. B. *Preparing for Ulysses: Politics and Veterans During World War II.* New York, 1969.

SAALBERG, JOHN J. "Roosevelt, Fechner and the CCC—A Study in Executive Leadership." Ph.D. dissertation, Cornell University, 1963.

SALING, THOMAS W. *History of the Bonus Expeditionary Force and the Battle of Washington.* n.p., 1932.

SALOUTOS, THEODORE. "The Professors and the Populists." *Agricultural History* (October 1966).

SANDS, WILLIAM FRANKLIN. "How Revolution May Be Caused." *Commonweal* (August 17, 1932).

SCHLESINGER, ARTHUR M., JR. *The Coming of the New Deal.* Boston, 1959.

——. *The Crisis of the Old Order.* Boston, 1957.

——. *The Politics of Upheaval.* Boston, 1960.

SCHRUBEN, FRANCIS W. *Kansas in Turmoil, 1930–1936.* Columbia, Mo., 1969.

SCHURZ, CARL. "The Pension Scandal." *Harper's Weekly* (May 5, 1894).

SCHWARZ, JORDAN. *The Interregnum of Despair: Hoover, Congress and the Depression.* Urbana, Ill., 1970.

SHIDELER, JAMES H. "The Neo-Progressives: Reform Politics in the United States, 1920–1925." Ph.D. dissertation, University of California, Berkeley, 1945.

SHIELDS, JAMES [O'SHEEL, SHAEMUS]. *Antigone and Other Poems.* Philadelphia, 1961.

——. *It Could Never Happen Here.* New York, 1932.

SHOVER, JOHN L. *Cornbelt Rebellion.* Urbana, Ill., 1965.

SINCLAIR, ANDREW. *The Available Man.* New York, 1965.

SMITH, GENE. *The Shattered Dream.* New York, 1970.

SNELLER, MAURICE P., JR. "The Bonus March of 1932: A Study of

Depression Leadership." Ph.D. dissertation, University of Virginia, 1960.

"The Soldier Bonus Controversy." *Congressional Digest* (June 1922).

SPOLANSKY, JACOB. *The Communist Trail in America.* New York, 1951.

SPRINGER, FLETA CAMPBELL. "Glassford and the Siege of Washington." *Harper's* (November 1932).

SPRINGER, GERTRUDE. "What Became of the B.E.F.?" *Survey* (December 1, 1932).

STILES, LELA. *The Man Behind Roosevelt.* Cleveland, 1954.

STOKES, THOMAS L. *Chip Off My Shoulder.* Princeton, 1940.

SYNON, MARY. *McAdoo.* New York, 1924.

TERKEL, STUDS. *Hard Times: An Oral History of the Great Depression.* New York, 1970.

TUGWELL, REXFORD GUY. *The Brains Trust.* New York, 1968.

TULL, CHARLES J. *Father Coughlin and the New Deal.* Syracuse, 1965.

U.S. CONGRESS. HOUSE. *Bureau of War Risk Insurance.* Report 130, 65th Cong., 1st sess., 1917.

———. *Farms for Soldiers.* Document 173, 66th Cong., 1st sess., 1919.

———. Committee on Un-American Activities. *Hearings.* "Communist Tactics Among Veterans' Groups," 82d Cong., 1st sess., 1951.

———. *Increase of Loan Basis of Adjusted Service Certificates.* Report 2670, 71st Cong., 3d sess., 1931.

———. *Laws Relating to Veterans.* 81st Cong., 2d sess., 1950.

———. *Message from the President of the United States to the House of Representatives Returning Without Approval House Bill 17054, An Act to Increase the Loan Basis of Adjusted Service Certificates, February 26, 1931.* Document 790, 71st Cong., 3d sess., 1931.

———. *National Soldier Settlement Act.* Report 216, 66th Cong., 1st sess., 1919.

———. *Payment of Adjusted Service Certificates.* Report 1252, 72d Cong., 1st sess., 1932.

———. *Soldiers' Adjusted Compensation.* Report 804, 67th Cong., 1st sess., 1921.

———. *Soldiers' Adjusted Compensation.* Document 396, 67th Cong., 2d sess., 1922.

———. *Soldiers' Adjusted Compensation*. Document 281, 68th Cong., 1st sess., 1924.

———. *Soldiers' Adjusted Compensation*. Report 313, 68th Cong., 1st sess., 1924.

———. *World War Adjusted Compensation*. Report 1020, 66th Cong., 2d sess., 1920.

———. *Veto Message on the Adjusted Service Certificates Act*. Document 197, 74th Cong., 1st sess., 1935.

———. *Veto Message Relating to Amendment of World War Veterans Act*. Document 495, 71st Cong., 2d sess., 1930.

U.S. CONGRESS. JOINT CONGRESSIONAL COMMITTEE ON VETERANS AFFAIRS. *Hearings*. 72d Cong., 2d sess., 1933.

U.S. CONGRESS. SENATE. *Compensation for Veterans of the World War*. Document 45, 67th Cong., 1st sess., 1921.

———. *Federal Laws Relating to Veterans of Wars of the United States* (Annotated). Document 131, 72d Cong., 1st sess., 1932.

———. *Homesteads for Soldiers and Sailors*. Report 482, 42d Cong., 3d sess., 1872.

———. *Soldier Bonus*. Report 821, 66th Cong., 3d sess., 1921.

———. *Veterans' Adjusted Compensation Bill*. Report 133, 67th Cong., 1st sess., 1921.

———. *Veterans' Adjusted Compensation Bill*. Report 756, 67th Cong., 2d sess., 1922.

———. *Adjusted Service Compensation*. Report 402, 68th Cong., 1st sess., 1924.

———. *Work and Homes for Returning Soldiers, Sailors and Marines*. Report 780, 65th Cong., 3d sess., 1919.

U.S. DEPARTMENT OF COMMERCE. BUREAU OF THE CENSUS. *Historical Statistics of the United States from Colonial Times to 1957*. Washington, D.C., 1960.

U.S. DEPARTMENT OF THE INTERIOR. *Annual Report, 1918*. Washington, D.C., 1918.

U.S. OFFICE OF WAR MOBILIZATION. *Report on War and Post-War Adjustment Policies*. Washington, D.C., 1944.

U.S. VETERANS ADMINISTRATION. *Annual Reports*. Washington, D.C., 1932–1940.

WALLER, WILLARD. *The Veteran Comes Back*. New York, 1944.

WARD, LOUIS B. *Father Charles E. Coughlin: An Authorized Biography.* Detroit, 1933.

WARREN, HARRIS GAYLORD. *Herbert Hoover and the Great Depression.* New York, 1959.

WATERS, W. W. *B.E.F.: The Whole Story of the Bonus Army.* New York, 1933.

WATSON, MARK S. Millions for Defense and Millions More for Tribute." *The Forum* (September 1932).

WEAVER, JOHN D. *Another Such Victory.* New York, 1948.

———. "Bonus March." *American Heritage* (July 1963).

WEBER, GUSTAVUS A., and SCHMECKEBIER, LAURENCE F. *The Veterans' Administration.* Washington, D.C., 1934.

WECTER, DIXON. *The Age of the Great Depression.* New York, 1948.

———. *When Johnny Comes Marching Home.* Cambridge, Mass., 1944.

WERNER, M. R. *Privileged Characters.* New York, 1935.

WEYL, NATHANIEL. "The Khaki Shirts—American Fascists." *New Republic* (September 21, 1932).

———. "Khaki Shirts and Fascism." *New Republic* (October 19, 1932).

WHITE, OWEN P. "General Glassford's Story." *Collier's* (October 29, 1932).

WHITE, WILLIAM L. "The Story of a Smear." *The Freeman* (October 22, 1951).

———. "The Story of a Smear." *Reader's Digest* (December 1951).

WHITNEY, COURTNEY. *MacArthur: His Rendezvous with History.* New York, 1956.

WILKINS, ROY. "The Bonusers Ban Jim Crow." *Crisis* (October 1932).

WOODS, JAMES RUSSELL. "The Legend and the Legacy of FDR and the CCC." Ph.D. dissertation, Syracuse University, 1964.

WORKERS' EX-SERVICEMEN'S LEAGUE. *Veterans Close Ranks.* New York, 1932.

ZINN, HOWARD. *LaGuardia in Congress.* Ithaca, New York, 1958.

Index

361